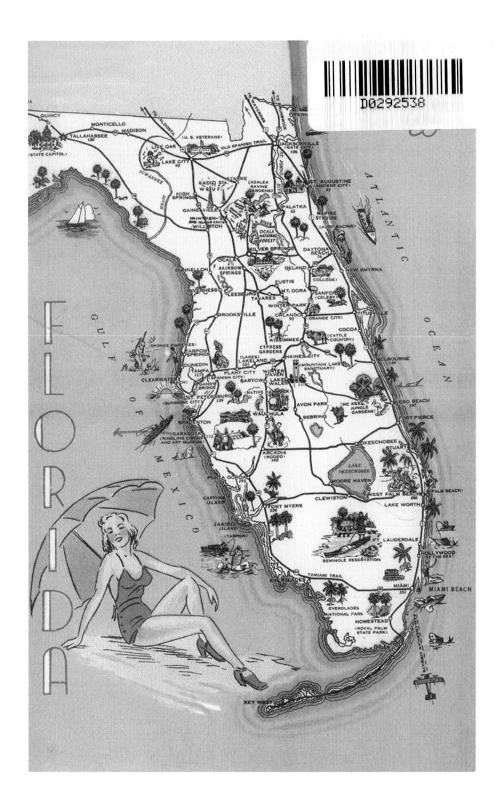

Alligators, Sharks & Panthers

Deadly Encounters with Florida's Top Predator – Man

by Charles Sobczak

Alligators, Sharks & Panthers

Deadly Encounters with Florida's Top Predator—Man

Copyright © 2007 by Charles Sobczak

Indigo Press L.L.C.
2560 Sanibel Boulevard
Sanibel, Florida, 33957

Cover design by Alex Whitehair of Whitehair Design and Molly Heuer
Layout by Maggie May

Although the author and publisher have exhaustively researched all sources to ensure accuracy of the information contained in this book, we assume no responsibility for errors, inaccuracies, omissions, or any other inconsistency herein. Any slights against people or organizations are completely unintentional.

ISBN: 9780967619903
Library of Congress Control Number: 2006927945

Indigo Press books may be purchased for educational, business, or sales-promotional use. For information and discount schedule, please write: Indigo Press, 2560 Sanibel Blvd., Sanibel, FL 33957, or e-mail indigocontact@earthlink.net.

First-edition paperback printing, October, 2006.
Printed in the United States by Whitehall Printing, Naples, FL

What Readers & Critics are Saying...

*"Author Charles Sobczak, a talented and perceptive chronicler of our tropical paradise, has struck literary pay dirt once again. His new book, **Alligators, Sharks & Panthers**, is a gripping account of the predatory creatures who live on our lands and in our waters and their effort to acclimate to man's ever burgeoning population in wildlife habitats. Sobczak's thorough historical research, compilation of fact, folklore and chilling documentation of actual attacks on humans intrigues and often terrorizes the stunned reader."*

Priscilla Friedersdorf, *The Island Sun.*

"Sobczak's work raises the most serious questions about human responsibility to other species—and to other generations. Do we wish to bequeath a world broken by climate change? Do we wish to bequeath a Florida diminished by the loss of the mystery of the panther? Do we wish to bequeath a Sanibel Island without the essential companionship of American alligators?"

Peter Blaze Corcoran, Professor of Environmental Studies and Environmental Education, Florida Gulf Coast University.

---

*"**Alligators, Sharks & Panthers** offers a perspective on Florida's wild predators in the context of human behavior and environmental pressures that may combine to result in disastrous events. Meticulous research details descriptions of actual attacks that draw the reader into the scene, while presenting an understanding of why these impressive predators do what they do.*

The author repeats sound advice throughout to avoid being a victim, and puts these events in their proper statistical context. The lessons taught are crucial to all who spend even leisurely time outdoors, especially along Florida's renowned waterways and beaches."

Fred Antonio, Director of Operations/General Curator, Central Florida Zoo

---

"It's nice to have a perspective from the animal's "voice." We all need to realize we share this wonderful planet with other amazing species. Thank you, Charles, for spreading the voices of the "Predators" of Florida."

Cory Hyde, The Calusa Group of the Sierra Club

What Readers & Critics are Saying...

"As an educator, this book is a wonderful instructional material to use in the classroom. By reflecting on past mistakes, this book will teach the next generation to appreciate and respect all that the Earth has to offer them.....

Rarely is there a book that will capture and hold the attention for both male and female students. This one does just that by its actual accounts and fascinating facts interjected with humor to instruct our youth that they need to care of our Earth and all of its inhabitants."

Diane Cortese, NBCT—The Sanibel School

---

*"Charles Sobczak's **Alligators, Sharks & Panthers** casts an unflinching and terrible eye at the tragedies that occur at the Florida borderline, between wilderness and "civilization." It is a sharp, critical perspective that reminds us how much we are encroaching on native wildlife, devouring habitat with an unchecked appetite. However awful and heart-rendering he depicts the predation of human victims, Sobczak unveils an ecological ethic that challenges the top predator to live responsibly, even humbly, within the great chain of life."*

Dr. James Brock, Associate Professor/Florida Gulf Coast University

---

"Intertwined with the messages of the collapse of our ecosystems, the author clearly turns the table on man as the top predator. Whether we outlast the other species remains to be seen. Or are we doomed by our own recklessness when it comes to our environment?

If you choose to read this book on a raft at the beach or on the bank of a creek, just remember you are in their territory!"

Mary Rawl, Director of PURRE, Fort Myers

"This book will teach you respect rather than fear as it explains the animals' habits and motivations and concludes that if we understand that we are the trespassers on their territory and behave accordingly, we will be safer. Sobczak points out that they, in turn, are protecting us. Because our efforts to provide enough natural habitat for the panther to roam, and if we keep the waters and environment natural and clean for the alligators and sharks, we are repaid by having an environment that is healthy enough to live in too."

Nola Theiss, *The Islander*

Introduction

In the spring of 2004, a little more than a year after the publication of my third novel, *A Choice of Angels*, I began thinking about writing a book unlike any other I had ever written. My initial inclination was to farm the book out to another writer, then publish it through Indigo Press. For a number of reasons, that approach never took hold.

For better or for worse, it was into this new, uncharted, nonfiction territory I was heading. The first title for the book was *Alligators, Sharks & Panthers: Deadly Encounters with Florida's Top Predators*. I soon began researching and reading about these three disparate creatures and their relationship with the seventeen million people who now call Florida home. My thinking was typical: they were the predators; we were the prey. As I studied the statistics, it became apparent that Florida, with its beaches, swaying palms, and theme parks led the world in wild-animal attacks.

Let me state, first and foremost, that I'm not a scientist, herpetologist, ichthyologist, or biologist. I'm a writer. Little did I know just how complex the subject-matter truly was and how difficult this book would prove to pen. Through the painstaking process, however, I gained a newfound respect not only for these creatures of tooth, fang, and claw, but also for the people who have dedicated their lives to studying them.

Shortly after I attended—along with Dr. Steve Bortone, a Marine biologist with SCCF (Sanibel-Captiva Conservation Foundation)—a lecture by the late Peter Benchley in the winter of 2005, the concept of this book began to change. By then, I had read much about the fatal alligator-attack files supplied me by the Florida Fish and Wildlife Commission, and had been questioning the entire premise of my own book. Was it, after all, that simple? Were they all killing machines and we merely their hapless victims? My sojourn was changing direction.

Hadn't we been the species that had harvested alligators' meat and hide, to the point that, in 1973, they had to be placed on the endangered-species list? Isn't the American crocodile the one that is barely hanging on in Florida? Aren't we the species that kills over one million sharks—many of them for nothing more that their fins—for each one of us killed by them?

Then, there was the panther problem. Try as I might, I could not find a single verifiable Florida-panther attack that had ended in a human fatality. The only exception had been the death of a slave along the Florida/Georgia border well over one hundred years ago—a story that bordered more on folklore than fact. On the other hand, the Florida-panther population, through both bounty-hunting and extensive development, had been reduced to approximately eighty animals, a ratio of 220,000 Floridians to every remaining panther.

I started to realize I had had it all backward. From that point on, the book was titled *Alligators, Sharks & Panthers: Deadly Encounters with Florida's Top Predator—Man*, because, despite the headlines, we are indeed the top predator, not only in Florida, but everywhere on the planet.

I learned that every member of the wild-cat family presently is either threatened, endangered, or already gone. I discovered that the magnificent tiger may be extinct within the next fifty years and that the number of great white sharks left in the vastness of the world's oceans has fallen to fewer than ten thousand.

As I learned how well-designed and beautifully adapted these animals are, I became increasingly frustrated with our lack of empathy and tolerance toward them. By meticulously perusing the attack files, I realized that, more often than not, it wasn't the alligator or shark that viciously attacked an unsuspecting victim, but careless human behavior that set the stage for the incident to occur, in the first place.

With our weapons, cutting-edge technology, and overwhelming populations, those animals now survive by our mercy. It was no longer about beast vs. man, but man killing beast, either directly—through hunting, netting, poisoning, harpooning, spearing, and trapping—or indirectly—by taking their remaining habitats away and replacing those forests and fields with yet another shopping center, citrus grove, freeway, or subdivision. In the case of sharks, by the seemingly endless red-tide cycles and, in the past fifty years, the destruction of ninety-three percent of Florida's fabled coral reefs.

True, alligators and sharks still kill some of us, but not in numbers that matter. Daily, nine people die on Florida's incredibly overcrowded highways and nearly three people are murdered in the Sunshine State. Scores die annually in hurricanes brought on, in large part, by our own hands through global warming. Alligators, sharks, panthers, lions, bears, wolves, snakes, and all other predators in the world are not the problem. We are.

Ironically, we are also the solution. This is where my journey ended. Or has it just begun…?

Charles Sobczak

Contents

Acknowledgments

There are so many people who dedicated copious time and effort to this book, I hardly know where to start. First and foremost, I thank my wife, Molly Heuer, for her sublime patience during the eighteen months I spent sitting on our living-room couch reading books on creatures whose apparent sole mission in life was to eat my family and me raw. From cougar attacks to shark, bear, lion, crocodile, and alligator attacks, Molly has heard it all and been instrumental in my keeping the book's focus all along.

My next bow goes to Precious Boatwright of the Florida Fish and Wildlife Commission in Tallahassee. Precious and her crew worked diligently photocopying and sending me the sixteen alligator-fatality files, without which this book would not have been possible. In the same capacity, I thank Alexia Morgan, research biologist with the Florida Museum of Natural History, Ichthyology Department, University of Florida, Gainesville, for her help gathering the names and dates of the ten fatal shark attacks contained herein, as well as her review and critique of earlier drafts of the shark sections.

My gratitude also goes to Professor David S. Maehr, Department of Forestry at the University of Kentucky, for his outstanding critique of this book's great-cats, puma, and panther sections. Professor Maehr's comments not only helped me better understand the current plight of the Florida panther but also the threatened or endangered status of every great cat on our planet.

Along these lines, I extend my deep thanks to Chris Lechowicz, herpetologist with the Sanibel-Captiva Conservation Foundation, for his reading and green-lighting of the crocodilian and alligator sections. Christie Sampson and Cheryl Parrott—currently working with the J.N. "Ding" Darling National Wildlife Refuge on a long-term study of the alligator's role in the ecology of Sanibel Island—equally deserve my gratitude for their invaluable information on Sanibel's current alligator population.

This book would never have come together had it not been for the dutiful and diligent proofreading of the rough manuscript by Anne Bellew and Patricia Kiely, both of whom spent countless hours into making this a better read and a much better book. In addition, I thank Maria Fernandes-Jaeger of Eagle Eye Editorial Services in New York (www.eagleeye-nyc.com) for fine-tuning the finished manuscript and giving her all in turning *Alligators, Sharks & Panthers* into the best read possible. My freshman English instructor once said about my writing, "The phoenix of your thought rises from the ashes of your grammar." At this point, only Maria can truly attest to the accuracy of his commentary.

I would be remiss if I omitted Jean Heuer, for reading and critiquing the early alligator and shark stories; Candace Heise, the diligent research librarian at the Sanibel Library, for finding the various microfilmed newspaper articles that were instrumental in putting this book together; Maggie May for her steadfast dedication to carefully laying out page after page of this book; Becky Kaplan, for allowing me to go through and pick out numerous postcards from her collection of vintage Florida postcards; and certainly my deceased grandmother, Clara LaPlante, and her long-passed sister, Great-auntie Delia, for leaving me their extensive Florida postcard collection. In that same vein, special thanks go to Walt's Postcards (www.thepostcard.com) for their help in locating several obscure alligator and shark cards.

Thanks, too, to Ernest Simmons for letting me use his elegant painting of a Florida panther, even though it is far better-looking in full color. I thank the Tasmanian Museum for its kind permission to use the "Native Tiger of Tasmania Shot by Weaver" photo (the image is reversed from the original). To learn more about the extinct Thylacine, visit the museum's Web site at www.tmag.tas.gov.au. In this same breath, I also thank the *Associated Press*'s Regalle Asuncion for her help in finding the panther photos, and Jessica Marx, for working with me on the amazing crocodile photo by Peter Beard.

Equally praiseworthy is Donald Spencer, for putting several excellent postcards—The Alligator Race, Florida Playmates, and the only color version of the vintage cover postcard I could find—in a zip file and e-mailing them for inclusion in this book. These postcards have come out of Spencer's excellent book, *The Florida Alligator in Old Picture Postcards*.

I especially thank Steve Specht of Silver Springs for allowing me the use of the photograph that now adorns this book's front cover and an inner page. The cover photo depicts Ross Allen—then curator of the Reptile Institute of Silver Springs and a trained professional—facing off against Big George, a fourteen-foot, seven-inch alligator weighing nearly half a ton, deliberately invading Big George's home territory to study his defensive reaction. At the time, Big George was believed to be the largest alligator specimen held in captivity. Had Big George taken hold of the invader, Allen would have been instantly killed. I, however, strongly warn you to heed this advice: don't ever try anything like it on either a wild or captive alligator.

The old cliché, "Last but not least," fully applies here as I thank all my fellow authors, from David Alderton to Carl Zimmer, for providing me so much excellent material on some of the most astonishing creatures we share Planet Earth with, including our own species, *Homo sapiens*.

Charles Sobczak
June, 2006

Three Boys

Justin VanGorder, Eric McLeod, and Bryan Jeffrey Griffin: Three boys doing what boys have always done...swimming late into the afternoon along a stretch of green, algae-laden water near a small Central Florida town named Travares...swimming near the Palm Gardens Marina on a warm June evening, in a slow-flowing stream aptly called the Dead River.

Every ingredient to an impending tragedy was present on that fateful evening of June 18, 2003. In hindsight, when the three boys returned for their last plunge of the day, a disaster seemed almost inevitable to the marina owner, the police, and the trappers who came to recover the body and kill the beast. But to the three boys, ages twelve through fourteen, it was never evident. At that age, we are all immortal; we live in the whirlwind of youth, pushing the envelope of existence with never a thought that, in the flash of an instant, our lives could end...and for Bryan Jeffrey Griffin, end it did in the murky waters of the Dead River.

*****

The story of these three boys brings me back not to the streams, lakes, and swamps of Lake County, Florida, but to my own childhood in the hills, rivers, and bays of northern Minnesota; back to 1956 and to another three boys...a tale forever etched in my memories...etched in tears.

When the incident occurred, I was a young boy of six attending kindergarten at St. Jean the Baptist Catholic School. We were living below the tracks in a rough-and-tumble neighborhood called Helm Street. We were poor. My father, Stanley, worked as a plumber, doing his best to keep ahead of five hungry children and a young, pregnant wife. Everyone living in the Helm Street neighborhood struggled to get by.

Located on Michigan Street a half-block to the west of our house was a large, rundown, and dilapidated apartment complex. The three-story back porch was unpainted and half-rotten—tenement slums, just a stone's throw from the Fitgers Brewery and the Clyde Iron Works; apartments where tenants paid their low rent month to month, never once on the first.

Two of the three boys lived in the rundown apartment complex with their grandmother. Their mother had a drinking problem and rarely came around—almost everyone living on Helm Street had a drinking problem. The grandmother, elderly and on her own, struggled to discipline her grandchildren, but was always met with little success. The two boys did whatever they felt like—skipped school, smoked cigarettes, and stole penny candy and toys from the corner store. Wild kids with no one to temper their wildness....

The story unfolded in early May, 1956. The surface of nearby Lincoln Creek was still frozen over, but the rushing water beneath it steadily carved the ice away. The three of them, two young brothers and a cousin who had come to visit that Saturday morning, went to see what Lincoln Creek looked like where the stream came pouring out of a four-block-long tunnel at the end of 27th Avenue W, less than two blocks from their wooden apartment complex. It was an especially warm morning for early May.

No one saw what happened. They were three boys—the oldest, 12; the youngest, 10—intrigued by the spring freshet, who had been left alone with their own lack of good judgment. Perhaps one of them dared the other to step out on the ice and get a closer look. Perhaps one or all three accidentally slid down the steep, muddy bank...no one will ever know. But at some point, one of the boys fell into Lincoln Creek and was quickly swept away by the raging stream. The told story was that the other boys tried to save him and they, too, were swept away. All three drowned.

The news ran through Helm Street like an air-raid siren bellowing bleak, dark noise. My mother burst into tears upon hearing it, having seen the three children stop by earlier in the morning to see if any of us kids wanted to join them. She wouldn't let my older brother Billy go; it was too dangerous. Timmy and Tommy Larson, my best friends at the time, were too young to be allowed to journey off that far, and so was I. In the end, no one joined them but death.

The story is still told that, when they found the three boys trapped beneath the ice of St. Louis Bay, cold and lifeless, they were holding each other's hands. In a grief that had no measure, their grandmother died soon after. The mother kept drinking.

*****

Nearly a half-century later and two thousand miles to the south, a different version of the same sad tale unfolded in Central Florida on that fateful day in 2003. Throughout the afternoon, the three boys had noticed a large, eleven-foot alligator swimming near them. Around 3:30, one of the boys went in to tell Keith Buse, the owner of the marina, that the big alligator had come closer than usual to the boat ramp. Buse went outside to see for himself. He found the animal submerged in two feet of water right beside the seawall. "I could have bent down and touched him," he later told state investigators.

Buse went back inside the marina to retrieve a pole and strike at the alligator so as to move it away from the seawall and the ramp beside it. By the time Buse returned outside, the reptile had moved off, lurking just twelve feet away but well out of reach of his threatening pole. A moment later, the gator silently submerged beneath the green water. Buse didn't like how the alligator was behaving and sternly warned all three boys to stop swimming in the Dead River and go home.

A little while later, Buse called the Fish & Wildlife Commission's Northeast Regional Office in Ocala to report a nuisance alligator hanging out in the vicinity of his boat ramp. The gator Buse had reported was familiar to him. He had seen it many times before, lurking around the fish-cleaning table, waiting for the returning bass-and-crappie fishermen to toss in the filleted carcasses. In other words, waiting to be inadvertently fed....

Buse didn't make an emergency call that afternoon because, by that time, the three boys had stopped swimming. Following Buse's advice, the boys had gone home for the day. Buse went back outside a half-dozen times to see if the big gator was still hanging around, but never saw it resurface. He closed the marina at six o'clock and walked across the road to his nearby home for dinner. This story should have ended there and then.

But at 7:30 that same evening, unbeknownst to Keith Buse, the three boys returned. They must have decided it was still too hot out that night and wanted one last dip before dark. They didn't see any sign of the gator, although at that time the shadows were long and it would have been all but impossible to spot a reptile beneath the green, obscured waters of the Dead River.

After swimming for a few minutes, Justin VanGorder and Eric McLeod noticed bubbles coming up from the bottom and the three boys hurriedly climbed out of the river.

"They're just dumb bubbles," said Bryan Griffin as he bravely jumped back into the river from the end of the boat ramp. From the patio beside it, the other two boys saw the alligator resurface and start swimming toward Griffin. They yelled at him to get out of the water and started throwing rocks at the approaching reptile. Griffin, however, swam out deeper, inexplicably ignoring his friends' warning.

At 7:45, the three-hundred-pound alligator seized the ninety-eight-pound boy. Griffin screamed and yelled to his friends to run and get help.

The alligator went into a death roll. In an instant, both alligator and boy vanished beneath a roiled surface. The last thing the two boys on shore saw was the twisting motion of the alligator's tail. Griffin was locked in the reptile's mouth, unable to free himself from the tons of pressure an alligator's jaws can exert.

In a few minutes' time, VanGorder and McLeod ran across the street and notified the marina owner, Keith Buse, that their friend Bryan Griffin had been grabbed by an alligator. Buse told his wife to immediately call 911 and report the attack. Buse grabbed his gun and ran back to the boat ramp. When he and the two boys arrived at the ramp, the gator was still underwater. Five minutes went by before the reptile resurfaced with the boy, motionless and bleeding from the head, still tightly locked in the massive alligator's mouth. The leviathan was swimming across the river, heading toward the bulrushes and thick brush that lined the far shoreline.

No doubt Buse assumed that Griffin was already dead, but he didn't dare take a shot at the gator while it was holding a boy's midsection in its mouth. It was just too dangerous.

As the alligator swam steadily toward the far shore, Buse grabbed the keys to one of his marina-rental pontoons and drove out to catch up with the reptile. The alligator, upon hearing the vessel approach, re-submerged with the body. Buse idled around the area for several minutes, but failed to locate the alligator and Griffin. By that time, Brenda Lawrence, manager of Buse's marina, and her boyfriend, James Hemstrought, had arrived on the scene. They got on a second pontoon boat and joined Buse in the search.

At 8:15, Lawrence and Hemstrought found Bryan Griffin floating under an overhanging tree on the opposite shoreline. Hemstrought reached down into the water and grabbed one of Griffin's hands. As he tried to pull the boy out of the water, Hemstrought noticed that the alligator just below the surface still had hold of one of Griffin's legs. The alligator fought back and pulled the boy out of Hemstrought's hands. The beast and the boy's dead body once again disappeared into deeper water.

Ten minutes later, a sheriff's helicopter deployed a buoy where they had last spotted the boy. A few minutes later, for a second time that night Hemstrought saw the boy's body. He bravely jumped into the four-foot-deep water and pulled Bryan Griffin out from underneath the overhanging vegetation. The deputies who had joined in the search helped Hemstrought pull the body from the water.

Bryan was limp and lifeless, with puncture wounds across his midsection where the alligator had grabbed him. The deputies administered

4

CPR while Brenda Lawrence navigated the pontoon boat toward the other shore and Palm Gardens Marina. From there, the EMS personnel placed Griffin in a stretcher and rushed him back to Leesburg Regional Medical Center. It was too late.

As it had been for the three boys beneath the ice back in 1956, it was too late for Bryan J. Griffin. All of them drowned, leaving grieving families and a river of tears behind. This morning or this afternoon and again tomorrow, there will invariably be a similarly tearful message delivered to an anxious mother somewhere in the world, who will never be prepared for the awful news that her boy won't be coming home. That boy's body will be found either beneath a dock or at the bottom of a steep hill, with his broken bicycle beside him or lying there, lifeless along the edge of the street he was told never to cross...and told repeatedly.

Those boys did not heed the warnings of their friends or guardians, nor can we expect them to a thousand years hence and ten thousand miles from here...for they are just boys, caught up in the eternal ritual of pushing the envelope of their own mortality. We miss them, holding each other's hands beneath the ice of their tragic misfortune. We weep for them. We always will.

They Bet Him a Can of Beer

It's not difficult to recreate the tableau at Bayfront Point Beach on September 15, 1981: Two couples hanging out together, lying on beach towels, soaking up the sun, taking brief dips in the surf, drinking beer, smoking cigarettes, and laughing. It's easy to picture the two couples enjoying a leisurely Tuesday afternoon away from the hustle and bustle of downtown Tampa, where all four worked in the hospitality industry pouring drinks, serving dinners, and catering to Florida's tourist crowds. Given the gorgeous, warm weather; the beach, the cooler full of beer, and the rest of the evening off, there was in all likelihood some serious partying happening.

Try to picture the four of them sitting on the beach, staring at the wide-open channel between the northern tip of Anna Maria Island and the distant shoreline of Egmont Key, midway across the Southwest Channel of Tampa Bay. Although no one will ever know what was said that afternoon, we can assume the conversation between them went something like this:

"How far do you think it is to Egmont Key?" Mark Meeker asked his bartending friend, William Schwerer.

"A couple miles at least."

"I think I could swim it," boasted Meeker, looking over toward his date, Angie Tucker.

"No way," quipped Schwerer's girlfriend, Margaret Lord.

"I'm sure I could; it's not all that far," declared Meeker.

"I'll bet you a can of beer you can't make it," challenged Schwerer.

"You're on," said Meeker, shaking hands with his friend to seal the wager.

At 4:30 P.M. that day, Mark Meeker, a twenty-six-year-old bartender who had just moved into the Tampa Bay area, waded into the warm gulf waters taking one last studied look across the calm surface of Southwest Channel toward Egmont Key. The plan they put together was simple: While Meeker started swimming alone toward the distant island, his three friends would head down the beach to rent a boat and pick him up upon his reaching Egmont Key. If they could find Meeker before he made it to the island, they would motor alongside him during the last mile or two of his marathon swim. Alas, it was an incredibly ill-conceived plan.

The last time Tucker, Schwerer, and Lord saw Meeker alive he was 250 yards offshore, swimming at a steady pace toward the distant island. As promised, just as Meeker disappeared from view, his friends walked south along the beach in search of a rental boat. By this time it was almost 5 P.M. on that lazy Tuesday. Labor Day had been more than two weeks since and most businesses on Anna Maria Island had already started to scale back their operations until the tourist season fully kicked in again around mid-December.

Schwerer and the two girls soon learned that nobody was interested in renting them a boat that late in the day. Schwerer went so far as offer one boat-rental operator $50.00 cash for a one-hour use of a boat. In 1981, that was a lot of money. But it was too late in the day and the shop owner was in the process of closing. He told the three they could come back and rent a boat in the morning.

They didn't have a plan B. After realizing they weren't going to be able to catch up with Meeker or ultimately meet him as planned, the three became worried about their friend's situation. No doubt their concerns had a sobering effect on their mood. They walked down to the nearby pier to talk with some local fishermen and ask if they had ever seen sharks in the area.

"It's loaded with sharks out there," said one of the anglers, pointing toward the deep channel that ran between the point and Egmont Key. "Besides," the fisherman added, "there's a very strong outgoing tide running in the inlet this afternoon. You wouldn't want to be out there alone today, that's for sure."

At 7:30 that night, three hours after Meeker began his lonely swim and the sun effortlessly slipped into the clear blue waters of the Gulf of Mexico, William Schwerer called the Coast Guard.

Meeker, he told the Coast Guard, was out there somewhere between Brean Point—the name given to the northern tip of Anna Maria Island—and Egmont Key, swimming alone and soon to be engulfed in darkness. The Coast Guard, realizing the gravity of the situation, promptly sent out four search-and-rescue boats and a helicopter in the hopes of finding the wayward swimmer. By then it was twilight, with a gathering darkness and poor visibility. Given the conditions that late in the day, it's easy to understand why the Coast Guard couldn't find any sign of Meeker. It reluctantly called the search off at midnight with a plan to resume before dawn.

In a statement given to the Sheriff's Department the next day, Angie Tucker, Meeker's girlfriend, told authorities that, just before he left, he had told them he wasn't a strong swimmer. Meeker was a five-foot, ten-inch man and weighed 180 pounds. At that junction, everyone anticipated the worst. The search resumed at first light, more than fourteen hours after Meeker had plunged in the water. There was no sight of him. The party, clearly, was over.

At 8:20 A.M. on Wednesday, Bud Protiva, owner of a fishing boat called the *Sea Jeep*, was fishing for Spanish mackerel between Passage and Egmont Keys. Protiva was thus quoted, "I looked over and said, 'I think I see a turtle,'...then I looked over again and said, 'My God, it isn't a turtle....'"

What Protiva and his fishing companion had discovered was the lifeless body of Mark Meeker, whereupon they radioed the Coast Guard. Since a CG crew was already in the vicinity searching for Meeker, it pulled up alongside the *Sea Jeep* within minutes. Upon recovering Meeker's body, Coast Guard officers found numerous deep gashes, each one several inches long, around the front and inside calf of his lower right leg. At first, the authorities weren't certain if the gashes had been the result of a shark attack or an accidental encounter with a boat propeller. They also speculated that the cuts might have been made postmortem.

Upon further scrutiny, they noted that Meeker had removed the drawstring from his swimsuit and had attempted to tie a tourniquet around his upper thigh. With that key piece of evidence, everything pointed to a shark attack. It was apparent that Meeker had been fully conscious when the shark bit him some time during the three-mile swim. In all likelihood, Meeker would have avoided being hit by a boat. Besides, had a boat come that close, Meeker would have certainly flagged it down and been rescued. An autopsy performed a few days later confirmed it indeed had been a shark bite that had inflicted the lacerations.

Whether Meeker died of blood loss or drowned because of his impaired swimming ability after the attack, it will never be known. Judging from the location of the body when it was discovered, it appears he had made it beyond Passage Key, one mile off the beach, and was on his way toward Egmont when the shark bit him. The wounds were deep and clean, with very little flesh torn off. After two bites, the shark must have swum off, uninterested in continuing with the attack.

Had Meeker been closer to shore, it's highly unlikely his wounds would have been sufficient enough to kill him. But he wasn't near shore. In all probability, when he was first attacked, Meeker must have already been exhausted, wondering why his friends were taking so long and struggling against a relentless outgoing tide. Even in the wide channels of Passage Key Inlet and Southwest Channel, a steady current can turn a three-mile swim into a six-mile one. Had Meeker never been bitten, chances are he would have drowned, nevertheless.

The shark that bit him was never positively identified. Meeker's splashing could have easily attracted a lemon, a bull, or a hammerhead shark. Hammerheads, especially the great-hammerhead, are known to prey on tarpon and tarpon run thick through the Southwest Channel. Given the fact that the bites on Meeker's leg weren't large, even much smaller sharks—the blacktip, Atlantic shovelnose, or spinner shark might have been responsible for the injuries. Once he was bitten, Meeker's fate was sealed. The fear he experienced that evening must have been overwhelming. Alone, bleeding, and fatigued in the middle of a channel as darkness befell him, Meeker must have realized he had little time left.

In the end, extremely poor planning and a lack of sound judgment put Mark Meeker in jeopardy the second he decided to take his three friends up on their foolhardy bet. Meeker's lack of local knowledge of the tides and about the presence of sharks in the channel made his three-mile swim a sure-to-happen disaster. The ocean has a way with those who fail to respect it…a cruel way.

Meeker had been working at Bigg's Lounge in the Riverside Hilton, in downtown Tampa, for three weeks before his fatal swim. During an interview conducted several days after the accident, Greg Leonard, the hotel manager, told the following to reporters for the *St. Petersburg Times*: "While he was here, he was an excellent employee and one who was very well thought of."

In the end, Mark Meeker lost the bet. There was no celebration held on the shoreline of Egmont Key. Meeker's wager— the can of beer— was never opened.

When a Child Is Lost

On June 28, 1988, Major Floyd Buckhalter, Regional Commander, South Region, of the Florida Game & Freshwater Fish Commission, wrote a letter of commendation to Randy Pearson, a professional alligator trapper, for his outstanding service in finding and helping to kill a large bull alligator around midnight on June 4, 1988. The following is a segment from that letter:

Dear Mr. Pearson:

Those of us involved in emergency-service positions become accustomed to stressful or unpleasant situations, but few could have been prepared for the recent alligator incident in the Gardens of Gulf Cove subdivision in Charlotte County, which ended with the death of a four-year-old girl. During that time, certain individuals and groups distinguished themselves by their determination to bring the situation to a successful conclusion.

Especially noteworthy was your performance as you went about the difficult task of body recovery and capture of the alligator. You accomplished this job with speed and accuracy, thereby affording the victim's family some peace of mind.

In reality, there was no peace of mind to be found neither for the family of four-year-old Erin Lynn Glover nor for the neighbors, friends, and relatives of the tiny, blond-haired girl who had been taken and killed by an alligator. There had remained only an unmovable mountain of sorrow.

Erin Glover, nicknamed Gizmo, was a bright little girl with an entire life ahead. She would start gymnastics classes within a week so as to help rein in some of her seemingly inexhaustible energy and enthusiasm. She loved to laugh, play, and tag along with her eight-year-old brother, Justin. For Gizmo, her smile epitomized who she was.

Erin Glover and her family lived one block away from Hidden Lake, a typical Florida dredge-line pond located a half-mile south of the Myakka River in Charlotte County. The Gardens of Gulf Cove subdivision—a modest, friendly community, not unlike the myriad Florida subdivisions sprawled across the state—had been platted out years ago in a small section of West Port Charlotte.

There was nothing out of the ordinary on that June 4, 1988. It was a typical warm Saturday afternoon with the thunderstorms of early summer slowly building to the east over Arcadia and the thermometer permanently stalled in the low '90s—the typical beginning of another endless, hot, and humid Florida summer.

No doubt the three children—Erin, her brother Justin, and a nine-year-old friend, Jason Kershanick—simply wanted to do nothing more than take Kershanick's six-month-old Labrador puppy for a wet, splashing walk along the sandy shoreline of Hidden Lake. The kids had walked along the edge of Hidden Lake many times before, as had all the children in the neighborhood. No one living in Gulf Cove took the threat of the resident alligators seriously. Up until that fateful evening in June, no one had reason to.

Around 6:20 P.M., the three children and puppy arrived at the edge of the water. The Lab puppy naturally dashed in and out of the water. The dog's behavior plus its smell, a strong canine odor which alligators are very adept at detecting, was a contributing factor in attracting the alligator to the area where the children were walking. Erin started tossing stones into the water and kicking her feet, splashing the water ahead of her while she ambled a few yards behind the two boys and the black Lab.

Suddenly, without warning, a hungry 350-pound bull alligator rushed toward shore and grabbed the thirty-one-pound girl by her midsection. Erin screamed, kicking off one of her tiny pink tennis shoes as she actually managed to fight off the initial attack. Her brother Justin and friend Jason turned around and stood in disbelief as the alligator bit Erin a second time, attempting to get a better hold of its prey. Then the beast dropped her.

As she tried to climb back to shore in the ankle-deep water, the alligator stood up on all fours and rushed at Erin a third and final time, this time seizing the child firmly in its powerful jaws. There was nothing the boys could do as the alligator turned around and swam off with Erin in its mouth.

Justin Glover and Jason Kershanick immediately ran for help. Kershanick was later quoted, "After it happened, then we ran. It was pretty quick. It seemed like a nightmare, a dream. But then the way she screamed, when I saw the blood after he went in, then I realized it was real."

Little Kershanick ran home to find his father and little Glover ran home to find his mother. When Mrs. Glover returned to the edge of the lake with her son, a neighbor, Nolan Jesse, overheard her screams and came out with a rifle. He saw the alligator surface with a light-colored object in its mouth but was afraid to take the shot, thinking he might accidentally injure the little girl. The alligator swam farther away from shore with Erin still locked in its jaws.

As darkness fell and the authorities were notified, the neighbors, police, trappers, game wardens, and paramedics gathered and searched the edges of Hidden Lake. Later that night, five professional divers arrived to scour the bottom. They thoroughly searched the surrounding cattails and bulrushes on the far end of the pond. Everyone involved must have dreaded and known the likely outcome, though a spark of hope still flickered in the hearts of both Erin's mother and stepfather, Ty Bowns.

That spark of hope was extinguished just before midnight, when two officers found the alligator still pushing the body of Erin Glover in front of it. They caught up to the animal in their boat and shot the beast with a load of buckshot from a 12-gauge. Once the alligator was seriously wounded, the two officers managed to grab the lifeless body of Erin Glover from its jaws. It took four more shots before the gator was killed, the decisive shot being delivered point blank through the animal's skull with a 357-Magnum.

When they finally pulled Erin's body into the boat, they discovered the true horror of the attack. The girl's left leg and foot were missing, severed in the pelvic region. The alligator had already started to feed on its prey. All the flickering flames of hope vanished. Erin Glover, a child of four, had been inexorably lost.

After dragging the alligator back to shore, the officers sliced open its stomach and biologist Steve Marin removed Erin's leg from the alligator's stomach. Erin Glover's body was brought to the Fawcett Memorial Hospital Morgue.

In the final conclusion, her autopsy report read:

Erin Glover, a four-year-old white female, died due to drowning and multiple injuries, which she sustained during an attack by an alligator. Most of the injuries seen were in nature postmortem, including the deep lacerations, fractures of the bones, and complete amputation of the left lower extremity. This extremity apparently was recovered from the alligator's stomach. No evidence of any significant underlying natural disease was seen. The death is classified as accidental.

*****

12

Upon further investigation it was discovered that the same alligator that had attacked and killed the innocent little girl had been fed repeatedly by the residents and any number of Florida "snowbirds" who lived along the shores of Hidden Lake. One neighbor admitted to having fed the animal himself over the years. It was common practice to feed the alligators throughout the '80s, even though everyone knew it was both illegal and dangerous.

Most of the time, this particular alligator, which had lived in Hidden Lake for at least five years before the incident, survived by eating ducks and turtles. Two years prior to Erin Glover's tragedy, a sixty-four-year-old retiree living by the lake called Fish & Wildlife to request that they remove this large gator from the pond. The retiree felt it had become too tame and too large to remain in Hidden Lake. After an investigation, the agency decided not to relocate or destroy the animal in question.

In defense of the gator, some residents of Gulf Cove felt it was irresponsible for the parents to allow the children to come down with a puppy to play along a lake known to harbor such large reptiles. Some had fenced off their back yards and kept their children and dogs away from the potentially dangerous predators. But the complaints and opinions did nothing to ease the pain of the family and friends over the loss of the beautiful child to a hungry leviathan.

A neighbor set up a memorial fund saying, "I've had recent deaths in my family but this really hurts. You could see her every day playing with her bike across the street. Now she's gone."

The only things found when the police first arrived on the scene that afternoon were the deep imprints of the alligator's tracks and one of Erin's pink tennis shoes, lying on the muddy sand.

Rose, another neighbor, said it best: "It's a tragedy...unreal. I can't understand how she's gone like that." But alas, she was indeed gone. Gizmo has left the world forever. Little Erin Glover would never grow up to be a gymnast or a dancer.

The next time you see a person feeding an alligator, remember a solitary pink tennis shoe lying on the sandy shore of a Florida lake and think of four-year-old Erin Glover.

Then, please report that person...in Erin's memory.

Nearly one hundred million
residents and tourists enjoy the
Sunshine State annually.

The Top Predators

There are over one million alligators living in the Sunshine State, one for every seventeen Floridians. Near and offshore, along our 1,197 miles of coastline, there are uncountable sharks, some of them killers, members of family groups known as mackerel and requiem sharks. Although now dramatically reduced when compared to their historic zenith, populations of Florida panthers still roam the hardwood hammocks and cypress swamps of Southwest Florida.

Attacks from these three predators are on the increase and have been driven up by stark statistics of six thousand new Floridians entering the state every week. The high ground—the East Coast ridge running from Jacksonville to Miami, across to the Gulf of Mexico's coastline and on to the panhandle hinterland—has, for the most part now, been developed. The impact of an exploding human population, coupled with an unprecedented real-estate boom over the past fifty years, has left Florida's wildlife, especially panthers, in grave peril. As new subdivisions spread farther and deeper inland, the indigenous wildlife either vanishes or learns to adapt to man-made changes: drainage canals become alligator holes, golf-course water hazards run rampant, and ponds become unintentional wildlife preserves. Alligators move in. Unfamiliar with the alligator's instinctual behavior to kill to survive, people get bitten, some of them fatally.

Every year, more and more Floridians and many of the eighty million annual tourists take to the water: swimmers, boaters, jet-skiers, sailors, anglers, para-sailors, and kayakers crowd our beaches and surrounding waters, inadvertently putting themselves at risk. Alligators, like sharks, are opportunistic—if it moves and splashes, it is edible. People, then, will invariably get attacked...some of them even fail to survive....

What is it about human predation by wildlife that so intrigues us? Insects kill millions of people a year throughout the world. Diseases such as malaria, St. Louis encephalitis, West Nile virus, and a host of other deadly pathogens are daily transmitted by mosquitoes in every corner of the globe, including Florida. Scores of other insects, including the tsetse fly of Central Africa, poisonous spiders, deer ticks, and parasites take an uncountable toll on human life. Annually, insects are responsible for tens of millions of fatalities worldwide.

But it is not the same. Insects kill us indirectly; in a way, without blame or bloodshed. They do not hunt us down and eat us.

After copious hours poring over books, magazine articles, researching the Internet, and speaking with scores of people, I am convinced there is a collective subconscious, a primordial fear within us that psychologically magnifies the threat of being bitten, dragged down, or downright devoured. Predators scare us to the core.

Ironically, the most dangerous large animal in North America isn't the panther, the grizzly, or the American alligator, but the common deer—both the white-tailed and the mule. In 2003 alone, there were 1.5 million reported accidents and 210 fatalities resulting from collisions between automobiles and deer. Because of skyrocketing deer populations throughout North America, collisions are on the increase. White-tailed and mule deer harbor ticks that carry the debilitating and potentially fatal Lyme disease. Again in 2003, over twenty-one thousand cases of Lyme disease were reported in the U.S.

Bees and hornets kill more people annually than do all of North America's top predators combined. Poisonous snakes also kill dozens of Americans every year. Nevertheless, these tragic incidents never seem to make the national news or draw the kind of regional attention an alligator, shark or a puma attack does.

I doubt you ever picked up a book titled *Deer, Bees, and Mosquitoes: Deadly Encounters with Bugs and White-Tailed Deer.* Insect-borne diseases, snakebites, and collisions with deer somehow remain distant. The bite of a tick doesn't send shudders down anyone's spine; the bite of a shark does.

It doesn't matter that statistics prove one's chances of being struck by lightning and killed in Florida are far greater than one's being attacked and slain by an alligator. On average, lightning kills fifteen people a year in Florida, but it's not the same. A lightning bolt doesn't hunt you down, wait in ambush, and seize you unawares. Ultimately, it is human instinct. The fact is our ancestors, spanning thousands of generations, have learned to avoid becoming prey. Those who neither learned nor had an innate, primal fear of predatory beasts have now vanished. Survivors—and you and I clearly are their descendants—have learned to develop an intuitive fear of those fish and beasts.

Times have changed, though. Homo sapiens are without question today's top predators on earth. Up until the past few hundred years, before the development of reliable, mass-produced firearms, most large predators were difficult if not impossible to destroy. Spears and arrows readily bounced off the thick, armorlike skin of a one-ton crocodile. Stone axes, spears, and primitive bows and arrows did little to stop the charging rush of a hungry lion.

Our ancestors survived because they innately feared the beasts that hunted them down and their fear was imbedded in us. It lies deep in our hearts and viscera, and cannot be purged from intellectually knowing it is highly improbable that anyone reading this book will someday be taken by a wild animal or a hungry fish. That fear magnifies the threat beyond measure, and thereby makes reason and statistics moot.

It is that same fear that drives our endless fascination with all creatures of fang, tooth, and claw. We want to know where they hide, how they hunt, and how we avoid making the next headline. In large part, this is what has driven me to write this book. I wanted to tell the stories of those whose encounter with an alligator, shark, or puma left them mortally wounded. I wanted to learn about the creatures of the swamps, the deep, and the forest in order to better understand how to avoid my own predation and to learn more about their vital roles in Florida's ecology.

As research took me further into their realms, I've learned that, of the three major predators in Florida, the most deadly is not the shark nor the panther, but the American alligator. Fortunately for Floridians, the only other indigenous member of the crocodile family, the American crocodile, is comparatively harmless. Although American crocs can grow much larger than alligators—up to twenty-three feet—there have only been a handful of historic attacks and only one fatality I could authenticate.

There has never been a recorded fatal attack by a Florida black bear, so it has not been included in this book. Elsewhere in the U.S. and Canada, however, both black and grizzly bears do present a viable threat and fatal encounters are not uncommon.

To be better understood, Florida's main predators need to be looked at in context. Florida harbors only two of the twenty-two species of crocodilians and a handful of the world's man-eating sharks. Besides the relatively harmless bobcat, statewide there is only one large cat, the Florida panther, and no evidence that the jaguar or any other member of the big-cat family has roamed Florida since the arrival of humans to our peninsula twelve thousand years ago.

I have also concluded that Floridians should consider themselves lucky. Unlike Australia, our coastal waters are rarely visited by great white sharks, by far the most notorious in the shark family. The American alligator doesn't compare with the Nile crocodile, either, when it comes to human carnage, and our endangered panther pales in comparison to leopards, lions, and tigers vis-à-vis annual worldwide death counts.

And yet, our predators must be respected, so hopefully this book will teach one how to avoid becoming a part of the food chain. One may also gain new insights into the role these creatures play in nature's delicate balance.

The ensuing stories will reveal how human tragedies occur when, through misfortune or mistake, our paths cross a hungry animal's and a life is lost. My deepest sympathy goes out to those who have lost a loved one—a son, a daughter, a wife, a husband, a relative, or any friend whom they will miss forever.

A few months after I began working on this book, Janie Melsek, a landscape designer on Sanibel Island and an acquaintance of mine, was taken by a twelve-foot alligator less than a mile away from my home. Janie was a lifelong conservationist and environmentalist who landscaped island properties using native plant species. She purchased many of her beautiful grasses, trees, and shrubs from the Sanibel-Captiva Conservation Foundation's Native Plant Nursery. The foundation has dedicated itself to preserving quality habitat for wildlife and native plant species on Sanibel and throughout Florida.

Because of her interest in native landscaping, Janie knew better than most of the potential danger posed by being around freshwater ponds. On many occasions, Janie used a spotter when working alongside freshwater canals or lakes. For whatever reason, the spotter was absent on the day that alligator grabbed her.

Janie understood the vital role alligators play in Florida's freshwater ecology. The only freshwater pond on Sanibel prior to human dredging was a large gator hole located near the center of the island. Gator holes provide habitat for fish and aquatic life and, most importantly, alligators keep predators such as raccoons and bobcats from invading bird rookeries.

Janie also understood the beautiful order and the importance of maintaining a balance in nature. She would have wanted a world where we could live in harmony, though not without a cost, with the Sunshine State's native flora and fauna.

This book is my tribute to Janie Melsek and to the natural world she so believed in. I miss her...as do all those who knew and loved her.

A huge Nile crocodile from Peter Beard's
book, *The Eyelids of Morning.*

CROCODILIANS

Translated from the Greek, the word *krokodilos* means "pebble worm" or "gravel worm." The first part of the word comes from the Greek *kroke* (pebble) and the second is a derivative of *drilos* (worm). Presumably, the name comes from a crocodile's habit of lying beside riverbanks, though it hardly resembles oversized worms. When crocodiles were first named over three thousand years ago, their range was far more extensive than it is today, extending as far north as southern Turkey and the eastern shore of the Mediterranean Sea, including the regions of modern-day Syria, Jordan, and Israel. Those populations have long since been hunted to extirpation, but the Nile crocodile was already familiar to the ancient Greeks.

There are twenty-two known species of crocodilians. Of these, roughly half have been known to prey on humans, though some with such rarity that they cannot realistically be considered man-eaters. Two out of the twenty-two known species actively seek out and prey on humans: the Nile crocodile and the saltwater, or Indopacific, crocodile. Both reptiles must always be viewed as killers.

In one incident alone—on the night of February 19, 1945, near the end of the Second World War—nearly one thousand people were killed by Indopacific crocodiles. The British Marine launch forces had cornered and trapped one thousand Japanese soldiers on Ramree, an island located off the eastern coast of what was then called Burma (nowadays Myanmar). The island is connected to the mainland by a large mangrove swamp over eighteen miles wide.

As the British forces pressed the Japanese into retreat, evening approached. Not realizing the mangroves were inhabited by hundreds of large crocodiles, the Japanese forces attempted to retreat to mainland Burma under the cover of darkness, during an exceptionally low tide.

On that evening, Bruce Wright, a naturalist and member of the British force that had cornered the Japanese, was sitting on a marine launch grounded on the tidal flats between the mainland and the island. In the stillness of that hot, moonless summer night, he described the sounds he heard in gruesome detail:

That night was the most horrible that any member of the M.L. (marine launch) crews has ever experienced. The scattered rifle shots in the pitch-black swamp punctuated by the screams of the wounded men crushed in the jaws of huge reptiles, and the blurred, worrying sound of spinning crocodiles, made a cacophony of hell that has rarely been duplicated on earth. At dawn, the vultures arrived to clean up what the crocodiles had left....Of about one thousand Japanese soldiers that entered the swamps of Ramree, only twenty were found alive.

One cannot imagine what a grave mistake those Japanese commanders made on that fateful evening. Unable to see the twenty-foot killing machines in the dark, their weapons were rendered useless. Wading through the labyrinth of channels and mangrove roots, the Japanese became easy targets for the crocodiles. All totaled, 980 perished.

There have been other appalling stories from the region that have rivaled, but never topped, that single night's death toll.

Rogue crocodiles, which develop a taste for, and are very skillful at, hunting human prey, have also been recorded. In the 1960s, a missionary in northern Irian Jaya, Papua New Guinea, reported that at least sixty-two local villagers had been killed or maimed by a single saltwater crocodile. Like some tigers, older crocs will often turn to human predation as they age and are unable to catch more difficult mammals such as wild pigs or water buffalo.

To this day, vicious attacks in Australia's Northern Territories are common. From the eastern shore of India to the Philippines, the "salties" continue to feed on the inhabitants of this vast, oceanic region. Reports of attacks throughout the region flourished after the great Tsunami of December 26, 2004.

Africa's Nile crocodile is also a killer. Because of Africa's Third Worldly, village-bound lifestyle, it is impossible to calculate the actual annual death toll from crocodiles on that continent. In 1953, scientist L. Earl estimated that as many as one thousand people were killed annually by crocodiles on the lower Zambezi River alone. Some scientists' current estimation is, on average ten people a day are taken by crocodiles in Africa. The annual death toll by crocs in the Dark Continent will never be known.

The awesome power of the Nile crocodile is exemplified by an incident occurred in a Tanzanian (Tanganyikan) game park in the late 1950s. In that park, a party of tourists was photographing a large four-thousand-pound female black rhinoceros while she drank at a local watering hole. As the rhino struck her prehensile nose into the discolored water to drink, the calm of the pond was shattered as a massive crocodile shot up and clamped down on her muzzle.

What followed is a grim testament to the tenacity and power of the Nile crocodile. Once locked onto the rhino's nose, the crocodile would not release its grip, and because it weighed over half a ton, the large rhino was unable to shake the animal loose. Although crocodiles and alligators will tire quickly under certain circumstances, the power of their jaws exerts a viselike grip: once they take hold of their prey, they seldom let it go. For over an hour, neither animal moved more than a foot in either direction; the two behemoths held their ground.

Eventually, much to the surprise of the observing tourists, the rhino became exhausted and slowly inched her way into deeper water. A half-hour later, the crocodile had dragged the rhino deep enough to get her head underwater. After a final flurry of activity, she rolled over and drowned. The croc won. By nightfall, the victor, along with the other crocodiles that inhabited the watering hole, had devoured the kill. The ranger estimated the crocodile to be fourteen feet in length.

A recent National Geographic Channel documentary was produced about a killer Nile crocodile known as Gustave. This single animal may be solely responsible for over two hundred deaths around Lake Tanganyika in Burundi. Gustave is estimated to be over nineteen-feet long and weigh in excess of two thousand pounds. Gustave has a habit of drowning, but not always eating, its victims. Its behavior is similar to that of leopards, which have been known to kill humans not for food but for sport. Despite spring-loaded snares and massive iron traps, all efforts to capture Gustave alive have failed thus far. From what is known, Gustave is still out there preying on unsuspecting villagers.

The annual worldwide mortality from attacks by all crocodilian species is only a calculated guess. Remote and isolated villages rarely report to the authorities any news about tribal members who fail to return from nearby rivers. Countries like Papua New Guinea, Uganda, and Sierra Leone have no way of keeping accurate statistics on either attacks or fatalities. In his book *Crocodiles and Alligators of the World,* David Alderton estimates that the annual number of fatalities worldwide is approximately two to three thousand, perhaps higher. Because of crocodilians' wide distribution, that number is greater than any other known predator—sharks, bears, wolves, and all the big cats combined.

The only animal known to kill more people annually is also a reptile: the dreaded king cobra of India and Southeast Asia. It is estimated that the cobra kills over twenty thousand victims a year in India alone. The bite of a king cobra is potent enough to kill a full-grown Indian elephant. In fact, snakes kill more people annually than any other animal, though they do so defensively and, except when a small child is taken by a large python, they never eat their victims.

*****

Of the twenty-two recognized species of crocodilians in the world today, all are members of the family Crocodylidae. From this family, seven are members of the subfamily Alligatorinae (see inserted chart #1). These include the American alligator, the Chinese alligator, and the entire group of South American caimans, as follows: the broad-snouted, the common, the black, the Cuvier's Dwarf, and the Schneider's Dwarf. Of these seven species, only two are considered dangerous to man: the American alligator and the black caiman.

A larger subfamily than the Alligatorinae one is that of true crocodiles, or subfamily Crocodylinae. These differ from alligators in several distinct ways: they have a narrower snout and the fourth tooth back in the lower jaw, the fourth mandibular tooth, is clearly exposed when the animal has its mouth closed. There are other anatomical differences but these are the two most readily observable.

True crocodiles, which number fourteen species, include the American, the Morelet's, the Cuban, the Orinoco, the Nile (with several distinct races), the African slender-snouted, the Indopacific, the Mugger or marsh, the Johnston's, the New Guinea, the Philippine, the Siamese, the Dwarf (also with several distinct races), and the False Gharial.

21

Crocodylidae

Alligatorinae

Alligator
(True alligator)
- American Alligator
  Alligator mississippiensis
- Chinese Alligator
  Alligator sinensis

Caiman
(Caiman)
- Common Caiman
  Caiman crocodilus
- Broad-Snouted Caiman
  Caiman latirostris

Paleosuchus
(Dwarf Caiman)
- Schneider's Dwarf Caiman
  Paleosuchus trigonatus
- Cuvier's Dwarf Caiman
  Paleosuchus palpebrosus

Melanosuchus
- Black Caiman
  Melanosuchus niger

Crocodylinae

Crocodylus
(True crocodile)
- American Crocodile
  Crocodylus acutus
- Cuban Crocodile
  Crocodylus rhombifer
- Morelet's Crocodile
  Crocodylus moreletii
- African Slender-snouted Crocodile
  Crocodylus cataphractus
- Nile Crocodile
  Crocodylus niloticus
- Orinoco Crocodile
  Crocodylus intermedius
- Mugger
  Crocodylus palustris
- Saltwater Crocodile
  Crocodylus porosus
- Johnston's Crocodile
  Crocodylus johnsoni
- New Guinea Crocodile
  Crocodylus novaeguineae
- Philippine Crocodile
  Crocodylus mindorensis
- Siamese Crocodile
  Crocodylus siamensis

Osteolaemus
(Dwarf Crocodile)
- Dwarf Crocodile
  Osteolaemus tetraspis

Tominstoma
(False Gharial)
- False Gharial
  Tomistoma schlegelii

Gavialinae

Gharial
- Gharial
  Gavialis gangeticus

Chart #1:
The Crocodile Family Tree

22

Of these fourteen crocodiles, several have been documented to take human life, including the Orinoco (which grows to over twenty-three feet), the New Guinea (over thirteen feet), and the marsh or Mugger of India (over thirteen feet). As noted earlier, the two species universally held to be man-eaters are the Nile crocodile of Africa (over twenty-five feet) and the Indopacific or saltwater crocodile (over thirty feet). These two species account for ninety-nine percent of all human/Crocodylidae fatalities and must be considered extremely dangerous.

One reason for this high-mortality rate is the sheer size of both the Nile and Indopacific crocodiles. There are undocumented sightings from the 1920s of Indopacific crocodiles exceeding thirty feet in length. These originated from the Segama River in northern Borneo. There, a rubber-plantation owner by the name of James Montgomery described a huge croc which the local Seluke tribe believed to be over two hundred years old. One day, Montgomery saw the animal on the bank of the Segama River. It was basking with its large body and head out of the water and only a small portion of its tail remained submerged in the river. When it finally moved off the bank, Montgomery measured the distance from where its head laid to the edge of the water. That distance was thirty-two feet, ten inches. It suggested that the crocodile's total length was thirty-three feet. A crocodile this size presumably would weigh over five thousand pounds.

In Australia's Northern Territories, officials have documented several saltwater crocodiles over twenty feet in length. One of them—measuring twenty feet, one inch—weighed in at 2,418 pounds. The relationship between length and weight is exponential in all crocodilians. Every additional foot of length results in a disproportionate increase in girth and weight. A sixteen-foot alligator may weigh in four times more than a twelve-footer. A Nile crocodile approaching twenty feet in length weighs in well over a ton.

There is one additional subfamily and only a single member in it: the subfamily Gavialnae, represented by what is the most unusual of all crocodilians, the Gharial of northern India, Pakistan, Nepal, Burma, Bangladesh, and Bhutan. Unless provoked or cornered, it has never been known to attack humans. Although it is near extinction in the wild, records from the 1800s indicate that mature males may have reached lengths of over thirty feet and weighed over four thousand pounds. It is the most aquatic of all crocodilian species and lives on an exclusive diet of fish. Its habitat includes the cold, swift-flowing rivers that descend from the Himalayas. Fossil records show that the Gharial have not changed substantially since the late Miocene era, some ten million years ago.

There have occurred two recent extinctions since recorded history, including a rare terrestrial crocodile which thrived until eighteen hundred years ago on the island of New Caledonia in the far-western Pacific. It was called *Mekosuchus inexpectatus* and grew to about six and a half feet. It resembled a large lizard, not unlike the present-day Komodo dragon and, as such, spent the majority of its life on land and not in the water. Jawbones and teeth indicate it might have thrived on mollusks and land crabs.

The second extinct species, *Crocodylus sinhaleyus,* was a native of Sri Lanka and vanished comparatively recently without leaving any direct descendants. Very little is known about either of these species except that human over-hunting and loss of habitat have contributed to their extinction.

Notice the long, slender fish-eating snout of the endangered gharial.

Crocodilians have roamed the earth for 230 million years and witnessed the coming and going of hundreds of thousands of species, including the dinosaurs. Over this immense time frame, they have ranged in size from the two-foot-long *Terrestrisuchus* (extinct) to the forty-five-foot monsters known as Supercrocs (*Sarcosuchus imperator*) that lived 110 million years ago. Supercrocs had skulls over nine-feet long and weighed an unbelievable twenty thousand pounds. They ate dinosaurs.

It is interesting to speculate how the crocodilian family survived the great extinction that occurred sixty-five million years ago. This cataclysmic event, which scientists now contend completely wiped out the dinosaurs, was the result of the impact between the earth and a giant asteroid or comet. A trace layer of iridium found imbedded in sediment around the planet helps confirm the hypothesis that this massive collision happened around sixty-five million years ago. The largest impact may have taken place near the Yucatán Peninsula, on the eastern coast of Mexico. Evidence suggests there may have been as many as six separate asteroid collisions during the same era, all of which occurred within a very short time span.

The blasts blackened the skies for several years, resulting in a complete collapse of the food chain. We can only speculate that several variables factored into the crocodile's amazing survival during that catastrophic time.

For the first few years, the ravaged landscape would have been rich with carrion, assuming that many of the multi-ton plant-eaters such as the brontosaurus starved to death from the lack of growing vegetation. Once the major herbivores were gone, the carnivores, like the Tyrannosaurus rex, soon followed. This profusion of carrion could have helped feed the remaining crocodiles for years after the impact.

Another advantage crocodilians had was their extremely slow metabolism. Even today's crocs can go into a state of suspended animation, which permits them to go as long as two years without eating. In fact, the large Nile crocodile that feeds during the annual wildebeest migration is known to eat only once a year. It can grow to over twenty feet in length. It's hard to imagine how long a Supercroc over forty-five-feet long would have been able to survive without food, but three or four years is not out of the realm of possibility.

Another possible factor in the crocodile family's surviving the great Jurassic extinction is, most crocodilians prefer aquatic over terrestrial environment. Both fresh- and saltwater environments are more stable after catastrophes such as the Jurassic collision, whereby the marine environment would have provided just enough food to allow crocs to make it through to the early Paleocene into the coming rise of mammals. Dinosaurs, as we are well aware, have vanished…haven't they…?

In the past fifty years, scientists have begun to take a second look at the relationship between dinosaurs and modern-day birds. Along those same lines, they now feel crocodiles and alligators are more closely related to birds than to other cold-blooded animals such as turtles, snakes, and lizards.

Their physical appearance certainly doesn't suggest a kinship. However, birds and crocodilians have elongated outer-ear canals, a muscular gizzard, a four-chambered heart, and other not readily observable anatomical similarities. Some of the best clues to the relationship lie not in their appearance, but in a crocodilian's behavior.

Crocodilians build nests, guard and help incubate their eggs, and after the eggs hatch, the female will remain with her hatchlings for months, sometimes even years, to rear them into adulthood. Like birds, they tend to return to good nesting sites year after year and are all very vocal, especially the American alligator.

It is astonishing to witness a half-ton female Nile croc gently picking up her foot-long hatchlings in the same jaws that can crush the skull of a wildebeest. She ferries her brood carefully to the nearest water, making several journeys until all forty to fifty offspring are safe. She will remain and guard over her hatchlings for months, sometimes years, afterward. Crocodilians have gizzards and, like birds, they swallow stones to help in the digestion of food. A large croc can have over ten pounds of rocks, known as gastroliths, in its stomach. There is one theory that these heavy gastroliths, in addition to helping break down food, are also used as ballast to offset the greater buoyancy of the larger animals, much like the five-pound lead weights a scuba diver straps on before a dive.

The acid in a crocodilian's stomach is the most potent digestive fluid of all known vertebrates. It is capable of breaking down fur, hair, and bone into usable proteins. Only metal, some plastics, and stones survive this powerful onslaught of acid. Larger crocodiles have been found with jewelry, handguns, and pieces of undigested wood in their stomachs.

Unlike most mammals, crocodilians are anaerobic by design. They are capable of tremendous but very short bursts of energy. Depending on their size, after just a few minutes of intense activity, they begin to fade. Their muscle tissue fills with levels of lactic acid that would kill most animals. Large alligators have been known to die from exhaustion after a prolonged fight while in the process of being captured.

The entire family of crocodilians is cold-blooded. They regulate their body temperature by alternately basking in the warm, tropical sun or cooling off in a nearby river, swamp, or lake. This feature greatly limits their range and explains why nearly all of the world's crocodilians inhabit tropical and subtropical latitudes.

There are advantages to not having to maintain a constant body temperature. An adult crocodile weighing one thousand pounds and which remains in a resting state over the course of a day burns only 190 calories. The daily caloric intake for an average male adult between nineteen and fifty years of age should be 2,900 calories. Allow me to be more graphic and impart a little silly perspective, for the sake of analogy: crocodiles as large as half a ton can exist on a little more than one-third of a single Big Mac a day (there are approximately 485 calories in a Big Mac). If humans weighed half a ton, they would need to eat forty Big Macs a day, with most of that caloric intake used to keep their body temperature at 98.6° F. The sad truth is, humans would probably weigh in at one thousand pounds if they ate forty Big Macs as day.

A crocodile's slow metabolic rate, by using only four percent of the calories a human would need to survive, allows it the ability to go for extremely long periods without food. Some larger animals have been known to go as long as two years without eating. Their slow metabolism, coupled with a very unusual four-chambered heart, allows crocodilians to hold their breath and remain underwater for hours on end.

Crocodilians have a cardiovascular system unlike any other creature on earth. Nile crocodiles, when submerged, are able to slow their heart rate down to four beats a minute. At the same time, they are able to close down various arteries on demand. In essence, they can put their arms and legs to sleep at will, redirecting their blood flow to only their heart, lungs, and brain for hours on end. They are the only animal known to be able to go into this kind of metabolic hibernation on command. Of all crocodilian species, American alligators are perhaps the best adapted to stay underwater for prolonged periods.

Crocodilians also have keen eyesight, especially in lowlight conditions, as well as an acute hearing and a well-developed sense of smell. They have been known to smell the rotting flesh of a dead elephant up to two miles from the carcass. They also have unique motion-detecting receptors along their lower jaw, which allow them to know when a potential prey has entered a still pond. This detecting ability doesn't always work in their best interest.

As a litmus test for whether or not an alligator has been fed, local law-enforcement personnel oftentimes will throw things into a known alligator pond to see if the animal responds by swimming toward the area whence the disturbance originated. If the alligator approaches the area, officials feel confident the alligator has been fed in the past, whereupon they quickly dispose of it. The trouble is, this response is a conditioned reflex. The motion detectors beneath an alligator's jaw are designed to pick up unusual vibrations in the water, which the creature will instinctively investigate and, if hungry, attack, drown, and consume the intruder—perhaps a raccoon, rat, duck, or snake that has entered the pond. This sensory ability is even more important during an alligator's nighttime hunting expedition. Hence, as a litmus test for finding out whether or not an alligator has been fed, this is completely ineffective. Ninety-nine out of every one hundred alligators will respond and swim toward objects being thrown into the water, edible or not.

Except for the Gharial, which has a very long, slender, and toothy snout, most crocodilians have around seventy to eighty teeth. Like those of sharks, these teeth are constantly being lost and replaced over the course of a lifetime. It is estimated that a large, mature animal over fifty years old wears out between two and three thousand teeth in its life span. Since it does not chew its food, those teeth are designed to grab and keep a firm hold onto the prey.

Like sharks again, the crushing pressure of a crocodilian's clamped jaws is legendary. The force exerted by a twelve-foot American alligator is over two thousand pounds per square inch. That is like having a Toyota Camry parked on your leg. Once a large alligator or crocodile clamps down on its victim, it is virtually impossible for that victim to break free. The quickest and easiest way for one to remove one's arm from the firm bite of an alligator is to cut it off.... Not a pleasant thought.

In one experiment, a scientist placed a two-inch-thick piece of steel plate inside the mouth of a huge crocodile. The animal bit down so hard on the metal, it drove several of its teeth through the roof of its mouth, indenting the steel plates in the process. The bite of a croc which weighs over a ton is tantamount to having a Hummer parked on one's leg—a military-issue Hummer, complete with armor plating and a mounted 50-caliber machine gun.

Oddly enough, crocodilians lack the powerful muscles necessary to open their mouth. This characteristic has been exploited for years by roadside alligator wrestlers as well as experienced gator trappers. Their use of duct tape around a closed saurian's mouth renders their powerful jaws useless. Because they lack molars and any real chewing ability, crocodiles rely on crushing their food and using gravity to aid in swallowing it. They lift their heads up out of the water and let the mangled food more or less fall into their stomachs.

Once they have their prey firmly grasped, many crocodilians immediately go into what is commonly called a death roll. For larger prey such as wild boars and water buffalo, several animals will work together to tear apart a carcass. Each animal grabs a leg, an arm, or a head and then rolls in an opposite direction of their counterpart, whereupon they rip the prey into edible chunks of flesh.

Crocodilians thus cooperate with each other and have far more intelligence than their walnut-sized brains would lead us to believe. Cuban crocodiles held in captivity at the St. Augustine Alligator Farm have been taught to respond to their names' being called the same way dogs do it. Since Cuban crocs are one of the most aggressive of all crocodilians, no one ever thought this possible.

They have a natural ability to remember and this ability serves them well in the wild. At Lake St. Lucia in Natal, South Africa, the annual mullet migration attracts a large number of crocodiles. Coming in from all parts of the lake and connecting rivers, these reptiles work together to form an effective blockade across a section of the lake known as the Narrows, roughly five hundred yards across. They do not break ranks during this annual feast and there is no fighting over positioning. Breaking ranks would result in loss of food for every animal participating in the mullet feast.

Another anecdotal example of crocodilian memory comes from a book by Dick Bothwell, *The Great Outdoors Book of Alligators and Other Crocodilia.* In a section he calls "The Unsafe Saurians," Bothwell recalls the reunion of a ten-foot nuisance alligator named Henry with Jim Philbin, the Florida wildlife officer who had captured the reptile years earlier.

The story goes that Philbin had taken the alligator out of a St. Petersburg creek because of its formidable size and the creek's proximity to nearby developments. The animal was moved to a special pen along St. Petersburg's Lake Maggiore Park's nature trail. There he was viewed by thousands of hikers and, under normal circumstances, would lie as still as a statue and ignore the peering visitors.

When Philbin showed up at the edge of the fence one day, Henry unexpectedly sprang to life. Hissing with fury, it plunged off its sunning mound, swam quickly across a small pond, and charged up the bank toward the spot where Philbin was standing. Henry clearly remembered the man who had placed him in this pen and no doubt would have continued his attack had the fence not stood between them. Philbin was unharmed, but it was obvious to both the zookeeper and the hunter that the alligator knew exactly who had been responsible for its incarceration.

This failed attack and Henry's memory of the very same man who had captured it years earlier exemplify how large crocodilians hunt. As shown on National Geographic Channel's spectacular video, *Crocodiles—Here Be Dragons,* Nile crocodiles know when the great wildebeest migration occurs. Every year when the herds approach, the crocs gather along the shoreline of Africa's Grumeti River in Tanzania and await their prey. The annual dinner bell is ringing....

As crocodilians mature, their diet changes dramatically. In their first years, most crocodilians eat small prey such as insects, minnows, tadpoles, and frogs. After they reach a size of three feet, their diet starts to include small rodents, ducks, shorebirds, and fish. When they become over eight-feet long, they add on larger mammals such as deer, antelope, pigs, snakes, and in South America, large rodents such as nutria and capybara. The species' true monsters such as the Indopacific and Nile crocs take prey as large as baby elephants, hippos, rhinos, and water buffalo.

They all hunt using stealth and surprise. Either totally or partially submerged, they slowly glide toward the victim until they are within striking distance. Then, without warning, they use the massive tails to propel themselves upward and forward toward the target. The Indopacific crocodile's tail is so powerful it can actually propel the entire length of the animal's body out of the water in a form of tail-walking similar to behavior we see in trained porpoises.

By lunging at their prey with incredible speed, the crocs get a firm bite on the hapless beast. In the case of zebras and wildebeest, they generally grasp the animal in the head or neck area; they seldom lunge at the animal directly, but spring up beside their quarry and swing the gaping jaws into the unsuspecting animal. Once the prey is bitten, unless it is able to wiggle free, the crocodile uses its strong legs to back down into the water, pulling the prey, head first, underwater. It takes only minutes to drown a large mammal, after which fellow crocodiles work together in a series of death rolls to dismember and devour their prey.

The speed of these attacks is astonishing. In one second, a wildebeest sees what had appeared to be nothing more than a floating log along the edge of the river exploding into a massive mouth filled with eighty bone-crushing teeth. Some shoreline attacks fail but, should the crocodile encounter the wildebeest crossing the river, the situation is far graver. The wildebeest has little chance after entering the croc's realm.

In the water—a crocodilian's natural environment—neither animals nor people have a chance. With the snakelike motion of their enormous tails, crocodilians are able to outswim horses or the fastest Olympic medalists. They can, for short bursts, move at incredible speeds. Unless the prey—animal or person—can reach safety at the shoreline, it has little chance. The crocodile quickly disembowels the victim or grabs it by the arm or leg, drowning it within minutes. Swimming in waters known to harbor crocodiles or alligators is extremely ill-advised.

On land, the odds favor mammals. For very short distances, the Johnston's freshwater crocodile of interior Australia has been clocked as fast as sixteen miles per hour. But again, because of the anaerobic nature of their energy, crocs tire quickly and are not designed to move well on land. In a head-to-head race, most four-legged creatures can readily outpace the cumbersome crocodilians. But over the short distance needed to seize a person, alligators are capable of catching even the quickest of humans.

It should be noted that the Nile croc has been known to capture people unawares at considerable distances from the water's edge. In the late 1800s, along the edge of Lake Rudolf in Central Africa, an explorer's cook, while preparing dinner, was unexpectedly grabbed by a large crocodile. The incident occurred at dusk, which is the time normally associated with such attacks. All crocodilians prefer to feed at lowlight or darkness, though attacks can and do occur at any time of the day.

Of course, this is a generalization of the family Crocodylidae and not an elucidation on each of the twenty-two known species. For example, it is highly improbable that an African Dwarf crocodile will take down many hippos. Each crocodilian species is uniquely adapted to its particular habitat. With that in mind, to better understand the part they play in the ecosystem, as well as the fatal and nonfatal human attacks that have occurred in Florida, let us first look at some of the remarkable characteristics of American alligators.

A Long Silence Broken

Oscar Scherer State Park lies a half-dozen miles south of Sarasota, on Florida's West Coast. The entrance to the park is just outside the historic town of Osprey. The core of the park's current 462-acre site was originally called South Creek Ranch, which was owned by Elsa Scherer Burrows. She was the daughter of Oscar Scherer, a man who had made his fortune from the invention of a process to dye shoe leather, which sent the fashion world of his time (ca. 1872) into a flurry of multicolored shoes. Upon her death in 1955, Burrows bequeathed South Creek Ranch to the state of Florida, with the condition that it name the park after her deceased father.

Oscar Scherer State Park opened to the public in 1956. The habitat within the park consists of pine and scrubby flatwoods, hardwood hammocks, and freshwater marsh. There is a three-acre swimming pond known as Osprey Lake and a backwater stream called South Creek, which runs down and through the park. The creek eventually empties into a bay behind Casey Key, where it joins the salty waters of the Gulf of Mexico.

In 1991, the state of Florida purchased an additional 922 acres abutting South Creek Ranch called Palmer Ranch. With the combined ranches, Oscar Scherer State Park now encompasses 1,384 acres and is home to one of the largest native populations of Florida Scrub Jays, an endangered species.

*****

Sharon Elaine Holmes was born on April 24, 1957, one year after Oscar Scherer Park had been opened to the public. Sixteen years later, on August 16, 1973, Holmes died there. No one—from the Florida Game & Freshwater Fish Commission, presently known as the Fish and Wildlife Commission, to her father, to the park rangers or the tour-boat operators—could have foreseen the tragedy that would befall the teenage girl. Holmes was the first modern recorded fatality from a Florida alligator attack.

In 1948, the Game & Freshwater Commission and Florida State began keeping records of alligator attacks statewide. Bear in mind that Florida's population in 1950 was still under three million people. The tremendous urban sprawl we have witnessed ever since had yet to encroach into the vast wetlands and marshes of the state. In 1948, any encounter with alligators was considered rare.

By the 1950s, the indiscriminate hunting and harvesting of alligators for their hide and meat had taken their toll on the populations. The alligator was finally placed on the endangered-species list the same year of Holmes's accident: 1973. It is estimated that there were fewer than 250,000 alligators left in the entire continental United States at that time. A decade earlier, in 1961, alarmed by the decimation of its native alligator population, Florida outlawed the killing of alligators within its borders. Nonetheless, illegal trapping and poaching continued, with little to no enforcement over the next dozen years, ceasing only when said killings became a federal offense.

With far fewer people living in Florida at that time and a dwindling population of gators, encounters and attacks were extremely infrequent. In 1943, five years before Florida decided to keep track of verified alligator attacks, the harvest of alligator hide had plummeted to a mere sixty-eight hundred units, down from the 1929 Florida record of 190,000. This represented a ninety-six-percent decline.

In 1944, one year after the most deplorable gator-skin hunt on record, the Florida government, in an effort to curtail its plummeting alligator population, banned the harvest of immature gators less than four feet in length.

By 1973, with the indigenous alligator population near collapse and illegal poaching still an ongoing problem, large alligators in the wild had become virtually nonexistent. Most had been killed and skinned and their hide secretly smuggled into Louisiana, where the sale of alligator by-products was still permitted. The few larger animals that survived the mass slaughter lived within the secure boundaries of state and national parks, though even there they were never really safe from poachers.

For two straight decades, the combination of a sparsely populated Florida and a decimated alligator population left the fledgling Florida Fish and Wildlife Agency with little activity to report. In its first eleven years keeping records, only five attacks were recorded, none of them fatal. From 1960 to 1971, not a single alligator attack was ever noted. Then, in 1972 five attacks were authenticated. In 1973, a quarter century after record-keeping had commenced, the first fatality in modern history occurred—Sharon Holmes.

*****

They called it Sally. It was a "him," but in 1973 it wasn't common knowledge that female alligators rarely exceeded eight feet in length. Sally measured eleven feet, three inches. They didn't weigh up attacking alligators back then, but an animal of that length would weigh around four hundred pounds. Sally had been living in the marshes, creeks, and freshwater ponds of Oscar Scherer State Park for fifteen years.

32

Sally was well known and well fed. It's important to understand that feeding an alligator in the wild was not considered illegal in 1973; in fact, quite the opposite. At the time, it was common practice to feed wild alligators, especially in the parks. Most tour operators in Everglades National Park fed alligators during their airboat or swamp buggy tours, and the tour-boat operators and concessionaires at Oscar Scherer State Park were no exception.

In 1973, any camper or tourist could go to the park's concession stand and buy a prepackaged bag of alligator feed. Those packets would either contain dried bread or another alligator favorite, marshmallows. The packets cost twenty-five cents each. The tour-boat operator at the time, James Fox, used a loud horn on his night tours so as to attract local alligators to the back of his tour boat before tossing them marshmallows and slices of white bread. It became a conditioned response, making it sometimes unnecessary to even bother feeding the gators at all. Gators were simply responding to the sound of the dinner horn and never once failed to make their hungry appearance. Business on those night tours was good.

Sally would have been one of those preconditioned alligators. In her prehistoric brain, people equaled food. Fox, the park personnel, and tourists and visitors to Oscar Scherer State Park did not know that, over the years, they had been feeding and training an eleven-foot time bomb. Sooner or later, an alligator of that size, lacking any fear of humans, would invariably try to eat one. In this respect, alligators are not dogs: they can and often do "bite the hand that feeds," sometimes fatally.

The park authorities knew that Sally had recently moved into the park's swimming area. On August 5, eleven days before the attack, two wildlife officers tried to catch Sally by using a snatch hook. They were going to relocate the large gator to a less precarious habitat than their local swimming pond.

Sally, having been fed on a regular basis, readily took the bait on the large steel snatch hook. Because of its enormous size and strength, it quickly straightened out the hook. Signs were posted at the main entrance to the park and on three different locations along the lake's edge, which read: **CAUTION, GATORS IN SWIMMING AREA!**

It's important to remember that there had not been a recorded fatality by a Florida alligator in twenty-five years. Given that fact alone, most people ignored the warning signs and kept on swimming. Alligators were perceived as harmless reptiles that fed on turtles, fish, and of course, marshmallows.

On Monday, August 6, park officers tried to entice Sally into a steel trap, as they remained concerned about having such a leviathan in the swimming area. Still licking the wounds from the straightened snatch hook, Sally wouldn't come anywhere near the cage.

The next day, they went back to the snatch hook, this time securing it with a heavy rope to a nearby tree. Sally once again fell for the baited hook, but it promptly straightened out the second snatch hook. A third hook was put out on August 8, with exactly the same result. The bait was gone, the hooks straightened, and Sally was still swimming in the pond.

Possibly tiring of getting her mouth torn apart by three enormous fish hooks, Sally appeared to have left the swimming area on August 9. Two officers had found a trail made by a large alligator while the animal was exiting the swimming area and apparently heading toward a nearby marsh. Sally, it appeared to everyone, was finally gone.

Just in case Sally returned, the park rangers had left another baited snatch hook in the pond and kept a nervous eye out for any sign of the four-hundred-pound beast. On August 10, they caught two smaller alligators in the steel cage originally set up for Sally, but the big gator had yet to return. Sally was not seen in the pond again until near midnight on the night of the incident. That night, August 16, 1973, the mutilated body of a sixteen-year-old girl was lying beside the alligator.

*****

Sharon Elaine Holmes was an adorable teenager, a student at Sarasota High School who had just finished tenth grade. She had light brown hair, blue eyes, and weighed 125 pounds. She was petite, standing only five-feet, four-inches high. Sharon was born in Vero Beach, on Florida's East Coast.

Her family had checked into campsite #25 on August 14, planning to stay through the 17th. They were camping in a tent. The camp registration indicates they were a party of seven; perhaps some friends had come along for the midweek vacation. School was starting in a few weeks and this was going to be Holmes's last days of summer fun before she entered eleventh grade.

The attack happened just after sunset. Sharon was the only person swimming in the lake at the time of the deadly encounter. The warning signs about the large alligator being in the lake had been removed a few days before, since no one had recently seen Sally in the pond.

Sharon Holmes's father, Burton Holmes, was standing along the shoreline. No one knows whether the alligator swam up from beneath Sharon or she accidentally drifted toward the animal while swimming. But at 8:30 P.M. on August 16, Holmes yelled, "Help me!" once, lifted both arms high up into the air, and was then pulled beneath the dark water.

Her father immediately swam out to save her, thinking Sharon was drowning. For every person witnessing the incident, there was no indication that an alligator had been involved. As her father swam toward her, Holmes resurfaced for a moment. She reappeared about ten feet away from where she

34

had first been taken, floating motionless in the water. Then, still not comprehending what was really happening, witnesses saw her disappear for a second time beneath the water.

By this time, Burton Holmes had arrived at the area where his daughter's drowning was occurring. He called out to shore asking for a boat and started surface-diving in an attempt to find and rescue his daughter. During one of his dives, he miraculously got hold of Holmes's arm and tried to pull her back to the surface.

"She's right under me. I couldn't hold on to her. She's right here under me," Burton Holmes told one of the men who had taken a small raft to assist him. "Sharon's on the bottom. Someone, call the police," he added. Burton Holmes did not know he was pulling against the strength of a four-hundred-pound reptile which had his young daughter locked in its jaws.

By now, there were others diving in the lake, trying to find the missing girl. Several canoes had made it into the area, and as darkness gathered, they dove and searched in vain for the teenager. Her father kept repeating, "I couldn't hold on to her."

Ten minutes passed and Sharon never resurfaced. It was already pitch black and the diving men were exhausted. The situation on Osprey Lake was bleak.

One of the witnesses ran to find a park ranger and report the drowning. In the ensuing hours, the edge of the three-acre lake filled with rescue workers, sheriffs, park rangers, onlookers, and divers. Search lights were set up and teams continually scoured the bottom of the lake for Holmes's body. For everyone involved at the time, it had been an unfortunate accident. From all appearances, Sharon Holmes had drowned.

About midnight, Deputy Sheriff Don Evans, working with Ranger Ed Midkipp, spotted Holmes's body along the south side of the lake's bank, near an overflow culvert. It was being guarded by an eleven-foot alligator. The alligator was Sally.

As they approached, Sally slipped back into the pitch-black waters of the pond. The two men recovered Holmes's body and brought it back to the awaiting ambulance by boat. The alligator had bitten off both of her arms and there were numerous bite marks to her torso and head. Holmes was dead. The men knew it the moment their flashlights had discovered the body.

Noticing her injuries, the rangers realized it hadn't been a drowning at all, but the first recorded fatal alligator attack in twenty-five years. The long silence had just been broken. Then and there, all came to this sobering conclusion: alligators can and will kill people if given the opportunity. Insofar as what Floridians knew about alligators, everything would have to be revised as of that fateful August 1973 night.

At seven the next morning, Game Commissioner L. Tappen Dennis shot Sally with a high-powered rifle. Returning back to shore with the dead beast, Dennis and Sheriff Evans asked Sharon Holmes's parents to please leave. Once they left, Robert Taylor and Dennis cut open the alligator's stomach, removed Holmes's left arm and hand and a portion of the right elbow, and took those to the medical examiner's office.

Holmes had not drowned. Her autopsy confirmed she had died of a massive internal hemorrhage as a result of her liver having been crushed. Once seized in the jaws of an overpowering reptile—capable of cracking open the shells of snapping turtles and of having a bite more forceful than a great white shark's—Holmes died instantly. The teenage girl from Sarasota, swimming alone and unarmed, had no chance against a two-hundred-million-year-old killing machine.

The swimming area at Osprey Lake was closed for two weeks following the incident. Reports of other nuisance alligators skyrocketed after the shocking news of Holmes's death made headlines across the state. Many people called for the complete eradication of alligators in Florida. Fish and Wildlife officers were in shock.

The incident spearheaded a series of discussions and ordinance changes, which resulted in a complete ban on the feeding of alligators a few years after the incident. The consistent feeding of Sally was noted as the major contributing factor in the final report.

The lesson learned from that grim encounter should never be forgotten. If you ever see anyone feeding an alligator, visualize Sharon Holmes's lifeless, limbless body lying along the banks of Osprey Lake on that horrid night of August 16, 1973. Think of Holmes not as a stranger, but potentially being your own daughter or son. Then pick up the phone and report the person feeding that reptile, be it a friend or a neighbor, to the local authorities. Sadly, it is far too late to save Sharon Holmes, but you can save the next potential victim. We now know alligators will attack and kill humans, especially those that have been fed. The long silence has been broken. Let us never remain silent again.

In an Instant

It was a windy day. The steady breezes rushed out of the west at fifteen to twenty knots, making the surface of Lake Ashby shimmer with whitecaps and waves. It was late March and North-Central Florida was reawakening from its brief appointment with winter. The days were growing longer and warmer. The nights no longer carried the threat of frost.

The family had driven to the park before—four, maybe five times over the past few years. It was an easy fifteen-mile drive from the town of New Smyrna Beach, Florida, to this small county park. On that particular Friday, the first day of a long Easter break, Lori Binford decided to take her two young sons, pack up the two dogs, invite a cousin, and head out to Lake Ashby Park for a midday picnic.

They arrived just past noon and found an open picnic table a few yards from the roped-off swimming area. The two boys, Adam and Evan, immediately dashed to the water's edge after getting out of the car. Evan, who was five years older than Adam, wanted to see how cold the lake water was. The two dogs naturally tagged along with the boys while their mother and their nine-year-old cousin, Cassidy, stayed to set the picnic table for a taco lunch.

The lake water was eighty degrees, warm enough to invite the two boys and their accompanying dogs to wade in along the shallow shoreline. Evan spied some pretty water lilies just beyond the place where Lake Ashby Creek meanders into the lake. In a small cove less than two hundred feet from the picnic table, a dense array of cattails, lily pads, and bulrushes rustled in the spring breeze. The two dogs were in heaven, splashing along the shoreline and glad to have finally been released from the confines of the back seat of the car.

Evan, the older boy, decided to pick some yellow water lilies for the picnic table. With Easter a week away, perhaps the two children felt that their mother would appreciate the flowers. Adam joined in and the two, along with the dogs, spent the next five minutes gathering water lilies in the knee-deep water.

A short time later, both children made their way back across the creek and delivered the hand-picked flowers to their mother. Lori Binford smiled and placed them on the picnic table. It would be a little while longer before the tacos were ready, so she allowed her sons to continue playing. Evan decided to take the flowers he had just picked and toss them back into the water near the swimming area. Adam, noticing that his brother's plan would leave the table without any water lilies at all, decided to go back to the cove and pick some fresh ones for his mother. He didn't tell his mother where he was going and, busy preparing lunch, she didn't notice him slip away. Little Adam was three and a half years old.

One of the dogs, catching the smell of the tacos, stayed back at the picnic table to beg for food while the other, a small basset hound, ran along with Adam. The family had only been at the park for ten minutes.

Prior to that afternoon, there had never been an authenticated alligator attack in Lake Ashby. A year earlier, two nuisance alligators had been reported by Robert Landreth to the Fish and Wildlife Commission. The investigating officer on official complaints #96-5-1548 and #96-5-1547 followed through and ordered both problem gators removed. Professional trapper Curtis Lucas was dispatched to Lake Ashby shortly after the complaint had been filed and on June 2, 1996, Lucas harvested two alligators from the lake—a ten-foot, eight-inch male and a seven-foot, seven-inch male, both of which matched the description in Landreth's formal complaint.

Neither animal had ever attacked or threatened anyone, but they were coming dangerously close to the swimming area. Landreth felt that their behavior indicated they might have been fed before. The wildlife officer elected to err on the side of caution and the two aggressive gators were successfully removed from Lake Ashby. Their meat was sold to market and their hide turned into shoes, wallets, and handbags. Five to eight thousand alligators a year are taken out of Florida's ecosystem through this process; it is a professional and reasonable way to deal with problem gators throughout the Sunshine State.

Knowing there were still large alligators in this thirty-two-acre shallow lake, the county had posted a sign near the entrance to the park. The sign read: No Animals in Water: Fla. State Code 1005. It never mentioned anything about the lake's alligators or the serious dangers they posed. The sign was put there to make certain no one allowed their dogs in the lake, because dogs are natural attractants for hungry alligators. All dogs, especially wet dogs, give off a strong scent that alligators are instinctively drawn toward. Along with the odor, a dog's splashing and erratic behavior in the water will invariably draw the attention of any nearby leviathan.

Lori Binford didn't know this. Her two young sons, one eight and the other three, wouldn't have noticed the sign nor likely paid attention to it, even if they had read it. They were just kids and dogs playing along a shoreline on a gorgeous, warm Friday afternoon two days before Palm Sunday.

When lunch was finally ready, Binford called over to her oldest, Evan, and he quickly came back to the picnic table from the shoreline. Looking around for her youngest, Binford spotted Adam in the distance and decided to stroll across the creek and go down to the cove to retrieve her boy. As she got near the lake, she noticed Adam was bending over picking up another water lily for her.

Binford was twenty yards away from her boy when she saw Adam appear to fall into the water. There was a sudden splash, a splash too large for a three-foot-tall child to make. In an instant, Adam vanished. Binford rushed into the shallow water where she had last seen her child, but Adam was gone. Later that day, Binford told investigators that she might have caught a glimpse of Adam being drawn down, beneath the choppy surface of Lake Ashby, and the thought of an alligator crossed her mind. She knew something terrible had just happened.

Binford soon stood knee-deep in the last spot where Adam had been standing. She searched frantically around the immediate area. No Adam. She began to yell, then scream, and this quickly gained the attention of a park employee, Quincy Harden. Harden, suspecting the boy had drowned, immediately called 911.

Within a few minutes of the call, the local police, along with the regional EMS team, were on the scene. After Binford described the incident in detail, everyone agreed that it did not appear to be a drowning but an alligator attack. The splash, they all concurred, had been too large for a three-year-old to make and everyone remembered the alligator-nuisance complaints from a year earlier. The first responders contacted Fish and Wildlife and the Volusia County Sheriff's Dive Team to assist in the ensuing search.

Curtis Lucas, the trapper who had worked in Lake Ashby the year before, was brought in and, just before nightfall, was told by Sergeant Curtis Brown from Fish and Wildlife to kill any alligator he found large enough to have made such an attack. Earlier that same day, the divers, along with a helicopter, a number of small boats, and a dozen volunteers set up a grid and started a thorough search of the cove in the vicinity where Adam had last been seen. They searched diligently until darkness set in.

Lucas and his fellow trapper Mike Taylor decided they would continue to search through the night so as to find the culprit gator. By this time, everyone involved realized the outcome would be grim.

The winds continued unabated, which made the search, even under a rising moon, extremely difficult. Sometime around 1:30 A.M. the next day, Lucas and Taylor returned to the command post in near-total darkness to inform Sergeant Brown they had caught a glimpse of a large alligator with what appeared to be a white object in its mouth at a considerable distance from where Adam had been taken. Because of the windy conditions, they had been unable to capture or kill the animal. The search would have to resume at daybreak.

At 6:30 A.M. on Saturday, March 22, 1997, the two trappers once again spotted the alligator they had briefly seen the night before. It was first light, and as they approached the beast, it submerged. They tossed a bright orange buoy over the side where the alligator had gone down and went about trying to snatch-hook the animal, but to no avail.

Twenty minutes later, the alligator resurfaced sixty yards away. The trappers quickly sped toward it, but once again the gator submerged beneath the choppy surface of the lake. Another buoy was deployed and, on that blustery morning, the trappers began the arduous task of attempting to snatch-hook the animal for a second time.

This time they succeeded. At 7:29 A.M., the stout snatch-hook caught hold of the alligator and for the next thirty-seven minutes the two trappers battled the powerful reptile. Trapper Lucas finally exhausted the animal and brought it to the surface, whereupon Sam Dreggers, who was assisting the trappers, shot the gator in the head three times with a 12-gauge shotgun. They all knew that the boy, still locked in the alligator's jaws, was no longer savable. Upon being shot, the alligator went into a death roll. In the process, Adam's body was finally released. It sank. Once again, the boy was gone.

Less than a minute later, the limp body of Adam Binford floated back up to the surface. Adam's left arm was missing. Curtis Lucas lifted Adam's body into the boat and placed it on the deck. The grim outcome everyone had anticipated was now official. Tears welled up in both trappers' eyes. The wind continued to blow in from the west and the Florida sun started its empty journey to zenith.

Using the snare and a second snatch-hook, the trappers and their assistants pulled the dead alligator onto a nearby boat. They headed back toward the command post a mile away.

The incident at Lake Ashby County Park was over. Adam Binford, the boy picking water lilies for his mom, had become the victim of the eighth fatal alligator attack in Florida since 1948.

The alligator was later measured at eleven feet and weighed in at 450 pounds. In the roiled surface of a heavily vegetated cove against a crocodilian of this size, Adam Binford never had a chance. Perhaps the alligator had been drawn into the shallows by the scent and the splashing of the two dogs; perhaps it had been silently lying in the lily pads all morning, awaiting a raccoon to come down the shoreline or a turtle to emerge from the surrounding vegetation. Alligators are always at their hungriest in the spring, as they come out of winter fast and head into mating season.

Lori Binford wept for hours on end when she heard the news on Saturday morning. Neighbors spoke well of the boy who had left the world on that windy Friday in March 1997. Adam Binford was smart, adorable, and well-mannered, according to all who knew and loved him. When picking lilies for his mother, Adam Binford died, but his innocence remains eternal. Somehow, life goes on.

A Florida Maneater.

Alligator Mississippiensis, aka. Florida's
man-eater, from a 1930s postcard.

The American Alligator

The name alligator is a derivative of the Spanish word for lizard, *el lagarto*. Shortly after these newly discovered creatures were named, the Spanish term became corrupted to *aligarto*, and over the centuries, eventually to *alligator*.

The first encounters with the reptiles by Hernando DeSoto, Ponce de León, and other explorers must have been frightening. During the 1500s, the indigenous wildlife would have included numerous alligators approaching, or possibly exceeding, twenty feet in length. It is estimated that as many as three to four million may have resided in Florida at the time of its European discovery. There can be no doubt that several members of the early-exploration parties were eaten by the immense beasts.

One of the first scientific descriptions of the Florida alligator comes from William Bartram, a naturalist who traveled into Florida during the latter part of the eighteenth century. Between 1773 and 1777, Bartram described his first encounters with those reptiles as follows:

> *"Behold him [the alligator] rushing forth from the reeds. His enormous body swells. His plaited tail, brandished high. The waters, like a cataract, descend from his open jaws. Clouds of smoke come from his dilated nostrils. The earth trembles with his thunder.*
> *"I was attacked on all sides. Several alligators trying to overset the*

canoe, two very large ones attacked me closely at the same instant roaring terribly and belching floods of water over me. They struck their jaws together so close to my ears as almost to stun me. I expected every moment to be dragged out of the boat and instantly devoured."

Florida natives killing an alligator: a dangerous and deadly endeavor.

Bartram had a flair for hyperbole. His description suggests that alligators were more closely related to dragons than to crocodilians.

Many misconceptions still persist today with regard to alligators. Comments such as, "They can run over thirty miles an hour for short distances"; "They can hold their breath for over an hour"; and "Their upper jaw is hinged, allowing their mouth to open fully when they bask in the sun" persist to this day despite scientific evidence to the contrary.

Only in the past fifty years have we really come to a better understanding of the behavior of *Alligator mississippiensis*. Extensive field studies, research, and modern scientific examination have debunked many of the myths surrounding this two-hundred-million-year-old reptile. Some of the best field observations and early studies of the alligator came from a book published in 1934 by E.A. McIlhenny entitled *The Alligator's Life History*. McIlhenny worked and lived on Avery Island, Louisiana, where some of the largest alligators ever documented were found. The McIlhenny family is still known today for its famous Tabasco sauce, which corporate headquarters are still on Avery Island.

The largest alligator on record was found by E. A. McIlhenny himself during the winter of 1890. After shooting it, he realized he was unable to move the reptile. Using his rifle barrel and measuring the animal several times to be certain, he calculated its length at nineteen feet, two inches. The beast weighed nearly three thousand pounds and judging by the wear on its teeth, McIlhenny felt certain it was nearing the end of its life.

The largest alligator on record in Florida was killed far more recently. It measured seventeen-feet, five-inches long and was shot in Lake Apopka in 1956 during an alligator hunt. However, a skull taken from the Sebastian River in 1886 indicates the animal was over eighteen feet in length and would have set a state record. Today, any alligator over twelve feet is considered extraordinary.

All larger alligators are males, and they are commonly called bull alligators. Females seldom exceed nine feet in length and most weigh below two hundred pounds. In the wild, both male and female gators can live over fifty years old. The longest-living alligator in captivity died at sixty-six years of age. It was brought to the Adelaide (Australia) zoo in 1914 and died there in 1978. Nile crocs, on the other hand, are believed to live over one hundred years of age in the wild.

Alligators grow rapidly at first, then slow down dramatically after reaching six to seven feet. Most authorities believe it is safe to say they grow approximately one foot per year for the first half-dozen years. This growth rate varies across their range, depending on environmental conditions and available food sources. In captivity, it's possible to raise a five- to six-foot alligator in less than four years, using heated tanks and a near constant feed supply. As a rule, alligators that live in the northernmost fringes of their geographic range grow and mature more slowly than those living in subtropical regions such as southern Louisiana and Florida.

In subtropical conditions, alligators are sexually mature when they are six-feet long, or approximately six to seven years of age. In the very northern parts of their range, it may take as long as eighteen years for a female to be able to reproduce. In Florida, during April and May alligators breed when the large bulls can be found bellowing throughout the state's many swamps and marshes.

Alligators bellow in the key of B-flat, a little-known fact discovered accidentally during a concert held at an outdoor zoo decades ago. If you go out into a swamp inhabited by these reptiles with any instrument or device capable of playing a loud B-flat, you will undoubtedly be answered by a bull alligator. It's a peculiar, if not somewhat impractical, fact.

In late June to early July, females start building their nests. After breeding, the male and female have very little to do with each other and, during incubation, the female often defends the nest from her mate. She generally lays between twenty and fifty eggs, though clutches of over eighty fertile eggs have been found.

The sex of her offspring is determined by heat. Eggs that remain in a higher temperature range, between 90°–93° F, become males. Those between 82°–86° F become females. If the temperature exceeds 93° F or falls below 82° F, the embryos can die. If the nest becomes submerged for more than several hours, the embryos drown. Seven out of ten born alligators are males.

The incubation period is between sixty to seventy days, with the hatchlings making a loud, chirplike barking noise as they near the time to break free of their eggs. The female alligator, upon hearing her offspring's chirping cue, instinctively returns to her nest and begins to uncover her clutch. Using her bone-crushing jaws, she sometimes helps break open the delicate eggs without harming the two-ounce babies within. Like the Nile croc, she often ferries her entire hatch in her mouth down to the nearby water.

Hatchling mortality is phenomenal. For the Nile crocodile, in the first two years of their lives, it is estimated that ninety-five percent of all eggs, embryos, and hatchlings are eaten. Alligators don't fare much better, with over eighty percent of every clutch perishing within the first two years. Predation comes from every possible direction: fire ants, raccoons, ospreys, rats, gar, other alligators, skunks, herons, snakes, and a host of other hungry creatures. Only when young alligators approach three feet in length, are they safe. The only predator they need to fear at that point are humans and rival bull alligators.

The vast majority of alligator hatchlings will not survive to sexual maturity.

The alligator's historic range included eleven states and the northeastern corner of Mexico, along the Rio Grande. Only the Dismal Swamp in the far southeastern corner of Virginia has lost its native population, thereby reducing the range to ten states plus a small section of northeastern Mexico. In approximate order of alligator populations, these states are: Louisiana, Florida, Mississippi, Alabama, Texas, Georgia, North Carolina, South Carolina, Arkansas, and Oklahoma. Oklahoma is an unlikely home for the alligator, but there is a small native population of hardy alligators harbored on the southeast corner of the state.

The American alligator has moved into the northernmost reaches of any crocodilian species, including its only known relative, the Chinese alligator.

In places such as Arkansas and the Carolinas, alligators have been found dead in iced-over ponds, their lone breathing hole frozen over.

Alligators have been known to survive in temperatures as low as 26° F for very short periods. They are able to maintain their vital functions in a state of semi-hibernation at the unbelievably low temperature of 41° F. Their optimal functioning temperature is 89° F. They can withstand temperatures exceeding 100°F without returning to the water, but only for very short periods. This calculates to a survival temperature variance of 59° F. When a human's internal core drops below 90° F, serious complications begin to develop. Humans die of exposure when their body core falls below 80° F. Surviving fevers or heatstroke that brings a human's body over 105° F can result in brain damage or death. Being warm-blooded, *Homo sapiens* have a survival temperature variance of less than 15° F, one-fifth that of alligators.

Another adaptation of the American alligator is that it will not eat when the water or air temperature drops below 60° F. Because of their cold-blooded nature, alligators' digestive enzymes do not function below that 60° F mark. The food in their stomachs will not only fail to digest, it will rot. In rare cases, this inability to break down its food in lower temperatures will kill the animal.

Throughout its range, the alligator goes into a state of hibernation during the winter months. The length of this hibernation period helps explain why females along the northernmost geographical ranges take three times longer to sexually mature. It also helps explain why most of the alligator's feeding activity occurs during the heat of midsummer. During this warmer time of the year, gators eat constantly to store fat in their tail and body to survive the approaching winter.

An alligator can hold its breath for over six hours. This amazing ability was discovered during a gruesome series of experiments conducted in the mid-1920s. Large alligators were held underwater until they drowned, surviving between 320 minutes to an incredible 365 minutes. This is far beyond the six-and-a-half-minute average-submersion time of the Indopacific crocodile, and longer than any other crocodilian.

There is an exception to this unique ability. In the past, it was not uncommon for alligator wrestlers to dive into pools and wrestle a submerged alligator up to the surface. It is an incredibly stupid stunt, but during some of those prolonged wrestling matches several large alligators unexpectedly drowned. A few drowned in less than a minute. It was discovered that, with any activity, the underwater breath-holding ability of the American alligator is drastically curtailed.

How fast can an alligator run? This question was answered best by an acquaintance of mine who was once pursued by a six-foot alligator through a shallow swamp: "Fast enough!" By getting up on all fours, smaller alligators can run between two and ten miles an hour. For the first thirty feet of its charge, a large alligator can probably match this speed, but on land they tire quickly.

In the water, we are no match for the alligator, a very important fact to remember when trying to avoid being attacked. The fastest Olympic swimmer is capable of swimming at twelve and a half miles an hour for a hundred meters. Most of us are lucky to swim at half that speed, or approximately six miles per hour.

Using their long, powerful tails, alligators can propel themselves through the water at over sixteen miles an hour. They easily overtake swimming dogs, deer, and even water moccasins. When fully engaged, most of their massive bodies are pushed out of the water in a form of semi-planing, like a boat hull, which spells disaster to their prey.

Over a decade ago, knowing this single fact helped to keep my brother Steve and me from getting bitten, possibly even killed, by a large, aggressive alligator in the "Ding" Darling National Wildlife Refuge on Sanibel. It was late afternoon and we were cast-netting for mullet off a small sand spit. Steve was visiting from Minnesota and we had plans to use cut mullet to fish for tarpon offshore on the following morning.

I was throwing an eight-foot net and we had accumulated half a bucketful of mullet when the unexpected saurian made its appearance. After every cast, I would wade back to the sand bar to empty the net of those one-foot-long mullet, whereupon my brother would pick the flopping fish up off the ground and toss them into our five-gallon empty-paint pail. I would then head back out into the shallow water to make another cast. We had collected over a dozen fish when we heard this loud hiss behind us.

Looking back toward the path along which we had come down to the water's edge, we were astonished to see a nine-foot alligator standing high up on all four legs hissing at us. Since it's unusual to find alligators in salt water, this was quite unexpected. We both froze for a second. Then Steve asked, "What should we do?"

I said I would throw the net at the alligator and then we should run into the mangrove forest twenty feet to the south.

"Don't go into the water!" I added, knowing that such a move would be akin to having a death wish.

I threw my net and, in my panic, missed the beast completely. Steve and I bolted for the gnarly roots of the red mangroves a few yards away. Seeing us flee, the alligator sauntered up to the flip-flopping mullet on the spit and quickly ate them. It then tipped over the bucket and finished off the rest of our evening catch. Shortly thereafter, it slid back into the salt water and swam away.

That alligator was never after us, but wanted to let us know we had better immediately surrender our catch to it or we would have hell to pay. Believe me, it wasn't a hard decision to make.

Realizing that the noise and splashing we were making was what probably drew the alligator's attention to us in the first place, we picked up our empty bucket and cast net and went home, deciding we would catch pinfish for bait in the morning. The lesson learned was, a person should never stand between a hungry alligator and its dinner. Once filled with lactic acid and pumped up into an aggressive attack mode, it will readily pick that person for its menu choice.

Finding alligators inhabiting salt water is rare. After reporting the incident to an officer from Fish and Wildlife, he explained that, although alligators seldom stay very long in the saltwater side of the "Ding" Darling Refuge, they do come into it to feed, especially at night. Alligators cannot leach out the salt that becomes absorbed through their mouths and body, and if they stay in the salt water too long, they can die.

In his book *Jaws Too,* published in 1985, naturalist George Campbell describes tethering two small alligators he had captured to a red mangrove tree on the gulf side of the Florida Keys. Campbell did not realize alligators were salt-water intolerant and, sure enough, both animals died within twelve hours.

They do forage and feed in salt water, and on rare occasions they have even been spotted along various beaches throughout Florida, but alligators cannot overextend themselves in a briny environment. Like shipwrecked humans who are sometimes forced to drink ocean water to survive, the salt disrupts their electrolytes and eventually kills them.

This is certainly not the case with American or Indopacific crocodiles. They have special salt glands located in the lower portion of their mouths, which help excrete the absorbed salt. They are both considered "salties" and spend a major portion of their lives in brackish or saltwater environments. Indopacific crocs have been found swimming in the open ocean as far as two hundred miles from any land. This explains their ability to inhabit an extensive oceanic range from eastern India to Papua New Guinea and beyond. They simply swim from island to island, easily able to withstand an oceanic environment.

Another important thing to understand is, like crocs, alligators can be extremely fast for an instant. That is all it takes to grab hold of a victim in its relentless jaws. A story I came across in my research best describes this incredible speed.

In her fascinating *Alligators: Prehistoric Presence in the American Landscape,* Martha Strawn relates a story told to her by an alligator hunter named LeRoy Overstreet. Overstreet describes an incident that occurred while he and a group of men were working a pocket seine in Lake Kissimmee, Florida. The net was over fifteen hundred yards long and, with one end firmly anchored on shore, a group of men would work the other end by swinging around and pulling the net back toward the anchored post, entrapping several tons of fish in its immense pocket.

During one of these seining operations, one of the eleven men accidentally stepped on the back of a large, submerged alligator. The water was about four-feet deep and all of them were working in their bare feet, so there was little doubt that this unlucky individual had his foot on the scaly back of a reptile. He immediately yelled over to Overstreet and the rest of the crew to inform them about his predicament. Knowing that alligators react only after you take your foot off them, the man's friends immediately dropped their seine and came to his rescue. It was common knowledge to the seining crew that, should a person accidentally step on a submerged gator, the reptile would turn and bite the instant that person took his or her foot off.

Using both boats they had taken along, the crew placed four men in each vessel and pulled up on either side of the man in peril. Two of the men in each boat held the vessels in place while four others took hold of the man standing on the gator, two on each side, grabbing him between them under his armpits. On the count of three, the four men hoisted him up as quickly as possible.

They didn't make it. The alligator, completely underwater, snapped around and caught the man's leg in its teeth. What followed was a horrific tug of war between the four men holding the victim and the alligator below, twisting and turning with the lower portion of that unfortunate man's leg in its mouth. A few minutes later, the men won out and the alligator reluctantly let go.

But the victim's leg was terribly mangled. Later that same day, the doctors considered amputating what was left of it. After days in the hospital and several operations, the doctors were able to save the man's foot and leg, though the incident crippled him for life.

What I find most amazing about this story is, what a feat that alligator was able to manage…underwater! The next time you are in a swimming pool, dive down four feet and try to move quickly. The water pressure will make even swinging your arm back and forth a slow, laborious process. Not for an alligator, though. It is capable of lightning-quick reflexes. Never be fooled by its slow, lethargic appearance: **Alligators are exploding logs.**

That's how they hunt. They sit as still and lifeless as a log along the water's edge, their heartbeat slowed to a near standstill, their breathing imperceptible. An errant raccoon will sometimes actually step on the deadly log to get a drink. So long as they remain on that log, the alligator will remain motionless. The instant the raccoon steps off, it's over. The saurian seizes the animal in its jaws faster than the human eye can see. Wildlife observers have reported witnessing alligators grabbing small birds on the fly.

Alligators, like all crocodilians, have an acute sense of smell. They can pick up the scent of dead fish or carrion miles from its source and will quickly traverse the distance for an easy, lifeless meal. Unlike the Nile crocodile, which favors fresh kill, alligators sometimes cache their food and many seem to prefer their meals well-aged. Several "gator holes" along undercut riverbanks have been found with the rotting remains of mammals, fish, and other gators waiting to be devoured.

They also have a keen sense of hearing. Between the motion detectors that lie along the bottom section of their lower jaw and their acute hearing, few animals are able to cross even a narrow stretch of water undetected. Splashing noises like my cast-netting on that chilly afternoon are noticed immediately. If the alligator is hungry, it will soon be swimming toward the cause of the disturbance.

Their eyesight is as equally acute. They have very good lowlight vision and have a special nictitating membrane that allows them to see underwater. This membrane protects their eye in a fashion similar to our wearing a mask when snorkeling and bears a striking resemblance to the nictitating membrane found in many shark species. The same light-sensitive receptors that cause an alligator's eyes to glow when hit by a flashlight at night also allow it to see better than we can in near total darkness. Most alligators hunt at dusk, throughout the night, and at dawn. However, it should be noted that they have been known to attack humans during any time of the day.

Their upper jaw is not hinged, another popular misconception; it is fused to their skull and incapable of opening any more than our own. Because they raise their heads when basking in the sun, it appears as though their upper jaw has a separate hinge, but that is an illusion.

Like the Nile crocodile, alligators have excellent memory. The late Ross Allen, founder of the Reptile Institute at Silver Springs, Florida, described a so-called "blinker" during an alligator hunt in the 1950s. Blinkers are large, bull alligators that have been either shot at or wounded by hunters using bulls-eye lanterns at night. Whereas most alligators will become mesmerized by the bright headlamp of either an electric or, prior to the invention of batteries, an oil-fueled headlight, older, more experienced gators will sometimes become blinkers.

When the light hits their highly reflective eyes, they simply close them and sink to the bottom. Once submerged, they either lie still on the bottom or swim away in the darkness. Sometimes hunters, in such cases, resort to a large snatch hook to catch these educated beasts, but more often than not blinkers must be trapped with baited hooks and not taken by rifle during a night-hunt. Blinkers, as Ross Allen soon learned, are very difficult to catch.

In 1948, Florida Fish and Wildlife began tracking alligator attacks inside the state. To date, there have been three-hundred-plus attacks, sixteen of which were fatal (authors note: at the time of publication, in May of 2006, there were three additional purported fatal, though unconfirmed alligator attacks). From 1948 through 1959, there were only five authenticated attacks, none of which resulted in death. From 1960 through 1971, there were no documented attacks at all. In 1973, Fish and Wildlife recorded its first fatal attack, that of Sharon Holmes, a sixteen-year-old who was swimming in Oscar Scherer State Park in Sarasota County. The alligator that attacked her was an eleven-foot, three-inch healthy male. He had been fed by visitors in the years prior to the attack. It was not illegal to feed alligators in 1973; it is now.

The only known fatality from American crocodile occurred in 1925. The story of that attack is fascinating. Zulu, the name of the crocodile responsible for the fatal incident, was an immense fourteen-foot female, or so it was thought.

The attack took place in Biscayne Bay, near Miami. A party of surveyors came across Zulu while doing fieldwork along the edge of the bay. Bear in mind that a conservation ethos wasn't exactly fashionable in the twenties. Florida was still predominately wilderness. The state's population in 1925 was only two million and Miami, a small but growing city.

One of the surveyors promptly took out a rifle and shot Zulu twice. Naturally, he was sure he had killed her, but as he approached the croc, the surveyor foolishly kicked her to ascertain. Indeed, Zulu wasn't dead: she promptly swung around and, catching the surveyor in her unforgiving jaws, went into a death roll and tore him into pieces. It turned out that Zulu was quite alive; the surveyor, in turn, was quite dead.

For some strange reason, the other surveyors decided not to finish her off (maybe they didn't like the guy who had shot her...). Now wounded and exhausted, they captured Zulu and sold her to a Mr. Anderson, who owned an alligator farm up the coast in Lantana. Over time, Anderson nursed Zulu back to health and a full recovery.

What happens next is even more bizarre. At Anderson's small, roadside tourist attraction of a farm, Zulu soon became top billing. The infamous headline, "MAN-EATING CROCODILE!!!" did (and still does) tend to draw in tourists. Zulu was placed in a small enclosure with a mere four-foot fence around her. There was a stile leading over the fence and tourists were invited to sit on Zulu's back for a photo op. Once they were secure on the fourteen-foot known killer's back, Anderson would call out her name, whereupon she would stand up, arching her huge body, open her deadly jaws and "pose" for the photo. Countless Kodak box cameras have captured the moment, but remarkably never once was anyone bitten or attacked by Zulu. My surmise is, in the 1920s alligators and crocodiles were still considered far more harmless than they really are.

Over the years, Anderson also taught Zulu to catch small, dead, or sickly alligators thrown to her from a nearby platform. She was so fast she was able to grab most three- and four-foot reptiles in the air, devouring them in a flash.

In the 1930s, roadside attractions like the Alligator Race were common in Florida.

After Anderson's death, Zulu was sold and moved to the Ross Allen Reptile Institute at Silver Springs. There, Zulu lived happily until 1952. In a final twist to her strange story, Zulu was killed by another crocodilian named Big George, a fourteen-foot, seven-inch, very aggressive American alligator which shared the pen next door to Zulu's. One day, Zulu accidentally stuck her snout between the logs that separated the two and Big George grabbed hold of it, holding tight until Zulu drowned. Big George, by the way, is the alligator pictured on this book's cover, along with his "trainer" and founder of Silver Springs, Ross Allen.

Zulu's killing of the Miami surveyor is the only known incident of a wild American crocodile taking a person's life. There have been a number of deaths resulting from children or adults falling into pens of captive animals, but nothing as bizarre as Zulu's tale. Judging by her size, presumably Zulu was a "him."

51

American alligators are cannibalistic, as are many of the world's crocodilians. The large bulls are known to be particularly fond of eating younger, smaller alligators, especially during the mating season. In one evening alone, the infamous Big George killed fourteen of his pen mates at the Ross Allen Reptile Institute. After that, he was kept apart from other reptiles. In the wild, this type of self-predation forms another natural control over the entire population.

Fortunately, Allen and the management of the institute never engaged Big George in any photo ops with their patrons. Big George would have made a quick work of both the child attempting to sit on his back and, quite possibly, the parents attempting to place him or her there. As a species, humans have a tendency to become all-too-familiar with animals that would just as soon devour them when having their photo taken. Its scientific term is anthropomorphism, and it defines thus: "Ascribing human form or attributes to a thing or being not human."

Alligators are hardly human. They are prehistoric reptiles who have not significantly changed in millions of years. Although we have not changed biologically in the past fifty thousand years, culturally *Homo sapiens* have changed tremendously over the past five thousand years. Prior to this, the overwhelming majority of people were still living on the fringe of the Stone Age. There was no writing, only little agriculture, and survival was a day-to-day experience. Our lives have changed dramatically as of the Industrial Revolution, particularly after we embarked on the ensuing, current electronic revolution.

It has only been since the invention and dispersion of mass-produced guns, both rifles and pistols, roughly two hundred years ago, that we

Big George, at fourteen feet, seven inches, was considered the largest alligator ever held in captivity. Big George was responsible for killing Zulu.

have finally prevailed against lions, grizzlies, and every other former top predator. Nowadays, in large part owing to our overwhelming success as a predator species, we tend to attribute certain human characteristics to animals that shouldn't really be humanized.

On the other hand, within the past fifty years, humans have started to recognize the valuable role alligators play in the ecology of the wetlands. One of the most fascinating examples of their importance was discovered by accident at the St. Augustine Alligator Farm some years ago.

In an effort to make a better observation area for visitors, an older alligator holding pen was redesigned with a large moat, which completely encircled a small, interior island. The island had several larger trees and, within weeks of the enclosure's completion, the staff was astounded to find birds roosting in the island's trees. Shortly thereafter, to everyone's complete astonishment, the egrets and herons started building nests in them, directly above the hungry alligators.

At first, the farm's staff and scientists were baffled by the birds' seemingly bizarre behavior. Why would egrets and herons build their nests directly above an island crawling with predatory alligators? The answer is counterintuitive in a way, but ultimately it makes perfect sense.

Alligators don't climb trees; raccoons, rats, opossums, snakes, bobcats, otters and a host of other egg-and-chick-eating creatures do. With the ground beneath the rookery teeming with gators and a very unsafe moat to swim, the birds were using the alligator population as sentries to stand guard over their nests. Yes, a fledgling chick or two was lost to the reptiles over the course of a nesting season, but the birds must have considered this a fair price to pay for the peace of mind provided by the gators.

Since then, rookeries have been noted in many alligator farms throughout Florida and Louisiana. It makes sense that birds would willingly spare a few chicks when compared with the damage a single raccoon can do to a rookery in an evening. When one takes large, predatory alligators out of the environment, one is unwittingly taking out future bird populations. An interesting study for the Florida State to undertake would be to collate the decline of wading birds in the Everglades with the decline of the alligator populations in the mid-1970s. In a strange Florida version of *Field of Dreams*, we may eventually start saying, "If you build alligator ponds, the birds will come."

For countless generations, our ancestors survived because they respected and feared crocodiles and alligators amongst a host of similar predators. As you read this, rest assured that the only reason you are here right now is because your great-, great-, great-, great-grandparents had the intelligence and instinct to not be caught and devoured by the local saber-toothed tiger or neighborhood cave bear. As a society, we have evolved exponentially over the past fifty centuries, from smoky caves to microwaves, from grunts to iPods. Alligators, on the other hand, haven't changed one iota.

Our tendency to think that, just because we have become civilized, alligators have elected to join us in our civility is plainly wrong. Someone can manufacture a cuddly, stuffed alligator for you to give to your children, but you had better explain to them that, if they see one of those animals in their backyard, they had better not attempt to give it a hug. That alligator will not hug them back but be infinitely more predisposed to grab hold of them and immediately go into a death roll.

If you go to www.google.com and click on its image's search engine under "Gators," you will be amused if not amazed by all the products and logos there have been designed revolving around this deadly, prehistoric predator. There are alligator potato chips, alligator jewelry, alligator chocolates, gummy gators, gator BBQ sauce and hot sauce, football teams ("Go Gators!"), swim teams, hockey teams, kitsch alligator ash trays, stuffed toy alligators, singing-alligator golf-club covers, gator ink pens, cute children's books about equally cute alligators, wind-up toys, sports bars, football helmets.... The list is endless.

The irony is, gators are and always will be cold-blooded, small-brained predators. A stylized cartoon of a gator might look great on a football helmet, but waist-deep in a swamp an alligator isn't cute at all. However much we try to humanize them, the truth is quite the opposite.

Our ancestors survived because they knew this. As more and more people filter into Florida and alligator populations continue to rebound, we must remind ourselves that wild alligators are not pets, nor tourist attractions or photo ops, least of all made out of some harmless, tirelike material, which merely lie there waiting for some fool to go up and touch it.

Alligators are exploding logs! Touch them and you can be maimed or dead within seconds. Swim with them and you will likely be drowned by them. Two hundred years ago, alligators, along with panthers, were the apex predators of the Sunshine State. Today, humans are. Panthers and gators have been here long before us, though, and have honed their killing skills over millennia. We are the new kids on the block; our self-confident nature sometimes lulls us into a complacency that can end up in disaster. Primal, complex, beautifully designed; necessary, instinctual, and most of all, dangerous—this is the American alligator.

A typical alligator caricature found almost everywhere across the South.

Alexandria Murphy Is Missing

Central Polk County, Florida, is awash with lakes, some of them fairly large, like Lake Marion and Lake Hamilton. Others such as Lake Alfred and Lake Fannie are midsized. Then there are those considered more oversized ponds, such as Spirit Lake and Lake Deer. Irrespective of their size, all those lakes—interconnected by a watery labyrinth of marshes, streams, and man-made canals—harbor alligators. Lake Cannon, a five-hundred-acre lake straddling the towns of Winter Haven and Inwood, is no exception.

Alexandria Murphy, or Ali, was born on October 7, 1998. Alexandria and her infant sister, Destiny, had been born in Tampa, seventy miles west of Winter Haven, where their father, Bruce Elijah Murphy, still lived. Since the relationship between Bruce Murphy and Alexandria's young mother, Jessica J. Lester, was not going well, Lester felt she needed some time to sort things out. Three weeks prior to the incident, Lester and her two daughters moved to Winter Haven with the children's great-grandmother, Gwen Lester, to put some distance between herself and her ex-boyfriend. Jessica Lester was nineteen years old and had given birth to her first child, Ali, when she was only seventeen.

Raising two daughters alone wasn't easy. Fortunately, Lester had a large, supportive family to fall back upon. Her grandmother, Gwen Lester, loved the two little girls and didn't mind taking them in. Gwen had lived in her modest home on 25th Street NW for two and a half years. It was a nice residential neighborhood, only a few blocks from the shores of Lake Cannon and Lake Cannon Park, where Grandma Gwen had taken Destiny and Alexandria to play a week before the accident occurred.

Saturday, June 23, 2001, started out like any other summer day: hot, clear, and humid in the morning, followed by typical afternoon thunderstorms and a drenching downpour. Lester's two girls were good children. Alexandria had her dolls and toys and loved playing with her little one-year-old sister. But Ali also had a wild side: she was a sweet but spunky child, with a disposition to freedom, who loved to climb up on countertops and the kitchen table. Lester had been seriously thinking of enrolling Ali in gymnastics or swimming class in an attempt to burn off some of her excess energy.

Around 2:30 on that lazy afternoon, Grandma Gwen took Ali through the back door to let the two-year-old watch her feed the ducks. The two pet ducks were kept in the Lester home's fenced-in backyard. Ali loved to watch them gobble up the duck food and waddle around the yard. After she fed them, Gwen left Ali alone in the screened-in porch and went into the other room to tell Jessica she was going to run to the corner store for some sundries but would return shortly.

"Ali's still at the back porch watching the ducks," Gwen told her granddaughter.

The back door had been left unlocked, but Lester knew the yard beyond it was fence-enclosed. Lester paid little attention to the situation; she was on the telephone with her mother, Ellen Lester, who lived in Safety Harbor, Florida, talking about her personal problems— Jessica's being nineteen, single, and separated from her daughter's father, Bruce Murphy.... What Lester didn't consider at the time was her daughter's love of climbing and Alexandria's childlike curiosity about the world beyond the backyard.

Little Ali Marie Murphy had considerable history in this regard. On the previous Thursday, two days before the incident, she had somehow managed to get out of the house on her own. A neighbor who lived a few doors down from the Lesters had discovered Ali standing beside the busy street with a pacifier in her mouth and a rubber ball in her hand. The neighbor, a Spanish woman by the name of Mary Ann Morales, thought it strange that anyone would leave a two-year-old alone on such a well-traveled street. Shortly thereafter, Morales watched in disbelief as Ali was nearly struck by a passing car. Right after this, Morales, knowing where Ali lived, went outside, picked up the little girl and returned her home.

Gwen Lester wasn't home at the time but her granddaughter, Jessica, was...on the telephone. Morales knocked on the door and Lester came over to let Ali in while still on the phone. Lester didn't say anything to the woman who had just rescued her daughter, not even a thank-you. Lester kept talking on the telephone the entire time and, according to an interview conducted by Family Services with Morales after the accident, Lester hadn't seem very concerned about the welfare or whereabouts of her daughter.

Several weeks before the incident, yet another neighbor had witnessed little Ali wandering in their backyard all by herself. Knowing where she lived, the kind neighbor walked the two-year-old back home after discovering her. In the end, neither neighbor was all that surprised by what eventually happened to Alexandria Murphy.

While Ali was left standing alone at the back porch and her younger sister, Destiny, slept, Jessica Lester remained on the telephone for another ten to fifteen minutes. Hearing the youngest cry in her crib, Lester said goodbye to her mother, hung up, and went to check on her children. After picking up Destiny, Lester walked over to the back door to see what Ali was up to. At that moment, Lester discovered Alexandria Murphy was missing.

At first, Lester thought that Grandma Gwen had probably decided to take Ali along to the corner store. Lester tried to find Gwen's cell-phone number to call and check, but couldn't find her number. Around 3:30 P.M., Gwen returned home from the store alone. Lester's worst fears were realized: Ali Murphy had vanished.

Intuitively suspecting the worst, the two women immediately started looking through the neighborhood for the little girl. By that time in the afternoon, a powerful thunderstorm had swept in; it was pouring outside. It wasn't the kind of weather any parent would want a little girl to be caught out in. For the next fifteen to twenty minutes, the two women frantically searched for Lester's child. Around 3:45 P.M., Lester called the Polk County Sheriff's Department to report a missing child.

The police responded immediately and a full-blown search was underway within the hour. Officers scoured the neighborhood asking everyone if he or she had seen a barefoot two-year-old girl wearing a pink nightgown and cartoon-character panties.

On that same afternoon, Greg Pearson and his friend, Tom Hatcher, were at a birthday party for James Dysard's thirteen-year-old daughter at the nearby Lake Cannon Park. When questioned by the police, Pearson told one of the officers that he had seen a little girl in a pink nightgown a while before.

Earlier, Hatcher and Pearson had run back to the latter's house to get a cooler for the soft drinks when they observed a little girl fitting Ali's description standing in a driveway near the intersection of 24th Street and Lake Cannon Drive. She was all alone, swishing a stick through a puddle in the pouring rain. He told the police he would have liked to do something about it at the time but didn't, lest a possible kidnapping or child-molestation accusation be made. In this modern and suspicious world, an act of human kindness can, after all, be all-too-easily misconstrued. Pearson and Hatcher drove by the exact same intersection less than an hour later but, by that time, the little girl was gone.

After their interview with the Winter Haven police, Pearson, Hatcher, and Dysard pitched in to assist the authorities in their search for the missing child. Dysard volunteered his boat and was soon scouring the nearby shoreline where a canal connects Lake Cannon to Lake Howard. Police, friends, family, local residents, and volunteers were checking everywhere in the immediate vicinity for little Alexandria.

In an effort to cover more of the five-hundred-acre lake, the Sheriff's Department had called in its search-and-rescue helicopter. As James Dysard slowly patrolled the shoreline, he noticed the helicopter was hovering over one particular spot on the lake, some thirty-five yards out from a sandy-beach area. Suspecting they had found something in the water, he motored over to get a closer look. It was then that he saw Ali, lying facedown in the water, still wearing her pink nightgown. She appeared lifeless. Dysard jumped from his boat into the waist-deep water and carried her thirty-two-pound body to the shore.

Laying her down at the water's edge, he noticed the numerous and severe wounds and knew at once that an alligator had been involved. She hadn't been dead for very long and, looking back across the water, Dysard observed a small alligator that had followed him toward the shore. It didn't take him, the EMS personnel, and the police much longer to realize Alexandria had been killed by an alligator. They covered the little girl's body with a blanket and went to inform Ali's mother of her daughter's death. Twilight settled on Lake Cannon and an eerie silence descended over the neighborhood. News of the tragedy spread, generating utter disbelief and anguish.

As Ali's lifeless body lay on the ground awaiting the medical examiner's (M.E.) arrival, the police called in local agent-trapper Pete Kinnamon to trap, kill, and remove the alligator. Kinnamon appeared on the scene just after 6 P.M. to catch the small alligator, which was still swimming in the area. Using a baited hook and a stout fishing pole, Kinnamon easily got the hungry alligator to take the bait. The professional trapper reeled the alligator in and proceeded to dispatch it with his bang stick. It was a small male gator measuring six-foot, six-inch long and weighing less than one hundred pounds. The necropsy on the animal was completed the following day. Along with other evidence, it confirmed this had been the animal responsible for Ali's death.

The M.E. arrived on the scene shortly after Kinnamon. The examiner inspected Ali's body and quickly confirmed that the two-year-old had been attacked and drowned by an alligator. At 8:20 P.M., the Polk Professional Removal Service transported Ali Murphy's body to the Polk County Morgue located at the Lakeland Regional Medical Center. An autopsy was scheduled for the following Monday.

In the summary of the police's follow-up investigation, it was determined that Alexandria Marie Murphy, left alone in the backyard with her two pet ducks, had somehow managed to climb over the four-foot fence and escape into the surrounding neighborhood. There was a white utility shed in the backyard and next to the shed, jammed between it and the chain-link fence, was a two-foot-high wire cage Grandma Gwen sometimes used to transport the ducks. Apparently the athletic, energetic Ali had managed to get up on that cage, and from there climb over the fence to get out of the yard.

Ali must have wandered around the neighborhood for some time, having been last seen alive by Pearson and Hatcher a couple of hundred feet from the shoreline of Lake Cannon. From that point, it can only be speculated that Ali, in the pouring rain, eventually wandered over to the water's edge and proceeded to play in much the same manner as she had been observed by the two men earlier—swishing her stick back and forth in the shallow water. With over a dozen alligators living in Lake Cannon, it was simply a matter of time before one of them would be drawn in to investigate the cause of the disturbance. Alligators are biologically hardwired to respond to anything making unusual waves or ripples in lakes, rivers, and ponds.

Swimming toward her, the gator would have found a three-foot-tall, thirty-two-pound little girl standing there, alone and vulnerable. The alligator instinctively decided to take advantage of the situation and attack. The gator apparently grabbed Ali by her arms, dragging her back out to deeper water and then drowned her. Several alligators along that stretch of shoreline had recently been reported for being too aggressive. Permits to remove them were, meanwhile, in the mail to Trapper Kinnamon when the incident occurred. Although some neighbors disputed later claims that the alligators had been fed, they all agreed that everyone who feeds ducks and tosses their fish-cleaning scraps back into the water is effectively all the same giving food directly to alligators. The feeding of Lake Cannon's gators, although done inadvertently, was cited in the final incident report as playing a major factor in the cause of Ali's fatal attack.

Because of the unusual circumstances surrounding the accident, a thorough follow-up investigation was conducted. Discussions were held by the official parties involved on the possibility of removing the younger child, Destiny Murphy, from her mother's supervision, in light of two-year-old Alexandria's having been found alone in the neighborhood on numerous occasions prior to the fatal attack on that Saturday. Ultimately, the entire incident was turned over to the State Attorney's office for further review and possible legal action to follow.

After careful scrutiny of all the facts, Lawyer John Aguero, Assistant State Attorney for Florida at that time, wrote the following to the Polk County Sheriff's Department:

Based on your investigation, it appears the death of Alexandria was a tragic accident. The actions of the child's mother and great-grandmother certainly do not constitute willful neglect, nor do they rise to the level of culpable negligence. Alexandria was almost three years old and was apparently able to climb an almost four-foot chain-link fence barefooted. In our opinion, the death of Alexandria Murphy did not result from criminal conduct on the part of any individual. We plan to take no further action in this matter.

Alexandria Marie Murphy was no longer missing; she was gone.

Under no circumstances should anyone ever consider an alligator his or her playmate!

Deadly Alligator Encounters

In 1948, the Florida Fish and Wildlife Commission (FWC) began keeping records of unprovoked alligator attacks across the state. Since then, there have been 346 alligator attacks in Florida. As this book was sent to press, sixteen of the Florida human/alligator encounters had resulted in a human fatality, and in late April/early May 2006, three women were killed in three distinct incidents in various regions of the state (Sunrise, Gainesville, and St. Petersburg, Florida) within a week's time, but details and confirmations of these attacks were not yet available from FWC. Another prior nine deaths may or may not have been a direct result of an attack, but given the extenuating circumstances surrounding those incidents, the exact truth regarding the nine deaths will never be known. Most probably, they must have drowned first and then their bodies must have been scavenged by alligators.

The FWC does not include attacks or deaths that occur during alligator captures, alligator hunts, or when the alligator involved is being held in captivity, such as injured animals brought into wildlife clinics or alligators kept in tourist attractions or zoos. It also does not count incidents where the exact cause of death is uncertain, such as drowning victims who were discovered by alligators prior to being discovered by recovery teams.

Louisiana, with over 1.5 million alligators within its borders, has documented only a handful of attacks, and to date has never recorded a single fatality. To the best of my knowledge, no one has investigated this statistical anomaly. In fact, outside of Florida in the remaining ten states that still harbor alligators, there have been very few attacks and no official fatalities. It would appear that the Florida alligator is more aggressive in its association to humans, although there are no studies available which have explored this peculiarity.

If you have a nuisance alligator in your area, one that appears to have lost its fear of humans, or if you see someone feeding, harassing, or molesting an alligator, you can and should report it to FWC by calling its twenty-four-hour Wildlife Alert Hotline at 888-404-3922. Callers can remain anonymous and likely will even collect a reward.

Despite the increase in incidents over the past thirty years, alligators and people can coexist peacefully. All it takes is basic understanding of the feeding and nesting habits of North America's largest reptile to ensure a healthy coexistence. Here are some fundamental tips that will help one coexist with Florida's alligators and some important tips to remember in the extremely rare chance one should actually be bitten or attacked by an alligator.

- **IF YOU RENT, INTEND TO PURCHASE, OR ALREADY OWN PROPERTY ON FRESH WATER IN FLORIDA:** Be aware of the fact that in all likelihood you will eventually encounter alligators in the pond, lake, river, or drainage canal you are living on. In the spring, which is mating season, and summer months alligators often move around, generally at night, when they are most active.

Several years ago, naturalist George Campbell studied the migration of Twiggy, a young bull alligator on Sanibel, back and forth across the island for a number of years. Over several weeks, Twiggy would move as far as six miles. Fresh water is the natural habitat of alligators; always assume, even if you don't see any, that there are alligators lying just beneath the black water. Contrary to popular belief, alligators can and will climb fences and have been known to enter swimming pools. Swim in designated swimming areas only and look carefully around any pool before you dive in.

- **DO NOT FEED OR ENTICE ALLIGATORS:** Baiting, feeding, or enticing alligators toward you in any manner is against the law. Alligators lose their fear of humans when they associate food with people. You may not be the person who eventually gets bitten by an emboldened alligator, but by feeding it you can contribute to an eventual attack and even the untimely death of a fellow Floridian. If you see anyone else feeding, harassing, or enticing alligators, inform him or her of the dangers of doing so. Be proactive and tell that person you plan to inform the authorities.

By feeding alligators, people create future problems for themselves and others. Log on to the FWC's Web site (www.myfwc.com/gators/nuisance/Attack) and read in particular about the stories of Sharon Holmes from Sarasota and four-year-old Erin Glover from Port Charlotte, to better appreciate why feeding alligators is a very bad idea.

If you witness someone illegally feeding an alligator, report the person to FWC commissioners at (863) 648-3203 or by calling their toll-free number at (888) 404-3922. Many municipalities have their own ordinances prohibiting the feeding of alligators, so you can also call your local police department. Feeding alligators is a misdemeanor punishable by up to sixty days in jail and/or a $500.00 fine. Above all, you could be saving someone's life if a conditioned alligator ultimately elects to bite the hand that feeds it.

Remember:
NEVER FEED AN ALLIGATOR!

• DO NOT FEED OTHER WILDLIFE IN THE WATER: Even the feeding of ducks, carp, and egrets can and often does attract alligators. Their instincts to investigate any unusual splashes on or along the water's edge will bring them closer to where the activity is taking place, thereby increasing the odds of a dangerous encounter.

Never discard fish scraps and other edible waste anywhere near where alligators can get into the habit of feeding on it. By doing so, you are still inadvertently feeding them. The fatal incident involving Brian Griffin at the Dead River near Travares, Florida, in 2003, occurred right beside a fish-cleaning station.

• DO NOT LET PETS SWIM, WALK, OR RUN ALONG A FRESHWATER SHORELINE KNOWN TO HARBOR ALLIGATORS: Dogs are especially vulnerable to alligator attacks and hundreds of pet dogs are killed or injured by those reptiles annually in Florida. An animal walking along a riverbank or fetching a stick in an inland lake containing alligators is at extremely high risk of being attacked. Cats and other pets are also grabbed by alligators, but due to their strong odor, dogs appear to be especially vulnerable.

The size of the dog provides absolutely no immunity from an attack. Once dragged into the water, a hundred-pound German shepherd is no match against a six-foot alligator. Dogs have also been known to inadvertently entangle their owners in the attack. Bob Steele, of Sanibel, was walking his dog on September 11, 2001, and died in just such an incident.

● **DO NOT SWIM OR LET PETS SWIM IN AREAS WITH THICK OR EMERGENT VEGETATION:** The areas with dense water vegetation such as bulrushes, water lilies, cattails, or any marshy, heavily vegetated ditches or canals are the favored habitat of alligators. Dense vegetation provides the ideal cover for a submerged animal and presents a clear and present danger to anyone who ventures into those swampy areas. Swimming or wading in any freshwater river, lake, or pond is inherently risky in Florida, but emergent vegetation greatly increases that risk.

● **OBSERVE AND PHOTOGRAPH ALLIGATORS FROM A DISTANCE:** Alligators are wild, unpredictable animals. Use a telephoto lens if necessary and avoid getting too close to a "sleeping" alligator. Don't be fooled by their lethargic appearance: they can and do explode in a heartbeat. Keep a safe distance away.

● **DO NOT SWIM, WALK DOGS, OR GO OUT WITH SMALL CHILDREN AT NIGHT OR AT DUSK ALONG FRESHWATER LAKES, CANALS, OR STREAMS:** The vast majority of Florida's attacks occur during times of low light, either sunrise or, most often, during sunset. Alligators are predominately nocturnal. Low light and long shadows provide them the opportunity to get closer to their prey before striking. Never swim in a Florida freshwater lake that has been known to harbor any alligators after dark. To do so invites disaster.

Swimming at night was one of the key factors in the death of Michelle Reeves in Ft. Myers in 2005. She had been forewarned of the dangers involved, but couldn't resist the temptation of a midnight swim. It proved to be a fatal mistake.

● **DO NOT, UNDER ANY CIRCUMSTANCES, APPROACH A FEMALE ALLIGATOR'S NEST:** Although a female alligator needs to stray from her nest to feed, she will always remain in the general vicinity. If she comes upon you while you are investigating or atop her nest, she will instinctively attack. A six- or seven-foot female alligator is capable of a vicious, sometimes fatal bite. If you stumble across a large mound of vegetation (it will look as if someone has shoveled up a pile of damp vegetation about three to six feet in diameter and two- to four-feet high) that even remotely resembles an alligator nest, leave the area at once. Female alligators defend their nests vigorously and you are in immediate and grave danger.

● **DO NOT TRY TO CAPTURE OR REMOVE AN AGRESSIVE ALLIGATOR YOURSELF:** Keeping a baby alligator as a pet is illegal in the state of Florida. When these pets are released back into the wild, they will have lost all trace of fear of people. What was once a darling two-foot pet will eventually become a lethal twelve-foot predator.

Never attempt to catch or kill a nuisance alligator yourself. Doing so is against the law and comes with strict penalties. Call the FWC and they will arrange for a professional trapper to come in and take care of the alligator. If merited, the local police and game wardens are trained to shoot alligators. Keep in mind that alligators and crocodiles are not easy to kill and any wounded animal represents a potential killer. Remember the story of Zulu, the wounded American crocodile.

● **IF YOU GET BITTEN, EVEN SCRATCHED BY AN ALLIGATOR, SEEK IMMEDIATE MEDICAL ATTENTION:** Alligators feed on carrion and live in swampy, stagnant water. Their mouths are a haven for bacteria and disease. Even the smallest scratch or cut from the bite of an alligator has a high probability of becoming infected. See a physician and have the wound examined and cleaned. The physician will prescribe the proper medications to prevent an infection. It was the infection, not the bite, which eventually killed Sanibel's Janie Melsek.

Report any attack, no matter how minor, to the FWC immediately. Once an alligator begins to shows signs of aggression toward humans, it will only be a matter of time before a person is seriously injured. Always resist the urge to seek your own retribution on the infracting animal. Leave this to the professionals who will capture, destroy, and dispose of the animal correctly.

● **IF YOU ARE ACTUALLY ATTACKED AND GRABBED BY AN ALLIGATOR:** Fight back immediately and use your hands to poke at or puncture its eyes or beat as hard as you possibly can on its snout. Alligators are not bears: Do not play dead.

Be aware that the alligator is likely to go into a death roll. If you are on land, get down on the ground and prepare to roll with it in either direction. If you are in the water, do everything you can to keep your head above water. Fight for your life.

If an alligator has a firm hold of you and is dragging you beneath the surface, struggle violently, kicking and beating on the alligator as hard as possible. By realizing that it has made a mistake trying to kill an animal that fights back, the alligator might abandon its attack and release you. If you do get free, get out and away from the water immediately, as the alligator may resume the attack at any moment.

• **DO NOT HESITATE TO CALL IN AND REPORT A NUISANCE ALLIGATOR:** The Florida Fish and Wildlife Commission receives up to fifteen

Cartoon courtesy Dave & Lee Horton

thousand complaints a year from Florida residents. Alligators are found in every one of Florida's sixty-seven counties. FWC officers listen carefully to complaints and, if merited, have the problem alligator trapped or harvested. They remove over five thousand alligators a year.

*****

The dates and descriptions of all sixteen fatal attacks in Florida, can be found on the FWC's official Alligator Attacks Fact-Sheet Web site: www.myfwc.com/gators/nuisance/Attack

Chart #2 is a summary of all attacks to date and the years in which they have occurred. Those attacks might have been as minor as an alligator's charging without attacking someone, to a minor scratch, or all the way to a finger, hand, arm, or leg being torn off. Most, if not all, of the attacking alligators have been harvested—destroyed is the official term, but in fact trappers are allowed to sell the hide and meat from most nuisance alligators taken annually.

The stories are based on the FWC's official incident reports; related newspaper articles and interviews; and official autopsies, necropsies, and related materials. To the best of my knowledge, they are accurate, though some discrepancies may occur due to conflicting reports by eyewitnesses and law-enforcement officials. Keep in mind that these are stories involving real people, most of whom have relatives and friends who revere their memory, just as I do Janie Melsek's. These are genuine human tragedies and my deepest sympathy goes out to everyone who has ever lost a friend or loved one to an alligator attack. Because of the sensitive nature of these attacks, I have kept personal interviews of friends and family to a minimum, relying on other publicly available sources for most of the details surrounding the events.

There is no doubt in my mind that alligator attacks will continue to occur in Florida, and with an even greater frequency than they have in the past. There are more alligators and more people and the odds are clearly in favor of these attacks' increasing in the years to come. Hopefully, the stories and the information herein will help you from ever having your name being added to the FWC's Web site.

Chart #2: Alligator Attacks
Courtesy FWC's Web site:
www.myfwc.com/gators
*years in which fatal attacks have occured

Year	Attacks
1948-59	5
1960-71	0
1972	5
1973*	3
1974	4
1975	5
1976	2
1977*	14
1978*	5
1979	2
1980	4
1981	5
1982	6
1983	6
1984*	5
1985	3
1986	13
1987*	9
1988*	9
1989	13
1990	18
1991	18
1992	10
1993*	18
1994	22
1995	19
1996	13
1997*	11
1998	9
1999	15
2000	23
2001*	17
2002	14
2003*	6
2004*	11
2005*	9
TOTAL	351

A Deadly Shortcut

There are essentially two ways for a boy to get from SW Hidden River Avenue to SW Pine Tree Lane in Palm City, Florida: the long way is to drive, bike, or walk south through the winding streets surrounding Lighthouse Point and the Palm Cove Golf Club until you reach SW Murphy Road. From there, take a left and head west two blocks, then turn north again on Pine Tree Lane for a little over a mile. On foot, this journey can take an average person an hour. The shorter way, the way fourteen-year-old Phillip Rastrelli took on September 10, 1978, is to head down the water's edge and swim across the canal, fewer than three hundred feet shoreline to shoreline. That route is far shorter and quicker...although in the end, it cost Rastrelli his life.

It happened on a Sunday, the day young Rastrelli was supposed to mow the lawn of his older brother's girlfriend's parents, Mr. and Mrs. Belcher. Rastrelli, a strong swimmer who had made that crossing several times before, was last seen by his brother, Mario Jr., standing on the bank of the Hidden River Canal in his swim trunks. It was still hot and steamy in early September, and the short swim across the brackish canal must have appeared far more inviting than a tedious three-mile bike trip.

No one had seen a large alligator in the canal recently, even though plenty of alligators were known to have frequented the area. The Hidden Creek Canal empties into the C-23 Canal and runs parallel to Bessy Creek, a creek which is more fresh water than brackish. Several neighbors admitted to having noticed a good-sized female gator with several smaller alligators in the canal not long before, but no large animals had been observed of late. Just a half-mile to the east, the C-23 Canal connects with the north fork of the St. Lucie River. The upper north fork of the river is a wildlife preserve and teems with alligators. Years later, in 1984, another fatal attack on another young boy would occur at Riverside Park, less than fifteen miles from where this Palm City incident occurred.

Mario Jr. didn't have the faintest idea of what had just happened when, an hour after his brother had plunged to swim across the canal, he jumped in to make the exact same swim to visit his girlfriend on SW Pine Tree. Upon Mario Jr.'s arrival, Joyce Belcher was quick to ask him why Phillip hadn't shown up to mow the lawn. Mario Jr., having watched his brother's entering the canal an hour earlier, immediately called his stepmother and father to inform them that Phillip was missing.

Within minutes, Mario Rastrelli Sr. and his son, Mario Jr., were in their boat searching up and down the canal for Phillip. After an hour of looking, to no avail, Joyce Belcher called the police to officially report the missing boy. The police arrived on the scene shortly after 2:14 P.M. and, along with members of the Palm City and District #2 fire departments, conducted an extensive search of the canal and surrounding waterways until darkness set in.

After questioning his parents, the authorities learned that Phillip Rastrelli had left his house angry: his father had told him he couldn't attend a rock concert in Fort Pierce later on that Sunday. But everyone concurred, their dispute had been little more than a typical father/son disagreement and no one in the family seriously believed young Rastrelli had run away. They checked a nearby tree house Rastrelli and his older brother sometimes frequented, hoping he was merely playing hooky, but he was not found there. They tried in vain to reach the young men's older sister, Leah Rastrelli, who lived in Tampa, to find out if, for some unknown reason, Phillip was with her. Leah, who didn't get along with her stepmother, was believed to be staying in Palm City on that weekend to attend a wedding.

Everything was put on hold until daybreak. The Rastrelli family garnered little sleep on the long night of September 11, 1978. Everyone, from friends to family, knew something had gone wrong that Sunday.

The search continued and expanded just after daybreak. Upon further investigation, a neighbor down the street from the Rastrelli residence, shared some new information with one of the officers. He had seen a large, bull alligator under a nearby dock the same morning Phillip had vanished. Later that afternoon, another neighbor called the police to alert them to a large number of vultures that were circling over an island located just to the west in Bessy Creek. The police immediately looked into it.

At 4:10 P.M. on September 11, after twenty-four hours of searching and waiting, the lifeless body of Phillip Rastrelli was discovered along the shore of the island in Bessy Creek, less than a mile from where Mario Jr. had last seen his young brother alive. The discovery was a gruesome one and confirmed that the boy had been attacked and killed by an alligator.

Over the course of a day, the alligator had begun to consume the young boy just as it would any other creature it might have seized while he or she attempted to swim across the Hidden River Canal. Once Rastrelli entered the brackish waters known to harbor the predatory animals, he became easy prey for any large alligator. The condition of the body was horrific, after being severely mauled by the offending gator. All that remained for the police was to find and destroy the animal responsible for the attack. Rastrelli's remains were taken to the morgue.

On Tuesday evening, after an extensive hunt, a huge alligator was captured near Bessy Creek. The gator was twelve-feet long and weighed more than five hundred pounds. It was shot and killed shortly after capture and the necropsy confirmed this was the alligator that had slain Phillip Rastrelli.

Because there were no witnesses to the incident, it is impossible to say exactly what happened. Based on similar events that have been observed, it is quite probable that the alligator, using the numerous motion detectors located along its lower jaw, instantly sensed the boy's presence in the water when Rastrelli began his short swim. In the water, alligators have an unbelievable advantage over human beings, regardless of how fit or how fast the person involved in an attack can swim. An Olympic swimmer cannot possibly outswim an alligator, let alone a fourteen-year-old boy.

The alligator, lying discreetly under a nearby dock, probably set out after Rastrelli within seconds after he had entered the canal. A young, healthy boy swimming across a still canal would make ample noise and motion to trigger a hungry alligator's instinct to kill. There was no indication the offending alligator had ever been fed by people. Given the circumstances, it probably wouldn't have made a difference. The alligator was hungry and a large, edible animal had just entered its realm. The decision to tackle and devour the slender, 125-pound boy was automatic for the reptile.

The alligator might have approached and grabbed Rastrelli from below or it might have overtaken him, grabbing his arm or leg while still swimming on the surface. Either way, it appears that Rastrelli didn't even have an opportunity to let go a scream or a cry for help before being dragged underwater. In the water, alligator attacks occur in seconds, not minutes. Once the prey is firmly locked in its jaws, all an alligator needs is to sink. Alligators can hold their breath for hours. Even the strongest swimmer cannot hold his or her breath for more than a few minutes, especially when fighting and thrashing about wildly, inadvertently using up precious oxygen in the process.

Struggling to free himself, Rastrelli probably drowned within minutes. The alligator, dragging the boy along by one of his arms or his head, swam north until it reached the C-23 Canal, then went west a hundred yards and entered the mouth of Bessy Creek. At some point, it dragged the body up onto the island and began dining on its catch.

The alligator had simply seen a feeding opportunity and acted upon it. Like any skilled predator, it instinctively weighed its options and felt it could tackle this good-sized swimming animal without too much trouble. On land, a teenage boy could easily outmaneuver and outrun the cumbersome five-hundred-pound predator. In the water, the boy had no chance.

Having recently seen only a small female with her hatchlings in the canal had left Rastrelli and his older brother, Mario Jr.—who made the same swim an hour later—with a false sense of security. Alligators, indeed all crocodilians, operate by using stealth and silence. Time and again, it is the alligator beneath the black water that takes a life. Swimming in any lake, canal, stream, or freshwater pond in Florida presents an inherent risk. Sadly enough, the three-mile bike ride, walk, or run Rastrelli might have chosen in lieu of the short swim statistically presented a much greater risk to the boy, with hundreds of pedestrian car fatalities annually in Florida.

Phillip Rastrelli had swum across the Hidden River Canal to mow the Belchers' lawn dozens of times before. No one is to blame for this misfortune: not his brother—who could have equally been killed by the same alligator when he swam the very canal an hour later—nor his father—for not letting Phillip go to the rock concert that afternoon—and certainly not the alligator—which was simply doing what alligators have done for millions of years and will continue to do for millions of years to come.

In the end, it was only a deadly shortcut.

Snorkeling the Wakulla

Edward Ball Wakulla Springs State Park lies a dozen miles south of Florida's state capital, Tallahassee. It is one of the largest and deepest freshwater springs in North America, pouring out more than four hundred thousand gallons of cool, clear, and fresh water every minute. A record 1.2 billion gallons of fresh water bubbled out of the Wakulla Springs on a single summer day in 1974. Presently, the park encompasses more than six thousand acres and abounds with native Florida wildlife—wild turkeys, deer, limpet, herons, and the reptile named Alligator mississippiensis. The water temperature remains a constant seventy degrees Fahrenheit and offers the perfect cooldown for the hot Florida summers. It gushes up from a depth of 285 feet and oftentimes is as clear as the surrounding air.

On a steamy afternoon in July 1987, George Cummings, a modern-art senior at Florida State University (FSU) living in Tallahassee, decided to drive a half-hour out of town and go snorkeling in the Wakulla River. It was the perfect way to spend a lax Monday afternoon during the heat of mid-July. For Cummings, July 13, 1987, became his last day alive.

Because of the extreme water clarity, Wakulla Springs is an ideal place to snorkel. The waters abound with freshwater fish: black bass, bream, mullet, gar, and several species of turtles; even the occasional manatee can be observed. From the outpouring of millions of gallons of water per hour, the grasses and aquatic plants sway in the current, which can sometimes run as fast as two miles per hour.

It is said that a person can still catch glimpses of ancient mastodon bones lying 185 feet below the surface. Park rangers keep the local alligators from entering the swimming area and the three-acre basin that forms the mouth of the spring. The river below the basin, however, teems with wild alligators and to prevent dangerous encounters, the park has a large, roped-off area set aside specifically for swimming and snorkeling. A visitor can look over the top of the springs from a viewing tower along the outside edge of the swimming area. There are warning signs posted everywhere about the dangers of swimming downstream…signs that are impossible to miss.

At 1 P.M. on that July 13, Cummings was brazenly flirting with disaster. A witness told authorities afterward she had seen Cummings snorkeling just outside the cordoned-off swimming area. She had promptly notified Mark, the lifeguard on duty that day, that there was a young man outside of the buoys. Mark had yelled over to the snorkeler and asked him to please return to the designated swimming area. Cummings reluctantly returned but dove

71

back under the ropes within minutes of having been reprimanded. Perhaps he only wanted to catch a glimpse of the mastodon bones lying deep beneath the surface.

With Cummings safely inside the swimming zone, the lifeguard returned to his post and the witness who had turned Cummings in, Julia, went back to playing with her children. Five minutes later, the lifeguard returned to the area to double-check on the errant snorkeler's whereabouts. Cummings again had left the safety of the buoyed area and was swimming beyond the floating dock in the non-swimming area of the river. Mark once again blew his whistle and signaled to Cummings to promptly return into the designated swimming area. For a second time in less than five minutes, George Cummings reluctantly complied with the lifeguard's request.

Julia had also noticed Cummings's second transgression, but after Mark's renewed warning, she resumed her playing with the children in the cool waters of Wakulla Springs. Mark, too, returned to his lifeguard's duties. George Cummings, however, had other plans.

Perhaps there were just more fish to view beyond the buoys, or perhaps Cummings—bearing an artistic temperament typical of the talented sculptor he was—had felt confined by the docks and ropes that protected him. For whatever reason, around 1:15 P.M., Cummings yet again disobeyed the orders of the lifeguard and slipped outside the safety zone for a third and final time. This time, he elected to float downriver with the cold, outflowing current. Amidst the scores of swimmers and visitors, neither Julia nor the lifeguard noticed his disappearance this time. With the river flowing quickly, Cummings soon was swept downstream a quarter mile, far from the watchful eyes of the lifeguard or park rangers.

*****

For fifty years prior to the attack on George Cummings, there had never been an incident of this nature at Wakulla Springs. In February 1999, a seventy-two-year-old Nobel Prize–winning physicist, Dr. Henry Kendall of M.I.T., accidentally drowned while doing research and diving in the springs, but there had been no alligator involved. Likewise, since Cummings's death in 1987, no one else has been killed or attacked by an alligator in the Wakulla River. With such a track record, there was no reason for the thirty people who had boarded Jungle River Cruise on that afternoon to expect to find even a deer, let alone a person, in the jaws of an eleven-foot gator.

The ticketed passengers boarded the small sightseeing boat at 1:20 P.M., mere minutes after Cummings had disappeared downriver. They were looking forward to their forty-minute cruise along the Wakulla River and a chance to glimpse one of the numerous large alligators known to inhabit the river's lower stretches.

Ten minutes into the cruise, the tour guide, Luke Smith, noticed a large gator named Rusty holding something in its mouth. "Looks like Rusty has caught himself dinner," Smith announced to the thirty-plus people on board. At first, Smith felt certain the alligator had a large turtle in its mouth. To help everyone get a better look at this rare sight, Smith put the tour boat into reverse and backed up to get closer to the animal.

When he did, he quickly realized that Rusty was not holding a turtle neither a small white-tailed deer. A cold chill must have run through Smith's body when he perceived Rusty holding a human body. Realizing that his cruise boat was filled with women and children, he quickly sped up and motored away from Rusty and its catch.

But some of the observant passengers also realized it wasn't a deer being dragged along in the alligator's mouth. Among the statements taken later that day by deputies and rangers, many on board quickly suspected it had been a person. One witness described the creature in the gator's mouth as resembling a doll, in large part because of the pale, lifeless color of the body. Others knew for certain it had been an adult man in the gator's jaws. As the Jungle Cruise completed its fateful journey that day, rumors spread on board about someone seeing a snorkeler floating downstream just minutes before the boat's departure.

At 2 P.M., the cruise boat returned to the dock and Luke Smith immediately got in touch with his supervisor, B.J. Givens. The two quickly took off in a small boat to verify the sighting. A quarter mile downstream, they found what they had feared: the body of a young man floating facedown beneath the clear water, with the alligator known as Rusty standing guard over its prey. They knew that, at that point, a rescue was out of the question. The man floating in the river was dead.

They returned upstream to notify the park manager, Dick Miller. The three of them, along with reporter Pam Whaley of the Wakulla News, soon headed back downstream to attempt to recover the body. As they approached Rusty, it swam off, and with the help of the paramedics also on the scene, the lifeless body of George Cummings was dragged out of the chilling waters of the Wakulla River.

One of the two boats remained and, as Cummings's body was being transferred to Tallahassee Medical Center's morgue, Rusty was located and shot by one of the officers using his sidearm. It had little effect. They shot Rusty several times, but the beast escaped into a swampy area just below where the initial attack had occurred.

Sergeant Chafin realized they were not going to kill the eleven-foot animal with a pistol and contacted George Byrd of the U.S. Fish and Wildlife Service to bring a rifle with a scope so as to finish off Rusty. Officer Byrd arrived sometime later and, after waiting for the alligator to come out of the swampy area, he shot and killed it with a high-powered rifle. Rusty sank to the bottom. Using a harpoon and ropes, the men had little trouble retrieving it from the cold, clear waters.

They dragged Rusty to a grassy area on the bank where photos of the reptile were taken. Eventually Rusty's body was taken to a Gainesville lab for a complete necropsy. At 4 A.M. on August 14, 1987, the body was in Gainesville awaiting dissection and the scientists got started.

The necropsy revealed Rusty as a large, bull male measuring eleven feet in length and weighing 415 pounds. The empty stomach indicated that Rusty had not eaten in more than two days. It was apparent that Rusty was hungry when it went after Cummings.

The tooth marks found on Cummings's leg were matched against the tooth patterns of Rusty's powerful jaws. The evidence was conclusive; there was no disputing that Rusty had killed George Cummings that afternoon.

Cummings had been bitten in several places, but there is no way of knowing exactly what happened that afternoon in the Wakulla River. In the water, even with snorkeling fins on, it is impossible for one to outswim an alligator. Alligators have been clocked to swim at speeds of more than sixteen miles an hour; an average swimmer cannot swim even half that fast.

Wearing a mask and using a snorkel doesn't help, as one's peripheral vision is drastically reduced. Dive masks and snorkels allow one to remain facedown in the water, and thus unaware of one's wider surroundings. George Cummings may have never even noticed the alligator approaching him. There were numerous bite marks on his body, any one of which could have been the initial strike. All an alligator needs to subdue its victim is to submerge the person until he or she drowns. From the autopsy report, that is exactly what Rusty did to Cummings: the same thing it would have done to a white-tailed deer or a wild boar that might have forded the Wakulla River that day. It is what alligators are programmed to do.

To the best of everyone's knowledge, Rusty had never been fed. Although familiar with the Jungle Cruise operators by their frequent mutual encounters, Rusty was a healthy, fully wild animal. By leaving the cordoned-off swimming area, Cummings, a strong, athletic twenty-nine-year-old man was killed.

In 1985, the same George Cummings had revealed a thirty-foot-high sculpture in Tallahassee titled "Homage to Kandinsky." In a letter dated July 14 to Lieutenant Kirkland, a nearby resident voiced her sadness at the loss of the young man, but argued that it hadn't been the alligator's fault. She insisted that they did not kill Rusty for having taken Cummings's life. Alas, it was already too late: too late for both the young man snorkeling downriver and for the alligator that took him.

To this day, the roped-off swimming area at Wakulla Springs is safe to swim and snorkel. To this day, leaving that roped-off area is not.

If it's fresh water in Florida—a canal, pond, river, swamp, or marsh—it harbors alligators!

A Skin Diver Disappears

In 1961, skin-diving was still in its infancy. The aqualung, invented by world-renowned marine scientist, Jacques-Yves Cousteau, and his engineer friend, Emile Gagnan, in 1943, had only been made commercially available in the U.S. in 1952. The television series, *Sea Hunt*, starring Lloyd Bridges as the skin-diving hero Mike Hunt was still being broadcast. The first episode of *Sea Hunt* aired in the fall of '58 and allowed television viewers their first glimpse of the newfound world of coral reefs, exotic sea creatures, and menacing sharks.

It would be another five years before the organization called PADI, Professional Association of Diving Instructors, was established. Neither diver nor instructor certification was available in 1961. The equipment, when compared with today's sophisticated scuba gear, was unreliable and barely affordable.

Because diving was so new, shark attacks on skin divers, as they were called then, were rare. William Dandridge, a healthy twenty-three-year-old from Miami, recently released from military duty, learned to dive while in the navy. The U.S. Navy was the first to recognize the military applications of skin-diving. Today's Navy Seals are regarded as the best-equipped and best-trained divers in the world.

It's unlikely that his being attacked and killed by a shark ever entered into Dandridge's thoughts on the morning of June 25, 1961. The last person to die in a fatal shark attack in Florida had been Richard Best in 1934 in Brevard County and, prior to Dandridge's untimely death, no Florida diver had ever been killed by a shark. As instructor Dandridge and his two pupils steamed out to a coral reef near Fowey Rock Lighthouse, Dandridge was probably far more concerned with checking their regulators and making sure the tanks were topped off with compressed air, rather than worrying about marauding sharks.

His students for the morning, Mr. and Mrs. James Quillian, were anxious to get started. At 8:30 A.M. on that bright Saturday, the three dropped anchor over a healthy stretch of coral roughly two miles east of Crandon Park Marina. Mrs. Quillian chose to remain on board for the first dive while her husband went down with the instructor. They entered the water just after nine with enough air in their tanks for a fifty-minute dive. It was the Quillians' third lesson with Dandridge.

Ten minutes into the dive, Mrs. Quillian was surprised when Dandridge popped up not far from the anchorage and screamed, "Help, help, help!" at the top of his lungs. Before she was able to respond to his desperate cries, he was inexplicably pulled back beneath the waves and vanished. She later told the police the only thing she had noticed was that his mask had been ripped off. From her vantage point several hundred feet away, there had been no sign of blood in the water or any indication that a shark was involved.

James Quillian surfaced five minutes later and asked his wife if she had seen any sign of Dandridge, since they had accidentally split up a while earlier. When Mrs. Quillian told her husband what had just happened, James Quillian dove back down to look for Dandridge but found nothing.

Soon thereafter, the Quillians hailed a passing boat, which in turn relayed a distress message to the Coast Guard. Within the hour, a helicopter and several Metro divers searched for any sign of the missing Dandridge for the rest of the day. A shark attack had never been seriously considered. Everyone assumed Dandridge had drowned.

The following day, June 26, 1961, the *Miami Herald* ran a brief article about Dandridge's disappearance. The article was based on the assumption that Dandridge had accidentally drowned. That same afternoon, Metro divers recovered William Dandridge's body not far from where he had vanished the previous morning. On June 27, 1961, the *Herald* ran a brief statement on page 3-A that Metro divers had recovered Dandridge's remains. Nowhere in the articles was there any mention of a shark attack.

But by all means it had been a shark attack. Whether the facts surrounding the case, at that time, were suppressed by the Metro divers, by William Dandridge's family, or by the *Miami Herald*, it will never be known. The International Shark Attack File has duly recorded the name, date, and place of the attack. We can only speculate as to why the *Miami Herald* hung on to the drowning story. Someone along the way was probably concerned that news of a fatal shark attack involving the fledgling sport of skin-diving might not be the kind of press local dive shops or the Miami tourist industry would welcome. The Miami Police Department might also have had its own reasons for the apparent cover-up.

As is usually the case, the exact species of shark that attacked Dandridge remains unknown. Unless a tooth breaks off, thereby supplying the medical examiner with either physical or DNA evidence—although DNA evidence wouldn't have come into play in 1961—there is no way of telling what kind of shark bit into Dandridge. Because he resurfaced and cried for help, it's difficult to believe his death was a drowning. Dandridge was a well-trained, professional navy diver in the prime of his life. Wearing a pair of flippers and less than one hundred feet from his vessel, it was implausible that he wouldn't have been able to make the short swim to safety.

Something had bitten Dandridge before he surfaced and cried for help, just as something bit him a second time as he shouted to Mrs. Quillian, thus his being mysteriously pulled back into the deep. Given the evidence, it's likely that both bites were to his legs, which seriously impaired his ability to reach for the dive boat.

In all likelihood, the animal responsible was either a tiger or a bull shark. Although great white sharks are known to cruise along Florida's extensive shoreline, especially during the cooler winter months, they seldom attack. On the other hand, tiger and bull sharks not only bite people, they also have been known to eat people, at least parts of them. Both species inhabit warmer waters and their diet, especially a tiger shark's, includes virtually anything they can eat, from turtles to tin cans. Given that the attack occurred in late June, when the waters of Biscayne Bay are warm, the evidence would indicate that Dandridge died from the bite of a large bull or tiger shark. Though he became one of the first, William Dandridge wouldn't be the last diver in Florida to perish under such sinister circumstances.

Towing in a large bull shark using chain for leader.

SHARKS

It is hard to imagine a single word in the English language that bears more psychological impact and imbedded fear than *shark*. One's screaming **"FIRE!"** in a crowded theater is the same as someone else's yelling **"SHARK!"** at a busy Florida beach: it will send shudders down anxious parents' spines and clear the water of swimmers in minutes.

Peter Benchley's 1973 novel and soon thereafter Steven Spielberg's film, *Jaws,* have redefined our mental image of this silent, stalking predator. Both book and film have left us with a lasting impression of the huge, menacing eating machine that attacks people, dogs, and boats with a ruthless sense of purpose. So striking were those images that in England, ever since the publication of Benchley's novel, people have referred to sharks as jaws.

More recent films such as *Open Water,* various PBS television documentaries, and Discovery Channel's annual shark week have only served to reinforce the stereotype: the dark, triangular fin slicing through the water; the tooth-filled mouth thrusting forward and biting at the metal bars of its cage; the clear blue water surrounding the camera turning black with the stain of blood.... A shark has attacked!

In the open ocean, large sharks, dolphins, and killer whales are the ultimate predators. Sharks have been honing their predatory skills for four hundred million years and have become extremely efficient at what they do.

Up to now, there are over four hundred known species of sharks. Dozens, perhaps scores of species, are yet to be discovered in the ocean's great depths. Sharks range in size from the largest fish in the ocean—the whale shark, which can attain lengths of sixty-seven feet and weigh in excess of fifty tons—to the rare and minuscule spiked-pygmy shark of the deep oceanic trenches in the western Pacific. The spiked-pygmy weighs less than a pound and attains a maximum length of six inches (refer to Chart #3 for further details about Elasmobranches).

The diversity and wide range of shark species cover every environmental niche, from the black, crushing depths of over two miles beneath the sea, all the way up to the shallow sand bars of temperate oceans. Sharks have managed to survive several mass extinctions and there is no doubt they will continue to survive millions of years hence.

Although attacks and fatalities do occur in cooler, temperate waters, most shark encounters happen in tropical and subtropical seas. As a species, sharks prefer a water temperature of 68° F, although the Greenland shark has been found swimming under the Arctic ice and the great white sharks of southern Australia prey on seals in water as cold as 50° F.

Most shark attacks on humans occur between latitudes 47° S and 46° N. This has more to do with man's unwillingness to enter water colder than 60° F than with the range of shark species. When we think of shark attacks, we tend to visualize the regions where most attacks occur: Australia, the South Pacific, Hawaii, California, and of course Florida.

Further, almost all shark attacks occur where the greatest number of humans has invaded the shark's domain: along the beaches, especially those where people surf. Most people are attacked between two and four in the afternoon, the hottest part of the day and when they are most likely to take a swim. Most shark attacks take place in waist-to-chest-deep water, although the downing of planes or the sinking of vessels at sea represent the most gruesome examples of shark attacks and human mortality.

One of the greatest illustrations of an open-ocean shark-feeding frenzy occurred on July 30, 1945, the same year of the retreating Japanese soldiers' slaughter by saltwater crocodiles. On that fateful night, shortly after midnight, the USS Indianapolis was hit by two torpedoes fired from a Japanese submarine. The ship went down in minutes, taking approximately 297 of her 1,197 crew. What happened to the nine hundred survivors lives in infamy in the annals of U.S. naval history.

The story of the Indianapolis began on July 15, 1945, when Captain Charles McVay and his crew took on a top-secret cargo in San Francisco Bay. Although the nature of that cargo still remains undisclosed, we can speculate with some degree of certainty that the *Indianapolis* was carrying the two atomic bombs that were dropped on Japan on the first week in August, 1945: Little Boy on Hiroshima on August 6, 1945, and Fat Man on Nagasaki, on August 9, 1945.

A 1937 photo of the doomed U.S.S. Indianapolis.

The *Indianapolis* departed from San Francisco on July 16, steaming toward a refueling stop at Pearl Harbor at a record-breaking twenty-eight knots. After refueling, and still sailing under a cloak of secrecy, she departed Pearl Harbor for the island of Tinian, on the Northern Mariana Islands. The ship arrived at her destination on July 26 and off-loaded the top-secret cargo.

McVay was glad to be finished with this unusual mission, a voyage that came complete with an entourage of navy brass, scientists, and extra marine security forces. The rumor mill on board was running nonstop during the assignment and all McVay wanted was to return to regular combat as soon as possible.

From Tinian, the ship made a short passage to Guam, one of the Marianas's southern islands, and unloaded the remaining navy brass and scientists. She then re-fueled, re-supplied, and departed from Apra Harbor, Guam, on July 28. Based on an average cruising speed of 15.7 knots, the *Indianapolis* was scheduled to cover the 1,171 miles between Guam and Leyte, in the Philippines, in approximately three days. There were reports of Japanese submarines along the route the *Indianapolis* was taking, but because of missed communications and the lingering cloak of secrecy surrounding her mission, Captain McVay was never informed of the submarines' presence.

What happened next laid the groundwork for the tragedy. Again, because of the top-secret nature of her mission to Tinian, the *Indianapolis* fell through

The Shark Family Tree

Elasmobranchs

Orectolobiformes

Orectolobidae
- Carpet Sharks
- Wobbegongs
- Some Nurse Sharks

Parascylliidae
- Collared Carpet Sharks

Brachaeluridae
- Blind Sharks

Hemiscylliidae
- Bamboo Sharks

Ginglymostomatidae
- Nurse Sharks

Stegostomatidae
- Zebra Sharks

Rhincodontidae
- Whale Sharks
  Rhincodon typus

Lamniformes

Cetorhinidae
- Basking Sharks
  Cetorhinus maximus

Lamnidae
- Great White Sharks
- Mako Sharks
- Other Mackerel Sharks

Alopiidae
- Threshers

Pseudocarchariidae
- Crocodile Sharks

Mitsukurinidae
- Goblin Sharks

Odontaspididae
- Sand Tigers or gray nurse sharks

Megachasmidae
- Megamouth Sharks
  Megachasma pelagios

Elasmobranchs

Carcharhiniformes **Squaliformes** **Hexanchiformes**

Carcharhinidae
- Requiem Sharks
- Tiger Sharks
- White-tip Sharks
- Black-tip Sharks
- Blue Sharks

Sphyrnidae
- Hammerheads
- Bonnet Sharks

Triakidae
- Smooth Hound Sharks
- Oil Sharks
- Leopard Sharks

Leptochariidae
- Barbeled Hound Sharks

Hemigaleidae
- Weasel Sharks

Scyliorhinidae
- Catsharks
- Nursehounds
- Swell Sharks
- Lesser Spotted Dogfish

Proscylliidae
- Finback Cat Sharks

Pseudotriakidae
- False Cat Sharks

Squalidae
- Spined Sharks
- Spiny Dogfish
- Dogfish Sharks
- Spurdogs
- Lantern Sharks

Scymnorhinidae
- Spineless Dogfish
- Dwarf Sharks
- Sleeper Sharks

Echinorhinidae
- Bramble Sharks

Oxynotidae
- Rough Sharks

Chlamydoselachidae
- Frilled Shark
  Chlamydoselachus anguineus

Hexanchidae
- Comb-toothed Sharks
- Cow Sharks
- Six- & Seven-Gilled Sharks

the cracks of standard protocol. Though her departure from Guam had been duly noted, no one in Leyte knew when she was expected to arrive. So, when the ship was torpedoed in the middle of the night on July 30, even though an SOS had been broadcast from the ship, no one went looking for her. The survivors of the sinking ship were abandoned at sea.

Four of the most gruesome days in the U.S. Navy history had elapsed before a submarine-reconnaissance plane noticed an oil slick in the ocean. Following the slick down-sea, Pilot-Lieutenant Wilbur Gwinn began seeing heads bobbing amidst the oil. He realized these were navy personnel and estimated the number at approximately 150. In the end, of the nine hundred men who had gone into the sea, only 317 came out alive, including McVay.

Some died of injuries sustained during and shortly after the sinking. Some went mad from drinking salt water and floating in the subtropical heat for four days. Most were attacked and devoured by sharks. On average, a sailor perished every ten minutes from a shark attack over the course of those dreadful four days.

Oceanic white-tip, tiger, mako, and blue sharks, among others, were the species attacking the helpless sailors. The sharks were initially attracted to the disaster area by the powerful sonic waves created as the huge cruiser sank. By using their lateral lines as sensors, sharks are capable of detecting unusual underwater motions such as struggling fish or active swimmers from over a mile away. The massive vibrations created by the sinking of a ninety-eight-hundred-ton heavy cruiser would have brought in sharks from hundreds of miles off. The splash of a plane going down or the sinking of a vessel in subtropical waters invariably attracts sharks. The *Indianapolis* disaster was no exception.

The U.S. Navy, looking for a scapegoat and not wanting to accept any responsibility for the disaster, unjustly court-martialed Captain McVay. Though the captain was cleared of all wrongdoing fifty-six years later, he never knew about the final verdict. McVay had retired in 1949 and in 1968, using his navy pistol, he committed suicide. In July 2001, the Secretary of the Navy ordered Captain Charles McVay exonerated of all wrongdoing in the loss of his ship and nearly all of her crew. Justice, albeit at a terrible price, had finally been served. It could be said that McVay became the last victim of this infamous navy disaster.

Although other ships went down with staggering loss of human life during WWII—the *Arizona*, 1,104 dead; the *Franklin*, 724 dead; and the *Bunker Hill*, 396 dead—none were nearly as appalling as the sinking of the *Indianapolis* and the fate that befell her nine hundred crewmen that late summer in the Philippine Sea. It is considered by many historians the worst U.S. naval catastrophe of WWII.

There have been many other ship disasters which have ended in bloody shark attacks. On February 26, 1852, the English frigate *Birkenhead* struck a reef south of the Cape of Good Hope in South Africa at 2 A.M., less than a mile from shore. On board were 490 English soldiers with twenty-five of their wives and thirty-one of their children. Besides these passengers and the soldiers, there was the crew: another 134 men under the command of Captain Robert Salmond.

Soon after striking the reef, Captain Salmond ordered first the evacuation of the women and children and then the last lifeboat filled with thirty of the soldiers. Six hundred men remained on board the sinking frigate.

The *Birkenhead* broke in half and sank thirty minutes later. Lieutenant Girardot, one of the surviving soldiers, later described the incident to his father: "I remained on deck until the boat sank. I was dragged under the water by the suction and a man caught my leg. I succeeded in freeing myself by kicking him and got to the surface, where I hung on to some pieces of wood. I remained in the water for five hours.... The sea was so high that many perished trying to reach land. Practically all those who found themselves in the water without their clothes were taken by sharks; hundreds of them surrounded us and I saw a number of men seized right next to me, but, as I was dressed...they preferred the others."

In the end, 455 lives were claimed by the accident, most of them from being devoured by sharks. When news of the disaster reached London, curiously no mention was made of the attacking predators.

A more recent example of ship disasters occurred in the Sea of China in 1987. The vessel was called the *Doña Paz*. Although originally designed to carry only 608 passengers, the *Doña Paz* was later reconditioned to carry fifteen hundred passengers and ferried them between the numerous islands of the Philippines.

On December 20, 1987, the *Doña Paz* left Manila with over three thousand passengers crowded onto her decks and berths. At ten o'clock that night, a small oil tanker collided with her and started a series of events that would result in the second worst maritime disaster in history.

The tanker's 880 barrels of kerosene caught fire minutes after the collision, setting the entire sea on fire. Of the three-thousand-plus passengers, only two women and twenty-three men survived—a survival rate of less than one percent. Sharks scavenged the corpses and played a significant role in the ultimate death toll.

The waters of the Philippines abound with tiger, sand-tiger, blue, oceanic white-tip, and great white sharks. Of the three thousand dead, only three hundred mutilated corpses were recovered. In the ensuing months, local fishermen were still catching sharks whose stomachs held human-body parts, presumably from the sinking of the *Doña Paz*.

Sharks are naturally attracted to any unusual or irregular motion that occurs in water. Nearby sharks arrive on the scene of these events within minutes. Others, sensing the event with their internal motion detectors, may take several days to arrive at the scene. Near the epicenter of the event, given the likelihood of blood in the water and the struggling, injured survivors, sharks always find ample opportunity to attack. The outcome is inevitable.

There can be little doubt that hundreds of people perish at sea annually as a result of shark attacks that take place when a boat sinks or people are otherwise involved in a maritime accident. Because the victims' remains are seldom found, the exact number of open-ocean deaths will never be known. They are seldom, if ever, included in annual shark-attack statistics.

Only a handful of the four hundred species of sharks attack people; at that, only a dozen do so consistently. These are the great white, the tiger, the bull, the blacktip, the blue, the mako, the oceanic white-tip, the whaler, the hammerhead, the nurse, the grey nurse, and the wobbegong shark. Many of these species are not indigenous to Florida waters.

The most famous of the twelve is the great white, known in Australia as the white pointer or the white death. Great whites are the largest predatory sharks in the world and their reputation is legendary. Although great white sharks have been observed swimming along the Florida coastline, they are not a common species. The reason might be that Florida's waters are generally too warm for great whites and thus most sightings of these magnificent predators occur during the winter months.

The size of great white sharks is incomprehensible. Like large crocodiles, the relationship between length and girth has to be taken into account. As a great white approaches twenty feet in length, its girth becomes monstrous. A nineteen-foot great white shark can weigh forty-five hundred pounds. To the question "How big do great white sharks get?" a reporter once asked a very astute Australian diver and his answer says it perfectly: "Big enough!"

A great white shark that weighs over two tons and measures twenty-feet long can swallow a man whole. Although bigger sharks have been sighted, those sightings have yet to be authenticated. One was a report of a thirty-six-foot great white taken in Port Ferry, Victoria, Australia, but there is some question to the validity of this claim.

Another anecdote involves an enormous great white shark that was stranded in a weir in New Brunswick, Canada, in the 1930s, which was estimated to measure and astounding thirty-seven feet in length. This claim, too, has never been verified.

The largest great white shark actually harpooned, weighed in, and verified was caught off the coast of Cuba in 1945. That fish measured twenty-one feet in length and weighed 7,302 pounds. Another immense fish was caught by fishermen off the Azores in the Atlantic in 1978. It was hauled ashore and measured by a reliable observer at 29.5 feet. It was too large to weigh, although it was estimated to be in excess of ten thousand pounds.

Sharks of that size have led some people to speculate that there may still be a viable population of the largest predatory shark known to have ever roamed the ocean: it is called *Carcharodon megalodon.* Its fossil teeth are still found today and measure six inches in length. A shark with teeth this large could grow to an amazing eighty feet in length.

There are few anatomical differences between a great white (*Carcharodon carcharias*) and the supposedly extinct *Carcharodon megalodon.* In his book *The Blue Meridian,* Peter Matthiessen speculates that present-day great white sharks are merely smaller specimens of the *megalodon.* There might, after all, be some truth to what the shark hunter Quint said to Hooper in Peter Benchley's novel, *Jaws.* Near the end of the novel, Quint speculates whether the *megalodon* is still out there patrolling

An enormous great white shark harpooned off the coast of Australia in the 1960s.

the depths of the sea. He adds that we would never find a dead one because sharks don't have air bladders; they remain buoyant by virtue of the oil produced in their oversized livers. In some species, their liver represents one third of their body weight. Although their natural oil allows them to float, all sharks have a negative buoyancy of approximately four percent.

If there are *megalodons* still swimming in the great depths of the ocean, they would sink when they died, thereby denying us the ability to ever authenticate their existence. Needless to say, an eighty-foot shark could never be caught by hook and line. The largest great white shark ever brought in on fishing tackle and certified as an IGFA—International Game Fish Association—record was caught in 1959 by Alf Dean off the coast of Australia, near Ceduna. It weighed an amazing 2,664 pounds.

The largest great white, in fact the largest fish ever taken by rod and reel, was caught off Montauk, Long Island, New York, in 1986 by Donnie Braddick. The fish was seventeen-feet long and weighed a whopping 3,427 pounds. The catch was disqualified as an official IGFA record because Braddick had used a whale carcass to attract it, which is illegal under IGFA rules. Even larger sharks have been hooked, but no one has been able to land a bigger fish than Braddick's great white.

The possibility of the continued existence of an extinct species such as the *megalodon* is nothing new when it comes to our limited knowledge of the ocean. The discovery of the coelacanth in 1938 off the coast of South Africa serves as an excellent example. The coelacanth had

An early mold of a megalodon's awesome jaws.

been believed to be extinct for over sixty million years when a specimen was brought ashore by a fisherman. Local anglers had known about the existence of this large fish for centuries and called it the oil fish. Coelacanths can weigh up to 130 pounds.

Since the 1938 discovery, numerous coelacanths have been caught near the Comoro Islands and scientists have succeeded in filming them in their natural habitat. They are no longer considered extinct.

The only thing we really know about the deep oceans is we don't know much about them at all. In a lecture by Peter Benchley I attended in 2005, he stated that thus far we have explored less than 1/2000th of the entire deep ocean. The world's oceans cover seventy-one percent of the earth's surface and thereupon we have only scratched the surface. Viewed from outer space, our earth isn't a lush and green terrestrial planet, but a blue planet. Nearly three-fourths of its surface is water and most of that water is comprised of the world's great oceans.

When one considers that the average depth of oceans is two miles and their deepest point—the Marianas Trench in the northwestern Pacific—is almost six miles deep, one is looking at an unimaginable volume of water. With different species of fish adapted to live and thrive at various depths throughout this liquid atmosphere, the possibilities of undiscovered species are endless.

The aqualung, a precursor to modern scuba gear, was invented in the 1940s, less than seventy years ago. Even with the best available equipment today, divers are rarely able to exceed depths of three hundred feet. There are only a handful of deep-diving submersibles in existence and, given the oceans' sheer enormity, how many square miles can a few bathyscaphes cover in a given year?

It has been said that we know more about the surface of the moon than we do about the ocean. Every decade, new discoveries are made, such as the megamouth shark in 1976, off the northern shore of Oahu, Hawaii. This new species is believed to be a plankton- or shrimp-eating fish similar in design to the basking shark. The one caught in 1976 measured fourteen feet in length and weighed 1,653 pounds. Since 1976, a total of eleven megamouth sharks have been caught and we still know virtually nothing about their diet, populations, or behavior.

Discovering an animal this large on land would be tantamount to finding the Yeti in the mountains of Nepal. The megamouth isn't alone, though, nor is it the largest undiscovered shark swimming in the deep oceans. Scientists in deep-diving submersibles such as the *Alvin* and the *Trieste* have observed even larger sharks of unknown species coming to feed on baits staked out on the ocean floor over ten thousand feet beneath the surface. Indeed, the world's great oceans remain clouded in mystery.

*****

Our views about sharks have changed dramatically in the past one hundred years, as has our knowledge of their behavior and biology. One hundred years ago, before a series of deadly attacks along the New Jersey coastline, it was widely believed that sharks would never attack a living person. Although open-ocean attacks were acknowledged, according to the scientific community at the time the concept of a shark attacking someone swimming along a beach was unheard of; a highly improbable occurrence, especially in northern waters. It was also held that a shark's bite was incapable of cutting through a human arm or leg bone.

Both concepts changed during the summer of 1916 in what is now commonly referred to as the "Twelve Days of Terror." On July 1, 1916, Charles Vansant was taking a late-afternoon swim in the Atlantic Ocean near the community of Beach Haven, New Jersey. As he swam just beyond the lifelines in chest-deep water, Vansant was suddenly hit by what most scientists now believe was a small great white shark or, as some scientists would also argue today, probably a bull shark. Although he survived the initial attack and was dragged to shore by fellow swimmers, at 6:45 that same evening Charles Vansant was pronounced dead. His death certificate stated, "Hemorrhage of the femoral artery, left side...bitten by shark while bathing."

In fact, the shark had torn Vansant's left leg off and, although he received almost immediate medical attention, the wound was too grave, making it impossible to stop the massive blood loss. Exsanguination, or one's bleeding to death, is the most common cause of demise after a shark bite.

The scientific community considered the event a freak of nature and resisted against attributing to a shark the cause of the fatal attack. Their skepticism disappeared when a second attack occurred at Spring Lake, New Jersey, on July 6, 1916.

Situated forty-five miles north of Beach Haven, along the Jersey shore, Spring Lake was an elegant summer resort at the turn of the twentieth century. Charles Bruder was an employee of one of the large, luxury hotels that lined the beach front. He was alone, enjoying a midday swim roughly 130 yards offshore when he was savagely attacked by a shark.

On its first strike, the shark completely bit off Bruder's right leg just above the knee. On the second attack, the shark tore off his left foot, biting clean through the bone. Although the lifeguards reached Bruder within minutes, his having both femoral arteries severed while in the water proved to be too much for the young, healthy Bruder to endure. When the would-be rescuers finally reached Bruder offshore, his last spoken words were, "A shark bit me. Bit my legs off!"

Charles Bruder died of shock and blood loss on the bottom of the lifeboat. He was dead by the time they reached the beach. Once back on shore, the doctors attending Bruder spent most of their time reviving the swooning women who had fainted at the sight of the legless and mutilated young man. News quickly spread of the second attack and the entire Jersey shore was closed down in the aftermath of the two consecutive attacks. The scientific community then based in New York and Boston was quickly revising its opinion that unprovoked shark attacks could never occur near-shore or that shark bites were incapable of cutting through a human's leg bone.

The twelve days of terror culminated on July 12, 1916, with a shark attack at Matawan. Matawan is located thirty miles north of Spring Lake and some sixteen miles up the Matawan Creek, a considerable distance from the beaches and resorts of the Jersey shore. In 1916, it was a small hamlet surrounded by lush farms and rural homesteads.

Around 2 P.M., three young boys had decided to beat the heat and go for a swim at the Wyckoff dock. One of the boys was eleven-year-old Lester Stillwell. While floating on his back over the "deep hole," Stillwell was violently attacked by what was then believed to be an eight-foot great white shark, but now is believed by many scientists to have been a bull shark. He was pulled underwater immediately, having only enough time to emit one blood-curdling scream before he disappeared into the dark waters of Matawan Creek.

What happened next is very unusual. Within the hour, the boys had let everyone in town know that their friend Lester had been attacked. As the townspeople gathered down at the creek, a young man named Stanley Fisher swam out to try to find the body in the deep water. After several attempts, Fisher finally located it and began coming out of the water with young Stillwell's lifeless corpse in his arms. In waist-deep water only a few feet from shore, the shark turned its attention to Fisher and bit him in the right thigh.

After a violent struggle, the shark released Fisher, who then made his way to the slope near the Wyckoff dock. As Fisher was being pulled out of the water, a stream of bright red blood shot skyward. His femoral artery had been severed and over ten pounds of flesh had been torn away from his thigh, whereupon it exposed the bone and raked the remaining flesh into torn and jagged strips.

Although he was rushed by train into Monmouth Memorial Hospital, once again it became too late. Stanley Fisher was pronounced dead at 6:35 that evening, his death a result of uncompensated hemorrhagic shock. Although it is doubtful that Fisher would die from such a wound today, given modern medicine's improved facilities and rapid evacuations, the world in 1916 moved much slower. The elapsed time between the attack and Fisher's arrival at the hospital was too long and the wounds too grave. Within twelve days, four people had been killed by sharks.

Rewards were immediately posted for the killing of the shark believed to be responsible for the two deaths at Matawan. Before the terror was over, a fifth victim, another boy named Joseph Dunn, was bitten downriver from Matawan, even though he survived the attack when two friends pulled him from the jaws of the shark.

What ensued over the next few days was nothing less than a witch hunt for the shark. Many townspeople believed the culprit was stranded in the Matawan Creek. Wire fences were strung up, portions of the river dynamited, and several locals spent hours firing shotguns and rifles into the creek, targeting anything that moved.

The shark escaped. Several days later, a great white shark was taken in Sandy Hook Bay near the mouth of Matawan Creek. Although we will never know for certain, that shark was quite possibly the man-eater that had taken little Lester Stillwell and fatally bitten Stanley Fisher. The fish was seven-and-a-half-feet long and weighed 350 pounds. Human flesh supposedly was found in its stomach, but it was never conclusively proven that it had been the offending shark. Because the Stillwell attack occurred so far up a tidal creek in a mixture of both fresh and salt water, contemporary scientists look to the bull shark as the more likely offending species.

Concerned Matawan citizens hunting for the killer shark in 1916.

After the New Jersey attacks, both the theory that unprovoked shark attacks never occurred near the shore that far north, as well as the assumption that a shark's jaws were not capable of biting through an adult's bone mass, were debunked. In hindsight, the only unusual segment of the four fatal attacks had been the fatal bite delivered to Stanley Fisher as he attempted to retrieve the body of Lester Stillwell. Statistically, sharks will attack the people involved in rescuing a bitten victim only 1.1 percent of the time.

In other words, if an individual swims out to save another who has already been attacked by a shark, that person has a near ninety-nine-percent chance that the shark will not turn on him or her. This statistic has remained constant regardless of how close one is to both the victim and the shark. This is definitely not the case with either alligators or cougars, which will readily turn on and attack any would-be rescuer.

The reason for this statistical anomaly is unclear. One possible theory involves the shark's ability to detect electrical fields. Sharks can detect minuscule charges of electrical energy by using a sensory organ known as ampullae of Lorenzini. This unique organ is named after the man who first described it in 1678, Stefano Lorenzini, although the exact function of the organ was not understood until three hundred years later.

The sensory system appears as a number of pores scattered about the shark's head. The plural-form word "ampullae" derives from the shape of the organ, which is similar to an ampulla, a narrow-necked bottle from the time of the Roman Empire. Every ampulla on a shark is filled with a jellylike substance which in turn appears to react to pressure and temperature changes, or as most now believe, small electrical charges produced by hidden prey in or under the sand.

The shark's electro-receptive system detects electrical fields so weak that one scientist compared it to the electric field of a flashlight battery connected to electrodes spaced one thousand miles apart. Sharks are able to filter out their own electrical fields while zeroing in on sting rays, mollusks, and other prey completely buried along the ocean floor and invisible to the naked eye.

Sharks frequently attack metal objects underwater, because the interaction of these metals and salt water can give off weak electrical signals through electrolysis. Sharks have been known to bite boat propellers, swim platforms, shark cages, and a host of other items which equally produce these minute charges.

One plausible explanation for why sharks bite and re-bite the victim and not the would-be rescuer is, once a person is bitten, his or her electrical field changes dramatically. An open wound leaks both blood and electrical energy. This may explain the precision with which an attacking shark always returns to bite only the individual whose electrical field emanates a stronger and more disrupted charge.

Further research needs to be done to better understand this "supernormal" sensory ability shared by many elasmobranchs. Elasmobranch is the scientific name given to the subclass of marine animals which includes all sharks, skates, and rays.

A shark's ability to detect very tiny electrical charges may explain its uncanny ability to navigate open oceans. Using the ampullae of Lorenzini may help sharks detect the magnetic fields surrounding the planet, thereby allowing them to intuitively know where the poles are at all times.

Although many sharks such as the white-tipped reef, the nurse, and the wobbegong remain rather stationary throughout their lifetime, some species such as the blue and the oceanic white-tip shark have been known to migrate thousands of miles annually. Until recently, before the introduction of global positioning radio telemetry and extensive shark-tagging programs, little was known about the migratory patterns of oceanic sharks.

In fact, before Valarie Taylor, a renowned shark expert and diver from Australia, stuck a great white shark with an instrument designed to measure the internal temperature of the fish in the early 1970s, we had no idea that any species of sharks were warm-blooded. Most fish and sharks are cold-blooded, or poikilothermic. A poikilothermic animal's body temperature is virtually the same as the surrounding water. Mackerel sharks—among them the great white, the mako, the porbeagle, and the thresher—are partially homeothermic, or semi-warm-blooded. Their internal body temperature can be up to 40° –50° F warmer than the surrounding waters. This explains how the great white shark can survive and flourish along the cold Humboldt currents off the California coast and why the mako and porbeagle sharks have such extended ranges.

One drawback to being warm-blooded is that of caloric intake. Alligators and crocodiles are cold-blooded and need only a tiny portion of the calories a human being needs on a daily basis. Warm-blooded sharks need substantially more food than their cold-blooded fellow predators.

This is possibly why great white sharks prefer high-fat, high-calorie foods such as sea lions, elephant seals, and other pinnipeds. One gram of fat produces nine calories of energy, whereas one gram of protein only produces four calories of energy. As a rule, then, cold-water, warm-blooded sharks rely on a high-fat, high-calorie diet. This may help explain a great white's tendency to bite a person once and then spit him or her back out. Humans just aren't fat enough.

The trouble is that a single bite becomes more than enough to kill. Great whites have been known to bite and then disregard several other non-fatty preys such as sea otters and penguins. Once again, the injuries sustained by the bite generally prove fatal, but the shark seldom returns to actually consume its mistaken victim.

The bite of a shark takes 1/400th of a second. That's the same as the fastest shutter speed on many thirty-five-millimeter single-lens reflex cameras. It is an event that happens so quickly, it is barely perceivable by the human eye. It also explains why a shark can bite a person repeatedly within a fraction of a minute. Their jaws extend outward and open and close in less time than it takes one to blink. A human blink takes 1/64th of a second, over six-times slower than a shark bite.

Great whites, as well as tiger sharks and all other species, have spring-loaded teeth. If a tooth should break off on a bone while making its first bite, the tooth behind it springs forward for the second bite, thereby allowing room in the jaw for the growth of a third replacement tooth.

Sharks are virtually swimming teeth. Over the course of a lifetime, an average shark may go through twenty thousand teeth. The shark's teeth are enlarged versions of its skin scales. In fact, the rough, sandpaper-like skin of a shark is none other than dermal denticles that cover its entire body. Their skin is so rough that people have been injured just from the abrasive nature of collisions with swimming sharks.

A shark's teeth are arranged in rows that move slowly forward like a conveyor-belt system, from the rear inside of the jaw outward to the front row of the teeth. This continuous tooth replacement occurs every two weeks in some species.

The bite force of sharks is awesome. Although they do not have the same bone-crushing power of the American alligator, they don't need it. Sharks have twice the biting power as African lions, coupled with teeth that are both serrated and razor-sharp. A shark's bite is fifteen times stronger than a human's and strong enough to damage oceanographic instruments such as cameras and recording devices. Only the American alligator has a stronger bite. The alligator's bite has only been surpassed by that of the *Tyrannosaurus rex*. Fortunately for humanity, the *T-rex* is extinct.

Because of their immense pressure, stunning speed, and razor-sharp teeth, shark bites are strangely painless in nature. Men have actually had a leg bitten off without even realizing it until they tried to swim to safety. Some years ago, a friend of mine who had been bitten by a shark told me all he had felt at that moment was a bump on his foot. He didn't even realize he had been bleeding and that a chunk of his heel had been missing until he visually verified the injury.

Sharks have only fair eyesight. Because of their other sensory abilities, they don't need to see all that well. Moreover, the various ocean conditions often prevent them from seeing distinctly even if they had better eyesight. Most sharks see grayish, blurred shadows rather than colorful details. Since their eyes are located on the side of their heads, sharks lack binocular or stereoscopic vision.

Many sharks have a nictitating membrane similar to that of alligators'. At the moment of attack, the membrane is pulled up and over the eye so as to prevent damage to the eye from a thrashing, finned fish, or a fighting pinniped. Some sharks actually roll their eyes back into their heads when biting, giving them a white-eyed appearance.

Although their eyesight is poor, it must be noted that many shark attacks have been thwarted by the victim's gouging or stabbing at a shark's eyes. They are sensitive and, for an animal that is otherwise covered in teeth, their eyes, along with the gills, present the only vulnerable targets for an unarmed swimmer.

Of course, their sense of smell is legendary. They may or may not detect odors that have little to no importance to them, such as the smell of gasoline or man-made chemicals and products, but for odors and scents that are important, like blood or bodily fluids, sharks are extraordinary in every regard. In some sharks, the olfactory lobes that analyze smell information make up two-thirds of their brain's total weight. Sharks are basically swimming teeth with better-than-blood-hound noses.

As they patrol through the water, and by and large most killer sharks swim slower than we walk, they siphon off water through two nasal sacs located near the front of the snout. Unlike human noses, a shark's olfactory organs are never used for breathing. They are solely used to process and pass along potential prey information to the brain.

Blood of any kind is first and foremost on the shark's list of preferred odors. Blood means there is an injured fish or animal out there. Sharks can respond to concentrations as low as one pinhead of blood in a bathtub or, a better example, one teaspoon in an average-sized swimming pool.

More recent experiments have shown that even this level of sensitivity may be underestimated. Some scientists believe there are sharks capable of detecting blood over one hundred times as diluted as that pinhead in the bathtub, but in fact sharks may detect one drop of blood in an Olympic-sized swimming pool.

This ability to hone in on blood or other bodily fluids is important for us to remember whenever we venture into the ocean. Certain human activities—spear-fishing, hand-lining, or chumming for fish—very likely attract nearby sharks. Going into the water with any kind of cut, abrasion, or while menstruating also increases one's chances of attracting sharks. Although it is unknown exactly how far away sharks are able to pick up a blood scent in the water, up to a mile is widely thought to be a reasonable distance. Once again, scientists contend that, with some species of shark, that distance could be over ten miles.

Human body fluids and excretions including sweat, saliva, urine, and feces are believed to be potent enough to attract sharks. Although little research has been done on this subject, sharks have a much higher statistical probability of attacking men than women. A man is nine times more likely to be bitten by a shark than is a woman

One theory about this anomaly is that men are more odoriferous in the water than are women. Some scientists have suggested the attacks might relate to the hormone testosterone found in men. A third explanation is that men tend to engage in aquatic activities that inherently create higher risks. Fishing, surfing, spear-fishing, snorkeling, and scuba diving still are, percentage-wise, predominately male activities.

Regardless of the cause, the outcome is well documented. It is estimated that ninety-three percent of all shark attacks, both fatal and nonfatal, occur to men. I can't help but think more than a few women reading this would find this statistic somehow justifiable...?

Sharks do not have a very highly evolved sense of taste. They can discriminate between bitter, sweet, salty, and sour, but they still lack the discerning palate of a good French chef. Then again, French chefs are not wont to devour everything raw.

Sharks, therefore, use a series of sensory inputs to zero in on their prey. From great distances, they are able to detect sounds that reach their lateral line sensor as unusual vibrations in the water. Further, sharks turn to their acute sense of smell following minuscule, if not molecular, traces of blood or other organic odors up-current. Once close enough to their prey, they again use their motion detectors and lateral lines to further zero in on the target. As they make the fateful approach, they engage a combination of eyesight and electrical detectors—their ampullae of Lorenzini—to bring them within striking distance. Finally, they resort to contact either by bumping the prey to verify that it's edible or by simply biting it and seeing how it tastes.

In 1/400th of a second, the animal in question, be it a tuna or a human, will have been bitten. Finding the taste to its satisfaction, the shark quickly turns around and continues to attack. From research on seal predation in the Farallon Islands off the northern coast of California, massive blood loss almost always terminates the prey long before the shark begins consuming it.

Many shark species began this predatory behavior very, very early. The sand tiger shark of the western Pacific gives birth to only one shark pup at a time. Although there may be four or five fetuses in the uterus during the early months of pregnancy, by the time of delivery the dominant pup has survived by cannibalizing its brothers and sisters inside the womb. As a human, it's difficult not to find this particular adaptation rather repulsive.

This intra-uterine cannibalism known as oophagy may also occur among mako sharks and other species in the order Lamniformes, including the infamous great white shark. Because so little research has been done on the reproductive biology of great white sharks, scientists can only speculate whether or not they rely on oophagy during fetal development. No mature great white shark has ever survived in captivity except for the record 198 days that a young great white once kept in the million-gallon tank of the Monterey Bay Aquarium.

Although there are some primitive species of sharks—about forty percent—that are known as oviparous, i.e., they lay eggs in waterproof egg casings (e.g., the Port Jackson shark), most species do give birth to live pups. The most common form of shark reproduction—roughly fifty percent—is known as ovoviviparity. In this form of gestation, there is no placental connection between the embryo and the mother. The embryos held inside of the mother's body are nourished by yolk stored in a yolk sac attached directly to the growing fetus. One theory is that the fetuses are safer in this environment than they would be in open-water egg casings. A second theory is that ovoviviparity, or a-placental viviparity, allows the fetuses to grow larger inside the womb but produces fewer offspring per pregnancy.

The most advanced system of shark reproduction is called viviparity, also known as placental viviparity. Only ten percent of all sharks utilize this technique. Early on, the embryos live on stored yolk, but as the pups grow they make a pseudo-placental connection by attaching the yolk sac to the wall of the uterus. This arrangement is similar to the placenta found in mammals. In this case, the pups are relatively large at birth. All requiem sharks—lemons, blues, and hammerheads—utilize this form of embryonic development.

The length of pregnancy and number of delivered pups per pregnancy vary widely amongst the four hundred species of sharks. Some sharks give birth to litters of ten or more, with pregnancies lasting nine months (e.g., the blue shark), while the gigantic basking shark may take up to eighteen months to give birth. The spiny dogfish, a small shark found off the U.S.'s eastern seaboard, has the longest gestation of any creature on earth: it carries the young for twenty-four months before it gives birth. The fertile tiger shark gives birth to as many as eighty pups at a time after a twelve-month pregnancy.

Once born, the pups are on their own. There is no parental care and, should their own father swim by them, it would consider its own children fair game and devour the progeny without hesitation. Some scientists believe that shark mothers have evolved a brief fasting instinct during and shortly after the birthing period, thereby giving her offspring some protection from their inclination to consume their own children. Either way, sharks are not exactly nurturing parents.

In many species, the young try to stay together in the shallow nursery areas where they are born until they grow large enough to head out on their own. Except for the great white pups, which can be nearly forty pounds at birth, most shark pups are vulnerable to attacks by other predatory fish, including other sharks, for the first few years of their lives.

For the most part, sharks mature and grow slowly. Alligators and crocodiles can breed within three to four years of birth, whereas larger sharks such as great whites and hammerheads may take up to fifteen years before reaching sexual maturity. Once again, data on these top predators are too insufficient to be conclusive. On average, it is widely believed sharks grow only six inches a year. As they mature, the growth rate slows down even further, with some studies of the cold-water Greenland shark indicating a growth rate less than one half-inch a year.

One theory for this slow-growth rate may be related to the shark's slow digestive system. Many species only eat once every two or three days and some have been known to go without food for several months at a time. A large great white shark weighing just over a ton needs to eat approximately eleven tons of food per year to survive. Like alligators, cold-blooded sharks survive on fewer calories.

Most sharks are thought to live up to twenty-five years, though this number is only a calculated guess. Because there are four hundred known species and studying sharks in their aquatic environment is a daunting task, information about the actual age of various species is limited. Great whites are believed to live at least twenty-five years while whale sharks may live over seventy years of age. The piked dogfish, a harmless three-foot shark found in the western Pacific, is thought to survive well over one hundred years.

This slow advance to sexual maturity makes many sharks extremely vulnerable to the pressures of overfishing. Unlike alligators—which mature early, breed annually, and have large litters—many shark species sexually mature late, breed only once every two years, and have as few as one pup per pregnancy.

Much more fieldwork and biological research need to be done in this area before we fully understand just how vulnerable sharks are to human activities. Practices such as finning and harvesting sharks for food or liver oil may prove to be too intensive to maintain a sustainable shark population. We will look more extensively at man's predation on sharks in the last section of this book.

*****

Shark attacks are on the increase worldwide. The year 2000 saw the highest number of unprovoked attacks ever recorded, with seventy-nine confirmed cases, according to records kept by the International Shark Attack File (ISAF). This is very telling when one compares the average fifty-nine annual cases within the decade 1990–1999, of which only 12.7 percent were fatal.

Since the year 2000, the average number of shark attacks has increased to sixty-seven unprovoked attacks per year. Unprovoked attacks are defined as incidents where an attack on a live human by a shark occurs in its natural habitat without any human provocation of the shark. Incidents involving sharks and divers in public aquaria, holding pens, on boats involving anglers catching sharks, or shark-inflicted scavenging damage to postmortem drowning victims are not included in this figure. One category which is not included in the unprovoked-shark-attack file, but in my opinion should be, is that of air and sea disasters. I could find no clear explanation in the ISAF's Web site for this obvious omission.

Most attacks involve swimmers or waders (43.5 percent), followed by surfers and windsurfers (35.5 percent), divers and snorkelers (15.5 percent), and the remaining 5.5 percent are attributed to body-surfing or other shallow-water activities.

The ISAF is overseen by the American Elasmobranch Society and is currently affiliated with the Florida Museum of Natural History located at the University of Florida. It has been keeping accurate records of shark attacks worldwide since 1958 and maintaining files on every confirmed unprovoked attack in the world. If and when available, these files include police and medical reports, newspaper clippings, photographs, audio/video tapes, and eyewitness accounts. Access to the files is restricted to scientific or medical research, as well as allowed or denied on a case-by-case basis.

By using older U.S. Navy research and by engaging in collaboration with other regions of high-incidence shark attacks such as South Africa, Australia, and Hawaii, the ISAF has assembled a massive collection of data, which include approximately 2,291 shark attacks and stretch from the year 1580 to the present.

This painting by John Singleton Copley portrays an attack by what appears to be a tiger shark.

Most attacks occur in the United States. Florida State leads the world in unprovoked shark attacks, but Australia has the highest occurrence of fatal attacks, in large part owing to the ubiquitous great white throughout its territorial waters. We will look more closely at the Florida statistics in the next chapter.

Over the decades, mortality rates have shown a slow but steady decline. In the 1940s, it was estimated that forty-six percent of all attack victims died as a result of their injuries. In the 1950s, this number dropped to thirty-five percent and over the following decades the mortality rate continued to fall. Since the year 2000 to the present, the fatality rate in shark attacks has dropped to an all-time low of 8.9 percent.

The decline in mortality is not due to the number of actual attacks, which has steadily increased from an average of twenty-eight annually in the '50s to sixty-seven per year nowadays. Nor has the viciousness or severity of attacks been a factor in this increased survival rate. The main reason for the reduction of fatalities lies in far better immediate first aid, faster medical evacuation, and improved treatment. This is especially true in Australia, where most major beaches are now stocked with shark-attack kits in much the same fashion as most buildings are supplied with fire extinguishers. These kits are stored in small waterproof bins along the coastline and provide quick access to tourniquets, bandages, and other essential medical supplies immediately needed after a shark attack. Widespread use of rescue helicopters and construction of state-of-the-art trauma centers have also greatly helped to reduce [human] mortality.

Technology, too, has come into play. If a person were attacked along a beach stretch in Florida in 1948, access to the nearest payphone would be blocks, if not miles, away. Today, cell phones are ubiquitous and, within seconds of a confirmed attack, ambulances or helicopters are on the way.

Technology is also partly responsible for the increase in reported attacks. When you go to the ISAF Web site (www.flmnh.ufl.edu/fish/Sharks/ISAF), you find a link to an electronic Attack Questionnaire in four languages, which asks Web browsers every sort of information relating to a regional shark attack. The World Wide Web allows formerly remote areas of the globe to be directly linked to the files stored in Central Florida.

As a result of this interaction, attacks that occur in Bora Bora or off some isolated stretch of sand on the eastern seaboard of Brazil may no longer go unreported. Access to the Web means that anyone, anywhere in the world with a computer can relay his or her attack information to the Elasmobranch Society and, once it's both properly verified and merited, that information is eventually included into the ISAF's databank.

Another reason for the increasing attacks is the rapid rise in overall world population. This is especially true in Florida, where since 1950 the population has risen from less than three million to its current seventeen million. Add to that number the more than eighty million annual domestic and international tourists who visit Florida, and there can be little doubt as to why shark attacks in the Sunshine State are on the increase.

The only reason attacks haven't risen even higher in the past few decades is probably due to the decimation of the world's shark population. At present, there may be less than ten thousand great white sharks left in the entire world and, despite the fatalities brought about by these fish in Australia and California, both regions have now placed the great white shark under complete protection. California was one of the first to do so when it passed Assembly Bill 522 in 1993.

Bill 522 was first brought to the California Legislature floor by scuba diver Assemblyman Dan Hauser in 1992, one year prior to its enactment. An unexpected endorsement of the great-white-shark bill came from a diver who had been brutally attacked by one. Eric Larson was mauled by a shark on July 1, 1991, off the California coast. The shark clamped down around Larson's left leg while he surfed. Larson pounded on the shark's head, only to have it release the leg and grab his arm.

Larson eventually freed himself and survived. It took over four hundred stitches to sew up his numerous wounds. There were many others who supported the bill including the Pacific Coast Federation of Fishermen's Associations; surfing, diving, and kayaking organizations; and a great many marine scientists, including Peter Klimley, author of *The Secret Life of Sharks*. As a newspaper writer for the *San Diego Union Tribune* put it, "Suppose you're a four-thousand-pound ocean predator with a mouthful of dagger-like teeth and a nasty habit of occasionally snacking on humans. Where do you look for friends? Where else but California, amigo?"

On October 11, 1993, Governor Pete Wilson signed the bill, thereby affording the great white shark full protection under the laws of California. California also leads the nation in complete protection of the puma. South Africa began protecting sharks in 1991 and Australia, except for a few isolated areas, has also recently signed shark protection into law.

When I attended the Peter Benchley lecture in 2005, sponsored by the Conservancy of Southwest Florida and held in Fort Myers, Florida, the author of *Jaws* concluded his presentation with a brief film shot in South Africa involving great white sharks, which are common off the eastern coast near Durban. I had been studying great whites for months prior to attending Benchley's lecture, so I had the usual preconceived notions about these ancient and deadly predators.

What I saw on that evening was astonishing. Because of increasing interest in seeing wild sharks, several tour operators out of Durban have switched from whale-watching to shark-watching. To attract the sharks to the stern of their boat for viewing by customers, the captains used large-cut tuna, hunks of beef, and other baits.

A few years back, one of the mates decided to pet one of the regular fifteen-foot great white sharks during one of their shark-feeding watching tours. As it turned out, the great white apparently enjoyed being petted and came back repeatedly for further stroking and caressing.

This eventually evolved to some of the strangest known behavior between a human being and an apex predator. Under no circumstances should anyone attempt this with any other wild shark, as the results can be disastrous. The film's climax was when that charter boat took along both Peter Benchley and Rodney Fox, who had survived a vicious great-white-shark attack in Australia in December 1963.

Fox's attack had occurred during a spear-fishing competition and left him with over four hundred stitches in his left side. The wounds were so grave that, had he not been wearing a wet suit, his entire stomach would have been torn open. A neoprene wet suit kept him intact just long enough to reach Adelaide and the operating table on which he spent the following four hours being sewn back together.

Over the years, Rodney Fox had not only "forgiven" the shark, he had also become a strong proponent of shark conservation. In that film, Fox and Benchley were taken out to pet a four-thousand-pound great white...and pet it on the nose, just above its razor-sharp, pearly-white, spring-loaded teeth, which could potentially open and close at a 1/400th of a second....

Like a swimming two-ton puppy, the Herculean great white shark would come to the boat's stern, stick its head three feet out of the water, and wait for anyone to reach over and rub the white underside of its snout. After convincing Fox that the shark wouldn't bite him, the mate, Benchley, and the camera crew watched in awe as Fox reached over and petted the distant cousin of the creature that had nearly taken his life over thirty years before.

The shark loved it. After thirty seconds of being rubbed on the snout, it fell backward into the water as though in some kind of sensory-induced trance. Remember that the underside of a shark's snout is filled with the ampullae of Lorenzini amongst a host of other exotic olfactory and sensory organs. Remember, too, that a shark bite takes 1/400th of a second. With one swish of its eight-foot tail fin (caudal fin), a shark that size would have been quite capable of launching itself completely out of the water and Rodney Fox wouldn't even know what had happened, had the shark decided to bite his arm off.

While watching the film, I couldn't help but remember that approximately ninety-six percent of all shark attacks on people have supposedly been cases of mistaken identity. Sharks bite first and then realize they've made a mistake. It is a known fact that only four percent of all attacks result in someone's actually being consumed. If we could clearly identify ourselves as humans and not supposed seals, great whites would have no interest in us as food; they would find us quite an endearing and friendly intra-species.

The movie went on to show that particular shark, along with several other great whites, coming back repeatedly for several more snout rubs and then vanishing into the depths of the Indian Ocean. I still cannot make sense of this unbelievable behavior and neither can the marine biologists with whom I've discussed this extraordinary behavior.

Were a human to ever try petting a wild puma or a grizzly bear, he or she would certainly die from trying it. Approaching a crocodile or an alligator in such fashion would, likewise, end very badly. Come to think of it, be they lions, snakes, or a host of other man-killers, there is nothing in the natural world—except killer whales and dolphins—that we can touch, let alone pet, and yet avoid being seriously, if not fatally, injured.

After years of patient observation, several researchers have gained limited access to a number of predators, but not before they, too, had modified their own human behavior. People like Farley Mowat and his wolves, Diane Fosse and her mountain gorillas, and Jane Goodall and her chimpanzees come to mind. On the other hand, more than a few wildlife researchers such as Timothy Treadwell and his girlfriend, Amie Huguenard, have been killed and devoured by their object of study. On October 8, 2003, Treadwell and Huguenard were killed and devoured by a grizzly bear which they had been attempting to study in coastal Alaska. By and large, the introduction of a stranger into wild settings is not tolerated by the animals involved, which makes the petting of a great white shark by Rodney Fox even more astonishing.

As a sideline, let me point out that it is a misnomer to call orcas killer whales. Killer whales are the only animal in the sea capable of killing a fully grown great white shark and have been observed doing so on several occasions. They have never been known to kill humans and there has never been a single confirmed death in the wild from an encounter with a so-called "killer" whale.

Ironically, however, the ocean's most dreaded shark is the multi-ton great white, which, it turns out, loves to be petted under its nose, just like a dog. That film made me realize how little *Homo sapiens* truly understand the natural world's apex predators.

104

He Always Loved the Sea

The sea has a way of turning tragedy into mystery. The death of William Covert is a case in point. Whether young Covert drowned first and was then scavenged by a shark or was attacked by a marauding bull shark and died fighting for his life will never be known. Because no one witnessed the incident and Covert's body was never found, one will never know for certain the sequence of events that led to his disappearance.

At the time of the incident, Covert had been in the Florida Keys for a little less than a month collecting tropical-fish specimens. The collected exotic fish were helping to pay for his post-graduate schooling. Covert was a 1993 graduate of Michigan State University in Lansing. He had graduated with a double major in marine biology and zoology. Covert was an experienced diver but, like all college students, was always pinching pennies to get by. His diving equipment was minimal at best. Some would say that, as much as anything, it was probably what killed him.

Covert and four other divers had headed out to dive and gather tropical fish along the edge of Florida's largest coral reef, roughly three miles off Indian Key and four miles southwest of Alligator Reef Light. Underwater visibility was thirty feet on that Wednesday. Given the respectable, though not ideal, water clarity, Covert's specimen-collecting was going well. Although there were three other divers in the water, only Covert had scuba gear. The other three were breathing by using regulators and hoses attached to an air supply pumped down from the surface. The last time anyone saw Covert alive, he was working along the outer edge of the reef, thirty feet from one of the other divers.

Unlike the other three, who were tethered to their air supply via hoses, Covert's scuba gear allowed him to venture much farther from Captain Tom Scaturro's dive boat. It was later estimated that Covert was at least two hundred feet away from the vessel when the attack occurred. With only thirty-foot underwater visibility at the time, no one witnessed what happened.

Forty-five minutes into the dive, Captain Scaturro checked Covert's downtime against his remaining air time and became concerned. Tom Scaturro put on his gear and went in the water to search for the overdue Covert. A few minutes later, Scaturro discovered Covert's dive tank and fish-collecting nets on the bottom but no Covert. Scaturro speculated that Covert had run out of air and probably returned to the boat. When Scaturro returned to his vessel, there was no sign on board of the missing diver.

The concerned captain called up the other three divers and began a thorough search of the immediate area hoping to find the missing Covert. What they found instead of the diver was very disconcerting. All that remained behind was a badly shredded T-shirt, a pair of torn BVD sweatpants pierced by thumb-sized holes, a mask, a torn dive belt, eleven pounds of dive weights, a regulator, and a dive tank with one hundred pounds of air remaining. Covert himself had vanished.

For the next five days, the search for William Covert continued. The U.S. Coast Guard, Florida Marine Patrol, Monroe County Sheriff's Department, Key Largo Volunteer Fire Department, and even some of Covert's friends from Michigan—who had flown down after hearing of his disappearance—conducted a massive search. After five days, the search was called off. No trace of Covert's body had been found.

From the outset, the debate about how Covert had died stirred controversy throughout the professional and scientific communities. Shark attacks on scuba divers are rare. The last authenticated fatal shark attack on a diver had occurred on June 24, 1961, to William Dandridge in Biscayne Bay, thirty-four years before.

The evidence left behind by Covert was inconclusive. George Burgess, Ph.D., director of the International Shark Attack File (ISAF), after reviewing the file, elected to not rule Covert's untimely death the result of a shark attack. Ten days after the event, Burgess said to the *Orlando Sun-Sentinel*, "This is a case of a botched dive, if I've ever seen one. If this is where we stand, I'm not going to call it a shark attack. The circumstantial evidence points too heavily the other way."

In his role as director of the ISAF, it is oftentimes left to Burgess to have the final say as to whether or not to include a fish bite or other mysterious diver's fatality as a shark attack. Barracuda have been known to attack and bite swimmers and divers, as have several other species of large predatory fish such as goliath grouper and moray eel. In the case of the vanished William Covert, Burgess decided it pointed to an accidental drowning first and the scavenging of Covert's body by sharks afterward.

As the authorities followed up with their investigation into Covert's death, they discovered he was diving without two key pieces of safety equipment: an air-pressure gauge and a buoyancy compensator. Pat Koch, owner of the Rainbow Reef Dive Center in Islamorada, knew Covert personally and had tried to sell him a pressure gauge only a week before his final dive. "He wouldn't spend the money," Koch told investigators. "He didn't come up when it was hard to breathe. He came up when he was out of air."

In the end, Pat Koch sided with Burgess. Covert drowned first and was then eaten by sharks. He added, "Unfortunately, Bill died because he broke every safety standard that we divers must follow. Sharks do what sharks do: scavenge and clean up the remains."

106

When the police finally checked Covert's tank, it still had one hundred pounds of air pressure remaining. A full steel tank of the style Covert was diving with contains 2,250 pounds of air at the start of every dive. With only one hundred pounds remaining, every breath Covert took at that point was like one's sucking through a long, skinny straw. Realizing he was out of air, some speculated that Covert dropped his tank on the ocean floor in an attempt to reach the surface thirty-five feet above.

If Covert failed to exhale properly during his ascent, he may have accidentally caused himself an air embolism. Surfacing from such a depth without exhaling causes the lungs to expand, forcing air bubbles into the bloodstream. These expanded air bubbles can then block blood from reaching the brain, possibly causing a diver to lose consciousness, or in a worst case scenario, result in death. The buoyancy compensator, an inflatable vest similar to a miniature life jacket, would have helped in Covert's ascent as well as in assisting him to maintain neutral buoyancy while swimming underwater.

Joel Dovenbarger, director of Medical Services for Divers Alert Network—a nonprofit agency that provides both medical and safety information to divers worldwide—said the following about Covert's dive, "Divers forget that the final destination of the dive is to get back on the boat." Speaking about Covert's lack of a pressure gauge, Dovenbarger added, "On a stupidity meter, it ranks pretty high."

While Burgess, Dovenbarger, and Koch felt that Covert had drowned before being eaten by a shark, there was plenty of evidence pointing the other way: that Covert had been attacked first and then died from trauma and massive blood loss soon thereafter.

"We're very confident this was a shark attack," stated Monroe County Sheriff's Detective Thomas Kiffney.

Covert's shredded T-shirt and torn dive belt were examined by Jose Castro, a shark expert with the Southeastern Fisheries Science Center in Miami, after they had been retrieved from the ocean's floor. After the examination, Castro, along with several other experts, reconstructed a far different series of events than that of an accidental drowning victim. According to their theory, the five-foot, five-inch, 170-pound Covert probably saw the shark minutes before the initial attack took place. He then shed his near-empty tank in an effort to swim back to the boat before the aggressive bull shark came in for him.

The shredded T-shirt indicates he probably lost his right arm first, while attempting to fend off the shark's first strike and then lost his second arm moments later. The tear across his dive belt would imply that the shark

107

then took a large bite out of his abdomen. With both arms amputated and bleeding uncontrollably, Covert would be completely unable to defend himself from additional attacks. Death would have taken less than five minutes.

Depending on the speed of the current that day, and whether or not Covert was diving down-current from the other divers, all traces of blood as well as his body could have been swept away long before Captain Tom Scaturro or any of the other three divers would have been able to spot anything.

Another consideration taken into account by Detective Kiffney and those in his camp was, Covert was an experienced diver and thus used to working at the relatively shallow depth of thirty-five feet. Given these two factors, it's highly unlikely that he would have been so foolish as to hold his breath and risk an embolism on his short ascent. Moreover, he still had one or two hard-pulling breaths remaining in his tank when he abandoned it, another discrepancy in the drowning theory.

The shredded T-shirt and additional evidence all pointed to a large bull shark being the most likely predator. Bull sharks are common in the Keys, as they are throughout Florida. A large Florida bull shark can approach four hundred pounds. Bull sharks are known to feed on humans throughout the world, from Lake Nicaragua in Central America to the Zambezi River in Africa. They are aggressive and more than capable of killing, then consuming, a full-grown adult. Once bitten and mortally wounded, it's possible that other, smaller sharks were involved in scavenging Covert's body.

There were even a handful of people who felt the entire incident might have been some kind of hoax. They went so far as postulate that Covert was still alive and the entire accident had somehow been staged. The Monroe County Sheriff's Department paid no attention to any of those claims. For them, the evidence pointing to a fatal shark attack was too indicting. This had been no carefully orchestrated hoax.

Lacking a body, Maryann Fiodelis, Covert's mother, had to petition the court for her son's death certificate. Speaking to the *Ocala Star-Banner*, Fiodelis said, "My son loved the sea." Covert had often told his mother, "There's nothing better than being out there. It's so beautiful to see the fish that you wanted and then to catch it."

Fiodelis thus concluded her interview: "He went doing what he wanted. That's the only thing that helps a little."

William Covert, a young diver and dedicated marine biologist, loved the sea. On September 22, 1995, he disappeared into his beloved ocean for all eternity.

Not Since 1913

It came as a shock to everyone involved when the shark-bitten body of Mike Harold Karras Jr. was discovered near Mickler's Landing, Florida, approximately five miles south of Ponte Vedra in St. Johns County, three days after the boy had disappeared in the surf. The last shark attack anyone could recall in St. Johns County had occurred fifteen years earlier, in 1961. That attack hadn't been fatal. After researching the county's records, Dr. Perry Gilbert from the Mote Marine Laboratory, noted that the last attack off any Jacksonville beach before the 1961 incident had happened forty-two years prior, in 1913. The 1913 victim survived to tell about it.

Like so many shark attacks, everyone initially felt the incident had been a probable drowning. Karras Jr. and his brother Ricky had elected to go swimming on a stormy day in an area prone to turnouts. Turnouts are a local term for what most people today refer to as rip tides. Rip tides occur along certain beaches and form a narrow but powerful undertow, which are difficult, if not impossible, to spot during rough-surf periods.

In 1994, while our family was on a trip to the Big Island of Hawaii, our older son, Logan, accidentally got caught in a rip tide along the island's south shore at what is considered one of the only green-sand beaches in the world. Logan was playing in the surf, which was impressive that day, when his younger brother, Blake, ran up to my wife and me and hollered, "Logan's drowning!"

We looked over in horror as our boy, only six at the time, was struggling to get back to shore while fighting against a small but powerful undertow located near the far edge of the beach. He was less than fifty yards away. Luckily, I was able to run down and reach him before he was washed out to sea. Although Logan had already swallowed some salt water and was frightened and exhausted, he recovered quickly. It was our first, and hopefully last, experience with turnouts.

In 1961, the two young Karras boys were last seen heading toward the pounding surf on a Sunday afternoon in the Boardwalk area of Jacksonville Beach. This stretch of beach is well-respected by the locals for its strong turnouts. The boys were from Tennessee and, in all likelihood, completely unaware of the dangers these strong rip tides can present.

No one saw them vanish into the sea, so the details of how it happened are lost. After searching for the children for several hours later in the day, Mr. and Mrs. Mike Karras notified the Jacksonville Police Department of their sons' disappearance. Upon investigating the weather conditions that day and the presence of several turnouts, the police assumed both boys had gotten caught up in a turnout and had drowned.

Three days later, the remains of Mike Karras Jr. washed ashore several miles south of Ponte Vedra. The body had two large shark bites to it. At first, the authorities felt that the boy had probably been bitten after drowning, but an autopsy conducted later in the week proved otherwise. Karras Jr. had died from exsanguination, or blood loss, and not by drowning. It was concluded that the teenage boy had died from the wounds inflicted upon him by a large shark of unknown species.

Upon further review, it was speculated that Karras Jr. may have been in the process of drowning when the shark hit him. Oftentimes, the wild thrashing and erratic behavior of a drowning victim will help provoke a nearby shark into attacking. A young boy frantically flailing his arms or kicking his legs would certainly create the vibrations a shark's delicate sensors are on the lookout for.

Like many shark attacks, the offending shark probably swam up to the struggling boy, circled him several times surveying the situation, and then elected to bite him. The shark bit him twice, once on his right leg and a second time on his left shoulder. Once it decided that that animal didn't taste like a fish or anything it had ever tasted before, the shark turned around and swam off. With two large bites to his body measuring ten-by-eight inches, the boy had only minutes to live before bleeding to death in the briny Atlantic water.

Scientists who examined the wounds estimated the size of the shark to be ten feet or longer, effectively ruling out the bull shark as the likely predator. In Florida, bull sharks seldom reach this length. A more likely candidate would either be a hammerhead, a great white, or a tiger shark. A great white was spotted off Jacksonville in March 2004. The fish was well offshore, but estimated by the anglers who happened upon it to be twelve-feet long and to weigh in excess of one thousand pounds. In the end, we will never know what kind of shark killed young Mike Karras on that Sunday.

His younger brother, Ricky, was never found. There is a possibility that the attacking shark must have turned to Ricky after biting his brother. Once again, lacking a survivor to tell the story of that day's events, we can only surmise what happened.

The beaches off Jacksonville are safe. The chances of any swimmer's actually getting bitten by a shark off any Florida beach are astronomically low. Even as recently as 1976, the chances of one dying from wounds received from a shark attack were as high as fifty percent. Today, thanks to quicker response, better medical help, and cell-phone technology—all of which help one to contact emergency personnel much sooner—that percentage has dropped to an all-time low of less than nine percent.

Turnouts along a beach are far more deadly than the sharks lurking near its far end. Many more people drown in the ocean than die at the hands of predatory sharks. In fact, statistically speaking, the two Karras boys were at their greatest risk during their drive down to Jacksonville from their home in Tennessee.

Losing both of their boys in one day was certainly devastating for the family. Since the accident occurred after Labor Day, there were no lifeguards on duty. As troublesome as this shark attack was, the contributing factor was the rip tide. Had both boys not been washed out into deeper water, the attack probably would never have taken place. It's really not sharks one must be concerned about when one enters the ocean…but the ocean itself.

At Rivergate Park

E leven-year-old Robert Crespo loved to fish. Throughout the summer of 1984, he and his best friend, Chuck Long, would come down to the newly opened Rivergate Park in Port St. Lucie, Florida, to fish. If the fish weren't biting, they would enjoy a summer swim. Some mornings, as early as 7 A.M., Crespo's neighbor, Delores Yurka, would see the two boys heading down to the north fork of the St. Lucie River with their fishing rods and bait buckets in hand.

Over the long, hot summer, the opening of Rivergate Park, located just across the street from where Crespo and his family lived, must have appeared a godsend to a young boy who loved the water. To this day, the brackish waters of the St. Lucie River teem with redfish, sea trout, ladyfish, and mullet. The park's boat ramp and docks also provided ample space for a couple of enthusiastic kids with fishing rods until their classes started up again in the fall.

On August 6, 1984, Robbie Crespo and Chuck Long once again headed down to Rivergate Park around 9 A.M. They had planned to take an early-morning swim and keep an eye on the anglers who were fishing off the dock near the boat ramp. On that particular morning, they had left their poles behind, but if the fishing looked good, the boys always had the option of heading across the street to Crespo's garage to pick up their tackle and join in the bite.

Around noon, Crespo and Long went back to Crespo's house for a leisurely lunch break. The only decision to be made after lunch was whether the two should continue swimming when they returned to Rivergate or switch over to fishing. Since it was still hot, the two boys donned their swimming trunks and left their fishing rods tucked away in the corner of the garage. Swimming got the nod.

Robbie Crespo and his family had relocated to Port St. Lucie three years before, after years living on Key West. As good as the fishing was in the St. Lucie River, the fishing Crespo remembered from the Keys was much better.

Around 2 P.M., both boys strolled back to their new, favorite park. They joined other local kids and spent the next few hours running jumps off the boat ramp's end and enjoying the water. Time passed without notice and in the next few hours nothing out of the ordinary happened. The fishing slowed down to a typical midday slump while a handful of kids swam, jumped, splashed, and wore away the hours in an unending chorus of shouts, taunts, and laughter.

But everything changed in minutes. At 4:32 P.M., Carol Fraser, fishing in a nearby boat with her husband Albert, noticed that a large alligator was swimming directly toward the two boys, who were still splashing about in the water a few yards off the boat ramp's end. The Frasers yelled to Crespo and Long to get out of the water, but only Long took notice.

Moving quickly to the safety of the dock, Long was already out of the water when he hollered back to Crespo something about a gator coming up behind him. Crespo, mistakenly, thought his best friend was kidding him and didn't heed the warning.

A moment later, Robbie Crespo turned around and saw the alligator steaming toward him, now less than ten feet away. Crespo made a valiant effort to swim to the dock, where Long was holding out a long fishing rod for him to hang on to, but he never made it close enough to grab hold of the rod. In the instant it took to make a huge swirl with its massive tail and without a single word spoken or shouted by the victim, the alligator grabbed Crespo by the leg and immediately dragged him under. Crespo, four-feet, four-inches tall and weighing a mere eighty pounds, became an easy target for an aged and hungry twelve-foot, five-inch alligator. The predator and his prey disappeared beneath the discolored waters of the St. Lucie River. The unimaginable had happened.

Everyone who witnessed the attack—the kids, the anglers on the dock, and the fishermen in nearby boats—were in shock. It had happened so fast.... Albert and Carol Fraser disembarked and ran to a nearby pay phone to dial 911. The police mistakenly thought Al Fraser had said they were at Lyngate Park, not the newly opened Rivergate. After first going to the wrong park, the police still managed to arrive at the scene only a few minutes later. The alligator and the boy were nowhere to be found. Everyone suspected that, by this time, the boy had drowned.

At 4:45 P.M., after more than five minutes under water, the alligator resurfaced some twenty-five feet from the end of the boat ramp. One of the officers fired his handgun at the animal as it swam toward the western shore. Charles Heppeard, Robbie Crespo's stepfather, who had been notified by Chuck Long, arrived on the scene and was stunned by the sound of gunfire and the police aiming at the animal.

"What the hell are you shooting at? My boy is still in his mouth," screamed Heppeard.

The officers, realizing that Crespo was, in all likelihood, already deceased, fired one more handgun round and one shotgun blast at the alligator, but both narrowly missed it. After the volley of gunshots, the alligator re-submerged and continued swimming away beneath the surface, the limp body of Crespo still firmly locked in its jaws.

At 5 P.M., Fish and Wildlife Commission's (FWC) Officer Stoney Lee arrived. Assisted by two police officers, Lee commandeered a boat from a local angler and went out in search of the alligator. A passing boater notified them he thought he had seen a large alligator with something in its mouth on the other side of the river, some quarter mile upstream from the park along the far western bank. The three men proceeded toward that general area in search of the gator and its prey.

They soon found the alligator in the area described, lying in four feet of water under some overhanging brush. Using a high-powered rifle, Officer Lee took aim and shot the alligator in the side of the head, whereupon the beast immediately let its prey go. The alligator was injured but not killed by the blast and once again slipped away beneath the muddy waters. Robbie Crespo's body, pale and lifeless, slowly sank below the surface.

Risking their lives, Officer Lee and a fellow FWC officer, Dale Knapp, jumped into the river in an attempt to recover the body. For fifteen excruciating minutes, they waded in chest-deep water hoping to find Crespo, but to no avail. A few minutes later, a second boat approached and the officers recognized the man driving it as Mike Rafferty, the Alligator Control Agent for Martin County, who had come to help.

The two officers told Rafferty they suspected the body had drifted out into deeper water. Rafferty produced a small grappling hook and started dragging the water just beyond the drop-off, not far from the western shore. On his second drag, he grappled the lifeless body of young Crespo and hauled it to the surface. They easily lifted the small body into Rafferty's boat, covered it in a blanket, and radioed the Port St. Lucie Police and EMS crew back at the boat ramp that the body had been recovered and the boy was deceased. Rafferty, then, transferred Crespo's body unto a police boat and returned to the scene to hunt for the alligator responsible for the attack, hoping to find and destroy the animal before nightfall.

At the boat ramp, Ramona Heppeard, Crespo's mother, was overcome with disbelief and grief. Hearing the news of her boy's death was expectedly devastating to the young, loving mother. Robbie Crespo was survived by two younger sisters, Becky and Mandy, then aged eight and three, respectively. Now it had been left to the two girls to comfort their mourning mother and father in the weeks and years to follow.

After Crespo's body had been removed from the accident scene, all that was left was for the wildlife officers to find, shoot, and kill the attacking gator. The hunt for the animal picked up where the alligator had last submerged, just after it got shot and finally let go of Crespo's body.

Just before 6 P.M., almost an hour since the last sighting, Officer Dale Knapp spotted what looked like an alligator's head surface one hundred yards south of them down the river. Knapp lay down in a prone position on the boat, took careful aim with a .270 rifle, and fired a second shot at the alligator. From that distance, it was impossible to tell if the salvo had hit or missed. In either event, the alligator submerged once again and the search continued.

At 6:30 P.M., with several boats and officers searching the vicinity, the alligator surfaced for the last time. Captain Ries, another FWC officer, took aim with the same .270 rifle and shot the offending gator point blank in the head. The animal died within minutes. They hauled the reptile up into one of the larger boats and brought it back to the boat ramp for further examination.

Both the physical exam at the scene and the necropsy that followed confirmed that this had been an old, infirm, and starving alligator. A healthy, twelve-foot, four-inch bull gator normally should weigh close to five hundred pounds. This particular reptile weighed only three hundred pounds. It was discovered that the other two rifle shots had hit it in the head but, because of its thick skull, neither bullet had penetrated the brain except for the very last round. There was no indication whether the hand- or the shotgun rounds fired earlier had hit the animal.

The alligator's stomach contained assorted material such as fishing line, sinkers, fishing floats, marbles, mammal hair, an old turtle carapace, crab shells, and a considerable amount of vegetation. A third of the gator's teeth were missing and the remaining ones were severely worn. Its age was estimated between fifty to seventy-five years, based on its poor health and well-worn teeth. By that time in August, most alligators are well on their way to putting on all the additional fat they need to endure the dormant winter months. That animal had no body fat at all.

The wildlife officers concluded the alligator's poor health and desperate hunger had contributed to its turning to humans for food. Like an aging tiger or a lion in failing health, older wild animals will sometimes turn to human prey because they lack the ability to catch and kill the creatures that make up their diet's mainstay. Although there were—and still are—hundreds of wild alligators throughout the north fork of the St. Lucie River, there had never been an attack on record. For years before this incident, an even larger thirteen-foot, nine-inch alligator had hung out not far from a rope swing located farther down the river near Prima Vista Boulevard. The local kids used the swing with hardly a thought to the resident goliath. In turn, the massive gator never threatened or even approached the children, though this scenario presented an obvious recipe for disaster.

The death of young Robbie Crespo in the jaws of a hungry alligator sent shudders down the spine of anxious parents and wildlife officials alike.

Tragedy has a way of bringing out the best and the worst in us; this became no exception. Crespo's stepfather, Charles Heppeard, told the following to newspaper reporters two days after the incident: "You bet I think someone is to blame. I think whoever is at fault is whoever's idea it was to make a park down there. There's no [warning] signs and people water-ski down there. But the people who put the park in never did any wildlife studies to see if alligators would be a danger."

An attorney from Gainesville, James Jamieson, soon jumped into the fray. In an interview with the *Miami Herald* shortly after the attack, he stated: "It just incenses the hell out of me!"

Jamieson was of course referring to the fact that the boy had been killed by an alligator in an unmarked public area. As it turned out, Jamieson had been in the process of filing suit against the state for an alligator-mauling incident that had happened to Christopher Palumbo in a lake on the campus of University of Florida, Gainesville. The lawsuit was for $2 million and Jamieson had good cause to voice his opinions on the matter.

The story of Robert Crespo's attack was picked up by dozens of newspapers across the state and eventually made it to the national television news. Rivergate Park was closed on the following day for posting. By the following Wednesday, signs were located throughout the park, which read: BEWARE OF ALLIGATORS—NO SWIMMING OR DIVING! The signs are still posted and swimmers no longer jump off the end of the boat ramp at Rivergate Park.

In defense of their decision not to post the park in the first place, wildlife officials argued that alligators are ubiquitous throughout the state. One officer said it best when he told a reporter, "We would literally, in this case, have to post every puddle and every ditch in the state of Florida."

A local trapper, Tommy Gore, confirmed that there are hundreds of alligators in the upper St. Lucie River and nobody can assure the townspeople that another attack will not occur in Rivergate Park. With more than one million alligators living throughout the state and their ability to move considerable distances both on land and through connecting freshwater systems of rivers, swamps, lakes, and man-made canals, encounters between alligators and people occur daily. Most times, however, alligators, even the larger ones, shy away from people. But once in a while the encounter goes wrong, and on August 6, 1984, Robbie Crespo became the fourth official alligator-attack fatality in the peninsula known as *La Florida*.

Many regional newspapers, including the *Orlando Sentinel*, later ran editorials about alligator awareness and education. People like Crespo and his family, who move up from an area that doesn't harbor any alligators— in their case, Key West—are often unaware of the potential danger. Swimming in any freshwater bed, or even brackish water—fresh and salt water mixed—presents a greater risk for the swimmer. Feeding an alligator increases the risk of attack tenfold, although there was no indication that the alligator that killed Crespo had ever been fed.

The uproar regarding the incident and the surrounding publicity created a groundswell of nuisance-alligator reports in the following months. Most reports were proven unfounded and the state's wildlife officers refused to remove most of the large reported alligators just because they existed. Over time, all legitimate alligator complaints were duly assessed and no human has been killed in the St. Lucie River since eleven-year-old Robbie Crespo died more than twenty years ago.

Alligators—even old, starving ones—are part of Florida's natural ecosystem. It's extremely difficult for one predator to be tolerant of another, especially those that prey on their own kind. But when Crespo and his friends jumped off that dock that afternoon, posted or not they had entered the natural realm of the American alligator. By doing so, the boys were at risk, even if a smaller risk than their getting hit by lightning or by a car while crossing the street toward the park. But said risk was nevertheless there and, as long as the boys continued to swim in a freshwater system known to harbor alligators, an incident of the sort could happen.

One of my main reasons for writing this book is to educate the greater public about the inherent dangers of alligators. A few years ago my son, Blake, who was fourteen at the time, and his friend David Roberts, got stranded on an island in one of Sanibel's many wildlife areas, the Sanibel Gardens Preserve. Both, knowing the dangers of hidden alligators, refused to swim across a thirty-foot canal. They were aware they would inadvertently create noise and splashing that might result in an alligator attack. Blake and David yelled for help for fifteen minutes and, after a passerby perceived their plight, they were then rescued by the Sanibel Police Department.

When you finish reading this book, please don't bury it in your bookshelf. Pass it along to a friend or relative. Donate your copy to the local library and tell everyone you know about these tragic stories. Educate your children, grandchildren, friends, and family about Florida's alligators and their rare but sometimes deadly behavior. In a way, the outrage produced by the fatal attack on an eleven-year-old boy in the St. Lucie River has never ended. Let Robbie Crespo's story and all others in this book act as a sign posted in every lake, swamp, river, canal, and stream across the entire Florida Peninsula, wherein it peremptorily reads: BEWARE OF ALLIGATORS EVERYWHERE! NO SWIMMING!

BLACK TIP SHARK

The blacktip shark is common throughout Florida's coastal waters.

Florida Sharks

Of the four hundred species of sharks in the world, approximately seventy-two are found in the U.S. Atlantic, the Gulf of Mexico, and the waters around Puerto Rico and the U.S. Virgin Islands. Of these seventy-two species, only twenty-five are known to frequent the coastal waters in depths of less than sixty feet. This is the water depth most commonly used by recreational Floridians. As a result, unless you are stranded offshore, the vast majority of Florida sharks are effectively harmless to man.

These inoffensive, deep-water species include the enormous but non-aggressive whale shark; the thresher; the Cuban ribbontail; the oddly shaped angel; the spiny dogfish; the bramble; the Florida smoothhound; the rare, deep-water sixgill; and the Atlantic sharpnose shark, amongst scores of others. These sharks are seldom, if ever, involved in unprovoked attacks, but each can inflict serious injuries if care is not taken when handling or encountering them in the wild.

Florida plays host to several of the world's most deadly sharks; these select few are responsible for most fatal attacks in the state. By far, the single most dangerous shark patrolling every foot of Florida's extensive coastline is the bull. Following closely behind the bull is the tiger shark.

Although responsible for the greatest number of overall attacks, the smaller Florida sharks—the blacktip; the spinner; the lemon; the Atlantic sharpnose; and the slow but powerful nurse—often bite but seldom, if ever, kill their victims. Although less common in the number of attacks, other dangerous Florida sharks include: the silky, short, and long-fin mako; the sandbar; and the dusky.

The bull shark is to Florida what the great white is to California and Australia. The bull is not only the most dangerous shark in our waters; it's also widely believed to be responsible for nearly all fatal attacks occurring in the Sunshine State.

It is extremely difficult to verify the specific shark species involved in fatal attacks. Under certain circumstances, it is all but impossible. Unlike alligator attacks, wherein the offending alligator is almost always identified, killed, and destroyed, finding the shark responsible for an attack is quite a daunting task. Once the attack is over, the shark disappears into the vastness of the Gulf of Mexico or the Atlantic, oftentimes never to be seen again. The chances of hunting down or finding an offending shark are inconceivable, given the sheer magnitude of the ocean. Aside from eyewitness reports and forensic evidence—bite patterns, possibly including the shark's broken teeth, and the extremely rare occasion where the attacking shark is captured or killed—medical professionals and scientists involved are generally left to guessing at the culprit species.

Aside from hammerheads whose distinctively shaped heads make them easy to identify, all other Florida sharks are easily mistaken and misidentified even by experts, given the speed and confusion of any attack. Anyone who has fished and caught a variety of sharks knows this. A blacktip looks much like a spinner shark; a large lemon thrashing about looks not so unlike a dusky or a silky shark.

In rare but extreme cases, there are only the victim's torn pieces of clothing or tattered swim fins left, which makes a positive identification of the guilty species completely impossible. In most cases, Florida's scientists point toward the bull shark as the likely suspect.

Bull sharks are found in all of the world's temperate oceans and remarkably in quite a number of freshwater rivers and lakes. They are extremely aggressive animals and when they encounter anyone in the water, just like an escaped convict, they should always be considered armed and dangerous. Bull sharks, because of their unique ability to adapt to freshwater environments, tend to frequent estuaries, rivers, bays, and other locations favored by man. It can be unequivocally stated that bull sharks are estuary sharks.

The scientific name for the bull shark is *Carcharhinus leucas,* which in turn makes it a member of the family Carcharhinidae, or what is commonly referred to as requiem sharks. Throughout the world, bull sharks have a long list of regional names, as follows: the cub; the Ganges; the river; the requiem; the ground; the Zambezi; the Nicaragua; the shovelnose; the slipway grey; the square-nose; and the Van Rooyen's shark. In Australia, the bull shark is interchangeably called freshwater whaler, Swan River whaler, and river whaler.

The bull is a cold-blooded shark with a dark grey body, graduating in shades of grey to an off-white belly. It is not a large animal when compared with tigers or great whites. In Florida, the average size for a bull shark is between 150 250 pounds. The maximum known size of a North American bull shark is eleven feet, with the largest specimens weighing over five hundred pounds. The current IGFA all-tackle bull-shark world record was taken by Phillip Wilson in 1986 off Dauphin Island, Alabama. Wilson's shark weighed 490 pounds. The Florida State record for a bull shark was set in 1980 by Pete Peacock while fishing off Key West. That shark weighed in at 389 pounds.

Bull sharks are shaped similarly to great whites. Their head and body are very thick, quickly tapering down to a wide, powerful tail fin. In the wild, they are believed to live up to twenty-four years. Bulls are capable of producing offspring between the ages of six and fifteen. Females give birth in the early summer in shallow, brackish waters after a yearlong pregnancy and generally have between one and thirteen live young per pregnancy.

Bull sharks have an elaborate osmotic system, which allows them to physiologically acclimate to fresh water. Bull sharks adapt from salt to fresh water, as opposed to what the Indo-pacific and American crocodile are known to do—adapt from fresh- to saltwater environments. For the bull shark, this unique ability serves them well. Bull sharks have been found twenty-three hundred miles up the Amazon River, hundreds of miles up the Mississippi and its tributaries—as far as Cincinnati, Ohio—and are the only known shark to inhabit freshwater lakes.

In Central America, bull sharks are common in Lake Nicaragua. Originally thought to be landlocked, it is now known that bull sharks negotiate the rapids of the 130-mile San Juan River, which flows into the Caribbean along the eastern coast of Nicaragua. They have also been found in Lake Yzabal, Guatemala.

The bull sharks of Lake Nicaragua have been known to attack and kill native populations. In the spring of 1944, a single shark attacked three locals from the town of Granada in Nicaragua. Two died as a result of their injuries. Presumably, one person a year is killed by the freshwater bull sharks of Lake Nicaragua.

In Africa, bull sharks are known as Zambezi, or river sharks. This African species grows considerably larger than those in Florida. Some have been recorded as weighing over 650 pounds and growing over twelve feet in length. In 1970, a prawn fisherman in Mozambique had his arm torn off by a bull shark. The shark swam off and returned a few minutes later to tear the head off the same helpless victim.

Zambezi sharks have been known to attack and kill hippos, crocodiles, water buffalo, and in like manner countless native Africans who come down to the coastal rivers to wash clothes or gather water. One woman was fatally attacked by a Zambezi shark in ankle-deep fresh water. Ironically, the Zambezi River is also a haven for Nile crocodiles. On occasion, the Nile crocodile has been known to prey on the river sharks swimming in the Zambezi.

The same story holds true in India, where they are known as Ganges sharks. Near the mouth of the sacred Ganges River, literally thousands of bull sharks gather to feast on the numerous bodies cast into the river for burial in the sanctified waters. This ritual has inadvertently resulted in a shark population that now relies on scavenging human flesh as its major source of protein. In a single year, twenty pilgrims bathing in the Ganges were attacked by bull sharks; ten survived.

There are many marine biologists who believe the most dangerous and deadly shark in the world is not the infamous great white, but the less highly profiled bull shark, which is known to attack and eat almost anything, including hammerhead sharks, sting rays, and porpoises. In a Mote Marine Laboratory (Sarasota, Florida) experiment to teach porpoises to injure or kill sharks, the trained porpoises readily attacked lemon sharks, but the moment a bull shark was put into the pen, the porpoises stopped their attacks and wanted no part of continuing with the experiment.

As an experienced Florida fisherman, I have had a number of personal encounters with bull sharks, all of which attested to this shark's fearsome reputation. On two separate occasions, while fishing inshore near the tidal creeks that empty out of Sanibel Island's "Ding" Darling National Wildlife Refuge, I've seen bull sharks in action.

Once I watched a two-hundred-pound bull shark devour a two-foot ladyfish in a single gulp less than six feet from the edge of my jonboat. Some years earlier, I wrestled a thirty-six-inch snook out of the mouth of an even larger bull shark swimming beside my starboard gunwale.

The most impressive sighting happened thirty-two miles offshore while fishing over an artificial reef west of Redfish Pass. Earlier in the day, we had lost a fifty-pound cobia while being gaffed, so I have little doubt that the cobia's blood trail helped to bring in this particular shark.

We were having an excellent day catching numerous snapper, grouper, and large amberjack, but we were surprised and startled by the arrival of the four-hundred-pound predator. I was finally getting a twenty-pound amberjack into the net when, from out of the depths, appeared a nine-foot bull shark. In the flash of an instant, the shark charged the exhausted amberjack and bit three-quarters of its body off. The attack took place less than five feet from the side of my catamaran and the water was crystal clear. The shark completely ignored the boat and quickly circled back to finish off "my catch."

The bite had been so clear-cut—slicing through the amberjack's half-inch-thick spine as though it weren't even there—that my fishing line didn't even break. Uncertain about what to do next, I reeled in the jack's head and remaining six-inch torso. The net was no longer needed: upon inspecting its remains, we were amazed at how clean the cut had been, as though a surgeon, not the teeth of a massive shark, had sliced through the fish.

Expectedly, the bull shark immediately returned and started looking for the rest of its prey. I'll always remember it looking up at me as I held that head in my hands. It likely considered jumping into our boat to get the rest of its feast. Having no use for what little of this large jack had been left, I unhooked its head from the jig, waited for the shark to make another looping circle, and tossed the remnants back in.

The shark got so close to my starboard gunwale's edge, I could have reached down and touched it as it swallowed the rest of the fish in a single bite. I then surmised, given its size, that bull shark would have equally swallowed one of my legs up past the knee without any difficulty. Mercifully, the shark made one last pass and vanished forever into the pale blue waters of the gulf.

Another deadly shark common to Florida's waters is the tiger shark. In Hawaii's coastal waters, tiger sharks are responsible for virtually every fatal attack. Tigers grow to be much larger than bull sharks and are called the garbage cans of the sea.

Tiger sharks are voracious eaters: they bite and oftentimes swallow almost everything that crosses their path. The list of stomach contents of captured tiger sharks borders on the absurd—copper wire, nuts, bolts, lumps of coal, boat cushions, clothing, tom-toms, unopened cans of salmon, driftwood, the head of a crocodile, a horse head, beer bottles, a husky dog in a sled-dog harness, wooden shoes, crayfish, crabs, leather coats, pigs, hyenas, monkeys, plastic bags, scuba tanks, and not surprisingly, human remains.

Among the man-killing species, tiger sharks are second only to great white sharks in size. There are several species of sharks that grow larger, e.g., the whale and the basking sharks, but these are filter feeders and pose no threat to man. The tiger shark is a prolific species of predatory shark; it gives birth to between forty and eighty live pups every few years, after a gestation period of between fourteen to sixteen months.

Their size is impressive. Two twenty-one-foot sharks have been captured in shark nets: one in New South Wales, Australia, in 1964, and a second off Mackay, in Queensland, Australia, in 1980. In 1922, a twenty-foot-plus tiger was taken in the Gulf of Panama, along Central America's Pacific Coast. These sharks weighed over six thousand pounds each. At that size, they would be capable of swallowing an adult human being whole.

The IGFA all-tackle tiger-shark record was a mere thirteen-foot, nine-inches long, but that fish weighed in at 1,780 pounds. It was caught in the Atlantic on June 14, 1964, by Walter Maxwell, while he fished with a 130-pound test line out of Cherry Grove, South Carolina. The Florida all-tackle state record for a tiger shark stands at 1,065 pounds. It was caught by Richard Baggs on June 20, 1981, off Pensacola. Baggs's tiger shark stands as Florida State's single largest fish ever caught by rod and reel, topping a record great-white catch of 686 pounds and finishing just ahead of a 1,046-pound blue-marlin catch caught off Panama City in 2001.

Given their inclination to inhale just about anything floating in the ocean and their enormous size, tiger sharks are considered extremely dangerous. Unlike most sharks, which have few distinctive markings, tiger sharks are aptly named because of the tigerlike colorations along their bodies. These striped markings fade as the animal matures. Several Florida fatalities among divers or swimmers have been attributed to tiger sharks.

A third large, menacing Florida shark is the great hammerhead. Although these immense fish have seldom been identified in Florida attacks, worldwide hammerheads are consistently ranked in the top-ten most dangerous sharks. Their distinctive heads make them the easiest shark to identify, although they can still be confused with either the scalloped hammerhead (up to four hundred pounds) or the much smaller bonnethead (up to thirty pounds).

The Florida State record for hammerhead sharks also stands as the all-tackle world record. It was taken in May 1982 by Allen Ogle off Sarasota, Florida. The fish weighed

Although this monster was caught in the South Pacific, tiger sharks this large have been found in Florida as well.

in at 991 pounds, although larger hammerheads up to twenty feet in length have been observed swimming in the open ocean. (Author's note: As this book was heading to press, a potential new world record hammerhead shark was

Florida harbors the largest hammerheads in the world.

caught five miles west of Boca Grande Pass. The fish took five hours to land after being hooked on 130-pound test line by Bucky Dennis of Port Charlotte. The hammerhead was fourteen feet, five inches in length and weighed 1,262 pounds. Even though the great hammerhead was once regarded by the U.S. Navy as the third most deadly shark in the ocean, research has shown that hammerheads are involved in only five percent of shark attacks worldwide. Very few hammerhead attacks have been fatal.

A. Peter Klimley, the world-renowned shark expert and author of *The Secret Life of Sharks*, believes most hammerhead attacks are defensive in nature. In 1931, a Florida woman was severely injured by a hammerhead off Palm Beach, but she survived the encounter.

Perhaps the best known Florida location for seeing hammerhead sharks in action is Boca Grande Pass, located in Lee County, on the state's southwestern corner. The pass is famous for its tarpon fishing and the sightings of "Old Hitler," a seventeen-foot great hammerhead also responsible for countless attacks on hooked tarpon.

Some years ago, I was boating in that pass and personally witnessed a great hammerhead attack a hooked tarpon. The entire incident took less than two minutes and was astonishing to observe. It was late May and both me and my brother-in-law's family had taken a boat ride from Sanibel to see if we could spot some of the tarpon schools that typically come into Boca Grande Pass during their annual spring migration. It was late afternoon when we arrived and, as we had anticipated, the schools of hundred-pound tarpon were there in droves, rolling, eating, and splashing in the falling tide.

As we watched them, we noticed that a young lady in a nearby flats boat had hooked into a good-sized tarpon. We decided to shadow her from a safe distance and observe the ensuing fight. As is typical of these majestic fish, the lady's silver king exploded out of the water repeatedly and gave us fifteen minutes of great entertainment. Just as she reached the final stages of the fight— the hooked tarpon was less than thirty feet behind the low-riding flats boat— Blake and Luke, the two boys up in my tuna tower, yelled, "Shark!" Within seconds, all of us spotted the two-and-a-half-foot-high dorsal fin raking through the water a few yards behind the hooked tarpon.

By this time, we were within fifty feet of the starboard side of the flats boat; it was easy to see that the shark was two and a half times as long as the tarpon it was about to strike. My guesstimate put the shark at fifteen feet plus, by far the largest fish I had ever seen.

The hammerhead swam right up to the exhausted tarpon and swallowed half of its six-foot body in the first bite. The fishing line instantly broke due to the tremendous torque of the shark's attack on the tarpon. The young woman in the stern of the flats boat was visibly dumbstruck and went pale as a ghost as she realized what had just happened.

With the upper half of the tarpon staining the surrounding waters black with blood, the hammerhead quickly turned around, circled back, and with a swooping second bite, it finished its dinner. The hundred-pound fish had been eaten in two bites. Given that hammerhead's size and the fact that the petrified fisherwoman had been sitting a mere six inches above the water line, it crossed our minds, and undoubtedly her own, that she could have equally been another two-bite victim.

Sharks, especially large hammerheads, frequent the pass throughout the tarpon season. In the summer of 2005, an Austrian tourist was bitten by a shark while swimming in Boca Grande. He was lucky to have gotten out of the pass alive.

The last major Florida shark worth mentioning is the mako. Although makos are regarded as deadly sharks worldwide, Florida has not experienced as many attacks from makos as other coastal locations. In Australia, for example, mako sharks are known as blue pointers and considered extremely dangerous.

The name mako comes from New Zealand's Maoris, who named it *mako-mako*, which translates as man-eater. Considered the finest game of all sharks, the mako is fast, jumps furiously when hooked, and reaches lengths of thirteen feet. The all-tackle world record stands at 1,115 pounds; the Florida record stands at 911 pounds for a mako taken off Palm Beach in 1962 by Audry Cohen.

By and large, the mako is a pelagic, offshore species. As a result, it is seldom implicated in Florida's predominately near-shore attacks.

*****

Florida State leads the world in shark attacks. This is not the kind of information a tourist is likely to find in a local Chamber of Commerce brochure, but the truth is, more shark attacks occur in Florida than anywhere else in the world.

Between 1670 and 2001, Florida recorded 474 unprovoked attacks, with California reporting 111 and Hawaii, 100. The combined total for all other coastal states, whether on U.S.'s western, gulf, or eastern seaboard, was 165. The Australian total was 323 and Africa's, 293. Attacks in other countries—all Pacific Islands, Asia, and South America combined—add up to only 369.

Most shark attacks are not fatal. As stated earlier, fatal shark attacks have fallen to an all-time low of an 8.9 overall percentage. Shark attacks have occurred in almost every coastal county in Florida, as follows: Bay, Brevard, Broward, Collier, Dade, Duval, Escambia, Flagler, Franklin, Indian River, Lee, Manatee, Martin, Monroe, Nassau, Okaloosa, Palm Beach, Pinellas, Santa Rosa, Sarasota, St. Johns, St. Lucie, and Volusia. Fatal attacks are far less common and have occurred in only eleven counties: Bay, Brevard, Broward, Dade, Duval, Indian River, Monroe, Pinellas, Santa Rosa, and Volusia.

In all of Florida—in fact, on the whole of Planet Earth—Volusia County stands as the most likely place for one to get bitten by a shark. Although it leads the world in attacks, only one person has ever been killed by a shark attack in Volusia County's offshore waters. Such a high-incidence rate can be

Territory	Total Attacks	Fatal Attacks	Last Fatality
Volusia	180	0	
Brevard	86	1	1934
Palm Beach	55	0	
Martin	25	0	
St. Lucie	22	0	
St. Johns	22	0	
Duval	19	2	1976
Florida Keys	17	1	1952
Indian River	15	1	1998
Broward	10	1	2001
Dade	10	1	1961
Pinellas	9	2	2000
Bay	7	1	1988
Collier	5	0	
Escambia	5	0	
Flagler	5	0	
Sarasota	5	0	
Lee	5	0	
Santa Rosa	2	1	1911
Franklin	2	0	
Manatee	2	0	
Nassau	2	0	
Okaloosa	1	0	
Gulf	1	0	
Walton	1	1	2005
General	7	1	1896
FLORIDA	**520**	**13**	**2005**

Chart #4: Florida Shark Attack History
Courtesy the International Shark Attack File.

attributed to one factor: surfing in and around Ponce Inlet during the summer months. Locally, it's common knowledge that, during the summer months, the waters surrounding this inlet swarm with small, hungry sharks.

Since most of these sharks are too small to inflict mortal wounds on anyone, surfers tend to ignore the risk, whereupon they get bitten regularly by small, inshore sharks such as blacktips, spinners, and Atlantic sharpnoses. The sharks average less than one hundred pounds and, although their bites usually require dozens, if not hundreds of stitches, they are almost never fatal. If one ever feels compelled to get bitten by a shark and live to tell about it, Volusia County, Florida, should be one's vacation spot. Since 1882, Volusia has recorded 180 unprovoked shark attacks, twice as many as its nearest rival, Brevard, which recorded eighty-six attacks in that same period.

*****

So, how is one prevented from getting attacked by a shark while living or vacationing in Florida?

• DON'T GO SWIMMING, DIVING, SNORKELING, OR WADING IN THE OCEAN:

It is that simple. Aside from an old *Saturday Night Live* skit involving John Belushi dressed as a "Land Shark," there has never been an unprovoked land attack by a shark. But before you make a lifetime commitment to chlorinated pools or safely posted freshwater lakes, ponds, and streams (remember, we also have alligators in Florida!), let us take a realistic appraisal of your chances of actually getting bitten by a shark while swimming along the Florida's shoreline.

According to compiled data by the International Shark Attack File, you are at far greater risk of being killed on a Florida golf course than while swimming. Within forty-four years, between 1959 and 2003, there have been 425 lightning-striking fatalities in Florida as opposed to eight fatal shark attacks. In other words, you are fifty-plus times more likely to be killed by lightning in Florida than be fatally bitten by a shark.

Since 1985, tornadoes in Florida have killed sixty-nine people; sharks have killed two people. Between 1990 and 2001, 1,401 Floridians lost their lives on bicycles. During that same time frame, three people were killed by sharks. Automobile accidents annually take almost three thousand lives in Florida; in the past sixty years, less than .02 people a year have died from shark attacks. In 1997, there were 1,120 homicides in Florida; no one was killed by a shark that year.

The list is endless and the odds against being killed by a shark attack are staggering. You have a ten-time greater risk of dying from complications of cosmetic surgery than from shark attacks. Worldwide, fifteen people a year die from shark attacks while 150—ten times as many— die from falling coconuts.

Smoking cigarettes, house fires, melanoma, accidental firearm discharges, one's choking on food while eating dinner, cancer, heart disease—even something as unlikely as falling off a stepladder while changing a lightbulb—pose much higher risks than do being bitten and killed by a shark. Chances are, only a handful of people reading this book will have ever even seen a shark while swimming, let alone be bitten by one.

Nevertheless, there are certain precautions a person can take to further reduce the risk of a shark attack. For people venturing offshore on a power or sailboat, there are many shark deterrents on the market, from complete floating body enclosures to chemical and electrically charged shark repellants. Information on these various devices can easily be found on the World Wide Web. Since most people reading this will never engage in long-distance offshore boating, let us look at some preventative suggestions to beachgoers, recreational snorkelers, and scuba divers:

● NEVER FEED SHARKS!

It might seem crazy to most of us, but there has been an ever-growing tourist industry across the Caribbean involving the hand-feeding of sharks by divers and snorkelers. Wisely, Florida has made it illegal to feed sharks in its territorial waters. Sharks, just like alligators, cannot distinguish between the hand that feeds them and the hand itself. Equating humans with food will eventually result in a hungry shark's turning its attention from the piece of raw tuna being handed it by an outstretched arm to the arm itself. Whether from a boat or when diving or snorkeling, never hand-feed or entice sharks with food.

● TRY TO STAY CLOSE TO A GROUP OF PEOPLE WHILE SWIMMING!

Sharks are far more likely to attack isolated individuals than those in larger groups. Once by yourself, you present an easier target for a shark to focus on and poise itself for a possible attack.

● DO NOT WANDER TOO FAR OFFSHORE!

Time and again, the person who gets attacked, just as Charles Bruder did in 1916, has swum much farther offshore than everyone else along the beach. If you feel you need a longer swim, swim parallel to the shore rather than deeper offshore.

• AVOID BEING IN THE WATER DURING TIMES OF DARKNESS OR LOW LIGHT!

Sharks and alligators, like many predators, prefer to feed during sunrise and sunset. Low light or darkness aids predators in their ability to get closer to their prey without being noticed.

• DO NOT ENTER THE WATER IF YOU ARE BLEEDING FROM AN OPEN WOUND, HAVE ANY KIND OF INFECTION, OR ARE MENSTRUATING!

Sharks have an extremely acute sense of smell. Blood of any kind is a natural attraction to all shark species. This is especially true for women who are not using any kind of sanitary device, such as a tampon.

• NEVER URINATE OR DEFECATE WHILE SWIMMING IN THE OCEAN AND NEVER SWIM NEAR ANY SEWAGE OR EFFLUENT OUTFLOWS!

Sharks have a natural curiosity about any organic compounds they detect. Scientists still have no idea what specific olfactory clues help to draw in sharks, but some suspect that any bodily fluids or excrement in the water attracts a shark's interest. Of course, swimming near any known sewage outflows poses its own set of health concerns, which far outweigh the dangers imposed by a possible shark attack.

• WHILE SWIMMING, DO NOT WEAR SHINY JEWELRY SUCH AS RINGS, ANKLE BRACELETS, OR WATCHES!

The flash of an ankle bracelet, given many sharks' poor eyesight, can easily be mistaken for the flash of light reflected off a swimming fish's scale.

• AVOID MURKY, DISCOLORED WATERS!

In roiled, murky surf, a shark is far more likely to bite a person by mistake than in clear, settled water. From a shark's underwater perspective, a splashing foot in a churned-up sea resembles a small, injured fish at the surface. Since it bites in a 1/400th of a second, a shark's victim has no time to pull his or her arm or leg away. Remember also that, especially in murky waters, sharks, with their poor eyesight, rely more heavily on their lateral lines as motion detectors to find prey.

• NEVER SWIM WHERE THERE ARE LARGE SCHOOLS OF FISH!

Along Florida's East Coast, huge schools of mullet migrate during spring and fall runs. Sharks follow these schools and kick into feeding frenzies, given the right set of circumstances. If you are swimming near or, God forbid, in one of these schools when a shark decides to attack it, you may end up as prey, too.

● DO NOT SWIM WITH PETS!

Dogs, because of their erratic swimming and splashing, are especially prone to attracting the attention of nearby sharks.

● NEVER SWIM IN DEEP CHANNELS OR NEAR ABRUPT DROP-OFFS!

Sharks frequent channels in search of prey and lurk beneath drop-offs waiting for unsuspecting fish to swim out over them. River mouths, tidal creeks, and man-made canals pose increased risks of attack.

● AVOID BRIGHTLY COLORED CLOTHING!

Most life jackets, because they are easier to see from a passing Coast Guard helicopter, are either orange or yellow. Over the years, yellow life jackets have been given the name yum-yum yellow, since bright, starkly contrasting colors, and even uneven tan lines, are thought to attract the attention of sharks.

● DON'T SWIM NEAR PEOPLE WHO ARE FISHING OFF THE BEACH!

Their bait is there to purposely attract fish. Whether cut or live bait or Spanish sardines, all of these serve the purpose of drawing game fish toward the angler. Sharks smell these baits and are as likely to be enticed into the area as are any other fish. If anglers are actively catching fish from the beach, the erratic motion of their catch's struggle is guaranteed to garner the nearby sharks' attention.

● SIGHTING OF PORPOISES IN THE WATER DOES NOT INDICATE THAT THERE ARE NO SHARKS IN THE AREA!

While it is true that sharks and porpoises are natural enemies, they have learned to coexist and will often feed on the same prey. Seeing porpoises, just as seeing diving birds or schools of fish, should tell you to be more cautious; there is clearly feeding activity going on around you.

● NEVER FISH AND DIVE FROM THE SAME BOAT!

If you have divers beneath your boat, please refrain from fishing while they are in the water. A friend of mine relayed an incident during which he was diving and noticed a large bull shark behaving erratically in the last minutes of his dive. He and his fellow diving friends wisely returned to their boat only to find that the boat's captain had hooked a tuna while they were diving. The struggling tuna naturally had attracted the bull shark. In the excitement, the shark could well have turned its attention to the divers.

• IF YOU ARE SPEAR-FISHING, USE EXTRA CAUTION!

A wiggling, wounded fish is what sharks eat. Understand that you have invaded the shark's domain. With a stringer full of bleeding fish on your dive belt, you are extremely vulnerable. Use extra caution and return to your vessel often to unload and get rid of your catch.

• IF YOU SEE A SHARK NEAR YOU, DO NOT PANIC!

Sharks can sense fear. The exaggerated motions of a panicked swimmer could well trigger an immediate attack. Remain calm and slowly swim or wade back toward shore and the safety of the beach.

• NEVER DIVE OR BOAT ALONE!

In this statement, there are far greater risks than that of shark attacks, but our purpose is not to discuss them here. If you are on a dive and have encountered an aggressive shark, ascend back-to-back with your diving partner and try to keep an eye on the shark at all times. If the shark approaches, hit it on the nose with a stick or spear gun. Most sharks will break off an attack that poses more trouble than it's worth.

• IF A SHARK BITES YOU, GET OUT OF THE WATER!

Do it as quickly as possible. It is virtually impossible to stop any bleeding while you are still in the ocean. The bleeding, in turn, will naturally excite the shark and increase the chances for a second attack. Remember, shark bites are often painless. If you feel a shark bumping against you, you may have to check if you've been bitten before you realize you actually have. Swimmers have been known to have their lower leg bitten off without knowing it.

• IF A SHARK HAS A HOLD ON YOU, JUST AS WITH ALLIGATORS, FIGHT FOR YOUR LIFE!

Playing dead will only ensure your ending up dead. Like alligators, sharks are not bears. Many victims have survived by jamming their arms deep into the shark's mouth to stop it from biting other parts of their bodies. Gouge at the eyes, under the nose, and at the gills, as these three areas are most vulnerable. Aside from a bang stick or a spear gun, most other weapons, including knives, are difficult to use when fighting with a shark and generally offer little help in fending off an attack. Shark skin is difficult to penetrate but is most vulnerable along a shark's underside and belly.

• ONCE ONSHORE, STOP THE BLEEDING!

Sharks know what they're doing. Great white sharks oftentimes will take only one bite of an unsuspecting seal, then back away to let it bleed to death before consuming it. A severed femoral artery in your leg gives you less than two minutes to live; you have a few more minutes if it's your arm. Use anything available for a tourniquet—the rubber strap of your dive mask, a torn T-shirt, a belt, or the drawstring from your bathing suit—so as to stop the bleeding. One girl was saved because a friend had the courage and foresight to actually stick his finger into the pulsing artery. Use compresses if the wounds are less grave, keep applying pressure, and elevate the person's legs to keep them from going into shock. Seek immediate medical attention.

• REPORT ANY ATTACK TO THE INTERNATIONAL SHARK ATTACK FILE!

Information on any shark attack is important to prevent future attacks and to further understand the relationships between humans and sharks. Go to www.flmhn.ufl.edu/fish/Sharks and click on the link that has the reporting form;

Cartoon courtesy Dave & Lee Horton

Never swim or water-ski near anglers who might be fishing for sharks!

it's available in four languages. Submit the completed form and let the ISAF decide if it qualifies as an unprovoked or provoked attack. All information is confidential and available only for qualified scientific study. If you have any doubt as to the validity of an attack, e-mail or call to discuss the incident before you fill out the form. ISAF's Web address is www.flmhn.ufl.edu/fish/Sharks/ISAF, and the phone number is 352-392-1721.

The Trouble with Feeding Sharks

In October 1999, the Florida Fish and Wildlife Commission (FWC) held a public hearing on the pros and cons of wild-shark feeding in Florida waters while scuba diving, a highly publicized and hotly debated topic. The first public workshop was held before a sizable crowd equally divided between commercial shark-feeding interests, including dive-shop owners and dive-boat operators, and a grassroots coalition of environmentalists, local divers, and concerned citizens. A petition signed by nearly four thousand Florida residents was submitted to FWC supporting a complete ban on shark feeding in the state.

In September 2000, FWC voted down a shark-feeding ban. Persuaded by dive-industry attorneys and numerous dive experts, FWC decided not to ban marine-life feeding and deferred to the dive industry to establish safe feeding guidelines, with substantial input from anti-feeding environmentalists. Regina Franklin, Executive Director of DEMA—Diving Equipment & Marketing Association—along with John Stewart, president of Dive Marketing International, and Bob Harris, a PADI-DEMA attorney, celebrated the decision as the most important victory for the dive industry in fifteen years.

"The [dive] industry as a whole recognizes the significant value of interactive [animal feeding, touching, riding, and petting] marine experience," an elated Regina Franklin said.

The initial battle against the feeding of wild sharks was lost. After the FWC decision, an organization called the Marine Safety Group vowed to continue its fight against the concept and practice of hand-feeding, baiting, and artificially attracting sharks and other predators for commercial exploitation. Attorneys for PADI-DEMA and staunch supporters of shark feeding like Jean-Michel Cousteau, son of the legendary Jacques-Yves Cousteau, angrily warned the Marine Safety Group to "stay the hell out of [our] way."

In a letter to FWC dated November 2000, the city of Pompano Beach expressed its liability concerns over future injuries that might occur as a direct or indirect result of shark feeding. Pompano Beach's city officials were well aware of the popular shark-feeding site operated by Diving USA just a mile off Fisherman's Wharf Pier. One mile beyond the bull-shark feeding station laid the rusting ruins of the *Ronald B. Johnson*. The sunken shipwreck is a part of the Pompano Beach Artificial Reef Program. As time would tell, Pompano Beach officials were right to be concerned about shark-feeding liability.

In February 2001, amid growing concern for public safety with regard to artificially attracting and enticing sharks, the city of Deerfield Beach, acting unilaterally, voted to ban shark feeding in its offshore waters. PADI and DEMA were dismayed by Deerfield Beach's decision but optimistic that FWC would continue to allow commercial exploitation of sharks by dive-boat operators and other vested interests. While one side argued that feeding sharks makes them equate humans with a food source—the same argument made against individuals who feed alligators—the other side contended that there was absolutely no evidence supporting such a position.

Early in July 2001, a bull shark attacked an eight-year-old boy off a beach in Pensacola, Northwest Florida, ripping his arm off in the process. The boy survived the attack, but suffered irreversible brain damage as a result of the extensive blood loss from his injuries. The attack in Pensacola kicked off what would soon be labeled "The Summer of the Shark" by both the national and Florida media. That same year on August 4, while swimming near a shark-feeding station in the Bahamas, Krishna Thompson had his leg bitten off by a bull shark. Citing the fact that the operators of Hotel Our Lucaya had never informed him of the nearby shark-feeding station, Thompson hired the late and world-renowned attorney Johnnie Cochran and filed suit against the resort for $25 million.

By September 2001, with Florida still in the national spotlight after a series of shark attacks throughout the summer, FWC reversed its decision to allow shark feeding. On September 6, 2001, FWC elected to fully ban shark feeding in state waters effective January 1, 2002. The Marine Safety Group, a longtime supporter of the ban, issued the following statement to the press:

> It is only a small, profit-motivated group—presently profiting from commercial exploitation of Florida's marine wildlife—that will be the "losers" when shark feeding is banned. The beach-going public "wins" because they no longer will have to worry about "spillover" dangers from nearby shark-feeding operations. The sport-diving community "wins" by regaining the opportunity for all divers to safely observe and explore ocean wild places and wildlife. Most of all, the sharks "win" because they get to go back to just being sharks, instead of manipulated stunt performers.

The battle still wasn't over. In October 2001, just before the final vote on the complete shark-feeding ban in November, PADI issued a last-ditch call-to-arms urging all its members to fight the proposed ban. A coalition of groups, including PADI, DEMA, Project Aware, and Jean-Michel Cousteau argued that responsible shark-feeding encounters help divers and snorkelers become dedicated conservationists. FWC carefully weighed both sides of the argument and, on November 1, 2001, voted to ban the feeding of all marine wildlife in Florida's state waters. Florida became the first state in the U.S. to officially ban shark feeding or shark enticing (chumming, et cetera).

*****

On September 16, 2001, four months before the shark-feeding ban went into effect and against this backdrop of the shark-feeding controversy, Eric Reichardt and fellow diver Mike Pizzio entered the Atlantic Ocean at 1:20 P.M., two miles off Pompano Beach. Using highly technical scuba gear—re-breathers, OC bailouts, deco gases, sophisticated gauges, wet suits, and accompanying tech gear—the two divers descended 265 feet toward the wreck of the *Ronald B. Johnson*. Reichardt went down in search of a rare tropical fish he had spotted a week earlier on another dive to the same reef, while Pizzio planned to explore parts of the wreck's interior. Both men were highly trained professional divers.

Though the shark-feeding station that the city of Pompano Beach had been concerned about was situated less than a mile from the wreck of the *Johnson*, it was unlikely either diver gave this fact any consideration before they entered the water on that afternoon. When Pizzio reached the bottom, he looked back toward the surface to see Reichardt still descending thirty feet behind him. That was the last time anyone saw Eric Reichardt alive. On the bottom, the current was running at 1.5 knots and visibility was limited to forty-five feet or less. Pizzio proceeded to swim toward the stern of the wreck. Once he moved into the leeward side of the ship to tie in his ascent cord, Pizzio glanced behind him fully expecting to find Reichardt approaching. There was no sign of the second diver.

Knowing the dangers of diving to three hundred feet, Pizzio abandoned his plan to explore the wreck's interior and started searching at once for Reichardt. After sixteen minutes of searching the area, Pizzio decided to resurface, hoping that Eric had done the same and was safe back on the boat. After decompressing and making it back to the dive vessel, Pizzio was dismayed to find no trace of Reichardt on board. Pizzio called the Coast Guard to report an overdue diver and proceeded to hail other boats, whereupon all offered to help in the search. By nightfall, a full-scale search was underway for Reichardt.

Three days passed before any sign of Reichardt was sighted. Then, on September 19, an offshore charter fishing boat called *Offsides* discovered the grisly remains of Reichardt floating two miles from the Pompano fishing pier and not far from the wreck of the *Johnson*. Reichardt's right arm and right leg were missing and his wet suit was shredded. Despite the numerous injuries to the head, torso, left leg, and arm, the Broward County Medical Examiner recorded Reichardt's death as an accidental drowning.

The M.E. contended that the shark wounds and amputations had occurred postmortem. Working on a tip that the injuries had possibly been sustained prior to Reichardt's death, George Burgess, Director of the International Shark Attack File (ISAF), made a formal request that Reichardt's autopsy reports, along with all collateral information, be sent to him for review by personnel. The ISAF, then, began delving into the real cause of Reichardt's untimely death.

Later on, in March 2002, a snorkeler swimming less than two hundred meters from a former Florida dive site where local dive operators had still been illegally feeding wild sharks, was savagely attacked by a nurse shark. Mercifully, the snorkeler survived the attack. As a result, authorities cracked down on illegal feeding operations throughout the state.

On April 9, 2002, after careful scrutiny of Eric Reichardt's autopsy report, Burgess contended that, although Reichardt had in fact drowned, he had been attacked by a shark beforehand.

"This gentleman ran into a shark," Burgess told reporters from the *Orlando Sun-Sentinel*. "And he drowned. And after he was dead, other organisms, including sharks, went after his body."

Dr. Joshua Perper, the Broward County Medical Examiner in charge of the case, agreed with Burgess that Reichardt may well have been attacked by a shark first, whereby it caused the drowning, but declined to officially reclassify the case as a fatal shark attack. Burgess elected to unilaterally include it as the only official Florida fatality from a shark attack in the year 2001, the so-called "Year of the Shark."

The evidence Burgess relied on to establish his claim that Reichardt had been a shark-attack victim consisted of extensive hemorrhaging from his left thigh. "You don't get hemorrhage unless you're alive. That indicates the bite occurred while he was alive. That's a shark attack...unless he encountered some sort of injury-making machine in two hundred feet of water. That's deep for an outboard motor. Just from the description, there's ample evidence that this was a shark."

Although the Broward M.E. conceded that there was merit to Burgess's claim, the official cause of death today remains on record as an accidental drowning. Burgess speculated that the first bite, probably from a bull shark, had been to Reichardt's inner left thigh. At that point, Reichardt may have lost consciousness or had his diving equipment ripped away. Either would have resulted in drowning.

No one will ever know with any degree of certainty what happened that afternoon over two hundred feet beneath the surface. Dave Earp, a professional lobster diver who was on board the boat the day Reichardt disappeared, stated the attack might have been brought on in part by the practice of feeding sharks at the nearby feeding station.

"I don't want to say that the attack was a direct result of shark feeding, but it obviously increases the chances of an attack. I'm a professional diver. I dive every day and I've noticed the increased aggression of bull sharks in the area."

On April 10, 2002, a day after Burgess had publicly announced his hypothesis that Reichardt had died from a shark attack, shark-feeding proponent and enthusiast Erich Ritter went into severe shock after a bull shark he was feeding in the Bahamas bit off a large part of his left leg during the filming of a TV adventure show. Ritter blamed his attack on murky waters, stating the bull shark mistook his leg for a remora. On June 6, 2002, after its government heard both sides of the argument, Hawaii became the second state in the U.S. to legally ban all feeding of sharks in its territorial waters.

In April 2005, Dr. Burgess, in response to the continued pressure from PADI, DEMA, Project Aware, and a dwindling number of dive tourism companies still supporting the feeding of wild sharks, said, "When you feed a shark, you are provoking it, so most shark attacks are not actually attacks, just responses to the environment. Throwing fish and blood into the sea is altering the way that sharks behave. Shark tourism is not seeing sharks in their natural habitat—what tourists are watching is a circus."

In June 2005, a South African diver, Henri Murray, 22, was swallowed whole by a great white shark estimated to be over twenty feet in length while diving in a well-known shark-feeding area. In September 2005, a group of South African scientists, marine environmentalists, conservationists, and concerned citizens proposed a complete ban on shark feeding in South African waters. Commercial interests, PADI, DEMA, and shark-feeding tour operators vehemently opposed that ban as well.

If Eric Reichardt were still alive today, he, on the other hand, would vehemently tell you about the trouble with feeding sharks.

A Capsized Catamaran

It was on a Saturday, early August. Florida was midway through its endless summer. The cool, refreshing waters of the Atlantic coastline beckoned. The winds were steady but manageable as the four young adults launched the seventeen-foot catamaran from the Granada Boulevard boat ramp off Ormond Beach in Volusia County. They set sail just after noon.

After an hour of sailing, Daniel Perrin, the twenty-one-year-old captain and owner of the cat, noticed that one of the two hulls was leaking. A small crack had opened up in the four-year-old Hobie cat style boat and Perrin decided to head back to shore. Once the four of them beached the vessel, they dragged it up and Perrin surveyed the extent of the damage.

Perrin had some duct tape in his truck and, in a decision that would later prove fatal to Cindy Wapniarski, he decided to fix the leak using duct tape instead of changing plans and leaving the cracked catamaran onshore. After repairing the catamaran's leak using nothing but the tape, Daniel Perrin, Cindy Wapniarski, Tami Ennis, and Randall Cohen, pushed the cat back out to sea for the last time. There wasn't a single life preserver, flare or a marine radio on board.

For the next several hours, things went smoothly. The tape held and the four enjoyed a glorious afternoon in the clear, indigo waters of the Atlantic. Around 6:30 that night, after soaking up salt water for hours, the duct-tape patch failed. As is often the case in the marine environment, things rapidly went from bad to worse. They were miles from shore when the boat started seriously taking on water.

In an attempt to drain the water, Perrin decided to pull the pontoon's drain plug, hoping that, by doing so, the water inside the cracked hull would drain out. His plan didn't work. In fact, Perrin's actions worsened the situation and the salt water started pouring in from the crack and the open-drain plug. As the pontoon filled with water, the boat capsized and the four sailors were dumped into open water as a huge thunderstorm approached and darkness engulfed them.

Clinging to the foundered boat, the four young adults miraculously managed to stay with the vessel through the intense storm and the long night that followed. Even though one of the pontoons had filled with water, the second pontoon held, keeping the cat afloat and allowing them to survive until daybreak. Their low profile in the water, coupled with their lack of a marine radio or any kind of flare or electric beacon kept them from being spotted by a passing angler or commercial vessel. It was the most grueling night of their lives.

At daybreak, the four young adults decided to abandon ship and attempt to swim to shore. The raging storm and steady current had now carried them between six and nine miles off the coast. Just before leaving the relative safety of the foundered vessel, Cindy Wapniarski told the other three that she wasn't a very good swimmer. Wapniarski was a secretary and part-time student at Embry-Riddle Aeronautical University. She had moved to Ormond Beach from Chicago.

Wapniarski's boyfriend, Randall Cohen, comforted her by stating he would stay with her throughout the marathon swim, helping her as much as he could. Reassured by his promise, Wapniarski, Cohen, Perrin, and Ennis left the floating cat just after sunrise and started swimming toward the distant condos looming over Ormond Beach. In an interview with the *Daytona Beach News-Journal* after the incident, Cohen was quoted, "I tried to carry her (Wapniarski), but it was exhausting. I couldn't do it for more than five minutes at a time."

Less than halfway through their monumental swim, disaster struck. Tami Ennis turned to witness Wapniarski thrashing about and yelling something about a shark. After millions of years of evolution, sharks have honed their lateral lines—a kind of motion detector—to focus their attention on the least efficient swimmer in any group, the most vulnerable prey, be it a fish or a swimmer. Wapniarski, at that point exhausted and swimming erratically, would have presented the easiest target. The shark instinctively honed in on the weakest link, just as any predator would.

Tami Ennis recalled the attack in a statement given after the incident, "Christy had yelled something about a shark. I saw her being picked up and down and saw the water change color around her. She came up too high and too fast."

Cohen swam to Wapniarski's rescue, but the damage was too severe. The shark had vanished back into the depths of the sea after having torn out the inside of her right thigh, from her groin to her knee, and bitten off her left leg. Cohen later told the *News-Journal*, "I swam with her for about fifteen minutes, but kept going under."

Bleeding profusely, Cindy Wapniarski died from exsanguination, or excessive blood loss, within minutes of being bitten. Realizing it would be impossible to swim the rest of the way with the added burden of bringing in a dead body, the three of them said their farewells and left Wapniarski's body floating lifelessly in the Atlantic. It would be another eight hours before the survivors staggered onto the beach not far from where they had put out to sea thirty-one hours earlier.

For the following three days, the Coast Guard searched in vain for Wapniarski's body; no trace of her was ever found.

In August 1982, one year after the fatal attack, Wapniarski's parents filed a $10 million lawsuit against North American Racing Association, Inc., the catamaran's manufacturer. Eugene and Joanna Wapniarski claimed that the crack in the pontoon was a manufacturer's defect and this defect ultimately led to the death of their daughter.

In 1984, after a lengthy trial, the family was awarded $450,000 in damages. The majority of the award, $360,000 (sixty percent) was to come from the manufacturer, with the balance, some $90,000 (twenty percent), coming from the boat's captain, twenty-one-year-old Daniel Perrin. The court also found Wapniarski herself responsible for twenty percent of the damages.

The lawyers representing North American Racing Association, Inc., appealed to the 5th District Court of Appeals, stating that it was the boat owner's negligence—by not having life preservers on board and by electing to try to fix a crack with duct tape, instead of bringing the boat in for professional repairs—that lay at the heart of the tragedy.

One year later, in 1985, after hearing the appeal, the 5th Circuit Court of Appeals overturned the lower court's ruling. The defendants argued that, even though the seventeen-foot vessel wasn't required to have positive floatation devices, the catamaran was still found floating a day later when it was discovered by a helicopter searching for Wapniarski's body. Had she remained with the vessel awaiting her rescuers, the association contended, instead of attempting to swim six-plus miles to shore, she would probably have survived the ordeal. In the end, only the $90,000 judgment against Perrin held.

Annually, Volusia County records more shark attacks than any other county in Florida; it could be argued, more than anywhere else in the world. Most attacks are minor bites received by the many surfers along Ormond Beach, Daytona Beach, and New Smyrna Beach. Of the hundreds of shark attacks that have been recorded in Volusia County over the years, the death of Cindy Wapniarski is the only attack that ended in a fatality, a fatality that should have never happened.

He Was Just a Boy

"I reached for his fingers," Sonny Wilson told the *Orlando Sun-Sentinel* reporters. "I touched them. He was pulling me, too. I didn't realize it was a shark. I thought it was just a wave."

Seconds later, nine-year-old James Tallasmon disappeared beneath the surf, one hundred feet away from the safety of the shoreline of Vero Beach, Florida. Up until those fateful few minutes, it had been just another day at the beach for the three visitors from Gifford, Florida. Gifford is a citrus-growing region a few miles north of Vero Beach.

It happened on a Saturday afternoon, November 21, 1998, around 2 P.M. Tallasmon and his mother's boyfriend, Sonny Wilson, 31, had been happily playing in the waves approximately one hundred yards north of the life-guarded section of Jaycee Park. Tallasmon had brought a toy squirt gun, which he was using to squirt salt water at Wilson. Tallasmon was a good swimmer and both were playing in water that wasn't even over his head.

Without any warning, Tallasmon suddenly began flailing and struggling to remain afloat. Wilson was only yards from him when the shark hit. Wilson's first reaction was that Tallasmon had somehow been caught up in an inexplicable undertow. Wilson reached out for the boy, but his tenuous grip wasn't strong enough to keep the shark from pulling the struggling boy underwater.

"He was looking at me but not saying anything," Wilson told reporters the following Tuesday. "Maybe he was already in shock."

Curiously, young James Tallasmon never screamed or spoke a word in the few seconds he had before the shark pulled him under. The dreaded word "shark" was never uttered from Tallasmon's lips. Up until the body was found the following morning, most believed his disappearance had been the result of a drowning, not a shark attack.

Billy Heffelfinger, 30, was playing football on the beach with a half-dozen friends when he noticed the struggling boy just offshore. Bravely rushing into the surf to his rescue, Heffelfinger reached the scene mere seconds after Tallasmon disappeared.

"I didn't see any fin, any thrashing, any lifting of the person out of the water," Heffelfinger told reporters from the *Palm Beach Post*. "It was like the kid had vanished and a shark crossed my mind because I said, 'You know, as much fight as he was putting up, he's got to at least splash or show some bubbles or something.' It was like he fought his last battle."

Heffelfinger, along with his friends, dove repeatedly into the area where the boy had last been seen, but the water visibility was incredibly poor that day, a factor that might have contributed to the shark attack in the first place. Wilson, having just watched the boy vanish, stood in disbelief. Noticing

Wilson was going into shock, Heffelfinger escorted him back to the beach and out of harm's way. Heffelfinger was then joined by several more beachgoers and nearby lifeguards in a futile attempt to locate the missing boy.

Within fifteen minutes, the local authorities were on the scene and a full-scale search for James Tallasmon was underway. Given the poor water visibility, the search-and-rescue dive team was rendered nearly useless. The water was reportedly so murky, they were unable to read their air-pressure gauges once they submerged. The search was discontinued after dark.

At 5:45 A.M. the next day, the search for James Tallasmon resumed. At this point, although there was speculation that it had possibly been a shark attack, most authorities felt it had been a drowning. The previous Tuesday, although yellow and blue flags warning of strong currents, baitfish, jellyfish, and Portuguese men-of-war had been flying along Vero Beach, shark-warning flags in the water were absent. Aside from a thirteen-year-old boy being bitten in the same general area ten days before this incident, sharks had not been a common sighting.

A little less than two hours into the search on that Sunday, at 7:22 A.M. divers literally bumped into what remained of James Tallasmon. Upon examining Tallasmon's remains, the case for an accidental drowning was dismissed. What the divers discovered was clearly the work of a shark, and a large shark at that.

Both of Tallasmon's arms had been bitten off. An even more gruesome discovery was made: James Tallasmon had been decapitated. All that remained of the boy was his torso and legs. There wasn't any other plausible explanation for the nature and severity of the injuries sustained by the boy. The medical examiner stated unequivocally that James Tallasmon had died of a fatal shark attack.

George Burgess, director of the International Shark Attack File (ISAF), after reviewing all the evidence, concurred with the M.E.'s findings. After examining the bite patterns and taking the surf and water conditions into account, Burgess initially opined that the offending shark had been a lemon shark. Lemon sharks can grow to be twelve-feet long and have been known to follow the southern migration of baitfish, which was occurring along the beaches at the time of the attack. However, upon more careful examination of the autopsy report and bite patterns, Burgess revised his conclusion and stated that the fish in question had probably been a tiger shark. The ISAF now officially records the death of young James Tallasmon as a result of an encounter with Galeocerdo culver, or tiger shark.

Speculating on why such a rare incident took place, several scientists and local authorities blamed the murky-water conditions and the annual late-November migration of schools of baitfish and mullet heading south toward warmer water. The diminutive size of the boy, who weighed approximately seventy pounds, also came into play. It was theorized that the shark might have mistaken the boy's splashing arm as a baitfish in the discolored water and then, finding little resistance from the child, dragged him beneath the sea. Had the shark grabbed a full-grown adult, it might have abandoned the attack because an adult can put up a far fiercer struggle.

Most shark attacks occurring in Florida are bump-and-runs. Sharks off Volusia and Palm Beach Counties, the two counties with the highest numbers of recorded shark attacks, tend to bite their victim once, only to discover that it's not a fish they've bitten into but something else. After an exploratory bite, the vast majority of sharks swim off, leaving the victim injured but alive. Most of these bites require stitches, sometimes hundreds of them, while the more serious bites result in missing arms or legs. Only a tiny fraction of this kind of attack results in death.

The quote that Burgess gave to the *Palm Beach Post* following this tragedy bears repeating, for it should come to mind every time somebody finds him or herself wading out into the ocean from any stretch of sandy shoreline in Florida: "The key to the whole situation, one bathers tend to forget, is that when you enter the ocean, you're entering a wilderness."

The world's oceans are some of the last remaining wild places on earth. Aside from the dangers imposed by sharks, there are dozens of other deadly, if not lethal, animals swimming in them. The blue-ringed octopus, the Portuguese man-of-war, the barracuda, and scorpion fish are only a few of potentially lethal animals living in the sea. As a species, we may have greatly reduced or eliminated our chances of getting maimed or killed by wolves, bears, alligators, big cats, and other wild animals. Short of poisoning the world's oceans, mankind will never be able to completely tame seventy percent of the planet's surface.

In the end, the only sure way to never get bitten by a shark is to stay out of the water. Given the tens of millions of swimmers entering the water along Florida's thousands of miles of shoreline every year, and the statistical likelihood of their actually ever getting bitten by a shark, such a fear is irrational. One's chances of getting hit by lightning, an extremely rare event in itself, are fifteen times higher than one's being bitten by a shark. The odds against getting killed by a shark in Florida are so astronomically high, they are virtually incalculable.

These statistics offer little solace to the friends and family of young James Willie Tallasmon, when his life was inexplicably cut short at the hands of an ancient and hungry predator. Try as we might, none of us can make any sense of a tragedy of this nature. It was a horrific incident and nothing will ever bring the innocent boy back.

Lifeguards at nearby Jaycee Park didn't close the beach the day after James Tallasmon was killed. There were still no clear signs of any sharks in the near-shore waters. The following weekend, the beaches and the breaking surf were crowded with Floridians and tourists enjoying life— just as it should be.

A 1920s postcard of the king of beasts: *Panthera leo*

Lion, Philadelphia Zoo, Pa.

THE GREAT CATS

The relationship between *Homo sapiens* and the great cats is far more complex and interwoven than our relationship with either crocodilians or sharks. For the most part, the great cats and humankind have concurrently evolved as two competing predatory mammals—one a sophisticated and skillful four-legged carnivore; the other, an adaptable, tool-wielding, bi-pedal humanoid. For nearly two hundred thousand years, we oftentimes rivaled one another for prey and dominion across a vast array of landscapes and environments. In the end, *Homo sapiens* won, though our victory has been bittersweet. Our technology and overwhelming populations have brought most of the world's great cats to the brink of extinction. The Florida panther, now numbering under one hundred animals, is representative of the plight of the great cats around the world.

Almost every species of the great cats has at least one subspecies now either threatened or endangered, or already extinct. In the next hundred years, it is believed that half of the world's great cats will vanish, including the majestic tiger. Many of the biologists with whom I have spoken hold little hope for the Florida panther, but we will look at the plight of the panther in a subsequent chapter. In the panther's case, its dangerous encounter with Florida's top predator,

Homo sapiens, has more to do with habitat destruction than anything else, but the result has been the same.

Not including the eighty recognized breeds of domestic cats, there are thirty-six species of cats; depending on how you classify the diminutive Iriomote cat, some scientists say thirty-seven species. While in the process of writing this book, a new, previously unknown species of cat—or catlike creature—has been discovered in the tropical rain forests of Borneo. Temporarily named the fox-cat and represented, at present, only by two high-resolution photos, the small house-cat-sized carnivore may be more closely related to the civet or marten. A discovery of this nature is extremely rare in today's crowded world, but depending on the outcome, it may possibly increase the number of known cat species to thirty-eight.

Despite the different physical size of cats, ranging from massive Siberian tigers documented at 790 pounds down to the five-pound black-footed cat of South Africa and Namibia, most cats look similar to one another and behave remarkably alike. All but the lions, which form prides, are solitary, territorial animals that, for the most part, live and hunt alone in their given geographical ranges.

Of the thirty-six species of cats, only a handful is known to prey on *Homo sapiens*. That very short list includes the lion, tiger, leopard, jaguar, and puma. The latter is the name we will use when talking about the cougar, mountain lion, and panther in a generic sense. Several other cats are large and strong enough to prey on

Domestic cats have flourished under our protection. There are an estimated eighty million in the U.S. and over one billion worldwide.

people, but actual fatal attacks by any of these species have never been authenticated. This list includes the snow leopard, the cheetah, the Eurasian and North American lynx, the ocelot, and the bobcat. There may be historical incidents where one of these cats have been known to attack, perhaps even kill, a human being, but these events have been extremely isolated and should not be considered part of their normal behavior.

Most of the three-dozen species of cats are too small to contemplate tackling a mammal as large as a human being. Over half of the species are no larger than a common house cat and oftentimes live in remote reaches of the planet. These include the diminutive Kodkod, the Pallas', the sand, and the

Felidae

Felinae

Felis
- Wild Cat
  Felis silvestris
  - Domestic Cat
    Felis silvestris catus
- Sand Cat
  Felis margarita
- Jungle Cat
  Felis chaus
- Black-footed Cat
  Felis nigripes
- Chinese Desert Cat
  Felis bieti

Otocolobus
- Pallas Cat
  Otocolobus manul

Catopuma
- Asiatic Golden Cat
  Catopuma temminckii
- Bay Cat
  Catopuma badia

Profelis
- African Golden Cat
  Profelis aurata

Prionailurus
- Leopard Cat
  Prionailurus bengalensis
- Fishing Cat
  Prionailurus viverrinus
- Flat-headed Cat
  Prionailurus planiceps
- Rusty-spotted Cat
  Prionailurus rubiginosus

Caracal
- Caracal
  Caracal caracal

Lynx
- Eurasian Lynx
  Lynx lynx
- Spanish Lynx
  Lynx pardinus
- Canadian Lynx
  Lynx canadensis
- Bobcat
  Lynx rufus

Leptailurus
- Serval
  Leptailurus serval

Herpailurus
- Jaguarundi
  Herpailurus yaguarondi

Oncifelis
- Pampas Cat
  Oncifelis colocolo
- Geoffroy's Cat
  Oncifelis geoffroyi
- Kodkod
  Oncifelis guigna

Oreailurus
- Andean Cat
  Oreailurus jacobita

Leopardus
- Ocelot
  Leopardus pardalis
- Margay
  Leopardus wiedii
- Little Spotted Cat
  Leopardus tigrinus

Puma
- Puma
  Puma concolor

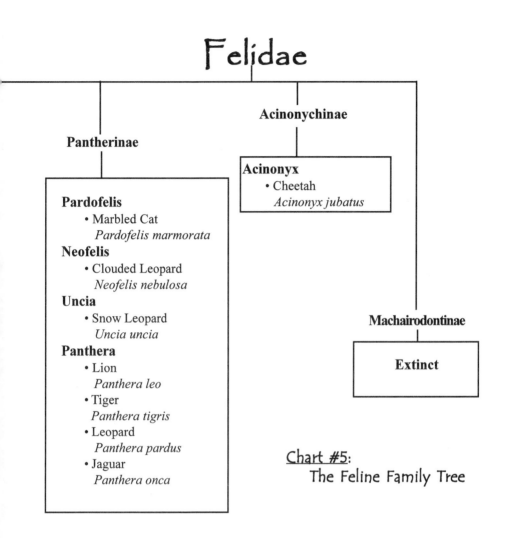

Felidae

Pantherinae

Pardofelis
- Marbled Cat
  Pardofelis marmorata

Neofelis
- Clouded Leopard
  Neofelis nebulosa

Uncia
- Snow Leopard
  Uncia uncia

Panthera
- Lion
  Panthera leo
- Tiger
  Panthera tigris
- Leopard
  Panthera pardus
- Jaguar
  Panthera onca

Acinonychinae

Acinonyx
- Cheetah
  Acinonyx jubatus

Machairodontinae

Extinct

Chart #5:
The Feline Family Tree

Chinese desert cat, to mention a few. For a complete list of the world's cats, please refer to Chart 5.

Of the five cats that place human beings on their menu, only three do so with regularity: lions, tigers, and leopards. The other two large cats, the jaguar and the puma, attack people so infrequently that, although individual attacks can be horrific, they are a statistical anomaly. Given the minuscule number of people who have actually been killed by a jaguar or a puma, calling either of them man-eaters is ludicrous.

Lions are a different story. Although there are scientists who contend that most man-eating lions are old or infirm, thereby incapable of capturing their normal prey, the majority now agree that this is a misconception. Lion populations are in trouble worldwide and it is easy to see why environmentally minded scientists would want to shy away from painting too grim a portrait of *Panthera leo*, the scientific name for the lion.

In my opinion, these scientists and biologists are sending the wrong message. Lions eat humans. Lions have always dined on us and, given the opportunity to do so, they always will. Lions readily eat baboons, chimpanzees, and monkeys. Why not humans? Take away man's guns, spears, and weaponry, place a solitary man on the Serengeti and he is an easy prey.

Humans can hardly outrun a lion, an animal that is capable of short sprints topping forty miles an hour (a gold-medal Olympic runner's top speed is twenty-five miles an hour), and I doubt any man in existence could outwrestle a five-hundred-pound cat armed with bone-crushing jaws, three-inch fangs, and razor-sharp claws. In hand-to-hand combat, my money is always going to be on the animal with the mane.

Just because lions kill us doesn't mean they are not worth saving. Many believe that it was our scavenging lion kills hundreds of thousands of years ago that allowed us to survive into the modern age. If nothing else, saving the lions should be our way of saying thanks. The role of lions in the ecosystems of Africa is essential to maintaining healthy, vital herds of ungulates such as zebras and wildebeest. They wean out the sick and infirm and keep the herd populations in check by taking the young and vulnerable, which in turn protect the grasses from overgrazing and subsequent erosion.

To understand how this system of major predator and prey works, just look at the erosion problems along the streams of Yellowstone National Park ever since we allowed the elk populations in the region to go unchecked. Field biologists soon realized that the eroding stream banks were hurting the native trout populations, and then pushed for the reintroduction of the wolf into the ecosystem. Wolves equal healthy trout streams, though at first glance such a statement seems absurd. Predators, especially top predators, have a vital niche in any given environmental system.

It is impossible to write about man-eating cats without first mentioning the two most infamous lions in the world, the Ghost and the Darkness. As of 1898, these two huge mane-less lions conducted a reign of terror for several years during the construction of the Uganda Railway in what is present-day Kenya.

They were immortalized in a journal-style book written by the man who eventually shot and killed them, Lieutenant Colonel J.H. Patterson, of the

British Army. His book, *The Man-Eaters of Tsavo*, was adapted to a feature film starring Val Kilmer and Michael Douglas called *The Ghost and the Darkness*. Both the book and the movie—despite the typical Hollywood liberties regarding the two lions' behavior—truthfully present the cunning and hunting skills of these two beasts.

Tsavo, both East and West Tsavo, is presently a national park in eastern Kenya. The name comes from a Masai word meaning "a place of slaughter." In the instance of the Ghost and the Darkness, a better description for the region could not be found. All told, it was estimated that these two lions were responsible for 135 railroad workers' deaths, plus those of an unknown number of natives from the surrounding villages.

Unlike the Serengeti pride lions, where the females do most of the killing, in the Tsavo region, the males do the majority of the hunting. The predominant prey in the Tsavo River basin is the enormous Cape buffalo, which can weigh up to eighteen hundred pounds. The Cape buffalo is a fearless adversary, quite capable of goring and stomping to death any lion brave enough to try taking one down. For a hunter, a wounded Cape buffalo is considered one of the most deadly big-game animals in the world.

Because of their choice of prey and the nuances of natural selection at work, the Tsavo males are much larger than grassland lions, often weighing in excess of five hundred pounds and standing over four-feet high at the shoulder. Because of their enormous strength and size, Tsavo lions have little difficulty lifting a 175-pound human body out of a tent, killing the luckless individual instantly, and running off into the surrounding bush to consume him or her. By December 1898, the Ghost and the Darkness had killed and eaten so many Indian coolies—the name Colonel Patterson used for the railroad workers brought over from India—that their killing spree shut down the construction of the Tsavo Bridge for a three-week period. The mighty British Empire was ground to a halt at the fangs of two man-eating lions.

The coolies thought they weren't lions at all, but angry spirits of departed native chiefs, who were determined not to have a railroad built through the Tsavo District. It took Colonel Patterson, using a .303 and a twelve-gauge shotgun, nine months to finally rid his project of the two menacing predators.

These two beasts were not old, infirm, or injured lions. Although one of them had had an old injury to one of its canines, it had long since been healed. The Ghost and the Darkness were two proficient killers in the prime of their lives, estimated to be between four and six years old, respectively. From its nose to the tip of its tail, the second man-eater killed by Patterson measured nine feet, six inches, and was capable of a vertical leap in excess of twelve feet.

In his book *Ghosts of Tsavo*, Philip Caputo makes a valid argument: not only are today's Tsavo lions also man-eaters, they actually teach their offspring how to hunt for humans. In recent years, their tactics have included ways to avoid being shot, as if they have learned that we carry weapons capable of killing from a great distance.

Caputo's book opens with a contemporary account of another man-eating lion that was terrorizing the Luangwa Valley in Zambia. The lion had killed dozens of local villagers when, in September, 1991, a big-game hunter by the name of Gilbert Hosek and two of his friends were reluctantly recruited into tracking and killing the Man-eater of Mfuwe, as the lion was known.

This lion, like most present-day man-eaters in Africa, would never return to the same village after making a killing raid into that village. Instead, it would consume its victim, then move ten, sometimes twenty miles away and attack a second village a night or two afterward. A fully grown male lion can consume between fifty and seventy-five pounds of meat in a single seating.

For lions, killing humans is done one of three ways. The first is a bite directly to the head, piercing the person's temples with its canines. This is perhaps the best method for the victim, as death is instantaneous. The second technique is to seize the victim by the neck, shaking him or her violently and instantly breaking his or her neck. Death occurs in minutes. The third is when the lion sinks its tusks directly into the victim's chest, tearing into his or her heart and lungs. This is the worst way of dying, as the victim may still be alive when the lion begins its meal.

Hopefully, the person is dead by the time the lion starts dining because the consuming portion of its victory is not pretty. Using its coarse-grained tongue, the lion first flays off the skin by repeated licking. The lion feasts on the blood, which comes rushing to the surface as the skin is methodically licked away.

The lion then bites into the stomach, disemboweling the person in the process. Removing vital organs and intestines, it generally eats the heart and liver first, as these two organs are rich in protein and other nutrients. It then turns its attention to the legs, eating the meaty thighs and buttocks first. It follows up with the shoulders and calves and, if still hungry, it will proceed to crack open some of the smaller bones for their marrow.

Lions bury the stomach and intestines. They never eat animal stomachs, though the reason for this is unclear. They seldom eat the head or genitalia, either. Lions leave the larger bones to the hyenas, which have much stronger jaws and can readily gain access to the rich marrow inside. The anxiously awaiting vultures and jackals finish off the scalp and whatever else is left behind. Within hours of the initial attack, virtually everything edible will be gone. Beetles and ants will scavenge any remaining coagulated blood or remnant morsels and here's the silver lining to this dark cloud: you won't have to worry about making your next car payment. Africa is so primal....

Less than five thousand years ago, many of our ancestors met just such a fate. At that time, lions were common throughout much of Europe, the Mideast, and North Africa. As civilization progressed, along with the technologies of copper, bronze, and iron, weapons were created not only to defend against these beasts, but ultimately also to exterminate them. Even in today's Africa, the hunting and killing of a lion by a Masai warrior is considered a great accomplishment.

But times have changed. Today, we consider any animal attack on a human being unprecedented and horrific. This is a symptom of cultural conditioning. A man-eating lion isn't horrific at all; it's just a big, hungry cat. In a lion's eyes, humans are just undersized, bi-pedal wildebeests. Any human characteristics we impute unto the lion's or any predator's behavior is strictly one-sided.

As a result of our so-called success over the past two centuries, lions are running out of places to thrive. In India, where up until two hundred years ago the Asiatic lion was common, there are only three hundred Asiatic lions remaining. There are 1.2 billion people in India—a number that increases by tens of thousands every year.

Do the math. There are four million Indians for every one Asiatic lion. The only remaining population of a species that once flourished from the Mideast to Nepal is confined to the 1,930-square-mile Gir Forest of northeastern India. By 1913, the Asian subspecies of lion had been reduced to twenty animals before it was rescued by Nawab of Junagadh, who took it upon himself to save this handful of the remaining king of beasts.

The only reason the Gir Forest wasn't destroyed in the first place was because, around 1900, it was infested with malarial mosquitoes and considered uninhabitable. Today the Gir Wildlife Sanctuary is just over eleven hundred square miles in size, and with malaria under control, the nearby natives resent the fact that they cannot have the pristine lion's land as well. It is doubtful, at this point, that the Asiatic lion will survive in the wild, as the pressure from the surrounding human population will someday overwhelm this speck of remaining habitat. In fact, desertification, a term that describes turning a forest into a desert by deforestation and soil erosion, takes a half-mile off the perimeter of the Gir Forest annually.

The Barbary lion, once common across much of North Africa, including the Atlas Mountains of Morocco, went extinct over a hundred years ago. The European lion, which was still present in Greece and other areas of the continent during the height of the Roman Empire, vanished sometime around the time of Christ. Both of these cats were used extensively in the infamous gladiator "games" held in the Roman Coliseum.

Without guarded sanctuaries dedicated to their survival, all of the big cats will ultimately vanish. There is no better example of this than the plight of the tiger.

Tigers, like lions, kill and eat people. The all-time record of human predation by lions occurred between 1932 and 1947 in Tanzania, where an estimated fifteen hundred people were killed and eaten by African lions. The record for tigers is far more impressive. Between 1920 and 1929, it is estimated

An old postcard depicting two Barbary lions—now extinct.

that tigers killed over seven thousand natives throughout greater India. Prior to WWII, it was not atypical for tigers to kill upward of fifteen hundred people a year in what was then an English colony. There is no International Cat Attack File or its equivalent maintained by anyone, so, like crocodilians, calculating human predation by cats is only a guesstimate. But if Siberia, China, Burma, Java, and the numerous other nations where man-eating tigers roamed in the 1930s had kept records, the number would probably exceed two thousand fatalities a year. Combined with the African lion and widespread leopard predation, the total human death count circa 1935 may have easily exceeded thirty-five hundred fatalities a year.

There was one infamous cat, the Champawat tigress of India, which was responsible for 436 deaths alone. As recently as 1915, a man-killing tiger was shot in Hong Kong after swimming to the island from nearby mainland. The last known Hong Kong tiger was hunted down and killed in 1942.

Tigers still take human lives in India, though with far less frequency than in years past. The chances today of a tiger killing anyone in Java are nil; the Javanese tiger is extinct, the last one vanishing sometime in the mid-1980s. The same holds true for the Caspian, the Bali, and in all likelihood, the Chinese tiger, which at last count had less than fifty remaining in the wild.

The only wild populations of tiger with sufficient numbers to take human prey are located in South-Central and Southeast Asia: India, Indochina, and Bangladesh. The largest single wild population of tigers in existence today lives in the Sundarbans Delta, formed by the confluence of the Ganges and Brahmaputra Rivers.

The Sundarbans, an Indian word meaning "beautiful forest," covers 3,860 square miles of low-lying islands and tidal mangrove forest. The region is rich in wildlife. The forest straddles both India (forty percent) and Bangladesh (sixty percent). It supports approximately five to six hundred of the world's largest cats and these tigers have historically always preyed on the local natives. In the decade between 1975 and 1985, 425 people were taken by man-eating tigers in the Indian portion of the forest, while 187 perished in the Bangladesh side. Only a small portion of the Sundarbans is preserved for these cats, and once the tiger population exceeds the forest's carrying capacity, roaming males looking for new territory outside that area are quickly exterminated. Their pelts, bones, teeth, and flesh find their way into an insidious wildlife black market.

It is now estimated that the total number of wild tigers in the world has fallen below five thousand. There are four reasons why their populations continue to decline. Unlike Africa—whose human population has been ravaged by HIV-AIDS, unending civil wars, and widespread starvation—Asia's human population has doubled since 1950, standing today at over three billion. With those numbers of people, there isn't room for a cat, which needs virgin forests and ample natural prey such as gaur (which can weigh over a ton), wild pigs, and the various Asiatic deer species to eat.

The second reason for the tiger's demise is, despite clear indications that the wild tiger may go completely extinct, sport hunting is still practiced in remote regions where tigers roam unprotected. For centuries, bagging a tiger was considered the pinnacle kill for any rifle-wielding big-game hunter. There are men and women out there who still consider it a sport. Around 1900, one Indian Maharajah was known to have said with regret, "My total bag of tigers is only 1,150!" I suppose we should have some kind of plaque ready for the person who shoots and kills the last living tiger, wherein it reads, "Congratulations, they're gone!"

A third reason for the tiger's steady decline lies in the two-by-four stud walls holding up your home. The world's demand for wood is insatiable. That beautiful teak furniture you recently purchased for your dining room was, in all probability, recently a forest of teak hardwood in Southeast Asia. Perhaps wild tigers left their scratches along its bark, marking their territories and sharpening their massive claws as recently as one year ago. Consumption of wood products worldwide—especially mahogany and teak—is inadvertently killing the few remaining world's wild tigers.

Perhaps the most pathetic reason for the demise of the tiger lies in traditional Chinese medicine. Ground-up tiger bone, tiger teeth, claws, even dried tiger eyes, all supposedly have medicinal properties that cure any variety of ailments—from impotency to arthritis. Of course, these potions can't cure idiocy, because scientific tests have repeatedly proven that these tiger-based medicines are useless. If you include the skins, which are still extremely valuable on the black market, a dead tiger could be worth tens of thousands of dollars to some Laotian farmer whose annual income might otherwise fall below $500 a year. Of course, he will shoot or trap a local tiger if given half a chance. From a population of approximately one hundred thousand animals in 1900, we are down to under five thousand.

The saddest news is, given the falling wild population and the limited genetic material remaining to keep the species from collapsing through inbreeding,

There are fewer than five thousand tigers remaining in the wild.

there is every indication that William Blake's "Tiger, tiger, burning bright," will be extinct within the next hundred years. This is unfathomable but true. The world's top predator, *Homo sapiens*, is in the process of completely wiping out the largest, most beautiful, and perhaps most exquisite predator in the world. Try to explain this to your children tonight.

The leopard is faring somewhat better, but its extinction meter is, likewise, running in the red zone. Leopard skin still is a valuable commodity. Its value increases steadily as the shortage of quality skins continues to drive prices up.

Of the three cats, leopards are much smaller than either lions or tigers. A large male leopard rarely reaches two hundred pounds. What they lack in weight, they compensate for by sheer cunning and unbelievable strength. John Taylor, a hunter in Africa for twenty-five years, once said, "If the leopard were as big as the lion, it would be ten times as dangerous."

Although far fewer leopards turn to man-eating than do lions and tigers, once they do, they take it to the limit. One of the most notorious leopards in history was the man-eater of Rudyaprayag, India. Between 1918 and 1927, this single cat terrorized a well-traveled route through the Garhwal Hills, which led to Hindu shrines high in the Himalayas. Over the nine years before it was killed, the Rudyaprayag leopard took 125 pilgrims. It survived countless efforts to be killed or trapped, but eventually a hunter by the name of Jim Corbett shot it.

Sixteen years earlier, Corbett had killed the leopard of Panar. Although far less famous, that Indian leopard had claimed the lives of four hundred victims. It is also interesting to note that leopards, like humans, are one of the few animals known to kill for sport. Pumas sometimes also share this dubious honor.

Like the proverbial fox in a hen house, leopards have been known to enter huts in India and Africa and kill everyone inside, consuming only the youngest and leaving the rest to rot. Their cunning and cruelty is well-documented and their strength phenomenal. Everyone is familiar with documentaries showing leopards dragging antelope weighing over two hundred pounds high up into nearby trees. They do this to keep the hyenas and lions from chasing them off their catch and stealing their dinner.

Leopards and pumas occupy the largest ranges of the world's great cats. Leopards can be found from Africa through parts of the Middle East, Asia, Siberia, and Sri Lanka, all the way into China, Malaysia, and Indochina. Not long ago, there were hundreds of thousands of leopards in the world, perhaps as many as a million. Today, leopards are on the endangered-species list.

During the 1960s, as many as sixty thousand pelts a year were harvested from wild-leopard populations. Within two decades, the leopard stocks in most of its ranges were reduced by ninety-five percent. They are now rare throughout their former range, although Africa still has sizable populations, estimated at around one hundred thousand animals. Leopards and their South American counterpart, the jaguars, have a recessive gene called melanism, which causes certain cats to appear almost pure black. These rare animals are what we have come to call black panthers. Hence, the term black panther can be applied to two distinct species.

The beautiful spotted coats of leopards resemble those of the only other great cat to grace the New World beside the puma: the jaguar. Like the leopard, the jaguar's coat has been its worst enemy. Jaguars have been hunted to the brink of extinction for their pelts throughout Central and South America. In Amazonian Brazil, during the 1960s, fifteen thousand pelts a year were stripped from the flesh of hunted, trapped, and poisoned

Leopard, New York Zoological Park

A leopard showing off its exquisite coat at the New York Zoological Park, circa 1929.

jaguars. Today, fifteen thousand is the estimate of the entire world's remaining population of these graceful animals.

Jaguars seldom kill people, but a handful of documented fatalities have been recorded. They look very similar to leopards, but when viewed side by side, the differences between the two species are readily apparent. The jaguar's spots are reversed. It's also stockier, shorter, has thicker legs, larger paws, and a far bigger neck, head, and jaw than a leopard's. If leopards are the backfield, picture jaguars as the linemen.

156

Jaguars were once commonly found within Continental U.S. along the Texas, Arizona, and New Mexico borders. Rare sightings of these cats still occur in those areas today. Most of the remaining jaguars live in South America, predominately in the Brazilian rain forests and the Pantanal wetlands of South-Central Brazil. Jaguars can weigh over three hundred pounds and prey on tapirs, peccaries, capybaras, caimans, turtles, birds, and even fish. Like tigers, jaguars love the water and are proficient swimmers.

Trading in any of the great cat pelts is strictly prohibited under the CITES (Convention on International Trade in Endangered Species) agreements, but unfortunately the black market for these pelts has driven the value of jaguar, tiger, and leopard skins to astronomical numbers. In 1996, it was estimated that the illegal trade in endangered or threatened plants and animals worldwide was between $10 and $20 billion. As horrific as these numbers are, the far greater risk to all of the world's great cats is habitat destruction brought by a human population that presently increases at the rate of seventy-four million a year.

Two other cats should be mentioned before we take a closer look at the current status of the puma and specifically the Florida panther: one of these is the snow leopard, which lives in the mountainous regions of Nepal, Tibet, Russia, Bhutan, India, Pakistan, Mongolia, and Afghanistan. Because of the remote, inaccessible habitats this cat favors, from the high Himalayas to the rugged mountains of Kashmir, very little is known about its behavior or the actual remaining number of snow leopards remaining in the wild.

To better appreciate how elusive this particular cat can be, read Peter Matthiessen's *The Snow Leopard*. In this articulate memoir, Matthiessen recounts his months of searching for a mere sighting of this nearly white, spotted cat amidst the deep ravines and towering peaks of northern Nepal. The current estimate of the wild snow-leopard population is under ten thousand, although this is only a calculated guesstimate.

Snow leopards are smaller (a large male will go up to 165 pounds) and stockier than leopards, but share one characteristic with them that has been a blessing and a curse—absolutely gorgeous pelts. Although officially banned, the black market trade in snow-leopard skins still thrives in the remote villages of Tibet and Kashmir. Snow leopards, too, are on the endangered-species list.

The second cat is the cheetah. The name is derived from the Hindu word *Cital*, which in turn comes from the Sanskrit word *Chiraka*, meaning "spotted one." Sadly, the cheetah is presently extinct in India, the very land that named it. The cheetah is the smallest of the great cats, with the largest males weighing 130 pounds. They are the fastest terrestrial animals in the world, having been clocked on the open plains of Africa at a documented sixty-eight miles an hour.

Formerly kept as private hunting cats in much the same manner as falcons and large hawks are kept today, cheetahs can be tamed. This characteristic has been their undoing in many regions of their former habitat. To fill the great stables of the Indian moguls, thousands upon thousands of cheetahs were taken from the wild. One ruler had a personal stable of one thousand wild cheetahs at his command while Akbar, a mogul emperor, boasted that he held over three thousand cheetahs in captivity in the mid-1800s.

The cheetah is unique in several aspects: chief among them, of all the cats, the cheetah has the smallest genetic variances known. There is grave concern that the cheetah population could quickly collapse from inbreeding, especially as the wild population vanishes. An even greater threat shared by all the great cats is the continual erosion of suitable habitat. Once common in Arabia, the last one seen there was in the 1950s. The last three wild cheetahs found in India were shot by the man who saw them in 1952. There are now under nine thousand remaining in Africa and eleven hundred being held in captivity in zoos and wildlife parks worldwide.

Cheetah pelts are still sold on the black market in Africa and the future of this sleek, unique cat is grim. Cheetahs will quite probably join tigers in extinction within the next hundred years.

Another leopard dies at the hands of the world's top
predator: Man.

Two Presents from God

In an interview with the *Palm Beach Post* taken a few days after the tragic death of her ten-year-old son, Donna Weidenhamer said, "We feel that Bradley, like all children, was a present from God." She was in tears as she spoke to the reporter.

The boy's father, Gary Weidenhamer, along with his baseball coach, Miguel Estrada, and several others, had miraculously managed to pull Bradley out of the jaws of an enormous alligator that seized the boy during a canoe trip down the Loxahatchee River, in Southeast Florida. Upon freeing the child, and noting the extent of his injuries, Bradley's father said, "It wouldn't have helped if Trauma Hawk—a Palm Beach County Sheriff's Department rescue helicopter—had been there the instant we got Bradley up from the alligator. The damage was too severe."

His mother later added, "We feel Bradley went to be with God the moment it happened."

The two deeply religious parents, members of the First Free Methodist Church of the Palm Beaches, knew that their gift had been returned to the giver. Bradley Weidenhamer, a fourth-grader who loved baseball, swimming, and biking had been bitten and killed by an alligator.

It happened around 12:30 on a beautiful Saturday afternoon on June 19, 1993. A few hours earlier, seven adults and six children had rented four canoes and put out from the canoe livery at Riverbend Park near the headwaters of the Loxahatchee River. From Riverbend Park, the river flows steadily north, across two small dams, then hooks back south-southeast at Jonathan Dickinson State Park, five miles north of Jupiter.

A popular day trip for both experienced and inexperienced paddlers, the river is a part of the Loxahatchee River Aquatic Preserve. The families were enjoying the day together, celebrating the end of their little-league season with a canoe trip and a picnic.

Wildlife abounds within the boundaries of the 11,500-acre park. Bobcats, gopher tortoises, sand-hill cranes, and Florida Scrub Jays inhabit the uplands while turtles, fish, and alligators inhabit the wetlands located along the stream's edge. The preserve has been called the Yellowstone National Park of Florida because of its rich and diverse wildlife sightings.

The vegetation is equally engaging. Five-hundred-year-old cypress trees tower over the river, while live oaks and sand-pine scrub forest compete for the higher ground. Water lilies, cattails, bulrushes, and a multitude of aquatic plants line the edge of the river. This emerging vegetation provides ample cover and ideal habitat for Florida's largest reptile, *Alligator mississippiensis*.

159

Along with dozens of smaller alligators inhabiting the waterway, there were two large gators familiar to park officials. Big George was one of them. Although Big George had killed a seventy-five-pound dog back in 1982, it had been skittish ever since and kept its distance from people. Big George was around ten-feet long and weighed close to 350 pounds.

The other large gator was known as Carl. It was slightly larger than Big George, measuring eleven feet, six inches and weighing over four hundred pounds. Carl was easily recognized by a large, golf-ball-sized lump located over its left eye. The scar, the rangers speculated, had probably been the result of an accident with a boat propeller years ago.

Several weeks before the attack, Carl had been reported to park officials as behaving aggressively. Richard Obach, the wildlife officer who investigated the report, concurred with the person filing the report. Obach had gone down the Loxahatchee mid-May 1993 to try to locate Carl and further verify the animal's behavior. Obach would then make a recommendation to his supervisor whether or not Carl should be permanently removed from the river.

They found the large gator a half-mile north of Trapper Nelson's camp, basking in a spot three quarters of a mile from where the fatal attack would occur a month later. Officer Obach splashed the water and called the alligator over toward the boat. Carl came readily, indicating the gator had probably been fed as of late. Carl did not appear to be afraid of people or their boats.

Obach reported the incident. Then, on Memorial Day weekend, while on a boating-safety patrol, Obach and Lieutenant Jeff Ardelean of the Florida Game and Fish Commission encountered Carl a second time that month. Because of its lump, Carl was an easy alligator to keep track of. This time, Carl kept clear of the boat and did not appear to be overly aggressive. The decision to remove Carl was put on hold.

On June 1, 1993, Richard Obach left on vacation. Don Scott, the park's superintendent, was taking him to catch his flight, during which Obach told his boss that the alligator known as Carl was, in his opinion, still a potential problem. Scott said that he would look into the matter. Given the two recent conflicting reports, the issue of what to do with Carl had been temporarily set aside.

Two weeks later, Carl fatally attacked Bradley Weidenhamer. The accident occurred at 12:30 P.M. on a Saturday in June. The water on the Loxahatchee was low that day and when periods of low water occur, numerous deadfalls and tree stumps that are navigable during high water become impassable obstacles for the stream's canoeists.

About a half-mile north of the Florida Turnpike overpass, well beyond the second dam and the Indian mound, the two boys riding in one of the lead canoes came upon a felled tree which was partially blocking the Loxahatchee. They got out to pull their canoe over the obstructing log. Bradley Weidenhamer stayed in the water, swimming and wading just a few strokes ahead of his canoe. The water in this section of the river wasn't more than four-feet deep.

What happened next no one will ever know for certain. Carl may have heard the splashing and, being hungry and naturally inquisitive, it swam over to investigate the activity. Because the water was so shallow, it is very conceivable that Weidenhamer may have accidentally kicked or stepped on the submerged reptile. If a person steps on an alligator, he or she triggers an automatic aggressive response the instant that person lifts his or her feet off the reptile. All that is known for certain is that, in an instant, Carl exploded out of the depths of the Loxahatchee and grabbed Weidenhamer by the head and shoulders, slapping its entire body on the water. Carl then submerged and started swimming away with the boy.

The people in the canoe directly behind the two boys were stunned.

"An alligator has Bradley!" one of them screamed. The boy's two parents, who had stopped to rest a few yards upriver along a sandy beach, came running to the rescue. By now the alligator had pulled Weidenhamer completely underwater, but his father could still see the son's white T-shirt through the brown, tannin-stained waters of the Loxahatchee. He reached down for the boy and caught him by the foot.

What ensued was a tug-of-war between a father, who had a desperate hold of his son's foot, and a four-hundred-pound alligator, which had Bradley's head and upper torso in its jaws. Initially the alligator prevailed, pulling Bradley back out of the hands of his father.

Gary Weidenhamer refused to give up and immediately grabbed his son's leg a second time, getting a better grip on it than he had the first time. Others soon rushed to Gary Weidenhamer's aid, including Mrs. Barker, a friend of the family, and Miguel Estrada, the baseball coach. As Weidenhamer and Estrada pulled on the boy's leg, Mrs. Barker and some of the others began to beat on the skull and body of the reptile with their canoe paddles. A few moments later, Carl reluctantly gave up its prey. It then proceeded to swim over to the far bank and crawled up it, looking back on the chaotic scene unfolding across the river.

The parents brought little Weidenhamer back up onshore and immediately started administering CPR. He wasn't breathing when they lifted him from the water, but within a few minutes they managed to resuscitate the boy. The head wound was extreme and there was blood everywhere. From statements made later, there can be little doubt that Weidenhamer's parents knew the gruesome outcome the minute they saw the extent of the damage done to their son's skull.

After getting the young victim back in the canoe, they still had a fifteen-minute paddle downstream to Trapper Nelson's Nature Center before they could get professional medical assistance. They wrapped the boy's head with a T-shirt to stem the bleeding and laid him in the bottom of the canoe for the journey downriver. One can only surmise how slowly those minutes must have passed as they paddled their way toward Trapper Nelson's.

Within minutes of their arrival, deputies, paramedics, and park rangers gathered at the canoe landing in an effort to save the boy. The Trauma Hawk arrived within minutes and flew Weidenhamer off to Jupiter Hospital. The doctors pronounced the boy dead at 2:16 P.M., roughly 105 minutes after the attack. The cause of death was extreme trauma to the head and shoulders. Carl, in one snap of its powerful jaws, had crushed Bradley Weidenhamer's skull, leaving him brain-dead and barely alive.

Mike Rafferty, a trapper from Palm City, was called to come in and catch the alligator. Carl was still in the vicinity of the attack when Rafferty shot it around 6:30 P.M. on that same day. The huge gator's body was brought by boat back to Trapper Nelson's. The necropsy on the animal was performed at 8:30 that night by Tim Regan of the Game and Fish Commission. The golf-ball-sized lump over its left eye was duly noted. The stomach, except for some vegetation and mud, was completely empty.

The alligator's body was buried and the head was removed to verify that the bite pattern of this particular animal was identical to the bite pattern of the wounds on young Weidenhamer. They were the same. Carl had indeed killed the boy.

Bradley Weidenhamer was an honor-roll student and played baseball for the Tigers, of the Lantana Little League. He was known as a good kid and loved by his coach, teachers, and obviously his family. Weidenhamer weighed forty-four pounds.

It is impossible to affirm that the alligator had been fed by other canoeists in the past. Carl's behavior in the weeks before the incident had been deemed inconclusive.

For millions of years, alligators have survived in Florida by catching and killing animals that come down to the river for a drink or that attempt to ford the river on their journey to greener pastures. Alligators do not discriminate between a deer, a wild boar, or a human being. It has been estimated that, on average, ten people a day die in Africa as a result of Nile-crocodile attacks not at all dissimilar to the attack on Weidenhamer. In Africa, crocodile attacks are so common they are viewed in much the same fashion as we have come to view fatal automobile accidents. A tragic but accepted reality.

No one calls for the eradication of cars after a fatal car wreck. Nor should we ever call for the eradication of all alligators after a tragic accident such as the death of a ten-year-old boy. Carl did not murder Weidenhamer. Alligators have no understanding of murder or vengeance. Carl was a hungry reptile that saw a feeding opportunity and acted upon it. Two innocent creatures died that day, a boy and the alligator that killed him.

After careful consideration and several heated conferences, the park officials decided not to kill the other large alligator, Big George, after the attack. "We don't remove gators just because they're there," a park official said to a *Palm Beach Post* reporter. "Alligators belong in the river," the official concluded.

The Loxahatchee River Aquatic Preserve and the Jonathan Dickinson State Park remain one of the best Florida locations for viewing an ancient, pristine, natural environment. The groups and individuals that still rent canoes out of Riverbend Park no longer let their children out to swim or wade as they paddle downstream. Big George still patrols its section of the Loxahatchee.

God had brought ten-year-old Weidenhamer into the world and God had made the animal that would take him from it. They had both been His creation and they were both gifts. Somehow, I believe young Bradley Weidenhamer would have wanted us to understand that.

A Rogue Shark Attack

The concept of a rogue shark is not a new one. The notorious "Twelve Days of Terror" that struck the northern New Jersey beaches during the long, hot summer of 1916 has long been attributed to the behavior of a solitary rogue shark. George Burgess, curator of the world-renowned International Shark Attack File, likens the actions of a rogue shark to that of postal workers and other murderers "who go off the deep end and just start shooting."

Beginning July 1, 1916, and ending twelve days later on July 12, 1916, it is widely held that a single eight-foot great white, or more likely a bull shark, was responsible for four fatal attacks and one serious injury along a stretch of the northern New Jersey's coastline and sixteen miles into the brackish waters of Matawan Creek. Despite concerted efforts from dozens of townspeople living along Matawan Creek, the shark responsible for the carnage was never found.

A different version of this same tale played out, to a lesser extent, on September 13, 1988, just south of Panama City, Florida. It was on that day that three different people were attacked, one of them fatally, by a single shark. This kind of shark behavior is exceedingly rare. Adding to its unusual aspect is the fact that most shark attacks, although seldom fatal, occur along Florida's East Coast, from the Keys to Jacksonville. The Gulf Coast elicits far fewer, but generally more severe, shark/human encounters.

The three attacks occurred near St. Andrews State Recreational Area, located across the bay from Panama City. John Martin, 38, was swimming just west of Shell Island in eight feet of water when the shark struck. The fish, estimated to be between six- and nine-feet long, was later identified by forensic scientists as a tiger shark. Tiger sharks are considered relatively uncommon in Florida waters, yet are responsible for almost all fatal attacks in the Hawaiian Islands. They also have a reputation for consuming just about anything they discover in the ocean— from inner tubes to ship's garbage.

Martin was swimming with his dog a short distance from his boat when a shark swam up and bit him in the leg. His girlfriend and another woman on Martin's boat witnessed the attack and tried to reach Martin immediately. Before they could, the shark returned and bit him a second time.

There are many shark specialists who believe that swimming with a dog in the ocean is risky. The erratic motions of a paddling dog, along with its smaller size and strong scent, are widely believed to attract the attention of sharks. That dogs are natural attractants to alligators is undeniable. By the same token, swimming with a dog may likely attract sharks and should always be avoided.

John Martin probably never gave it much thought before he jumped into the water with his pet. But after two large bites to his body, Martin wasn't thinking at all; he was bleeding profusely. His girlfriend, along with her friend and a passerby on a second boat, tried in vain to lift Martin back into his vessel. Severely injured, Martin himself was unable to be of any help to the would-be rescuers. After failing to get him on board, they eventually towed Martin to the beach, where he soon died from a combination of extreme blood loss and drowning, both due to a shark attack.

Less than thirty-five minutes after John Martin's fatal ambush, Dennis Hadden, 42, and his wife Ann, 41, were also wrestling with a shark. They were in the same vicinity, wading back to shore in four feet of water when the attack took place. It's important to note that, after a thorough investigation, it was determined that the murky, discolored water in the region played a significant factor in all three attacks. Recent heavy rains typical of mid-September, along with an excess of decaying vegetation, had left the waters around St. Andrew Bay turbid and cloudy. In conditions of poor visibility, sharks have been known to bite people in error. The trouble is an erroneous shark bite can be just as fatal as an intentional one.

The shark that attacked Ann Hadden was estimated to be six feet in length, although the muddy waters made an exact estimate of the fish's size impossible. The shark swam by very close to them and at first they thought it was a porpoise. They had never seen a shark that close before and couldn't believe it would be so bold. After swimming near them for mere seconds, the fish zeroed in on Ann and bit her on the forearm. Seeing his wife's arm in the shark's mouth, her husband started kicking at the fish. Wanting to avoid a fight, the shark released the arm and swam off. The Haddens had been unaware of Martin's death in the jaws of probably the very same shark a half-hour earlier. Although requiring multiple stitches, Ann survived the attack.

On average, somewhere between twelve to fifteen people are attacked and bitten by sharks every year in Florida. Murky water and cases of mistaken identity, wherein the shark perceives the flash of a swimmer's foot as a fleeing mullet or other potential prey cutting through the water, are often contributing factors in these attacks. Most encounters, however, result in stitches, not funerals.

Nonetheless, there are days when everything seemingly goes wrong. For John Martin and his orphaned pet, September 15, 1988, was just such a day.

The majestic *Puma concolor*, one of the few great cats in the world with an increasing population, especially in the western U. S. and Canada.

The Puma

"Let us remember that the mountain lion is in all physical respects a cat, simply a cat multiplied by 20."
Earnest Thompson Seton, *Lives of Game Animals*

Puma concolor, or *Felis concolor*, as it was called until very recently, is the scientific name for cougar, or puma, as I prefer to call them. The Florida panther is a subspecies of the puma. The name *Felis concolor* means "cat of one color," which is an accurate description of this exceptional cat. The new name, *Puma concolor*, translates as a powerful animal of one color, with the prefix puma derived from the Inca.

The puma stands alone among all the world's cats for the sheer number of names it has been called over the centuries: puma, cougar, mountain lion, panther, American lion, catamount, painter, Mexican lion, deer tiger, red tiger, leon, leopardo, as well as numerous Indian names including yutin, mitzli, pagi, ingronga, chim blea, and ig-mu-tank-a. All totaled, the puma has eighty-three denominations of record in English, Spanish, and assorted Native American dialects.

Today the trend is toward calling the cougar by its Inca name, puma. Pumas are extremely powerful. Many biologists would argue that, for its size, the puma is the strongest cat of all, even stronger than the athletic leopard. In

Florida, we call pumas panthers, though there has never been a verified or documented case of a melanistic, or black puma. There have been historical, albeit rare, sightings of black pumas but, lacking physical evidence such as actual photographs or a pelt, these have been dismissed as folklore.

Pumas rival leopards in the enormous extent of their range. Like all the other great cats today, their historical range has been decimated by habitat destruction, bounty hunting, and in both North and South America, ever-encroaching human populations. At the time of Columbus's discovery of the New World in 1492, it was suggested by one biologist that the puma population in the Americas could have been as high as one hundred million animals.

This number seems astronomically high and I doubt its validity, but using the current Florida range requirements of one male to every two hundred square miles and between three and four females (these calculations do not include puma kittens) within that range, we arrive at an average of 4.5 cats per two hundred square miles. This assumes poor but suitable habitat. It should be noted that out West, where game is plentiful, the range of a male could be as low as ten square miles, so this is a forgiving average.

When combined, the North and South American landmass is more than sixteen million square miles. These two continents represent 28.1 percent of the earth's total landmass. The puma's historical range covered the majority of this area, from Nova Scotia, clear across northern Canada as far north as the Yukon all the way to the Straight of Magellan in Tierra del Fuego. The far North, including Alaska, has never been known to harbor pumas, but these adaptable cats can and still do inhabit parts of the Alaskan panhandle.

Although the estimated human population throughout the region in 1492 was approximately 53.9 million, most of the indigenous peoples were located in Central and South America amidst the densely populated cultures of the Mayans, Aztecs, and Incas. In contrast to those crowded population centers, North America, where the puma had only minimal competition from the jaguar along its southern range, held an estimated four million Native Americans. Pressure on the puma from such a small human presence across such an immense landscape would be statistically insignificant.

By using 4.5 pumas per two hundred square miles as a baseline figure, and keeping in mind that the puma population in the now-decimated eastern hardwood forest was possibly as high as 4.5 cats per fifty square miles—offset by a density in the arid lands of the western U.S. of probably 4.5 cats per four to five hundred square miles—we arrive at an impressively estimated number: 365,000 pumas.

As astonishing as this number is, we must understand that around the year 1500 North America's natural wealth of flora and fauna would have made the present-day Serengeti Plain appear close to desolate. The buffalo (there were three species back then; two are presently extinct) and bison population in 1492 has been estimated between sixty to one hundred million. The Serengeti herds of Africa are one-tenth of that number today.

The following is just one example of the abundance of wildlife in early America. In 1790, nearly three hundred years after the discovery of the New World, Black Jack Schwartz rallied his friends and neighbors in Snyder County, Pennsylvania, to hold a ring hunt, or animal drive, to rid the surrounding forest of puma, wolves, and other troublesome varmints, as he referred to them.

Killed within that fifteen-mile radius were: 41 panthers, 109 wolves, 112 foxes, 114 bobcats, 17 black bears, 1 white bear (probably an albino), 2 elk, 98 deer, 111 buffalo, 3 fishers, 1 otter, 12 wolverines, 3 beavers, and over 500 smaller animals. According to his detailed account of the drive, a single fifteen-mile circle held over 1,124 animals, many of them large mammals such as the eastern buffalo, white-tailed deer, and elk. Half of the species killed in Schwartz's drive are extinct in Pennsylvania today—the buffalo, puma, wolverine, fisher, and wolf. Because a large herd of wild bison broke through the ranks, it was estimated that over one hundred animals escaped the mass slaughter.

The passenger pigeon was estimated to have a population of five to seven billion birds in 1492. Today, the passenger pigeon is extinct.

The number of pumas remaining in the wild today sadly echoes the declining numbers of all the world's great cats. In North America, where the puma is currently enjoying a steady rebound in population, the number of cats is estimated to be more than thirty-five thousand. In Central and South America, where statistics and accurate population numbers are far more difficult to obtain, the number is considerably lower, perhaps half the North American population—approximately seventeen thousand animals. As the earth's top predator, in a five hundred years' time we will have taken a population that was as high as 365,000 down to ten percent of that number. The good news is, in every state where the cat still roams except Florida, the puma population is recovering from the record low reached in the mid-1950s. Given today's trend, it is unlikely the puma will join the tiger and the cheetah on the path to extinction.

Depending on whom you ask, there are somewhere between fifteen and twenty-seven subspecies of puma. Personally, I think there are only two: the greater puma, which inhabits all of North America, and the lesser puma, which inhabits all of Central and South America. The differences between the many subspecies throughout their ranges, in my opinion, are little more than localized adaptations to specific environments. There are many biologists, such as David Maehr, author of *The Florida Panther: Life and Death of a Vanishing Predator,* who would argue otherwise.

The major difference between the North American and the South American puma is size. All subspecies of puma can interbreed. But there are considerable size differences between the two populations.

In North America, when one looks at the western mountain pumas and the Canadian cats, size is a factor. The largest unofficial puma ever recorded was killed in 1874 in Bellingham, Washington. This animal presumably tipped the scales at over four hundred pounds, but the record was never properly verified. From nose tip to the end of its tail, the cat measured over ten feet long. There are claims of many pumas shot during the settlement of eastern U.S. between 1600–1800 that approached, even exceeded, three hundred pounds.

The official size record is still given to a puma that was shot and killed by J.R. Patterson on a bounty hunt in the mountains near Hillside, Arizona, in March 1917. That cat, whose intestines and organs had been removed at the kill site, weighed 276 pounds and measured eight feet, seven and three-quarter inches tip to tail. Patterson claimed his five-dollar bounty after bringing this enormous cat in.

Whereas North American cats tend to be larger, including the Florida panther (which can exceed 150 pounds), Central and South American pumas average just over a hundred pounds for a male cat, with the females generally well below that. The primary reason for this size difference is related to the size of their respective prey.

The prey of choice for all North American cats is deer—white-tailed deer in the eastern edge of their range, mule deer and elk in the West. These are large animals and, just as the mane-less lion of Tsavo evolved to grow large enough so as to take down an eighteen-hundred-pound Cape buffalo, the North American puma has evolved to a size capable of handling these large ungulates.

In fact, the puma's weight-to-prey ratio is the highest of all the great cats, averaging 2.4 to one. That means, whereas the average catch of an African lion is one to one (a wildebeest weighs roughly the same as the average lioness) and the snow leopard 1.4 to one (snow leopards feed predominately on goats and sheep, which weigh only slightly more than they do), pumas feed on animals that weigh two and a half times as much as they do.

That's just an average and, although it's an impressive ratio, it doesn't do justice to the ferocity and skill of the puma. In one anecdotal tale from the frontier era, the famous Daniel Boone and his brother witnessed a spectacular sight on one of their buffalo hunts. They came across a puma in the process of taking down and killing a full-grown American bison. They calculated the bison weighed eight times that of the animal attacking it. Complaining that witnessing such a gruesome spectacle was very disturbing, they immediately shot both the puma and the bison. Typical top-predator behavior.

Out West, pumas take full-grown elk on a regular basis. A large bull elk can weigh over seven hundred pounds. The average western mountain lion weighs between 150 and 175 pounds. Pumas have devised a special technique for taking down elk, which generally prevents them from being killed or injured in the process.

Although nowhere near as fast as their closest relative, the cheetah, pumas are capable of tremendous bursts of speed over short distances. They have been clocked at speeds up to fifty-five miles per hour but, because of their smaller lung capacity, pumas can only maintain this speed for a few hundred feet—roughly the length of a football field. They tend to hunt, like most cats, during low-light conditions, both morning and evening, but have also been known to make a kill during broad daylight and in total darkness.

Pumas, like tigers and leopards, are ambush hunters…as are house cats. They stay low, tails flicking back and forth in anticipation, and slowly creep to within striking distance. Once committed to the attack, pumas kick into gear, sometimes leaping forty feet in a single bound while in pursuit of the prey. They are also capable of sheer vertical leaps of more than twelve feet, which would allow them to easily clear, say, a regulation basketball hoop—if not the entire backboard.

Using this tremendous speed and ambush ability, pumas kill full-grown elk by using the forward momentum of the animal itself. They sneak to within striking distance, then explode into a full-blown charge. Naturally, the elk's response is to bolt, whereupon the puma, in full stride, leaps unto the back of this six-foot-tall deer. Straddling the elk, rear claws digging deep into its hide for stability, the puma quickly reaches its two front legs around the elk's long neck and pulls that elk's head back and up as hard as possible.

The elk's body continues with the forward motion, and as the puma pulls in the reins, it breaks the elk's neck. The puma generally goes down with the fatally wounded ungulate, but more often than not it somehow manages to avoid getting itself killed in the process.

It obviously doesn't always go as planned. There have been reputable reports of dead pumas lying beside dead elk. Having a seven-hundred-pound animal land on you while going thirty miles an hour can also result in puma mortality, just as Tsavo lions occasionally die during their attacks on two-ton Cape buffalo. Mistakes, even fatal ones, happen during the bedlam of any predatory attack. Injuries are very common, especially when the animal being preyed upon is capable of fighting back, such as wild boars, badgers, or bobcats.

Throughout their range, pumas prefer deer. We have two native species of deer in North America, the whitetail, which average 150 but can exceed three hundred pounds, and the mule deer, which average two hundred pounds and can exceed 350 pounds. Pumas have also been known to kill livestock, especially in the West, where they feed on domesticated sheep, goats, cows, and even horses.

Lacking a local population of deer, pumas will kill and eat just about anything. In Florida, where deer are small and sometimes sparse, some panthers have turned to feral pigs for a large part of their diet.

Pumas need roughly five thousand calories a day to survive, or twice that of an average male human. Female pumas with cubs need fifty-five hundred calories a day to successfully nurse and raise their offspring. If hungry, wild pumas have been known to eat just about anything, including grasshoppers, lizards, snakes, and mice.

Whereas most North American pumas thrive on large game, Central and South American cats prey on smaller animals, including rabbits, capybara, monkeys, opossum, sloths, coatimundi, vicuña, marsh deer, and iguanas. They have also been known to attack and kill domesticated alpaca and llamas, which, although large, are easy prey compared to an elk or a buffalo.

Aside from the smaller prey base of the Central and South American puma, another contributing factor to their lesser size could be a result of competition from the jaguar. Although in recent times the jaguar has been severely over-hunted and is now considered rare, historically it lived and competed with the puma throughout most of its southern range. Large prey such as tapirs and caimans were probably left to the larger, indigenous cat—the jaguar.

Pumas can mate at any time of the year. When the female comes into estrus, which lasts as long as nine days, she sometimes attracts several competing suitors. This seldom ends well, as male pumas are exceedingly territorial and intra-species rivalry is one of the leading causes of death among wild pumas. During the period the female puma is in heat, she will mate repeatedly with one or more males if possible.

Following a successful pregnancy, she will carry between one and five kittens for ninety to ninety-six days. Male pumas have no compunction about killing and eating their own offspring, when given the opportunity. In this, they resemble both male alligators and male sharks.

Upon birth, the female puma assumes total responsibility for rearing her kittens. They are born blind, weighing under a pound, and should their mother not return to the den for any reason, her kittens are easy targets for predation by other animals. If left alone, starvation occurs within days. The kittens nurse until they are between five and six weeks of age, when they start feeding on meat, insects, and whatever other suitable protein brought in by their mother. Although extremely rare, pumas have been observed eating berries and other wild vegetation.

Over the next year or so, the kittens remain with their mother as she teaches them the hunting skills they will need to survive. Generally, after a year, one of the mother's suitors chases the kittens off and they are on their own. In a healthy environment, young male pumas will either find suitable unoccupied territory or kill an older cat and claim that cat's former range. In Florida, where there are so few remaining unclaimed ranges, intra-species rivalry is the leading cause of death of pumas.

The females find it somewhat easier. Provided there is enough prey, they can carve out a small section of forest beside their mother or replace an aging female's range through natural mortality. In the wild, pumas seldom survive past ten years. They almost never die peacefully in their sleep as they do in zoos, where pumas have been known to live as long as twenty-five years.

In the wild, the leading cause of death amongst pumas is starvation. That is followed by fatal automobile accidents. After that, we have injuries sustained during a kill and predation of the young by other animals, including intra-species cannibalism by male pumas. Next is human predation in the form of trophy and, though rare today, bounty hunting. Finally, we find territorial combat amongst males. Females seldom fight each other for range rights and are only rarely killed by males.

Dens are generally located in dense cover. In Florida, saw palmettos are preferred, but rocky crevices and shallow caves can also serve as suitable locations. The males seldom sleep in the same location for more than a night or two. If they return to the same spot to sleep, it is probably due to their having a large kill located nearby what they are feeding off.

As they wander their ranges—in the West it can be as large as five hundred square miles—male pumas mark the perimeters of their given turf by creating puma scrapes. These scratch hills, as they are sometimes referred to, will include urine and fecal material, which clearly indicate to a potential rival male that that territory is taken. In Florida, several panther mounds have been found as well. These mounds are larger than the scrapes, although the reason why Florida panthers create these mounds remains unclear.

Pumas cannot roar. They lack the physical anatomy necessary to produce the famous lion's roar. In part, that is why a puma's subfamily (felinae) is not included in the subfamily of lions, tigers, and leopards (pantherinae). Pumas can and do purr, though considerably louder than house cats. They also make chirping noises when calling for their kittens as well as many of the sounds we associate with house cats: mews, hisses, spits, purrs, and growls. Although it is still a hotly debated topic in some circles, pumas apparently do scream.

The screaming is more than likely a form of caterwauling done by a female puma in heat, but there are those who contend the infamous swamp screamer's sound is usually produced by either a bobcat or an owl. By and large, the puma is a relatively silent animal.

Historically, pumas are anthropomorphically considered a "bad" animal. As predators, humans have both consciously and subconsciously divided the animal kingdom into good and bad animals. Like "Bambi," deer are good. They are also herbivores. Ironically, most of the species placed in the "good" category taste "good" as well.

The so-called "bad" animals are those with which humans have historically competed: Pumas are bad; sharks, alligators, wolves, and grizzly bears are so far into the "bad" column, they are just about gone. Two species of Florida wolf were so "bad," they are now " 'extinctly' bad."

Teddy Roosevelt once said the following about pumas: "The big horse-killing cat, the destroyer of the deer, the lord of stealthy murder, facing his doom with a heart both craven and cruel." He was talking about a large cat he and his hunting party had treed on the rim of the Grand Canyon in 1913. Immediately after saying it, Roosevelt shot and killed the puma.

Indeed, since the Spaniards' arrival in 1492, the puma has been ruthlessly stalked and slaughtered. Its disappearance from the U.S. landscape follows the slow but steady western progression of settlers across the continent. Pumas were plentiful in Massachusetts around 1800. By 1840, they were gone.

The list of the last-known kill or verified sighting of a puma in eastern U.S. follows a steady pattern of localized eradication: from Alabama, in 1921, to Wisconsin, in 1950. Several states such as Delaware and Alaska probably had small populations of pumas, but never in numbers sufficient enough to claim they were an indigenous species. Although pumas are excellent swimmers, Hawaii was always a long shot for puma habitation. There are no Hawaiian pumas. So where are the remaining pumas in North America?

Florida, somewhere around 70; Arizona has 3,000 to 4,000; California, where Proposition 117—the California Wildlife Protection Act (1990)—places a permanent ban on all mountain-lion hunting, over 6,000 pumas, with numbers steadily climbing; Colorado harbors over 3,000 cats; Idaho has 2,500–3,000, and increasing rapidly; Montana, because of its size, pumas are quite common, but the exact number is unknown—perhaps as many as 5,000; Nevada holds 1,500; New Mexico, another 1,500; Oregon has 3,000 or more; in Texas, the number is unknown but climbing, perhaps 1,000; Utah holds 3,000; Washington, at least 1,500–2,000; Wyoming has an unknown number, but the pumas appear to be returning to much of their former range.

The balance of north American pumas are located in Canada, where remnant populations are still possible in New Brunswick and Ontario. By far, the greatest Canadian puma populations exist in Alberta and British Columbia, especially on Vancouver Island, which harbors the world's most dense population of pumas. There is also a sizable population in the mountainous regions of Mexico.

Pumas were still bounty hunted until the 1950s, when most of the states discontinued the practice. In California alone, between 1907 and 1963, the state doled out an incredible $389,345 to trackers and hunters as a monetary reward for killing 12,461 pumas. In 1917, the posted bounty on a puma was $20 for a male cat and $30 for a female. Pumas, especially the nuisance cats that have turned to domesticated animals as their major source of prey, are still taken in California despite the official ban. Between 1972 and 1999, an additional 1,401 pumas were shot, trapped, and killed in that state alone. The majority of those cats were confirmed nuisance animals with repeat offenses.

For the most part, this is how man treats competing predators.

Sometimes, certain pumas deserve getting shot. Like the leopard, the puma sometimes appears to kill for sport. An alligator, a lion, or a tiger will take a human to feed, but none of these predatory animals have ever been known to kill for sport or to take another mammal down only to abandon the carcass.

Such is not the case with the puma. In this regard, pumas behave much more like humans than most other predators on earth. Perhaps that's in part why people have traditionally loathed pumas as much as, if not more than, wolves. One story above all exemplifies this strange, aberrant animal behavior.

In a book published in 1964 by Stanley Young and Edward Goldman entitled *The Puma, Mysterious American Cat*, the authors describe a horrific incident that occurred in Glade Park, Colorado, around 1900. According to reliable reports, a single puma slipped into a herd of bedded ewes and over the course of the night, single-handedly killed 192 sheep. The puma ate a few bites here and there but left the overwhelming majority of the sheep to rot. This weird behavior is far more characteristic of humans, such as the recent mass shooting at Columbine High School in Colorado or the killing of hundreds of students and teachers in Chechnya.

There are other chilling tales in which pumas have been known to kill for no apparent reason other than for the thrill of killing. While tracking a puma in western U.S. around the turn of the last century (ca. 1900), a bounty hunter reported a gruesome tale. The puma he was hunting was apparently very adept at killing, but would eat only a tiny portion of each kill.

The hunter followed the cat for a week before treeing and shooting it. Over the course of that week, he would often come upon and document the cat's grizzly progress across the terrain. One night, the puma would kill a deer, eating only its liver and heart, both of which are very high in protein and other nutrients; the following night, it would be an elk, with the puma once again eating only the richest parts, generally licking up the blood then eating only the liver and heart. Nearly every day the puma continued this behavior, leaving its dead behind to be fed upon by coyotes, wolves, ravens, and wolverines.

There are many other reports of pumas killing far more sheep out of any given herd than they could possibly eat in a night. Like a fox in the chicken coop, perhaps the instinct to kill somehow intoxicates the puma into committing to a behavior that is exceedingly rare in wildlife. It should also be noted that the majority of these mass-slaughters occur when the puma is attacking domesticated animals, which, for the most part, have lost their natural instincts to flee.

Native Americans did not universally revere the puma. Across the North American landscape, the jury on the puma was split, with roughly half the tribes admiring the power and cunning of the cat and the other half considering it a pariah. As a result, the puma was often considered fair game and hunted for food—several historic accounts all agreed that puma meat was considered a delicacy, just as were bison and deer—whereas the bear, especially the grizzly bear, was almost universally respected.

Notwithstanding the puma's lowly position among many Indian tribes, Native Americans did a far better job of respecting nature and the realm of the puma than did the encroaching Europeans. The various Indian tribes often differed in appearance, in religious rites, in language, and in demeanor, but all North American tribes held a deep respect for the flora and fauna that shared their environment.

Native Americans lived off the land and were quick to realize that any dramatic changes in the salmon, bison or deer populations could have devastating consequences. They worshiped Mother Earth and understood that all life, including their respective tribes', sprang from her abundance. The concept of mankind's dominion over nature, which springs from the Judeo-Christian philosophies of the European pioneers, was foreign to Native Americans. One cannot own the land and control the forces of nature.... To think against those lines was incomprehensible to North America's Native tribes.

To shoot the buffalo and leave it on the plains to rot in the sun was so far outside of their realm of the human/wildlife relationship that American Indians must have thought the Europeans had gone mad or been possessed by demons. With our slow, though hardly steady, return to ecological principles, we are learning that the indigenous people of America were far better stewards of the land than we have been, especially when we first arrived in the New World.

The senseless mass slaughter of buffalos in the late 1800s brought them to the brink of extinction.

Years ago, Native American Luther Standing Bear wrote: *"We are the soil and the soil is of us. We love birds and beasts that grew with us on this soil. They drank the same water and breathed the same air. We are all one in nature. Believing so, there was in our hearts a great peace and willing kindness for all living, growing things."*

Everyone in America has grown up with the image of the crying Native American overlooking a crowded, smoggy city from a lonely precipice. What most of us have never understood is that Native Americans have had their own dispiriting history. During the migration of the Clovis people southward from the former land bridge across the Bering Sea, over fifty-seven different megafauna species were wiped out.

It is true that, when Europeans first set foot on North America, Native Americans lived in relative balance with the natural world. But it's also noteworthy that this hadn't always been the case. The Indians learned, over a ten thousand years' time and with great wisdom, to live in harmony with nature.

No doubt the puma killed Native Americans by the tens of thousands. With a puma population numbering in the hundreds of thousands and an indigenous human population of around four million natives armed only with bows, spears, and primitive weaponry, predation by pumas on most tribes was undoubtedly a constant threat.

Although there are earlier anecdotes of puma-versus-human encounters, the first authenticated attack on a European settler was recorded in 1751 in Chester County, Pennsylvania. The victim was Philip Tanner, attacked by a puma while inspecting a stand of timber he had been planning to fell along the edge of his land. The timber ran along Pigeon Creek. The details of the attack are unknown but the epitaph on his tombstone reads, "Here lye the body of Philip Tanner who departed this life May 6, 1751—age 58 years." A chiseled puma crouches on the face of that tombstone, reminding all who pass near it that Tanner died at the hands of a wild cat.

Scattered accounts of both fatal and nonfatal puma attacks continued through the 1800–1900s across the entire historic range of the puma, from Maine to California. The only known fatal attack by a Florida panther occurred around 1800 and was immortalized in 1885 by Theodore Roosevelt in his book *The Wilderness Hunter* (1893). Roosevelt loathed pumas and described them as "a beast of stealth, and rapine, ferocious and bloodthirsty as they are cowardly."

As attacks on the settlers moving westward across the nation were quite common during those times, Roosevelt probably felt justified in his disdain for the puma. You can still get a feel for his hatred of it in his description of the only known historical fatality inflicted by a Florida panther on a human:

> *Early in the present century (1800s) one of my ancestral relatives, a Georgian, moved down to the wild and almost unknown country bordering on Florida. His plantation was surrounded by jungles in which all kinds of beasts swarmed. One of his Negroes had a sweetheart on another plantation, and in visiting her, instead of going by the road he took a short cut through the swamps, heedless of the wild beasts, and armed only with a long knife, for he was a man of colossal strength, and of fierce determined temper.*

> *One night he started to return late, expecting to reach the plantation in time for his daily task on the morrow. But he never reached home, and it was thought he had run away. However, when a search was made for him his body was found in the path through the swamp, all gashed and torn, and but a few steps from him the body of a cougar, stabbed and cut in many places. Certainly that must have been a grim fight, in the gloomy, lonely recesses of the swamp, with no one to watch the midnight death struggle between the powerful, naked man and the ferocious brute that was his almost unseen assailant.*

After studying and reading about countless alligator, shark, and puma attacks, I can say without hesitation that expiration by puma ranks as the worst possible cause of predatory death. Fortunately, it is the most unlikely cause of any Floridian's death amongst the three predators described in this book.

The greatest chance of being killed comes from the American alligator, with shark mortality second and panther mortality nil. The black man killed in the woods of North Florida/South Georgia represents the only authenticated fatality from a Florida panther ever recorded. There have been several attacks since that time, but none have proved fatal. The Florida panther is so rare today that even seeing one could take years of patient effort; getting killed by one is virtually an impossibility.

But people do get killed by pumas in the U.S. and Canada, and do so with some regularity. Whereas a fatal shark attack is quick and in many cases nearly painless, a fatal attack by a puma is absolutely horrendous by comparison. I would much prefer death by an alligator, which generally drowns its victim within minutes, than death at the hands of an animal quite fond of eating one alive.

Before we delve into puma-versus-human attacks, let me stress again that pumas are not bad or evil animals just because they kill us. In fact, when compared with lion and leopard attacks, death by puma is extremely rare. There is an interesting, albeit speculative, explanation for this.

Whereas lions, leopards, tigers, and crocodiles co-evolved with humans, American alligators and pumas never saw a human being up until approximately twelve thousand years ago. Geologically speaking, this was yesterday. Sharing interior Africa, leopards and lions watched mankind ascend from an apelike creature with limited natural defenses to a gun-wielding mega-predator. Humans have always been on their menu because they had always been one of the available local prey.

When the Clovis people arrived in America, the top predators by and large didn't know what to make of those strange, two-legged beings invading their territory. Did they taste good...? Were they hard to catch...? Confirmed by the rarity of fatal attacks even today, humans are certainly not on the main menu of any North or South American predator except the shark, and even at that, only four percent of the time is a shark-attack victim actually consumed. We should consider ourselves lucky in this respect. In the new world, humans have become a special order of prey.

Puma versus unarmed man is never good; puma versus boy is worse. In August 1998, a six-year-old boy was attacked by a puma while walking along a logging road twenty miles west of Dupuyer, Montana. Little Joey Swift was walking behind a friend, who was riding a small pony. As they went by an especially thick section of under-story, Joey noticed a puma hiding in the dense brush.

178

He started backing up and hollering, "No!" Then Joey did what most of us would naturally do when confronting a large feline predator: he turned and ran. With pumas, our natural tendency to run triggers their natural tendency to chase. A boy might be able to reach a speed of fifteen miles and hour; a puma can run over fifty miles an hour for short distances. For humans, outrunning a puma is out of the question.

Within seconds, the puma overtook the boy, knocking him down to the ground. The cat then bit him on the back of his head and back, finally grabbing him by the skull and dragging him off into the dense brush.

The boy's mother, hearing her son's screams, responded immediately. Together with two men who were in the vicinity, she rushed in to rescue her boy from the attacking cat. Perhaps the puma felt outnumbered, but for whatever reason, the cat abandoned its prey and ran off into the surrounding woods. People who witnessed the entire event—and there were over fifty within earshot of the incident—would tell authorities that the puma couldn't have been in contact with Joey Swift for more than sixty seconds.

During those sixty seconds, the puma inflicted numerous bite wounds, claw marks, lacerations, and contusions to the child's head, shoulders, and abdomen. Over two hundred stitches were required to close all the injuries received in a minute's time. Pumas are capable of inflicting devastating injuries within seconds.

The attacking animal was killed later that same day by Tom Flowers. Treeing the puma with trained dogs, Flowers used a twelve-gauge shotgun loaded with slugs to take down the young, one-hundred-pound male cat.

Today, with the increase in the puma population throughout most of its remaining range, attacks are equally on a steady increase. Two regions in particular seem to hold the greatest number of puma attacks and fatalities: California and British Columbia (B.C.).

Within the past fifty years, most of the fatal encounters between humans and pumas have occurred in those two regions. British Columbia is immense, covering 366,255 square miles—over six times the size of Florida—and although it probably harbors fewer pumas per square mile than California, its sheer size and large, unbroken stretches of wilderness compensate for that. It is estimated that B.C. has a population of over four thousand pumas. Vancouver Island, nearly two hundred miles long and over forty miles wide in the middle, harbors the world's single largest population of pumas, estimated at over one thousand cats.

Vancouver Island is rich in wildlife, including a puma's favorite prey, the deer. The island has been the site of repeated puma attacks. A study compiled in 1991 revealed that twenty-nine out of the fifty puma attacks reported in North America at that time had occurred in B.C. In March 1992, Tim Loewen was stationed at the cashier's booth in the historic Empress Hotel's underground parking ramp. The Empress Hotel is located in downtown Victoria, on Vancouver Island, B.C. The Empress is famous for its traditional afternoon high-tea and considered by many one of the finest hotels in the world.

A nearby cabby, having just seen a puma entering the parking lot, honked and shouted over to Loewen, "You got a cougar in here!"

"What?" Loewen responded in disbelief.

"A cougar just walked into your parking lot," the cab driver repeated.

After working through his disbelief, Loewen dispatched a bellman to seal off all the doors into the underground garage. Initially, they felt ridiculous, looking for a puma in a parking garage beneath a fine, upscale hotel. Within minutes, they were no longer laughing.

While driving their Jeep around the dark, underground parking area, a full-grown puma slid silently past their headlights. It was apparently true: a cougar had come for high-tea.

Loewen called Bob Smirl, a Vancouver conservation officer, and proceeded to make certain every hotel guest was removed from the area. Within the hour, Smirl arrived with two hounds-men, two hounds, a tranquilizer dart gun, and a 30/30 Winchester carbine. Loewen raised the mesh gate and three very nervous men, two dogs, and two guns descended with flashlights on the trail of a trapped puma.

The dogs instantly picked up the scent and within minutes located their quarry. Smirl's first shot missed the cat and the dart ended up in an air duct. The second dart found its mark and soon the puma was lying limp on the garage floor. Luckily for the cat, the 30/30 was never used.

Officer Smirl and his helpers emerged a while later with a large, handcuffed puma in Smirl's arms. Placing the tranquillized cat down on the tailgate of his truck, he let fifty people from the large crowd that had gathered touch the soft pelt of the sedated animal. The media had a field day and the story made international news through the CBC (Canadian Broadcasting Corporation). To this day, a picture of the limp puma being evicted from the parking garage of the Victoria Hotel hangs in its elegantly furnished lobby. The puma was relocated to the far northern end of Vancouver Island, where it lived out the remainder of its life.

This particular incident ended well. Another puma story, this time from the little town of Princeton some 120 miles east of Vancouver Island on the mainland, ended tragically. Of all puma attacks I've reviewed, the sheer horror and heartbreak of this fatal puma attack stands alone.

It occurred on August 19, 1996. Cindy Parolin, a thirty-five-year-old mother of four, was on a horseback ride through the Similkameen backcountry.

Three of her children were with her: David (13), Melissa (11), and Steven (6). The four of them were riding along a logging road to meet Les, her husband, and Billy, their ten-year-old son. The surrounding forest was heavily timbered and, although Parolin almost always carried a rifle with her, she had decided to leave the gun at home on this particular camping expedition.

Suddenly, the horses became agitated and nervous. A small puma burst from the surrounding woods and charged the horse carrying the six-year-old boy, Steven. The puma leapt up onto the horse's neck and bit at the young boy's foot, tearing off his shoe in the process. Naturally, the horse reared, throwing Steven to the ground. The puma was on top of the boy instantly, biting him directly in the head.

The boy's mother screamed at the cat, dismounted from her horse and, breaking a branch off a nearby dead tree, charged the cat. She hit it as hard as possible in the ribs, knocking loose the puma's grip on her son's head.

The puma, undeterred, now turned its full attention to the mother. Cindy Parolin, at five-foot-five and average weight, was extremely fit. An avid camper and outdoors-woman, Parolin was also an experienced karate expert. As the cat came at her, she punched it hard in the face, then the two fell to the ground together, wrestling violently as they did.

Parolin yelled to her oldest son, David, to pick up Steven and get out of the area at once. The horses had bolted off and were of no help. Taking turns carrying the injured Steven the one mile back to their car, the three children reluctantly obeyed their mother and went for help. Parolin was now left alone with a frenzied sixty-three-pound male puma.

Leaving Melissa and the injured child at the car, David ran to find help. An hour later, around 7:30 P.M., several would-be rescuers returned to the scene of the incident. Parolin, screaming and badly injured, was on the ground with the cat crouched over her. Using rocks to safely pry the cat away from its victim, the rescuers managed to get the cat to turn its attention to them.

As the puma started coming directly toward them, rescuer Jim Manion fired a shot only to have his gun jam. He started backing up toward his pickup truck. The puma hesitated just long enough for Manion to get his rifle working again. Within seconds, as the cat made a full-blown charge at him, Manion fired a round from the hip. The bullet hit the cat full bore, lifting the puma off the ground and killing it instantly.

Manion rushed over to Cindy Parolin.

"Are my children safe?" she asked the man who had just silenced her attacker.

"Yes," he replied.

Parolin seemed to relax a bit upon hearing the good news, then added, "I'm dying."

Parolin was pronounced dead on arrival at Princeton General Hospital on that same night. Her scalp, face, and torso had sustained too many injuries and the resulting loss of blood killed her before the rescuers were able to get her to the emergency room for a transfusion.

Parolin's boy, Steven, survived. He suffered extensive scalp lacerations. In less than a minute's time with the boy, the cat had created the need for over seventy stitches to close all the wounds.

The battle between Cindy Parolin and the puma must have been horrific. Pumas attack, then retreat; attack, and then retreat, all the while inflicting more and more wounds to the victim and wearing him or her further and further down in the process.

The valiant stand by this unbelievably brave mother is one of the most heart-wrenching tales I have ever encountered. How many times have mothers said they would rather die so as to save their children, only to find a story that exemplifies that very commitment…?

At her funeral several days later, with over six hundred mourners present, the Reverend Chris Haugland said, "God was with Cindy Parolin every moment of her life, strengthening her to do what she had to do."

Time and again in puma attacks, it is the youngest and most vulnerable that tends to be singled out by the marauding animal. You cannot blame the puma for its behavior because, if you consider the viewpoint of the predator, taking the elderly, injured, or young is the path of least resistance.

Years ago, while our family was on vacation in Stewart, British Columbia, we happened upon a once-in-a-lifetime wildlife viewing. While camping in Stewart, we were told about a salmon run in Hyder, Alaska. The run was drawing in a great number of grizzly bears from the surrounding coastal-range mountains. Finding the mining road that wound up beside Salmon River, we ventured ten miles east to the spawning grounds and viewing area, where we were told the four of us—my wife Molly and I, and our two boys Logan (9) and Blake (7)—could watch the bears.

Hyder, Alaska, epitomizes wilderness. There was a small, fenced platform overlooking the gravel beds of the stream, but to and from the parking lot not a single fence stood between those three 350-pound grizzly bears and us. The bears were located below us, not more than seventy-five feet away. They were feeding on the dying, spawned-out salmon. The entire scene was straight out of a National Geographic Channel special.

We watched for quite some time and, as is typical, the boys started rough-housing. Upon noticing our kids' behavior, a female ranger quickly rushed over to us.

"Don't let your boys run," she stated emphatically. "Even though the bears are stuffed from eating the salmon, if they see something the size of your children running, they could instinctively attack and kill them."

Both my and Molly's jaw dropped. Although we had always camped and spent years outdoors, Molly and I had never had experience with grizzly-bear behavior. The ranger was carrying what looked to be a 45-caliber handgun, but one look at those sleek, healthy bears and you realized that a single handgun might not be enough to stop an unexpected charge.

Molly and I quickly grabbed the boys and told them to settle down immediately. We cautiously walked back to our vehicle and continued on. This was not the backwoods of Minnesota, where I grew up. These were very big, very real grizzly bears, capable of taking out one of our children in a single swipe of their paw.

I have never seen a puma in the wild, although once, while camping in the Bighorn Mountains of Wyoming, a large cat had been seen the day before we arrived. Although my research for this book has taught me to respect them, I wouldn't necessarily be afraid of seeing one someday while out trout-fishing or hiking in the backcountry. Statistically, I'm still well aware that I'm at a far greater risk of dying while driving to my trout stream than I would be by coming across a puma in the wild. Chances are, it would simply slip away into its element much like the lynx I did see years ago while canoeing the Cloquet River in northern Minnesota.

Although pumas tend to pick children as their victims, that isn't always the case. One of the most compelling puma attacks, this time directly on Vancouver Island, occurred on January 26, 1951. It was on that day that Ed McLean, a telephone lineman working out of Kelsey Bay, on the island's northeast coast, had turned in for the night in one of the telephone company's line cabins.

Earlier in the day, McLean had noticed a small puma prowling around the perimeter of the cabin but, having seen the cat on several occasions in the past, he ignored it. There can be little doubt that this was due, in part, to the small size of this particular animal, an immature female weighing only fifty-six pounds.

Around 9 P.M., after bringing in some firewood and getting into his heavy-wool underwear for bed, McLean noticed the young puma standing right outside his front door. He hurriedly blew out the gas lantern, thinking the light might somehow be attracting the cat's interest.

Within seconds of McLean's extinguishing the lantern, the hungry puma leapt right through the window of the front door, ruthlessly attacking. The cat grabbed hold of McLean's right elbow, hurtling both of them to the floor of the cabin. McLean managed to get the puma pinned down beneath him, but the cat continued to bite into his arm and shoulder. Using its hind legs, it viciously clawed at McLean's torso and legs.

Knowing he couldn't keep up this hand-to-hand combat for long, McLean remembered that he had placed a butcher's knife on the kitchen table after dinner. He pushed the cat away from him, got up from the floor and grabbed for the knife. As he did, the puma sprang at his right hand, biting it so hard that the man's thumb was virtually severed. Somehow, McLean managed to hang onto the knife, using only his four fingers, and then began stabbing at the animal's throat.

The cat kept clawing at McLean's head and shoulders, but the knife was hitting the bones and the cat's energy was slowly fading. "My arms were chewed up so badly, I didn't have strength enough to get away from her until she grew weak from loss of blood," McLean later told the *Vancouver Sun*.

With his body mauled and bitten from nearly head to toe, McLean somehow managed to drag himself out the front door of the cabin. As he cleared the doorway, the puma had regained just enough strength to come at McLean once again but before the puma could reach McLean, he slammed the door shut, trapping the wounded animal inside the cabin.

McLean, now outside in late January, wearing nothing more than his wool underwear and bleeding profusely, suddenly realized that the nearest telephone was at another telephone-company line cabin six miles across Kelsey Bay by boat. Going back into the cabin was obviously not an option, since the puma, although gravely injured, was still intent on killing him.

Barefoot and bleeding, McLean stumbled down to the dock and prepared to row across the open waters of the bay to the distant line cabin. Luck was with him as both the wind and tide aligned in the direction he was heading; otherwise, given his weakened condition, McLean would probably have been swept out to sea that evening and died.

Arriving at the other cabin late into the night, shivering-cold and delirious, McLean finally made it to the telephone and began dialing for help. It's important to remember this was 1951 and the 911 emergency telephone system we all take for granted didn't exist at the time. After several attempts at trying to reach help, a fading, disheartened McLean realized that he would have to try to make it through the night before reaching anyone for help.

Finding a sleeping bag that was stored at the cabin, McLean crawled into it and fell into a near-coma-like sleep. Mustering the last bit of energy he had, at nine the next morning, twelve hours after the puma had leapt through his glass window, McLean reached the Kelsey Bay home office by phone. Two of his friends and associates, Fred Dingwall and Bill Fersch, immediately drove out to rescue him.

When they got to McLean, he was near death. Suffering from exposure and severe blood loss, McLean was unconscious. Both the sleeping bag and the mattress he slept on were drenched with blood and the dried blood on his wool underwear was so thick that later, at Lourdes Hospital in Campbell River, his clothes had to be cut away.

From the hospital, where McLean had been rushed to the ICU to receive numerous transfusions and countless stitches, the two men went back out to the line cabin on the other end of Kelsey Bay, where the attack had occurred. Rifles drawn, the men peered in through the broken window of the front door only to find the puma, still alive but gravely wounded, lying on McLean's bed. When the cat realized there were men at the front door, it raised its head and looked for a moment as if it were about to muster yet another attack. The men took aim and shot the animal on the spot.

Further investigation revealed that the adolescent female puma was starving to death and its hunger had apparently driven it to such extreme predation. McLean remained in the hospital four more days. He was treated for blood loss, exposure, a mangled hand, and a badly chewed right elbow, along with uncountable other claw marks and lacerations. He survived and three weeks later was allowed to return to Kelsey Bay, where he continued to work for the local telephone company.

This true account says volumes about the sheer tenacity and strength of the puma. Armed only with a butcher's knife and outweighing the cat nearly three-to-one, an adult male was still unable to kill a fifty-six-pound cat. The agility and endurance of pumas are legendary. If pumas were as inclined to hunt and attack humans as their distant cousins—leopards, lions, and tigers—human mortality throughout their range would be staggering. Pound for pound, the puma is the strongest cat in the world.

On the other hand, this life-and-death struggle speaks volumes about the strength and tenacity of Ed McLean. The fact that he was able to reach the knife, subdue the panther, and row six miles across the bay to the nearest telephone is remarkable. Pound for pound, humans are one of the most persevering animals in the world.

*****

Aside from mainland British Columbia and Vancouver Island, the other hot spot for puma attacks is Cuyamaca Rancho State Park in southern California. Decades earlier, before California's Proposition 117 was passed, sightings of pumas were considered rare events in Cuyamaca Rancho. Once the ban was in force, and given the large mule-deer population that had built up during the puma bounty-hunting years, the cat population rebounded immediately. It's important to note that, given ample prey and safe haven, female pumas can reproduce quickly, having two or three litters annually, with as many as five kittens per litter.

Pumas are a resilient species and the increased frequency of California attacks is a direct result of a rebounding population. Humans have to understand that they cannot have it both ways. If we increase the number of top predators in the wild, we directly increase our chances of being killed by one. The irony is, pumas kill far fewer humans than deer. In 2003, deer/car collisions took over two hundred lives in the U.S., in addition to injuring tens of thousands. As a species, every ecological decision we make has its unintended consequences.

Four years after the ban on hunting wild pumas in California became law, a woman was attacked and killed by a cat at Cuyamaca Rancho. She was the second puma fatality that year in California. The first woman to die in a puma attack in 1994 was Barbara Schoener, 40, of Placerville, California. Schoener was killed while jogging one early morning in the Auburn State Recreational Area near Cool, California.

On December 10, 1994, a second fatal attack occurred in Cuyamaca Rancho, in San Diego County. The victim was fifty-six-year-old Iris Kenna, an avid bird-watcher and naturalist. She was walking along a park road during the early morning when she must have come across a hungry puma. Being alone and petite, Kenna was an easy target for the healthy, 116-pound male puma.

Recreating the incident later from evidence at the scene, rangers speculate that, initially, it appears as if Kenna confronted the cat face to face. Perhaps, as the puma became more aggressive and emboldened, Kenna panicked and ran. Running inevitably triggers a chase response in any predator, and this puma was no exception.

Catching Kenna within seconds, the puma knocked her down, biting her in the back of the neck and tearing off her backpack and glasses in the process. According to the autopsy report, her death wasn't instantaneous, though. Kenna was so badly injured in the initial onslaught that there was little, if any, struggling involved. Within a few minutes' time, Kenna's neck was broken and she was dead.

After killing her, the puma behaved in exactly the same fashion as when one takes down a deer or a peccary. It dragged Kenna's limp body into a brush-covered area some fifty feet from the road she had been walking down, not more than a mile from the Paso Picacho Campground, a small campground located in Cuyamaca Rancho Park.

Around 11 A.M., two hikers walking the same route Kenna had taken came across her bloodstained backpack and broken glasses lying along the path. Seeing all the bloodstains in the sand and quickly realizing something terrible had happened, the two hikers returned to the campground and told the rangers what they had found. Fifteen minutes later, following the drag marks into the surrounding bush, the rangers found Iris Kenna's lifeless body, partially covered with sticks and leaves in the same manner pumas cover deer carcasses.

The rangers, knowing immediately they had a killer puma on the prowl, evacuated Cuyamaca Rancho State Park, closing it off to arriving campers. Although the rangers searched for hours for the attacking puma, it was nowhere to be found. The rangers realized that, if they waited, the puma would quite possibly return to feed on Kenna's body after dark. They set up a blind and proceeded to wait for the puma's return, even though they had removed her body shortly after discovering it earlier in the day.

At 9:45 that night, true to its instincts to survive and feed, the cat returned. Using flashlights and high-powered rifles, the rangers shot and killed the animal. A necropsy showed the puma to be a five-year-old male in prime condition. It wasn't starving, wounded, or showing any indications of injury or disease. It was simply a puma that had elected to try eating one of those strange, two-legged animals that frequented its range.

Many of the citizens of San Diego were outraged. They wondered what the Legislature was thinking when it had banned the taking of pumas four years earlier. Although upset over the twin fatalities that year, one of the local ranchers put it best when he said, "When you enter the park, you enter the food chain, and you'd better know the risk."

With California's tally reaching six thousand pumas and climbing, there can be absolutely no doubt that human fatalities will continue to rise in the state. As Ron Woychak, a resource officer for nearby Cleveland National Forest, said in an interview with the *San Diego Union-Tribune* a few days after the incident, "State parks like Cuyamaca serve as game reserves. With its no-hunting restrictions, the park is a magnet that draws in the deer the lions prey on."

The lesson is, if one chooses to recreate in an area where pumas have an unlimited supply of wild prey to pursue, chances are sooner or later one of these wild cats will turn its attention to the newly arrived primates that now number over thirty million in the state of California. In the entire North America, according to some of the most recent data available, since 1900 there have been forty-one fatal puma attacks and 185 nonfatal encounters with pumas. It is safe to say that, between sport hunting, bounty hunting, trapping, and the poisoning of pumas, humans have killed an excess of one hundred thousand cats since 1900, probably twice that number if any reliable statistics were available. The odds are not in the puma's favor—forty-one humans killed by wild pumas to one hundred thousand pumas slaughtered by humans. We, as a species, cannot have our cake and eat it, too. To save the puma, the alligator, and the shark, a few of our kind must invariably die.

A Mother and Her Offspring

Nearly thirty years ago, Punta Gorda, Florida, was a sleepy little village lying along the south shore of the Peace River. The great explosion of Florida's development had only just begun and it would be decades before Punta Gorda Isles and thousands of vacant lots platted in North Port and Port Charlotte would be filled in with homes, duplexes, and condominiums. Late September 1997 still was a quiet time in South-Central Florida.

Palm Shores, located ten miles north of historic downtown Punta Gorda, was a half-empty subdivision carved out along some five navigable canals that emptied into the Peace River. The water in these canals is slightly brackish—a mixture of salt and fresh water, which chemistry changes hourly with the rising and falling of the tides. Back then, alligators occasionally patrolled the waters, but hardly were a common occurrence in Palm Shores.

So, when fifty-two-year-old George Leonard climbed into his canal late on the afternoon on September 28, 1977, to do some repair work on his dock, he never expected to encounter an alligator. His neighbor later told the police that, aside from the seven-foot alligator that had attacked Leonard, he hadn't seen another alligator in any of the canals of Palm Shores in more than a month.

It was around dusk when the incident occurred. As it happened so long ago and had only been the second fatal attack in Florida, to this date the details remain sketchy, lost to the passage of time. It had been four years since Sharon Holmes had been killed just outside of Sarasota. By this time, the residents of Florida had settled back upon the impression that Sharon Holmes's death in the jaws of an alligator had been an outright anomaly. Undoubtedly, the thought of running into an alligator in his backyard canal never crossed George Leonard's mind as he pounded away at some bracing and worked past sunset repairing his sagging dock.

And yet, time and again it's the unexpected and the unanticipated that always happens when dealing with wild animals. Leonard didn't realize that not only was there a healthy, seven-foot alligator swimming through his canal on that day, but also that she had two baby alligators by her side, which she was aggressively protecting.

No one saw the actual attack except Leonard himself, for he survived the initial encounter. With his lower right arm half-torn off, Leonard told the responding officers that an alligator had grabbed hold of his arm just as he was climbing back onto his dock. The alligator immediately went into a death roll, breaking his bones and leaving his right arm dangling in pieces of torn skin and ligaments from the elbow on down. The alligator let go after biting him and Leonard, bleeding severely and rapidly going into shock, still managed to get inside, tourniquet the arm, and have his wife call for an ambulance.

Because Leonard survived the attack, the initial report of the incident is that of an alligator bite, not a fatality. In fact, Leonard survived his wounds for three days, until the following Saturday, October 1, 1977, when he finally succumbed to blood clots, infections, and complications resulting from the severe trauma to his right arm. The doctors in Punta Gorda had attempted to surgically reattach the arm, but blood clots and infections developed and it was discovered during the autopsy that one of those clots had ultimately killed Leonard. He was still in the hospital recovering from the attack when he died.

The small female alligator that had bitten Leonard was killed the same night the attack took place. After patrolling the area for several hours, two local police officers located the seven-foot alligator swimming in one of the canals and shot her, point blank, in the head. One of Leonard's neighbors, Lee Anderson, wanted the police to "kill every gator you see!" The police informed him they weren't allowed to do such a thing, but they would search out, find, and kill the culprit alligator. At the time, alligators were still on the endangered-species list. When they finally found the animal, the police officers were probably a bit dumbfounded by the small size of the offending reptile.

It wasn't until a few days later that a Florida Fish and Game officer who was following up on the investigation discovered the underlying reason behind the attack. Hiding under a dock a few doors down from the incident's scene, the officer discovered two tiny baby alligators. With their distinctive yellow-and-black markings and no other female alligator to be found, it was obvious to the wildlife officer the two little gators belonged to the female that had charged and bitten Leonard.

The wildlife officer knew that female alligators fiercely defend their nests and offspring. Only birds—which are closely related to alligators—and all members of the crocodilian family have such a strong maternal instinct. Most reptiles, like Florida's loggerhead turtles, lay their eggs and disappear back into the wild, leaving their progeny to fend for themselves. Not alligators or crocodiles: Some have been recorded as remaining with their clutch for over a year.

George Leonard, hammering away at his dock, unknowingly became a threat to this ancient, primordial mother. From a clutch of up to four dozen, she only had two of her offspring remaining. Most of her clutch had succumbed to any number of predators—great blue herons, raccoons, bald eagles, osprey, tarpon, male alligators, and gar, among other indigenous wildlife—which are quick to seize and devour small, ten-inch reptiles.

Between eggs being preyed upon by everything from snakes to fire ants, and offspring being eaten by fish, feral pigs, and wading birds, fewer than twenty percent of any clutch might survive to maturity. With two offspring left, that dedicated alligator mother was not about to let Leonard take the last of her brood. Weighing less than one hundred pounds, she had no intention of killing him when she swam over and bit his arm. Leonard, after all, weighed almost twice as much as she did. In her eyes, he was after her babies and she was going to send him a message: "Stay away or else!"

In this regard, humans—most mammals, actually—and alligators behave remarkably alike. One of the most dangerous places for one to ever be is between a bear and her cubs, a bitch and her pups, an osprey and her chicks, a lioness and her lion cubs, or a mother and her child. In every instance, the mother will defend her offspring to death. It is instinctual for her to defend the babies from every apparent threat to their well-being. In the end, it was just the rare combination of Leonard's hammering on his dock at the very time that a female alligator had inadvertently swum into the canal with her last remaining babies.

Whenever anyone encounters these black-and-yellow-striped immature gators in the wild, or inadvertently stumbles across an alligator nest—active or inactive—he or she must leave the area immediately. In the water, it is impossible to outswim an alligator; on land, they can charge a person at a surprising speed. A seven-foot female alligator that is defending her offspring is a formidable, potentially lethal opponent. Because their mouths are teeming with infectious bacteria, even a small bite can ultimately prove fatal.

Of course, George Leonard had no intention of hurting this mother's offspring, but she couldn't possibly have understood it. She was just being a good, protective mother.

Sometime After Midnight

In a written statement to Deputy Sheriff Nick Parker on the same morning they discovered Grace Eberhart's body, Dena Black, a neighbor and dear friend, stated:

> *I am a close, personal friend of Grace Eberhart. About the first of June, she began to experience severe pain in her back. She found out she had a recurrence of cancer and was very distressed. She said to me at the doctor's office, "I'm not going to live like this."*
>
> *I knew that Grace was very depressed about her condition. Her husband Frank is mentally handicapped and her children live in the North, making everything seem worse. She never said anything about her feelings after that. She had been to several different doctors—quite a few visits from June until now. She had taken a lot of medications and had received radiation therapy on her hip and was scheduled to begin chemotherapy again soon.*

It happened on a Sunday, October 3, 1993. At 7:30 A.M. on that clear and cool fall day, the placid waters of Lake Serenity off Wildwood, Florida, were riled by an unknown disturbance. Jack Horrock, while reading his newspaper over a fresh cup of coffee and occasionally peering out of his lanai window, was the first person to note the unusual behavior of several alligators located in the middle of the small, one-and-a-half-acre lake. At first, he thought the gators must be mating, as they were actively splashing about and behaving in an untypical manner. But something was wrong with that scenario, contemplated Horrock, because he remembered that alligators always mate in the spring.

After watching the gators more closely for a few minutes, Horrock assumed they were playing with a dead heron or a pillow. After his wife, Beverly, handed him a pair of binoculars, Horrock saw that it rather appeared to be a human body the alligators were mauling. He couldn't believe his eyes. Nothing like this had ever happened in the quiet mobile-home community of Continental Country Club, located approximately five miles southeast of Wildwood. Horrock had no idea who the person floating facedown in the lake was, but without question he knew that the person was dead.

Minutes later, after learning that his neighbor, Francis (Frank) Eberhart had been desperately searching for his wife, Horrock notified the security guard, George Stine, about several alligators surrounding a body in Lake

Serenity. Horrock then called the Wildwood Police Department to report a Signal Seven (a fatal incident). The police were on the scene within minutes.

Deputy Sheriff D. Button arrived at Lake Serenity at 8:09 and, shortly thereafter, while standing on the banks, verified that three gators were indeed biting and mauling what appeared to be a male or female human body. Button called Sergeant Fergason and told him to contact EMS. He then phoned the Florida Game and Wildlife Commission. Those agencies' officials were soon on their way to Continental Country Club. As they awaited additional help, Button and Fergason taped off the area along the lake to secure the killing scene.

They found a solitary five-foot alligator near the bank and, believing the animal might have been involved in the attack, they shot and killed it. By 9:30 A.M., the police captain, the EMS personnel, several more police officers, and a Fish and Wildlife officer had already arrived and retrieved the body from the lake. Shortly thereafter, it was confirmed by the neighbors that it indeed was the mutilated remains of Grace Eberhart.

During the time the body had been in the water, the alligators had begun the process of tearing apart and devouring it. Eberhart's right arm had been completely torn off, as had the lower half of her left arm. There were numerous bite marks across the entire body and the neck had been severely broken.

Her husband, suffering from advanced Alzheimer's, was notified by the authorities that his wife's body had been found. He arrived on the scene later that morning, blessed his wife's body, and returned home to call the funeral home. The officers further questioned Frank Eberhart when he had last seen his wife alive but, because of his deteriorated mental condition, his answers were ambiguous and confusing, therefore of little help in trying to ascertain how the accident had come about.

Doing the best he could, Eberhart eventually told the investigating officers that his wife had been very depressed of late. The night before, sometime around 10 P.M., Grace Eberhart had come in to tell her husband where he would be able to find a large sack of money she had been saving. He informed the officers that his wife had recently learned that her cancer had returned. He also said he had told his wife it might be a good idea for her to go to the hospital again that Sunday, but she didn't respond. Grace Eberhart was living in constant pain, having already endured a mastectomy on her right breast, and due to the numerous tumors pressing on her spine, she had been living with a time-release patch containing the potent painkiller Fentanyl. Her oncologist had just informed Eberhart that this time her cancer was terminal.

*****

Eberhart loved Lake Serenity. Before she had been re-diagnosed, she used to stroll down to the edge of the lake to sit and read. Beside the lake and up a steep bank from the water's edge, the Homeowners Association had placed a small bench for the quiet enjoyment of the community's fifteen hundred residents. The Eberharts' modest double-wide manufactured home was located 150 yards from that bench.

However, since June after the distressing news of her cancer's return, Grace Eberhart had not returned either to read in the afternoon or to take in the morning paper as the sun rose over Central Florida. She withdrew into herself, despondent over her deteriorating health, her husband's worsening Alzheimer's, and the constant pain she endured. With her kids thousands of miles away, she suffered alone.

Like everyone living at Continental Country Club, Grace Eberhart knew that numerous gators frequented the lakes, ponds, and canals near Wildwood. A few days earlier, on Friday, October 1, two nuisance alligators had been shot and removed from one of the other country-club lakes by two state wildlife officers. The two gators had been behaving aggressively and, as a precaution, Fish and Wildlife had decided to kill the animals.

The residents in the small community had never fed the alligators and were well aware that feeding them is both dangerous and illegal. The alligators would come and go freely out of Lake Serenity via a canal that connected the lake to the much larger Lake Okahumpka to the west and a series of drainage marshes to the east, which eventually connected to a large, swampy area abutting Lake Harris. There were, and there still are, hundreds of alligators throughout the entire region. Years later, a boy would die in the jaws of an alligator not far from Lake Harris in the Dead River, which lay just east of Leesburg, less than twenty miles from Lake Serenity.

"She [Grace Eberhart] was such a nice lady," neighbor Beverly Horrock was later quoted.

"She was so sweet. She was such an angel and everybody who knew her thought the same," Mary Smith, another neighbor, told a newspaper reporter that same Sunday afternoon.

The entire incident shocked the quiet community and people wanted some kind of action taken against the numerous alligators. Over the next several days, altogether five gators were either shot or trapped out of Lake Serenity. One of them, a nine-foot, six-inch male, had both of Eberhart's arms in its stomach. The other reptiles had little else in their intestines besides sticks and acorns, verifying the fact that they were all hungry and none had been fed by the local residents.

But in the incident's summary report, some serious questions remained. Lieutenant Gene Newman was perplexed by the fact that the location of the initial bite mark, coupled with the lack of water in her lungs, seemed to indicate that Grace Eberhart had been in an upright position, wading in the water up to her chest, when she was attacked. The report speculated that perhaps she had tumbled down the steep embankment in the dark and rolled into the water. The only other viable explanation was that Eberhart was lying down right beside the edge of the water when the gator bit her. Both scenarios seemed highly improbable.

There were no indications of her being dragged down into Lake Serenity from the bench area, so that possibility was ruled out. Moreover, there had been her strange comments to her husband the previous night about where to find the money, as well as her comments made five months before to her friend Dena Black.

The autopsy verified that Eberhart had died from an alligator bite to the head and neck. It appeared that the attacking alligator had seized her and rolled, breaking her neck and instantly killing her. At the medical examiner's office, her autopsy clearly revealed to the coroner that Eberhart was indeed riddled with cancer. The pericardial sac surrounding the heart was circumscribed by a cancerous tumor; the left lung held a small tumor; there were additional tumors in her pancreas, liver, stomach, and in a portion of her right lung; her left breast, ovaries, uterus, urinary bladder, and tubes had already been removed from previous treatments. Given the extent of the current cancer, Grace Eberhart clearly had very little time left to live.

Ultimately, her death was ruled an accident. Frank Eberhart was never told about the alligator attack and was institutionalized shortly thereafter. Their children sold the mobile home.

Sometime after midnight on October 3, 1993, Grace Eberhart wandered out beneath the cool night sky of Central Florida and never made it back home to her failing husband and her lonely, fading life.

This painting by Ernest Simmons depicts a Florida panther at rest in a saw-palmetto grove, one of its favorite habitats.

The Florida Panther

"Do we save the Florida panther or do we save panthers in Florida? According to geneticists, the first option is no longer possible. I myself prefer the second option."

Walt McCown, Florida Game Commission Biologist

In December 1983, James Billie, then chairman of the Seminole tribe, went deer hunting on the Seminole reservation with a friend. Using a flashlight strapped to his rifle while hunting at night, Billie fired at a pair of green eyes reflected in the beam, and thereby killed one of the most endangered subspecies in the world: a Florida panther.

Working on a tip, a Florida wildlife officer investigated the incident the very next day. The officer found the hide from the dressed panther hanging over a cypress pole near Billie's home. Billie was charged with killing an endangered species. He fought the charge, stating he had every right to kill a panther—in this section we will refer to the puma by its common Florida name, panther—

on reservation land. Three years later, in 1986, Billie was ordered by the state's appeals court to stand trial for the shooting.

In October 1987, Billie went to court in LaBelle, Florida. Two charges were brought against the Native American: 1) James Billie had intentionally killed the animal and 2) the killed animal was an endangered subspecies— *Puma concolor coryi*, a protected species as defined by the Federal Endangered Species Act.

Because Native Americans have a legal right to harvest wild game on their land, so long as it is used for the tribe's sustenance, the first count proved moot. The second charge was all that mattered. If Billie's lawyers could prove the panther in question wasn't an endangered species, then Billie clearly had had a right to shoot the wild cat.

Therefore, on the second count—the killing of a *Puma concolor coryi* (the Florida panther's scientific name, after naturalist Charles B. Cory, who first described the animal in 1896)—Billie's defense team quickly went to work on what specific qualities define a subspecies. Their argument was whether or not the Florida panther was substantially distinct from the non-endangered western puma. If they could discredit the subspecies status of the Florida panther, then James Billie had to be found not guilty.

Historically, they argued, only three characteristics have set the Florida panther apart from its western cousins: 1) a distinctive cowlick, or mid-dorsal whorl found along the animal's back, located just behind the neck; 2) a crook in the end of the tail consisting of the last three vertebrae; and 3) a series of white flecks found on the shoulder, neck, and head region of the panther.

The white flecks were ultimately discovered to be discolorations from tick bites while the cowlick and crooked tail were later proven to be genetic mutations resulting from prolonged inbreeding within the remnant Florida population. The defense effectively undermined the case for the subspecies status of the Florida panther, stating that the similarities to the western counterpart far outweighed three tiny abnormalities caused by tick bites and inbreeding.

The prosecution argued the Florida panther does exhibit other differences from pumas, cougars, and mountain lions. *Puma concolor coryi* have slightly longer legs, smaller heads, slimmer tails, and a darker coat and tend to be, on average, slightly smaller than their western cousins. But do these variations make the Florida panther a true subspecies, or are they little more than local adaptations to a warmer, wetter environment? The defense argued that the panther isn't a subspecies at all, but merely an eastern version of the non-endangered western puma. In the end, Billie was acquitted on all charges.

The argument that acquitted Billie has been reused effectively several times since so as to turn prospective panther habitat over to agricultural and developmental interests. While there is an element of truth to this argument, local variations such as longer legs, smaller heads, and other Florida-panther adaptations are the same criteria used to designate subspecies status in a vast array of the world's fauna. Why should the *Puma concolor coryi* be handled any differently?

As disappointing as the decision to acquit Billie was, there were far more pressing issues facing the Florida panther. By 1995, realizing that inbreeding was slowly eroding away the forty to fifty remaining panthers through a combination of low-sperm counts and genetically induced heart disease, the U.S. Fish and Wildlife Service amended its panther policies. The panther was reclassified as an endangered remnant population, though still considered a distinct taxon, and Texas pumas were trucked in to infuse fresh genetic material into the handful of remaining Florida panthers. Within a few years, their population rebounded to an estimated seventy-five to eighty-five animals today.

Even with this increase in population, the Florida panther, no longer a "pure" strain, still survives in a tenuous and largely political landscape. It is a disheartening habitat filled with the perils of private-property rights, wavering endangered-species status, mercury poisoning, automobile accidents, feline leukemia, inbreeding, legal maneuvering, and big money. Given this current environment, the Florida panther's future is anything but certain.

It is ironic, but five years prior to James Billie's trial, in 1982 Florida schoolchildren chose the Florida panther as the state animal, rejecting both the manatee and the alligator in the process. Conservationists see the panther as a "flagship," or "umbrella species." Both terms mean that, under the panther's all-encompassing protection, humans indirectly afford equal protection to far less glamorous creatures like the humble gopher tortoise and the limpkin. Panthers, like grizzly bears and condors, are what many biologists refer to as charismatic mega-fauna. These exceptional animals tend to elicit a far greater emotional response from humans than do lesser creatures whose disappearance from the face of the earth isn't as important to us. Animals like the Englewood mole or the Seminole silt snail do not muster enough human empathy to grab our attention. If they perish, well, frankly, who cares?

But when we save vast tracts of land from agricultural or residential development for the endangered panther, we inadvertently save the land for every living thing within the panther's realm. If there is one thing that can be said about the Florida panther, it is one land-needy animal; this is a characteristic we should be thankful for.

Up until the invention of the transistor, very little was known about the Florida panther. I will discuss the invention of the transistor and its long-term ramifications on the world in this book's last chapters, but for now it's important to understand that, without the transistor, radio collars may have never been invented, and without radio collars, the panther might not have even made it into the twenty-first century.

By 1976, it was commonly held that the Florida panther was extinct in the wild. In 1980, the Florida Game and Fish Commission began studying the last-known viable habitat of the Florida panther, a respectable area of land that included Everglades National Park, Big Cypress National Preserve, Fakahatchee Strand State Preserve, the Seminole Indian Reservation, extensive private lands, and what is now the Florida Panther National Wildlife Refuge. All totaled, these lands comprise approximately 3.4 million acres.

In the early 1980s, sightings of the Florida panther may have been rare, but knowledge about its ranges, prey, biology, and behavior was nonexistent. If the panther were to be "saved," we would first have to know two things: 1) if there were any panthers left to "save," and if there were, 2) what would we need to do to "save them."

That's where the transistor came in. Radio telemetry, the electronic tracking and studying of panthers through the extensive use of radio collars, is what has kept panthers alive over the past thirty years. Biologists such as Ken Alvarez, David Maehr, Chris Belden,

Minuscule transistors, through the use of radio telemetry, help to save the few remaining Florida panthers.

and the dogs run by hounds-man Roy McBride, of Texas, came together in the early 1980s to begin the first scientific investigation of a very elusive subject—the Florida panther.

After investigating a thousand reports of sightings, tracks, and four confirmed fatalities—one by a turkey hunter, three by car accidents—Belden and McBride treed, darted, and collared the first Florida panther in February 1972 in Glades County. Panthers, behaving like other pumas, generally tree in response to being chased by dogs. It is an endearing behavior because a one-hundred-pound puma, head-to-head with three or four much smaller cat hounds, could easily stand and fight, potentially maiming and killing all of them. Leopards do exactly that when pursued by trained dogs in Africa. They generally run off for a short distance, then come to their senses, turn around, and kill all the pursuing hounds.

Panthers are quicker and stronger, but luckily for everyone less aggressive than leopards, so they settle for a nearby bald cypress or any suitable tree and scramble up. Once treed, the panther settles in and waits for the barking dogs to grow bored of the chase and leave. The barking of a well-trained hound changes timbre once it trees a cat. All the researchers need to do, then, is follow the barking to the base of the tree and look up. Many times the treed cat is a bobcat, which behaves in the same fashion, but persistence over the years has resulted in collaring the majority of all the remaining panthers in Florida.

When they reach the treed panther, researchers use a sedative-laden dart gun to shoot the animal in the rump or shoulder. The only remaining problem is how to get a huge, drugged-out cat safely down from a crook somewhere up a fifty-foot-high tree. Again in his informative book *Florida Panther: Life and Death of a Vanishing Carnivore*, David Maehr tells several humorous tales about these extrapolations. In the end, the solution came with the invention of an inflatable, portable crash bag, which dramatically reduced the incidents of injury to falling panthers.

Not that radio telemetry didn't and still does have its detractors. In 1983, the fledgling Florida Panther Recovery Team had its first major setback. After two years of successful tracking, darting, collaring, and re-releasing wild panthers, they accidentally killed one. It happened on January 17, 1983, after a successful treeing and darting of a healthy animal. The panther unexpectedly died while under sedation. Speculation was that the dart had hit an artery and the panther's heart had stopped beating.

The public outcry was swift and unforgiving. Some naturalists had been arguing that radio collars were already having a negative impact on a population already perilously close to extinction. The collars, they claimed, could interfere with the panther's ability to stalk and kill prey, or become entangled in vegetation while it was swimming—and thereby drown the cat—among a host of other fairly ludicrous assertions. Now, the very program that had been instigated to save the elusive animal had become responsible for killing one of them.

The Panther Recovery Team weathered the public outcry and, after months of meetings, re-evaluations, and a new set of capture guidelines, went back to collaring panthers within six months of that fatality, this time with a wildlife vet in tow. What they have since learned is indispensable information to the future of the Florida panther. Since the 1980s, collars have become smaller and the information retrieved from them increasingly sophisticated. When the batteries start to wear down, the cat is easily located (remember, these are tracking devices), treed, darted, inspected for disease, tooth wear, et cetera, given a new battery, and released. The transistor was, in fact, saving the cat.

What they learned early on was that the Florida panther's range was one of the largest for pumas in all of North America, some two hundred square miles per male. To put that number into perspective, the average lot size for a residential property in Cape Coral, Southwest Florida—which was once all prime panther habitat, by the way—is 10,000 square feet (100' X 100'). Currently, that one-fourth-acre parcel sells for approximately $50,000, plus or minus. There are four lots in every acre (and 43,560 square feet to an acre), with the excess square footage allowing for roadways, utility easements, drainage easements, and the like. There are 640 acres per square mile.

Using simple arithmetic, we can extrapolate that there are 128,000 acres in the two-hundred-square-mile range of a single male panther. Divided by four, those 128,000 acres could potentially produce 512,000 homesites. At $50,000 per homesite, a single Florida panther—which has no bankable assets aside from human empathy and its goodwill status as the designated official state animal—will need $25.6 billion worth of land to survive. This is the arithmetic of extinction.

Let's not forget that the male panther's range might include two or three females and possibly, if it has been lucky of late, a litter of three kittens. If you take that $25.6 billion and divide it by seven panthers roaming this hypothetical preserve, you arrive at a value of more than $3.6 billion per panther in habitat needs. That figure reflects the future development value of that land.

And that is the panther's problem, in a financial nutshell. Habitat extinction will ultimately lead to panther extinction, just as assuredly as bird hunts lead to the extinction of the passenger pigeon. Panthers need room to roam, and room in Florida is in high demand and short supply.

As demand continues to climb for future groves and subdivisions, a by-product of this rampant growth is habitat fragmentation. Fragmentation is a term used to describe circumstances when large, unbroken chunks of land are split up into smaller, splintered islands of woodlands surrounded by roads, orange groves, shopping centers, and neighborhoods. To get from island to island, the panther has to cross highways, navigate through backyards and buildings, and somehow remain undetected. Coyotes have proven very effective at this. Panthers tend to either pack up and leave or get hit by automobiles. Between 1994 and 2004, forty-five panthers were struck and killed by cars.

In the end, Florida's top predator, *Homo sapiens*, is far more land-hungry than the panther. Besides, man has the cash, the expertise, and the mechanical equipment to make it all happen. The economics of sustaining a viable Florida-panther population is presently untenable, **unless** we are willing to place some serious restrictions on future growth throughout Florida's vast interior.

It must be pointed out that the leading killer of panthers is panthers. After decades of study, scientists have estimated that intra-species mortality among Florida panthers results in thirty-seven percent of all panther deaths. Collisions with automobiles can and do kill panthers, but the underpasses built after radio telemetry showed where panthers cross Alligator Alley (Interstate I-75) have greatly reduced this risk. Neither James Billie nor anyone else is known to have willfully shot and killed a panther in decades. There can be little doubt, however, that quite a few deer hunters, mistaking the cat's dark-brown coat for that of a deer, have, in all likelihood, killed and carefully buried any number of panthers, but reporting these accidental shootings would be a rare event for obvious reasons. There are many other causes of death amongst Florida panthers, including rabies, infections, pseudo-rabies, feline leukemia, heart failure, and starvation, but far and away the leading cause is territorial panther-to-panther fighting.

This intra-species killing isn't entirely the panther's fault. Once a litter is born, the male kittens are doomed to destruction at the hands of the local warlord—the alpha-male animal in whose territory this blind, helpless one-pound kitten has been born. Unless the fathering panther is hit by a car or dies of disease within the next eighteen to thirty-six months, it or one of its nearby associates will sooner or later encounter the juvenile cat and, given the opportunity, kill it for trespassing on the older male's turf. Sometimes, as if to drive home its point, that older male will eat its young prey as well.

Young females stand a far greater chance of survival, provided there's enough prey to sustain them. Females usually share their much smaller ranges— approximately seventy-five square miles per cat—with other females without incident.

While it is true that, theoretically, the juvenile cat can wander off into the world to establish a new two-hundred-square-mile territory, its chances of finding a viable habitat in which to do so are presently nil. To the west, lie the exploding metropolises of Naples and Golden Gate. Unless it were well-moneyed and had a great credit rating, that juvenile cat's chances of setting up shop in an area that has some of U.S.'s highest real-estate prices are nonexistent.

To the south, lies Everglades National Park. With over two million acres, the park might first appear like an ideal place to look for a new home, but research has proven the Everglades to be ideal for alligators and aquatic-loving wildlife such as wading birds, bass, and water moccasins, but a poor habitat for panthers.

Ideally, panthers—whose numbers before the Spaniards' invasion are estimated to have been fourteen hundred in Florida—like the same habitats humans do: upland wetlands, coastal ridges, pine flatwoods, mixed-hardwood forest, tropical-hardwood hammocks, and most ironic of all, their best former habitat—the entire coastal ridge, from Jacksonville to Miami.... Could those ten million people living there at present please move somewhere else?

If you want to know where panthers thrive, think deer. Deer will traverse a swampy area, sometimes spending quite some time with their hooves submerged in the river of grass. Given the opportunity, however, most deer prefer dry feet and uplands to unbroken fields of saw grass. Panthers love habitat defined by slash pine, dense palmetto, and scrub oak and similar terrain. Submerged swamp is marginal panther habitat, at best.

Directly to the east of the current panther ranges, there sprawls the megalopolis of Lauderdale/Hollywood/Boca Raton/North Miami/Weston/ Homestead/ Miami...ad infinitum. No new available two-hundred-square-mile ranges in that direction, either. In fact, the current trend from both coasts is a steady, bulldozer-driven march toward the once swampy interior of South Florida by developers on either side of the state. The long-term consequences of this development will soon spell disaster for the coastal residents who allow it.

To the north of the current Florida-panther domain, lies the Caloosahatchee River. For reasons still unclear, the panthers, especially females, have made little progress north of the river. Perhaps it's because Florida panthers co-evolved with Florida alligators and they are instinctively aware that swimming wide stretches of open water could spell disaster. But panthers, although not prone to taking to the water, are still good swimmers and the width of the Caloosahatchee does not, at first glance, appear to be all that formidable.

Prior to the dredging of the Caloosahatchee, from Lake Hicpochee to Lake Okeechobee and the man-made creation of Canal C-43, the Florida panther had an eleven-mile-wide corridor through which it could gain access to northern and Central Florida. As it sits today, the Caloosahatchee forms an unbroken moat across a potential fertile region for future population expansion of the species. Over the long term, Floridians might look into filling in C-43 and re-establishing a viable wildlife corridor for the panther's northern expansion into areas such as the Babcock-Webb Wildlife Management Area (79,013 acres), the Babcock Ranch (with 91,000-plus acres, although currently under an option contract for future development), and the Fisheating Creek Wildlife Management Area.

Another potential option would be to build panther overpasses along the river similar to the underpasses built under Alligator Alley. Expensive, but not in light of the present value of $3.6 billion per cat. Since all of these potential northern habitats are more upland in nature, chances are the panther ranges would adjust downward accordingly. A male Florida panther's range might recede to under one hundred square miles per cat, possibly less.

In any event, it is easy to see that human beings, Florida's top predator, have managed to pen in the remnant population of panthers to a marginal habitat that appears to be able to support a stable population, for the moment at least, of roughly seventy to ninety cats. That's not enough of a viable population to preclude inbreeding and the eventual decline of the species. Avoiding that outcome would require a population between two and three hundred panthers, according to geneticists and scientists who have studied the issue.

In reality, only five percent of the total panther habitat available in pre-Columbian Florida still exists. That's why I have a problem with the estimate of fourteen hundred panthers in Florida around 1492. It has been calculated that in 1513 the deer population of Florida was four hundred thousand. Many of the Native American tribes who lived in Florida at that time derived much of their sustenance from the sea, such as the Caloosa Indians along the state's West Coast. The pressure on the deer herd was minimal and it is doubtful that panthers needed large, two-hundred-square-mile ranges during that era.

Using the same rough guide of 4.5 cats per one hundred square miles, we arrive at a pre-Columbian population of 2,429 cats (53,997 square miles divided by 100, times 4.5 pumas per range), although I suspect even this number is on the lower end of the actual number circa the 1500s.

Early settlers coming down into Florida from Georgia speak of wild cats being very numerous throughout the state. Although there has never been an authenticated Florida death at the hands of a panther, there are a number of anecdotal tales of human-versus-panther encounters.

Hernando de Soto, one of the earliest explorers of the peninsula, observed that the local Indians had to stand guard over their burial sites for fear that the resident panthers would eat their dead. Later in the 1700s, William Bartram, the Quaker naturalist who traveled deep into the heart of Florida, wrote the following: "They are very large, strong, and fierce, and are too numerous, and are very mischievous."

Bartram noted that the settlers of the time called them "tygers." Reminders of that name can still be found in Florida today, depicting locations such as Tiger Islands, Tiger Creek, and Tiger Hammock. Other colloquial Florida names for the panther are: swamp devils, swamp screamer, night crier, slough walker, and swamp lion.

From the mid-1800s onward, the die was cast for the remaining panther population. Unlike wolves, panthers do not instinctively avoid steel traps or human scent. Using dogs, which often accompanied the Florida Cracker families, the panther was easily treed and shot. Local Indians were paid to kill the cats and the cats' prey—the indigenous whitetail deer—to make way for cattle herds and other domestic livestock. A deadly cattle disease, the Texas fever tick, was being transmitted by deer. It finally reached Florida in the 1920s and, in 1939, an open season was declared on deer throughout the state. An estimated 8,428 animals were killed over four years of unlimited culling. With the deer gone, the panther population plummeted.

In 1887, a $5 bounty was posted for any panther scalps brought in. That bounty hung over the panther's head until the mid-1950s. In 1895, near Juno, on Florida's East Coast, two young boys were badly mauled by a female panther while in the process of skinning her kittens. The boys lived to tell about the incident, but neither the female panther nor her unfortunate litter survived.

Around 1900, in the sleepy southern settlement of Miami, it was reported that a panther ran alongside a young woman bicyclist who was carrying home a beef brisket in her basket. Although she was somewhat unnerved by the incident, in the end the cat elected not to attack.

In 1890, somewhere in either Alachua or Levy County, cattleman Bronson Lewis heard a disturbance in one of his cow pens. Investigating the commotion, Lewis soon discovered a full-grown panther crouched over a dead calf. The cat, defending its catch, immediately sprang on Lewis, knocking him to the ground.

During the ensuing battle, Lewis somehow managed to find a rope, wrap it around the cat's neck, and tie the attacking beast to a nearby stump. He then proceeded to beat the tethered cat to death using a fence rail. According to accounts, Lewis was literally torn to pieces in the life-and-death battle with the panther. Miraculously, he managed to survive, but it was months before he recovered and the damage inflicted by the struggle left him crippled for the rest of his life.

East of Ocala, by the Oklawaha River, it was said that a young woman, heavy with child, was walking back to her cabin after visiting her parents nearby. During the late 1800s, there was a common myth which held that Florida panthers have a particular affinity for pregnant women so, when the young woman heard the scream of a panther behind her, she quickly ran for the safety of her home.

In an effort to distract the cat, it is told that she started removing her clothing one piece at a time, hoping that the cat would stop to investigate the various garments and allow her enough time to make it home unharmed. Every time the young lady would drop a garment, she could hear the panther behind her snarling over the clothes, viciously tearing her clothing to shreds. By the time she arrived home, she was completely naked. The panther circled her cabin several times, but by the time her husband returned home later that night with his rifle, the panther had slipped back into the surrounding woods. Although entertaining, the credibility of this particular encounter appears to be questionable. I'm sure it made for good campfire stories circa 1882.

A bit earlier, circa 1870, another panther story out of Arcadia is probably a bit more reliable. On that year, seven local hunters decided to take their dogs out to replenish their lard supply with local hog fat. Electing not to bring along any guns, these hardened pioneers used their dogs to hunt down the feral pigs, pinning them to the ground, whereupon the men would slit their throats to kill them. In today's world, such a primitive methodology would appear incredulous, but we have to remember that in 1870 gunpowder and ammunition were scarce and expensive, and slitting a hog's throat was free.

In any event, it is said that the men, who had been on horseback following some distance behind the dog pack, soon discovered that their dogs had treed a panther in one of the local hammocks. Realizing they wouldn't be able to kill a panther with a knife, they sent one of the men back into Arcadia to fetch a rifle. Shortly thereafter some of the dogs broke off and started pursuing a second panther in the same hammock. This time, the cat elected to stand its ground and started engaging the dogs in a ferocious fight. Dogs were extremely valuable to settlers in the 1800s and losing a single dog was unacceptable to the five remaining hunters. It is said that one of them, Thomas Albritton, walked right into the mêlée and, using only his powerful fist, knocked the panther down to the ground. He then took out his hog-killing knife and slit the panther's throat, killing it instantly. Shortly thereafter, when the rifle arrived, they turned their attention to the treed cat and shot it dead.

They beheaded both panthers to claim their bounty and returned to the Albritton household, where they held a feast in honor of the hero of the day, Albritton himself, and his sledgehammer fist. The menu, according to *DeVane's Early Florida History*, consisted of "vegetables from the cow-penned garden, grated corn pone, potato pone, cassava pone, buttermilk and curd, homemade rice and red-eye gravy, corn syrup and honey." Although a somewhat fanciful story, it shows one just how tough Florida Crackers must have been to take on a puma one-on-one barehanded.

Another tale from that era, though slightly earlier still in 1858, hails from Sarasota, on the state's western coast. A local settler was splitting and squaring logs for the floor of his cabin along Oak Creek, just east of town. His young daughter, aged twelve, was washing dishes on a table in their yard while her younger brother played beneath it. A panther dashed in from the surrounding bush and grabbed the boy by the foot. The daughter bravely grabbed her brother and tried to pull him away from the wild cat. The panther quickly turned on the girl but the commotion soon drew the attention of the father, mother, and their two dogs.

Feeling outnumbered, the panther abandoned its attack on the twelve-year-old and ran under the crawl space beneath their cabin. The man then grabbed the adz he had been using all morning, raised a floorboard that had yet to be nailed down, and slew the cowering panther with his adz. It is claimed to be the only known puma death at the hands of an adz.

It is interesting to note that the Sarasota attack, once again, points to the puma's preference for children. Although no one was killed in the incident, we have to accept the likelihood that, if Florida increases its resident panther population, there is always the remote chance that, sooner or later, someone will be fatally attacked by a panther somewhere in the state. Denying such a probability is foolish. Are we willing to accept the risks associated with the reintroduction of the panther into larger ranges, knowing that sooner or later someone is likely to be killed by one…?

The answer should be a simple Yes. We accept the risks inherent in every high-speed lane added to the interstates and highways across our peninsula, yet we recoil at the very notion that we might lose a single human being to an alligator, shark, or panther. In 2004 alone, 2,936 Floridians died in automobile accidents. If we are genuinely concerned about Floridians' welfare, then we should ban automobiles. Road rage alone kills more Floridians annually than all animal attacks combined. It is social conditioning that allows people to accept over sixteen thousand intra-species human murders in the U.S. in 2004 alone. These deaths have come at the hands of a far more dangerous animal, *Homo sapiens*, though we still shudder at the thought of a single panther fatality. Of course, should a panther mortally attack someday, the offending animal must be destroyed, but we must stop there.

We should rejoice in the fact that panthers aren't leopards and that our native alligators aren't Nile crocodiles. If panthers were as prone to eating humans as leopards, the death count during the early history of Florida would have numbered in the thousands. Pumas were stronger, larger, and more ubiquitous in the Sunshine State during its early settlement. Luckily for all of us, panthers are reclusive cats and tend to shy away from development and human interaction. If American alligators had the same aggressive nature of their African cousins, the Nile crocodile, the death count from alligator attacks could top one hundred a year, instead of sixteen over a fifty-year-plus span.

Another promising development over the past decade has been a change in policy to provide better deer-browsing habitat. After the Fakahatchee Strand was logged in the 1940s, the deer population briefly flourished because the high canopies of the ancient cypress trees were removed, thus opening up the forest floor to new growth and ample browse. Over the decades, the trees grew taller once again and the deer population fell accordingly. Nowadays, the U.S. Fish and Wildlife Service conducts controlled burns and has even gone so far as to cut down cabbage palms, in order to maintain a healthy under-story and open, grassy areas to help the deer population increase.

Unlike panthers, white-tail deer have tiny home ranges. In one study, it was found that, given ample forage, up to seventeen adults used 480 acres, while the two bucks from that herd used 1,116 and 2,591, respectively. Compare these numbers to 4.5 panthers per 128,000 acres and you will see that, given half a chance, those same 128,000 acres could potentially hold 4,600 deer. A full-grown panther can survive on one deer kill per week. Improve the deer population within its current range and you might save the Florida panther. Think of deer as panther fertilizer, if it helps.

Why do we need Florida panthers? Because, as David Maehr puts it near the end of his *The Florida Panther:...*, "If we allow a self-sustaining population of panthers to exist in Florida, there may be some reason to think we can learn to manage ourselves as well. Instead of gauging human prosperity by our ability to sustain economic growth, we will learn the wisdom of a sustainable, dynamic balance as exhibited by Florida panthers. If nothing else, the panthers we studied demonstrate that coexistence with people is possible. A lasting balance can be built on the efforts of agencies and people who understand that creativity, honesty, and imagination are the keys to success. With changing times and changing paradigms, there is no need yet to write the panther's epitaph."

There are new resources evolving in Florida, which have given us a new, unforeseen weapon in the fight to save the panther. They are called HABs, which is short for Harmful Algae Blooms. Over the course of this writing in late 2005, HABs had just begun to wreak havoc on cities along the Gulf Coast and, to a lesser extent, along sections of Florida's East Coast as well.

Harmful Algae Blooms include outbreaks of red tide (*Karina brevia*) as well as toxic blue-green algae. What do these have to do with panthers? The answer is, land management and the repercussions of unchecked growth.

As coastal communities—from Tarpon Springs to Marco Island along the gulf, and Jacksonville to Miami on the east—approach complete build-out, land developers look increasingly at the last remaining untouched acreage in the state, Central and South-Central interior Florida. Babcock Ranch, with almost ninety-two thousand acres, is representative of this current trend. Farther north, developments near Orlando, such as Celebration, have already gained a solid foothold and continue to expand.

Presently, there are options by the Bonita Bay Group for large tracts of former sugar holdings. Entire cities are being mapped out and planned, with populations of over fifty thousand residents, complete with schools, hospitals, and commercial developments. The watersheds are already strained to the breaking point with excessive nutrient runoff, which in turn feeds into nonstop, year-round red-tide outbreaks.

As I write this, a HAB of red tide off Sarasota has remained in place for ten straight months. A toxic blue-green algae bloom in the Caloosahatchee River has killed most of the estuary and the abundant sea life within it. As we allow the interior of the state to be developed, we are inadvertently killing the coasts. Once these PUDs (Planned Urban Developments) get firmly entrenched, the runoff will increase and environmental degradation will continue to haunt coastal cities and towns.

There are health risks involved as well. Breathing red tide is dangerous, especially to people with asthma or respiratory problems. Blue-green algae can cause skin lesions and rashes. The endangered manatee is known to succumb to long-term red-tide exposure, and their reaction to the blue-green algae bloom is still unknown.

As the water and air quality of the coastline collapses, property values, tourism, marinas, fishing interests, and a host of related industries will equally crumble. There is an outside chance that the entire Gulf of Mexico could eventually become a dead zone.

A beautiful Florida panther from a 1930s postcard.

For the first time in human history, we might want to seriously consider putting ourselves under the panther's "umbrella" of protection. With every 128,000 acres we carve out for Florida's top carnivore, we save those two hundred square miles from the most dangerous mechanical predator in the state—the bulldozer.

Every hour, almost twenty acres of Florida land are cleared. Every day, somewhere around 450 acres are readied for condos, townhouses, and shopping centers. Every year, nearly 164,000 acres are lost to development. At the present rate of growth, we are losing Florida's remaining cattle ranches and wilderness at twice the rate of destruction of the Amazon rain forest.

I'm not going to give you any advice on how to handle a deadly panther encounter in the wild because, unless you're a biologist with the radio-collar tracking device in hand, your chances of seeing one of the approximately ninety Florida panthers in the wild are even fewer than winning the Florida Lotto. And, should you find yourself fortunate enough to actually see this extremely rare carnivore, the chances of that panther's attacking you are too low to calculate.

As our coastal communities struggle with water pollution from an already stressed environment, and our lush, subtropical state disappears beneath an endless onslaught of asphalt and rooftops, it may not be as much a question of our saving the panther, but of the panther's saving us.

Wrong Place, Wrong Time

The eternal, gut-wrenching enigma surrounding death and how it unexpectedly happens to any of us—why she decided to go out to pick up a gallon of milk that evening instead of waiting until morning; why the other driver ran the stoplight and broadsided her; why he chose to go out fishing alone on such a windy day and how they found the capsized boat first, then the body; or what could possibly have compelled them to finish the back nine on such a stormy day and how the bolt that killed them came out of nowhere—will never cease to mystify us.

The devastating impact of sheer coincidence always leaves us reciting the dissociative mantra of accidental death, "They were at the wrong place at the wrong time. It was tragically meant to be."

In reality, to be killed by an alligator is no different from any other accidental death. In this particular case, no one had been feeding the alligator. The victim hadn't been doing anything out of the ordinary, behaving recklessly or throwing caution to the wind; taunting or teasing the beast into attacking; he hadn't had any idea the beast was even there. It just happened. An opportunity presented itself to a two-hundred-million-year-old predator and it promptly acted on it. A man was seized, drowned and, had it not been for another's intervention, he would have been eaten, just as would a deer, a raccoon, or another smaller alligator be preyed upon.

This was the case in the death of Kevin Albert Murray of North Port, Florida. Murray was a forty-one-year-old consummate bachelor. He had just finished mowing the lawn at 13170 Irwin Drive in the northwest section of Port Charlotte, on a sweltering afternoon in mid-July 2005. He was tired, sweaty, and looking forward to an ice-cold beer and a weekend of fishing, reading, and good old-fashioned relaxation. After he completed the yard work, Murray decided to take a quick jump in the cool, brackish waters of the canal right behind the house. One jump into the Apollo Canal, and then it would be time to head home. Regrettably, that jump would also prove to be his last.

Murray was in the prime of his life. An avid outdoorsman and a skilled fisherman, Murray had moved to Florida decades before, along with his mother and father. He knew better than most about the potential dangers posed by Florida's largest reptile. Typically, Murray would have used the backyard shower at 13170 Irwin Drive to cool off, but he had been known to leap into the canal before. Murray must have thought, What are my chances of splashing down next to a hungry, four-hundred-pound, twelve-foot, two-inch alligator? It had been a calculated risk, but also an extreme long shot that anything that happened shortly after could actually happen.

Kevin Murray had been employed by Quality Lawn Care for the past three years. They serviced most yards along Irwin Drive, all but one which abutted the Apollo Waterway. That canal flowed westward, eventually joining the dark, tannin-stained waters of the Myakka River. The Myakka's headwaters lie in Sarasota County, some twenty miles north of where the attack took place. The entire freshwater river system teems with hundreds of native alligators. In 1988, four-year-old Erin Glover had been killed in Hidden Lake less than five miles from where Murray died on that July evening. Hidden Lake is an offshoot of the same system. Alligators were a common sighting along the Apollo Waterway, and those were truly wild alligators—never fed and very large.

It was around 7 P.M. when Kevin Murray made his single, fateful leap. The neighbors watched in horror as, within seconds of Murray's hitting the water, a massive gator grabbed him by the arm and immediately pulled him under. Murray, fighting for his life, miraculously managed to retake the surface for one last gasp of air. Then the leviathan, weighing almost three times as much as he did, submerged again. No one saw either Murray or the gator that had grabbed him for almost an hour, nor had they even noticed the large gator swimming in the area prior to the attack. With the alligator's ability to hold its breath for hours, Murray had no way of knowing what lay beneath the still surface of that canal.

The Charlotte County Sheriff's Office received the 911 call at 7:17 P.M. and deployed to the scene shortly thereafter. State alligator trappers Tracy Hansen and Bo Davis pulled up to Irwin Drive at 7:40 P.M., preparing to hunt for Murray and the alligator all night if necessary. It was no longer necessary: Within minutes of their arrival, the alligator resurfaced holding a lifeless Kevin Murray in its powerful jaws. It was across the canal, hiding in some bushes as the sunlight faded. With its prey drowned and defenseless, the alligator was in no hurry to proceed.

The two trappers, along with two Fish and Wildlife officers, boarded a boat and motored toward the animal. As they approached, the alligator released Murray's body. Taking advantage of this opportunity, they grabbed the body and returned it to shore, knowing they would soon be back to kill the offending gator. It was clear to everyone involved there would be no rescue, just a body's retrieval.

Around 8:15 P.M., all four were back in the boat shining lights across the water's surface looking for the killer. The beams soon picked up the bull alligator's highly reflective eyes. Using an arrow and crossbow with a barbed dart connected to a strong nylon line back to the bow, in the same fashion as one would a harpoon and line, the trappers shot the alligator in its midsection.

They dragged the animal, twisting and thrashing about wildly, back toward the boat.

One of the wildlife officers shot the gator, point blank, in the head with his revolver. It was over. They tied a noose around the alligator's head and started to troll it back to the dock along the Apollo Waterway. Within a few minutes of being shot, the alligator regained consciousness and started rolling and thrashing about for a second time. The point-blank gunshot to the head had only stunned the beast. The officer fired a second round into the alligator's skull just behind the left eye. This time, the bullet found its mark.

Within hours, it was all over. Kevin Murray was dead. The animal that had killed him was also dead. To this day, the Myakka River still flows idly out to sea and alligators patrol the river from above Lake Myakka to its mouth in Charlotte Harbor.

Everyone who knew Murray spoke well of him. His mother and father, along with fellow employees, friends, and relatives were heartbroken. Death had found Kevin Murray without his having ever beckoned her; nothing more, nothing less.

Somewhere in the world at this very moment, someone else might be found in the wrong place at the wrong time. He or she will, likewise, perish and death's enigma will perpetuate itself. At times, life can be very unfair.

One Bite of a Bull Shark

One bite: that was all it took to kill Thadeus Kubinski on a disturbing Wednesday afternoon a few days before Labor Day weekend. It wasn't the bite of a sixty-pound blacktip, nor the chomp of a one-hundred-pound lemon shark that killed Kubinski; it was the devastating bite of a four-hundred-pound bull shark, which left him bleeding to death ten feet off his dock on Boca Ciega Bay, Florida.

"Probably the most dangerous fish, pound for pound, in the ocean," said Bob Hueter, director of the Mote Marine Laboratory's Center for Shark Research, in an interview with Kevin Lollar of the *Fort Myers News-Press* in 2001. "They (bull sharks) have the highest recorded level of testosterone of any animal tested," Hueter added. "What we don't know is if that correlates with aggression. It might."

Anna Kubinski, who was swimming alongside her husband in the Intracoastal Waterway when the attack occurred, would have little argument with the aggressive nature of bull sharks. She watched in horror as the monster shark swam up and bit her husband in his right side mere minutes after he leapt into the bay from their dock. The powerful jaws and serrated teeth of the shark left numerous puncture wounds, extending from just under Kubinski's armpit all the way down his upper hip. Given the size of the bite to Kubinski's torso, it was all but impossible to stop the hemorrhaging. Kubinski bled to death in minutes.

Most serious shark bites, such as the near-surgical amputation of a person's arm or leg, afford a first-responder the opportunity to put a tourniquet around the limb and slow down, possibly even stop, the bleeding. But a large bite to the torso affords no such opportunity. Kubinski had been stabbed with fifty small daggers in a 1/400th of a second. The wounds were too many, too deep, and too uncontrollable. Kubinski died of exsanguination, or blood loss, at the scene. It was speculated that, even if paramedics had been waiting on the dock when Kubinski was pulled back out of the water, his chances of survival would have been next to zero.

The attack occurred in murky-water conditions around 4 P.M. The dock was located behind Kubinski's house overlooking Boca Ciega Bay. The home is in St. Petersburg Beach, west of St. Petersburg. After a long, hot day, the couple decided to take a brief dip before dinner. Anna had noticed a school of jumping mullet nearby, but never thought those mullet might have been fleeing the jaws of a large shark.

Anna elected to enter the water via their dock ladder while her husband decided to jump in. It was the last leap he ever took. Some scientists felt that Kubinski's large splash, coupled with the abundance of prey in the nearby waters, might have inadvertently attracted the attention of the surrounding shark. Reacting instinctively to the sudden commotion of his jump, the shark swam directly toward Kubinski and engulfed him in its mouth.

The shark instantly realized it was biting into something quite unlike the mullet it had probably been feeding on and spit Kubinski out. Although freed from the jaws of the shark, Kubinski's injuries were horrific enough to kill him.

Hueter, in a follow-up interview with the *Fort Myers News-Press*, said the following about bull sharks and humans: "They're one of the big-three species that are a concern to humans. The other two are tiger sharks and great whites. All three reach large size, are worldwide in distribution, and have teeth that are evolutionarily designed for shearing—taking out chunks of flesh—as opposed to grabbing and holding. They can cause serious damage.

"The difference between bull sharks and the other two is that bulls are more coastal, so they get in contact with humans more on a day-to-day basis. This is probably not a case of an aberrant shark. Bulls have been found in Boca Ciega Bay for decades or centuries. Hundreds and thousands of people have been swimming with bull sharks and didn't even know it."

This particular incident is similar to most fatal California shark attacks. In California, where the water is much cooler, the predominant species is the great white. Time and again, those immense sharks, some of them weighing two tons or more, will accidentally bite a surfer or abalone diver only to spit him or her out after it realized the catch was not the harbor seals or sea lions they had been mistaken for.

Like Rodney Fox, who was bitten by a great white in southern Australia, some of those bites require more than four hundred stitches to repair. If medical attention isn't given immediately, the unchecked blood loss usually proves fatal. Sharks will swim off thinking they've made a harmless mistake; hardly harmless, because the victim generally dies.

After Kubinski's attack in 2000, there was talk about closing St. Petersburg's beaches over Labor Day weekend…a familiar echo of the fictional town of Amity, New York, after the shark attacks in Spielberg's classic film *Jaws*. However, since the chances of another fatal attack were astronomically low, all beaches along Florida's West Coast remained open that year for the last big summer holiday. No one was attacked.

Thadeus and Anna Kubinski had swum in the Intracoastal Waterway since they first moved into their home in 1984, some sixteen years before. Neighbors interviewed after the attack said they didn't recall ever seeing any sharks prowling along the canals and waterways of Boca Ciega Bay. Chuck Maines, who had lived in the area for forty-seven years, put it best: "It's just a fluke. It's really, really strange."

Shark attacks are really, really strange and very, very rare…but one should not try telling that to Anna Kubinski.

He Must Have Wandered Off

The last few years of Samuel Stewart Wetmore's life had not gone well. Seventy years old, divorced, and suffering from the onset of senile dementia, Wetmore had withdrawn from life, dissolving into a private world of fading memories and despairing loneliness. Sometimes the neighbors would discover him wandering the streets of East Venice, Florida, appearing lost and confused. They would kindly return him to his home on Whippoorwill Drive and feel sorry for him. Who wouldn't...?

Eight months earlier, his son, Michael Yansan-Wetmore, had intentionally relocated to Venice from up North along with his family to help care for his aging father. He later told the police that, since his father's dementia had developed about one year earlier, he seldom came out of his room. Old Wetmore, who had moved to Venice in 1989, used to love photography, humorous writing, and taking long, leisurely strolls to nearby Woodmere Park. Now he had become a recluse. To all who knew him, it was sad to see what was happening.

When the Venice police knocked on Sam Wetmore's front door at Whippoorwill Drive the morning of May 4, 2001, Michael Yansan-Wetmore was quick to answer. The police asked him if he knew where his father was. Yansan-Wetmore let them in and told them his father was probably still sleeping in his bedroom, just as he always was. But, upon checking, the son found the bedroom empty. Then they told Yansan-Wetmore about the incident.

The last person to see the elder Wetmore alive had been the son's girlfriend, who had checked in on him sometime on Wednesday afternoon. Sometime between that afternoon, May 2, and Friday morning, May 4, 2001, Sam Wetmore, without anyone's noticing, must have wandered off alone into the surrounding neighborhood. No one remembered seeing him leave on Thursday night nor witnessed the actual attack. How Wetmore ended up in a small retention pond several blocks from his home will forever remain a mystery.

The residents living along Bellaire Drive were familiar with alligators. Besides the two retention ponds, which had always held a few resident alligators, the creek that ran just north of the ponds had a name anything but misleading: Alligator Creek. In a door-to-door survey of the residents conducted after the tragedy, only one household could ever remember observing anyone feeding the numerous gators behind their homes. That feeding had been done by some careless renters who had long since moved away. All residents of the small subdivision respected the local alligators and Fish and Wildlife determined it was highly doubtful that any illegal feeding had factored into the death of Sam Wetmore.

It was a resident who lived at 516 Bellaire Drive, William Brennan, who called 911 to report the Signal Seven (a fatal incident) on Friday, May 4, at 10 A.M. A few other residents of Bellaire Drive had noticed something unusual floating in the pond the day before, but thought it was another alligator with something stuck over its head, like a plastic bag or a piece of torn cloth. There was another slightly smaller alligator swimming nearby the one with the bag stuck over its head, but no one had actually paid much attention.

On that Friday morning, as the sun rose over East Venice, Brennan realized it wasn't an alligator at all floating in the pond, but a body. The plastic bag turned out to be Sam Wetmore's shirt. Brennan called the police. The first Venice officer arrived on Bellaire Drive shortly after ten and confirmed that someone was floating facedown in the pond. From the outset, it had been obvious that any rescue attempt would prove futile. Whoever was floating in the retention pond, had been dead for quite some time.

As they surveyed the scene, at first the police and wildlife officers naturally leaned toward the assumption that this had been an accidental drowning, not an alligator attack. The small gator guarding the corpse was hardly the kind of animal that fit the typical Florida-alligator-attack profile. According to the necropsy conducted the following day, the gator was an eight-foot, four-inch female weighing a mere 130 pounds. She was carrying undeveloped eggs inside and was probably going to be busy laying a new clutch soon. Aside from being blind in one eye and missing her right front foot (probably from fighting), she was in good health. Several weeks after the accident, a dozen yearling alligators were discovered near an old nest hidden in the bulrushes. It was concluded that the hatchlings were probably hers.

Unless protecting their nests or hatchlings, attacks by female alligators on full-grown human beings are extremely rare. Most gator attacks involve large bull alligators, oftentimes weighing in excess of four hundred pounds. Surely Wetmore must have drowned first, the authorities speculated, and was later mauled by the female gator. Of the twenty-five confirmed deaths involving alligators in the state of Florida ever since records started being compiled in 1948, nine have been ruled as death by drowning. Sometime after the drowning, the dead body had eventually been mauled or mutilated by scavenging alligators. It was understood by everyone involved on that Friday morning that the autopsy would ultimately determine what had happened to Sam Wetmore.

The police had little trouble scaring the small gator away from the body and proceeded to retrieve the victim. It was in poor condition when they finally brought it back to shore. The left arm had been torn off, the right arm badly chewed, and there were multiple abrasions, lacerations, and puncture wounds throughout the body. It was apparent that it had been in the pond for quite some time. It was positively identified as Sam Wetmore by a neighbor. Wetmore's son was then notified of the accident.

But to the surprise of everyone involved, Wetmore's subsequent autopsy ruled out drowning and confirmed that somehow an alligator had indeed killed the elder. Perhaps Wetmore had stumbled down the steep bank in the darkness and fallen into the pond, and before he could scramble back out, the female gator might have grabbed his left arm in defense of her hatchlings and torn it off in a death roll.

Whatever had happened, the autopsy indicated that Wetmore had bled to death due to his traumatic injuries. That could mean only one thing: what killed him had been an alligator attack and not accidental drowning.

Much mystery surrounding the incident still remained. Although he wasn't legally drunk, toxicology confirmed that Wetmore had been drinking prior to being attacked. Although he had always worn his glasses, they were later found on top of a dresser in his bedroom at home on Whippoorwill Drive. There was no blood found on the bank surrounding the pond and, to this day, no one has any idea when the actual attack occurred. Because no one witnessed anything, the general theory is that it happened sometime in the middle of the night. The medical examiner placed his time of death roughly twelve hours before Wetmore's body had first been discovered, but that timeline doesn't really add up.

Wetmore had last been seen by his son's girlfriend on Wednesday afternoon. The residents of Bellaire Drive were confident they had seen something floating in the pond early Thursday morning, but the actual body wasn't discovered until Friday a little after 9 A.M. No one saw him—not his son Michael, his son's girlfriend, or a neighbor—all day Thursday.

In his final summary, Sergeant Mike Frantz didn't suspect foul play nor felt that anyone had been negligent with regard to Wetmore's demise. It was concluded that he had simply gotten up sometime after dark on Wednesday night or early Thursday morning, and in his advanced state of dementia, wandered alone out of the house. A combination of drinking and his failing mental state caused him to journey well over two blocks from his home, where it appeared he must have slid down a steep embankment into the retention pond.

The resident female alligator, upon hearing a loud splash in her habitat, proceeded to head over and investigate the possibility that whatever had made the splash would be edible. Shortly thereafter, she must have come upon a confused and vulnerable old man. Even though Wetmore outweighed her by forty pounds, the female alligator must have

217

chosen to try and take down this strange animal that had fallen into her domain. Perhaps Wetmore was splashing around, trying to regain his balance and climb back out of the pond. Any kind of erratic behavior in the water naturally attracts nearby alligators; this case proved to be no exception. There is also the strong possibility that the female alligator was just defending her clutch against this large, bipedal invader.

After Wetmore's body was taken to the Sarasota Medical Examiner's office, Trapper John French was called to the scene by Fish and Wildlife. At first, he tried to use a baited-hook approach to capture and kill the female gator, but it didn't work. He then took out a crossbow device with a sturdy line attached to it, and proceeded to shoot the animal with the barbed arrow. Using the attached line, he pulled her back toward him and killed her. Adding to all other inconsistencies to this story is the fact that no human remains were ever found in her stomach, leaving the question as to where Wetmore's left arm had vanished. It was then speculated that there may well have been a larger gator involved, but for the time being it was nowhere to be found.

Still believing that another animal must have been involved in the death, French left a baited hook out for four days in the vicinity of the pond. No other alligator ever showed to take the bait. On the fifth day, the baited hook was removed. The neighbors never reported seeing any large alligator return to the pond during the weeks and months that followed.

Michael Yansan-Wetmore summed up the situation best in an interview, a few days later, with the *Sarasota Herald-Tribune*: "I have no idea [what happened] and never will. All I know is, he was in the wrong place at the wrong time. Two species collided in the night and they both lost."

A pregnant female alligator and a reclusive, senile old man who must have wandered off into the dark of night.... Michael Yansan-Wetmore was right: They both lost.

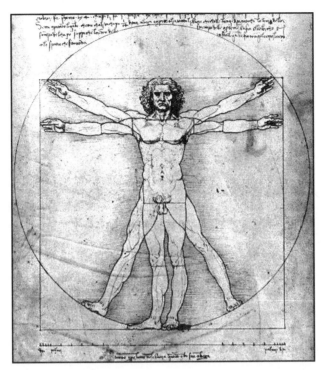

Leonardo Da Vinci's *Vitruvian Man.*

EARTH'S TOP PREDATOR: MAN

Roughly 170,000 years ago, somewhere in South Africa a woman gave birth to a new humanoid species—*Homo sapiens.* This contemporary theory of our origins is known as the "Eve," or "Mitochondrial Eve" theory. Using the mitochondrial DNA technique, scientists Allan Wilson, Mark Stoneking, and Rebecca Cann have determined that all living peoples are descendants of a single mother who lived in the broken savannahs of South Africa approximately fifty thousand generations ago. This new species was the latest installment in a long line of erect-walking apes, which introduced the evolutionary journey of mankind in Africa over five million years ago.

There were other living species of humanoids on earth at the time of "Eve's" birth: the *Neanderthals, Homo erectus,* and *Homo floresiensis,* the latter being a new human species whose remains were recently discovered in a cave on the island of Flores in Indonesia. The newcomers from Africa, *Homo sapiens,*

219

seldom, if ever, interbred with their contemporaries, whereupon all other variations on the humanoid form, over time, became extinct. Beginning 120,000 years ago, *Homo sapiens* migrated north and eastward out of Africa toward the Middle East, Europe, Asia, and Australia.

Our closest relatives—the chimpanzees and gorillas—were left behind in the equatorial forests of Africa. These African apes, especially the pygmy chimps known as bonobo chimpanzees, still share almost ninety-nine percent of our DNA. Another distant cousin of *Homo sapiens* is the orangutan of Southeast Asia. Over the past century of observation and research, we have learned that these wild animals use tools, are capable of recognizing themselves in the mirror (i.e., have a rudimentary sense of self-awareness), and have been known to murder members of competing, rival chimp bands.

Linguists have taught

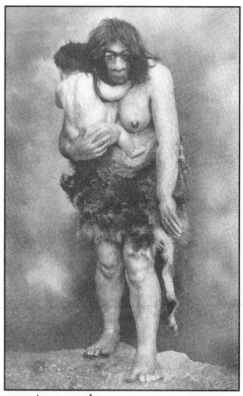

Looking at this re-creation, it's easy to see why *Homo sapiens* chose not to interbreed with the *Neanderthals*.

chimps and gorillas to use sign language and, like us, they share another common human emotion: they mourn. A mother chimp, upon losing a newborn at birth, will sometimes carry the baby for days as if personally lamenting her child's loss. In the years ahead, provided that threatened wild chimpanzee and gorilla populations survive, there can be little doubt that additional discoveries will unveil even more similarities between humans and our closest living relatives—the great apes.

Similarities notwithstanding, humans were still unique. Although chimps and apes display some limited ability at tool-making and intertribal communications, *Homo sapiens* have, without question, evolved light-years beyond them. Somewhere around 100,000 years ago, it is hypothesized that the

Hominids

Earliest Hominids

Aegyptopithecus
Sahelanthropus tchadensis
Orrorin tugenensis
Ardipithecus
- *Ardipithecus kadabba*
- *Ardipithecus ramidus*

Australopithecus
- *Australopithecus anamensis*
- *Australopithecus bahrelghazali*
- *Australopithecus afarensis*
- *Australopithecus africanus*
- *Australopithecus garhi*

Paranthropus
- *Paranthropus aethiopicus*
- *Paranthropus boisei*

Homo Genus
- 'Handy Man' – 2.4–1.5 million years ago (MYA)
  Homo habilis
- 'Peking Man' – 1.8–0.7 MYA
  Homo erectus
- *Homo ergaster* – 1.8–1.24 MYA
  Also proposed as "Homo erectus ergaster"
- Heidelberg Man – 800 thousand years ago (TYA)
  Homo heidelbergensis
- *Homo sapiens idaltu* – 160 TYA
- 'Hobbit' – 12 TYA
  Homo floresiensis
- 'Neanderthal Man' – 250–30 TYA
  Homo neanderthalensis
- Humans – 200 TYA–present
  Homo sapiens

221

human race discovered and mastered the making and use of fire. As our species migrated farther northward, our tool-making ability improved exponentially.

The physical earth was, and in all probability still is, oscillating between freezing-glacial and warm inter-glacial periods. As our ancestors migrated into harsh northern latitudes, survival for this clever, creative animal was no longer as easy it had been in lower, equatorial latitudes. Humans needed clothes to endure the frigid winters as well as better tools and weapons so as to take down the mega-fauna of the Pleistocene—the woolly mammoths, mastodons, and ground sloth. Humans needed fire to protect themselves from cave lions, saber-toothed tigers, and wolves.

As our ancestors migrated northward at the rate of less than one hundred miles per generation, our skin color became fairer and whiter. The cold and dark expanses of northern Europe and Asia, where the oblique winter sunlight was a mere fraction of the sun's intensity in the Tropics, favored those tribes that bore offspring with lighter skin. A fair skin was critical in helping humans absorb vitamin D from the sun, thereby avoiding the once common disease of rickets. As a debilitating disease, rickets attacks the bone development of young children, whereby they become bow-legged and handicapped. These weakened and disabled progeny were undoubtedly incapable of enduring the harsh conditions early man faced.

With the human life span during the Pleistocene averaging less than twenty-five years, coupled with a world of brutal day-to-day survival, children who developed rickets were, out of sheer necessity, abandoned by the tribe. Over tens of thousands of years, the black-skinned tribes of Africa eventually became the white-, yellow-, and brown-skinned tribes scattered around the world. Other selective adaptations took place: some subspecies grew heavy beards, developed sweat glands, and acquired extra layers of fat to protect them from the cold. Nostrils narrowed to pre-warm the glacially chilled air, while brain sizes across the globe steadily increased so as to cope with the advancement of language and the development and use of increasingly complex tools. The races, the subspecies of the modern world—the Australoid, Mongoloid, Caucasoid, and Negroid peoples—were born from these variations.

From Eskimos to Pygmies to the Chinese to the Germanic tribes, the various sub-species of *Homo sapiens* ultimately spread across every continent, filling almost every environmental niche on earth. People took two things with them everywhere they went: tools and an uncanny predisposition for violent ecological upheaval. *Homo sapiens* are the ultimate invasive species.

To survive in extreme conditions, humans formed packs similar to those of lion prides. Recent studies into human behavior indicate that the wandering bands started small but eventually averaged 150 individuals. To this day, hunter-gatherer tribes in contemporary New Guinea contain roughly 150 people; most army companies organized across modern nations average 150 individuals; NFL football teams, including special teams, trainers, coaches, and doctors and their spouses' average 150 people. It is a socially viable number wherein the individual can know how everyone within the greater organization reacts to his or her respective social status within the group. It is the optimal size for the human variation of the lion pride.

Language, or its precursor thereof, was born around fifty thousand years ago, perhaps much earlier. The ability to communicate accelerated the dispersion of the human race across the planet. Tribes were formed both as a means of self-defense and as predatory groups whose objective was to take away the territories and hunting grounds of neighboring tribes. Competing humanoid species of the Pleistocene, such as the *Neanderthals* and *Homo erectus*, were likely eliminated by these aggressive, intelligent tribes emanating from the Dark Continent. Most anthropologists now believe that *Homo sapiens'* advanced ability at language, as well as at communicating complex concepts and information, has played the decisive role in their ultimate victory.

This theory states that the single biggest advantage *Homo sapiens* held over *Homo erectus* and the *Neanderthals* was their ability to communicate complex information using oral traditions—in essence, telling their offspring which plants were safe to eat, when the herds would return, who was the enemy, and who was the friend. Without communication skills, all the knowledge our rival hominoids had gathered was lost with each passing generation. In essence, *Homo sapiens* outwitted their competition.

Our territorial imperative set the groundwork for our ultimate survival. From the earliest times, we waged war on each other with an intensity equaled only by the war we were simultaneously waging on our environment. Using fire both as a weapon and a tool, we torched forests and grasslands and left a long, bloody trail of extinction behind us as we conquered and dominated the living earth. From the outset, upon leaving the "Garden of Eden" of Africa, we were bent on relinquishing our hitherto blissful ways and peaceful proclivities.

Thenceforth, like modern chimpanzee bands, we readily assailed and killed any rival *Homo sapiens* tribe or any competing hominoids that intentionally or accidentally wandered into our territory. At the root of all our wars is a combination of this intense territorial imperative coupled with our relentless sense of tribalism. We are one species and, even though we can interbreed with every other human, the root of our racism—manifested as yellow, brown, black, and white supremacy—has lain deeply buried in our hearts. We instinctually mistrust "the other tribe."

223

As a result, we have incessantly formed mini-tribes. We join social clubs; we attend different churches; worship different gods; practice different political philosophies; and have sought to identify with our respective race, like-minded social organizations, and kin villages, cities, states, and nations. Everyone shares an overwhelming need to belong and to feel a part of the greater whole. We root for our favorite teams; stratify according to specific social and educational statuses; and above all perceive ourselves through the specific prism of familial background and our interaction to kinship. Over millennia, we've managed to cluster ourselves around mini-tribes in immeasurable ways. From the caste system of India to the Royal Family of England, the story of tribalism has unabatedly permeated every layer of the human experience.

We have systematically ravished environments. There is no such thing as the innocent savage of pre-Columbian America or the blameless, unspoiled inhabitant of the Pacific Islands. Gauguin's paintings of Tahitian natives belie the bitter truth behind the Polynesian migrations. From the day the first *Homo sapiens* were born, they have been slaughtering uncountable species of wild flora and fauna with a skill unrivaled by any other creature on earth. Man has been the quintessential natural born killer.

It is well known that the Clovis peoples, who may have arrived in North America as early as twenty-two thousand years ago from across the Bering Strait—which had been dry at that time due to the heavy glaciations at the time and their resulting lowered sea levels—killed over fifty species of mega-fauna within a few thousand years' span. The slow, massive beasts that inhabited North America were no match for the spear-wielding,

Although guilty of causing numerous extinctions early on Native Americans have learned to live in harmony with nature.

intelligent apes that advanced into their territory, and thus became easy targets for such skilled, tenacious, and adept hunters.

With their beautifully designed Clovis spearheads and atlatls—the latter a unique device that exponentially accelerates the speed and distance of a thrust spear—and the widespread use of fire, the prehistoric forebears of future Native American populations dexterously wiped out the three-ton ground sloth, giant beavers, woolly rhinoceros, and a myriad of large herbivores that flourished in the forests and rich grasslands of their virgin landscape. With their new environs' more temperate climate and the wealth of easily hunted protein, the new Native Americans migrated southward into Central and South America, where in time the New World's great civilizations would be born.

Right up until the European invasion of the New World—to Westerners, it was deemed a "discovery"; to Native Americans, an "invasion" and an "outright usurpation"—the American Indians still practiced a form of hunting now commonly referred to as "the Pleistocene overkill." Overkill hunting techniques included the banding together of several tribes to drive entire herds of bison over cliffs and into deep ravines, where they could be slaughtered in mass. Archeologists have noted that, given the astronomical number of animals killed in those drives, it would be impossible for Native Americans to use or harvest all the quarry. Archeological digs indicate that as many as one thousand bison were killed in a single stampede.

Native Americans weren't the only tribes partaking in the Pleistocene overkill—the first beginnings of what Richard Leakey has aptly christened "the sixth extinction." Leakey contends that the practice of hunting species into extinction ran rampant across the planet over thirty thousand years ago and continues unchecked today. Today, there is no Holocene or so-called modern era; there is only a sad continuation of the Pleistocene overkill.

In Australia, the Aborigines were busy wiping out dozens of marsupial species including giant kangaroos called Procoptodon goliaths, diprotodonts, and a co-evolved marsupial version of the leopard named Thylacoleo. Across islands worldwide, from Polynesia to Madagascar to the Hawaiian Islands chain, seafaring peoples were wiping out untold numbers of flightless birds such as the massive elephant bird of Madagascar, the moas of New Zealand, and hundreds of species of ground-dwelling pigeons like the dodo. Both large and small land tortoises, similar to the Galapagos tortoise we know today, were extirpated or hunted to extinction from hundreds of islands across the Pacific basin.

In Europe and Asia, the rise of mankind came at the expense of hundreds of animal species, including the Irish elk, Balearic cave goats, aurochs, massive cave bears, and wild horses. Everywhere on earth *Homo sapiens* came, saw, conquered, and left a bloody trail of extinctions and radically altered environments.

During that same time frame, both in the south of France and on the sandstone cliffs of the Australian outback, *Homo sapiens* took another evolutionary step and began recording the nuances of the world around them for all of their posterity to share and marvel at. Deep within the caves of Lascaux and Altamira in today's South-Central France and on the sandstone rock-faces of the Americas and Asia, art was born. Beautiful cave paintings, pictographs, and etched drawings depicting hunting scenes and wildlife were sometimes signed by a stenciled handprint on the stone wall beside them. They formed the early precursors to writing and still stand as an important benchmark in mankind's history.

Perhaps humans had evolved to the point where, for the first time in their long struggle to survive, they found enough free time to capture and reinterpret the creatures, the hunts, and the nature that surrounded them. With the birth of art, humans no longer merely worshiped gods, but started aspiring to be like them. Humans realized that they, too, could invent and create.

Ten thousand years ago, everything began to change for these nomadic tribes sprawled across an immense and hostile landscape. There were presumably fewer than five million people on earth and, although they had decimated scores of late-Pleistocene species, their environmental impact on the planet had been minimal. Over the next few thousand years, through trial and error, people learned that some of the animals they had relentlessly pursued and hunted could be tamed and harvested at their discretion. Humans, thereon, domesticated cattle, sheep, goats, and poultry. Subsequently, there came the revolution of agriculture.

No longer needing to follow the herds for survival or to rely on a meager harvest of wild fruits, grains, and vegetables, we learned we could stay in one place and prosper. Our cultural evolution was thus ushered in. The first great civilization sprang forth in the fertile valley between the Tigris and Euphrates Rivers in ancient Mesopotamia. The modern world was born and, as the need arose to manage and coordinate that new world, written language was invented. The formation of city-states, laws, armies, metallurgy, art, and an avalanche of information quickly followed. Nowadays, with the recent invention of electronic communications and the World Wide Web, this unmitigated process has continued and is yet to show any relenting signs.

As human populations grew worldwide, our impact on the earth's environment accelerated. Somewhere in the lush Fertile Crescent, the ancient tale of Gilgamesh, the warrior-king of Mesopotamia, was born. According to the legend, Enlil, the chief Sumerian deity in charge of looking after the well-being of the earth, entrusted the demigod Humbaba to defend the forest from invaders. But the warrior-king Gilgamesh killed Humbaba and leveled the great cedar forest, whereupon Enlil sent down these curses on the de-foresters: "May the food you eat be eaten by fire; may the water you drink be drunk by fire." Some five thousand years later, with the onset of global warming and an overpopulated world that cuts down two football fields of ancient forests every second, Enlil's sinister curse may yet come to pass.

The town of Nineveh, located on the outskirts of today's Baghdad, was used as an example of environmental devastation in Paul and Anne Ehrlich's book, *One with Nineveh*. I've chosen to call what happened there the "Mesopotamia Syndrome." Similar versions of it can be found throughout history. Whether or not the warrior-king Gilgamesh had been responsible, the city of Nineveh collapsed under the pressure of too many people making too great a demand on their surrounding environment.

They built their metropolis using cedar from forests that now seem unfathomable when we behold the dusty and inhospitable Iraqi landscape. It is a process of over-harvesting called desertification and it continues unabated across the modern world—India, China, Brazil, Rwanda, Haiti, and even here in the U.S. In fact, some version of desertification occurs in every nation and continent on earth. Once forests are cut and cleared, the top soil becomes exposed to the relentless heat of the sun, where it bakes into a hardened crust. In places like the Sahel of North-Central Africa, the winds sweep across the surface and huge dust storms develop. When the rains return, the top soil is swept downstream, no longer held in place by the detritus and roots of the forest. Erosion soon carries away the rich top soil, leaving only sand and dust behind. The surrounding micro-climate, once kept moist through the transpiration and the sponge effect of the forest, quickly turns dry and forbidding.

After the cedars of Nineveh were felled, the warrior-king turned to the north and took down the once extensive cedar forests of southern Turkey. After that, came the great oak forests of the southeastern Arabian Peninsula, and then the juniper, fir, and sycamore forests of Syria. As recently as two thousand years ago, the entire North African coast was heavily forested and rich with wildlife such as ibex, monkeys, and Barbary lions. It is now the northern edge of the Saharan desert.

The Mesopotamia Syndrome continues as *Homo sapiens* go on leveling the remaining redwoods, tropical rain forests, and the coniferous forests of Siberia and northern Canada. As those forests fall, the species that inhabit them are effaced in like manner.

Since the rise of civilization, mankind's assault on the checks and balances of nature has accelerated at a breakneck pace. It has been calculated that, at the time of Christ's birth, there were only 250 million people throughout the entire world. Although heavily populated urban centers such as Rome, Alexandria, and Jerusalem (yes, the monotheistic religions' Holy City was heavily forested at the time of Christ) were already feeling the strains of their dense populations, we as a species had only exerted minimal global impact.

Very little changed in the ensuing fifteen hundred years. Birth rates were held in check by equally high death rates. During the Dark Ages, infant mortality remained high and the average human life span stayed below forty years. The human race hit the five-hundred-million mark around 1550. By that time, the Western world was emerging from the stifling grips of a medieval theocracy (thus the moniker Dark Ages) into a new, humanistic and rationally oriented, scientifically based world known as the Renaissance.

From the first Christian/Muslim contacts through the Crusades, much of the classical literature of Greece and the techno-cultural Arabic/Persian customs found their way into Western society. A couple of centuries later—starting with the Mongol conquests and Marco Polo's travels, and culminating less than three centuries afterward with the Iberian voyages of discovery as far as China and Japan—a body of Chinese scientific knowledge was equally introduced to Europe, chief among them the invention that would ultimately decimate wildlife then and now: gunpowder, and shortly thereafter, the invention of firearms.

For wild animals, the invention of firearms changed everything. From the conquistadors to the pilgrims, Western explorers rapidly set their stake across the entire globe, bringing with them diseases, rats, and weapons capable of killing the most ferocious creatures at very little risk to the rifle-wielding hunters. Indigenous populations died by the millions from smallpox, influenza, and the common cold, while even highly advanced cultures like the Aztec, Maya, and Inca succumbed to the European behemoth and were exterminated everywhere.

The rate of plant and animal extinctions accelerated dramatically after 1550 and pushed the natural world into the quickened pace of the sixth great extinction. It is important to understand that 99.9 percent of all the creatures that have ever existed on earth are extinct, with most of those extinctions occurring during brief and violently disruptive periods throughout history. There have been five previous mass extinctions: the end-Ordovician (440 million years ago), the Late Devonian (365 million), the end-Permian (225 million), the end-Triassic (210 million), and the end-Cretaceous (65 million).

The end-Cretaceous extinction may well have happened overnight. The extinction of dinosaurs is now widely believed to have been the result of a collision between an asteroid or comet and the earth, which struck the Yucatán Peninsula near the present-day town of Progresso. It left what is called the Chicxulub crater—nearly three hundred kilometers (187 miles) wide. The impact was so tremendous that huge basalt lava flows occurred on the opposite side of the planet from the tremendously unleashed force. That collision's volcanic reverberations can be found today in the Deccan Traps of India. These are sheet flows of lava that form a series of plateau-like steppes across a broad plain in Central India.

Amidst the scientific community, there is no doubt today that something catastrophic collided with planet earth sixty-five million years ago, whereby it set off a chain of events that promptly led to the end of the 140-million-year reign of the dinosaur. This concept of abrupt environmental change is called Catastrophism. Although the concept of rapid, cataclysmic upheavals was initially rejected by the followers of Darwinian evolution, more and more people in the scientific community are seeing the merits of this theory.

In Darwin's evolutionary world, natural selection, over long and expansive periods, causes animals to make tiny gradual adaptations until they are best suited to survive in a given environment. Simply put, it is the survival-of-the-fittest theory, or adaptive evolution.

This was the case with dinosaurs. The earth was warmer in the Jurassic and thus covered in lush, tropical and subtropical vegetation, which provided ample forage for animals to grow so large as to defy our concept of functionality. There were dinosaurs that weighed as much as blue whales, smaller dinosaurs the size of our SUVs, and tiny, chicken-sized dinosaurs as well. All combined, those dinosaurs filled every imaginable niche of the Jurassic ecosystem.

But in one instant, every adaptation dinosaurs had undergone over the preceding 140 million years was rendered obsolete. It was no longer survival of the fittest but survival of the luckiest. Eighty-foot-long brontosaurs, which needed tons of forage a day, were doomed when, within months after the meteor's impact, a darkened sky killed almost all living plants. The lucky ones, then, were the tiny, ratlike mammals who scurried beneath the feet of the giant beasts. The lucky ones were also the sharks and fish that had never relied on terrestrial calories. Additional lucky ones were the alligators, which survived on the plethora of carrion that must have scattered the earth's surface as dinosaurs starved to death and vanished.

The concept of Catastrophism is important to grasp, for there is every indication we are currently entering an era of Catastrophism brought about by the behavior of one single species: *Homo sapiens.* We are all trapped on this spaceship called earth and teetering on a complete ecological disaster. In upcoming decades, environmental degradation will overshadow every other issue that currently faces mankind, from terrorism to poverty.

I like to compare our current situation to the story of telephone lineman Ed McLean, who fought the cougar in his cabin on the tip of Vancouver Island back in 1951. In our case, we are both the man struggling for survival against a hungry beast and the beast itself. Locked in our cabin three rocks from the sun, we are in the midst of a life-and-death struggle with ourselves. Indeed, we have met the enemy…and it is us.

How we fare against our preprogrammed instinct to propagate and survive will determine the outcome of the struggle. For the moment, I can unequivocally state we are losing. But the human spirit has proven time and again to be as resilient as Ed McLean was on that cold, wintry night. Wounded, bleeding, half-naked, and delirious, McLean still managed to get into his row boat, row across a bay, wrap himself in a sleeping bag, and muster enough energy to make the phone call that saved his life the next morning. We have the knowledge, the tools, and the intelligence to win this battle, but not if we continue to deny the depth of trouble our species is in.

Once *Homo sapiens* had guns, they went on a rampage against the 4,776 species of mammals, ten thousand species of birds, and uncountable fish, amphibians, and fauna that shared this planet with them. From 1600 onward, especially at the hands of the whalers and early explorers, the rate of those extinctions skyrocketed. Under normal circumstances, the earth experiences a natural loss of twenty-five species per century. This is referred to as the background extinction rate.

It occurs because, over time, landscapes change, natural migrations occur, competing species invade ecosystems, and natural catastrophes, among several other factors take their toll on living organisms. According to Leakey's *The Sixth Extinction*, in this era of contemporary Catastrophism, the rate of extinction for both flora and fauna has been 120,000 times higher than normal. We are currently experiencing the loss of species at the staggering rate of thirty thousand per year. This number may actually be on the low side because mankind still has no idea how many living species of plants, fish, reptiles, insects, birds, and mammals there are on the planet. The estimated range for the earth's total number of living species runs from ten to over one hundred million. Every year, we lose tens of thousands of species that have yet to be scientifically identified in just-cleared tropical rain forests. In effect, creatures become extinct before we even know they ever existed. The invention and indiscriminate use of firearms have been essential elements in this mass extinction.

Between 1500 and 1900, *Homo sapiens* had a gruesome field day with his lead balls and gunpowder. The list of amazing creatures that have vanished bears a sad testimony to this nearsighted hunting spree. Here is just a sampling of some of the animals with which we will never have the pleasure of sharing our time on earth: wolves such as the Newfoundland white, the Texas grey, the Kenai, the great plains lobo, the Shamanu, the Tasmanian (aka thylacine), and the warrah or Antarctic wolf; the Mexican silver grizzly and the Kamchatkan bear; the Cape lion and the Sumatran tiger; the Oregon and the Caucasian wisent bison; aurochs; the blue-buck antelope; the Bubal hartebeest; the Schomburgk's deer; the Portuguese ibex; the quagga, a zebralike horse; the tarpan horse; the Steller's sea cow, a thirty-foot manatee which lived in the Steller Sea and was wiped out in a record twenty-seven years by whalers; the Toolache wallaby; the Christmas Island musk shrew; dozens of species of moa; and uncountable ground pigeons...to mention but a mere handful.

Not with standing their lethal track record, firearms meant little when compared with the far more devastating technology that increasingly drives this mass extinction forward into the twenty-first century—the internal-combustion engine. Fossil fuels may provide all of us a momentary lifestyle of luxury

Collection: Tasmanian Museum and Art Gallery
Weaver, circa 1869, with a Tasmanian wolf (Thylacine) he had just shot to collect his bounty. The last Thylacine died in 1933.

beyond measure, but these fuels and the machinery they propel may someday prove to be the key element in our demise.

Nothing has done more to accelerate our assault on ourselves than gas- and diesel-powered machines. Skidders, heavy trucks, road machinery, and most of all the ubiquitous chainsaw have allowed us to deeply penetrate some environments and take out immense tracts of jungle forest once believed to be un-harvestable, let alone developable.

Every year across the globe, *Homo sapiens* cut down and clear an area equivalent to the entire Mexican territory. What few forests remain become so

231

fragmented and damaged, it is only a matter of time before their remnant wildlife populations join the growing list of extinct species.

That expounded, let us return to the first section of this book and take a look at the plight of crocodilians across the globe.

*****

Amazingly, there still are twenty-two species of crocodiles in existence, but of that number only two are not endangered or threatened in the wild—the American alligator and the South American caiman. All crocodilians have suffered from habitat loss, illegal poaching, and pollution.

By far, the most endangered species is the nearest living relative to the American alligator—the Chinese alligator. The exact number is unknown but the consensus is, there are fewer than 150 Chinese alligators still living in the wild. The just-completed Three Gorges Dam on the Yangtze River further threatens this fractious wild population. On the other hand, China has a human population of 1.3 billion people. That equates to 8.6 million people for every remaining wild Chinese alligator.

The same situation applies to the gavial—or gharial—of northern India, where the population has dwindled to below one thousand crocodiles. Meanwhile, India boasts a human population approaching 1.1 billion. By using high-powered rifles, Bushmeat hunters in Africa have systematically decimated local populations of Nile crocodile, thereby causing this once plentiful reptile to obtain its current position on the CITES' (Convention on International Trade of Endangered Species) Red List, or Appendix #1—considered at great risk for extinction or extirpation—in most poorer nations across the African continent.

Unlike many species, alligators and crocodiles survive and thrive in captivity.

Given the likelihood of human populations' approaching ten billion people within the next fifty years, over half of the remaining crocodilian species will become extinct in the wild. Because alligators and crocodiles fare better than most animals in captivity, their habitation in places such as the Madras

Crocodile Bank in India, the St. Augustine Alligator Farm in Florida, and myriad zoos, farms, and animal trusts across the globe will hopefully save them from complete extinction.

While it is always a tragedy when someone gets killed in the jaws of a hungry alligator, the fact is that *Homo sapiens*, as a collective species, are killing these crocodilians at a ratio of nearly one million per each loss of human life. Our technology has gotten light-years ahead of our compassion and our understanding of the natural world. Conversely, our cultural evolution has lagged behind our technological prowess. We are leaving future generations with a world devoid of wildlife. Our motto might read thus: "Shoot first and ask why we needed to kill them later."

The same grave prognosis applies to sharks. In my research, I've discovered that the once bountiful spiny dogfish—a small, three-foot-deep water shark inhabiting temperate oceans—has been over-fished in numbers that stagger the imagination. During the 1920s, in one season alone, twenty-seven million dogfish were hauled in off the coast of Massachusetts. They were once so plentiful that they were caught, dried, and burned like cordwood for heating fuel. In 1938, in Placentia Bay, Newfoundland, Canada, some 10.4 million pounds of dogfish were harvested in an attempt to reduce the local population. Most were simply discarded.

Today, the spiny dogfish is in serious trouble. They have the longest-gestation period of any vertebrate in the world, some twenty-four months, and the females don't become sexually mature until they reach between eighteen and twenty-one years of age. We didn't know this back in the '20s and '30s when fishermen harvested them indiscriminately. But the combination of long gestation and slow sexual maturity has made them extremely vulnerable to over-fishing. In 1996, the Center for Marine Conservation issued an "action alert" on the remaining dogfish population.

The great white shark, perhaps the most feared and exquisitely designed of all oceanic predators, is, likewise, in serious trouble. Trophy-fishing, long-lining, and needless killing have helped to reduce great whites' populations throughout their range. The great white, along with the basking and the whale shark, are all in Appendix #1 of the CITES' list of endangered fish. The total population of great white sharks is estimated to be below ten thousand, although no one knows for certain how many are left in the vast expanses of the world's oceans. California State, Australia, and a number of other nations have officially banned the killing of great whites, but these are still being legally taken throughout much of their range.

The practice of finning is another horrific example of mankind's deplorable relationship with wildlife. Finning occurs when a shark is caught, taken on board, and stripped of all of its fins. The carcass is then tossed back into the ocean while the fins are brought back to market to be sold to Japanese and Chinese dealers for the making of shark-fin soup, considered a delicacy in the Orient. Between 1980 and 1990, China alone imported over one billion pounds of shark fins annually. The fins represent less than ten percent of a shark's total weight; the remaining ninety percent are left to rot in the open ocean.

Despite the obvious similarities with the infamous Florida plume hunters of the late 1900s—who killed entire bird flocks for a mere handful of hat feathers—the market for shark fins starting in the 1960s was actually promoted by the U.S. National Marine Fisheries Service (NMFS). Around 1961, the Chinese and Japanese fishing fleets had already wiped out the sharks from the Arabian Sea, off the African coast of Nigeria, and along both coasts of Mexico, so they turned to the still plentiful shark populations of the U.S. The idea of killing an animal for a few pounds of fin meat is so bizarre, it seems inconceivable.... Then again, buffalo tongue was considered a delicacy in this country before we nearly lost that species to extinction. Only the buffalo's tongue was cut out of a one-thousand-pound animal and the rest left to slowly decompose under the Western sky.

By 1997, the Atlantic shark population was, in the words of a repentant NMFS, "in a precarious state." In the U.S., shark catches were reduced to no more than two sharks per vessel per trip and finning was totally banned. But the dangers posed to the remaining shark populations continue to grow.

The Taiwanese Gillnet Fishery reported a shark by-catch of 297 tons in 1986–87. The following year, that number dropped to 20.7 tons, or less than one-tenth of the prior harvest. As demand for inexpensive protein grows, coupled with our escalating human populations, the relentless pressure on sharks will continue.

Illegal harvesting through the use of sunken long lines, shark nets, and reef poisoning help to decimate the world's remaining shark populations. Environmental degradation, including pollution from offshore drilling, pesticides, nutrient runoff such as nitrogen and phosphorus, plastic trash, and an ocean filled with human garbage, all combine to imperil the shark's oceanic habitat.

In 1993, the NMFS established a management plan to protect thirty-nine species of shark in the Atlantic and Gulf waters. This zone called the Exclusive Economic Zone extends two hundred miles from shore, limits the overall annual shark catch by fifty percent, and prohibits "direct fishing" of five species: basking, sand tiger, Bigeye sand tiger, great white, and whale shark.

The list of managed sharks includes most of the known "killer sharks" such as the blacktip, dusky, bull, Galapagos, tiger, lemon, great hammerhead, and silky shark. A complete list of these sharks can be found at the NMFS' Web site (www.nmsf.noaa.gov). For the two dozen people who are killed every year by shark attacks, we annually kill over twenty-five million sharks. Given the likely prospect of more offshore drilling and the need to feed 6.5 billion humans, the scenario for the future of all sharks is very dismal, at best.

All fisheries, from sardines to tuna, are in serious trouble worldwide. Because of the demand for bluefin tuna especially in Japan, a single bluefin can command over $50,000 in profit for a fisherman. With this kind of money on the table, it is little wonder that the bluefin-tuna harvest has dropped a staggering ninety-four percent from its historic highs. Worldwide, the large, pelagic fisheries such as marlin and swordfish have fallen to a meager ten percent of their former levels. The once bountiful five-hundred-year-old cod fishery off Georges Bank, on U.S.'s northeastern coast, has totally collapsed, and the taking of any cod off the coast of eastern Canada has been prohibited or severely restricted since the early 1990s.

Earlier in this book, we looked at two human/animal bloodbaths that occurred near the end of WWII: the saltwater-croc attack on the Japanese forces off the coast of Burma and the shark attacks on the sailors of the USS Indianapolis in the Philippine Sea. However, we haven't yet discussed the behavior of the species that set the stage for these disasters to occur in the first place.

While the loss of almost two thousand men to sharks and crocs is unfortunate, hadn't we plunged ourselves into a horrific world war, neither incident would have occurred. The two bombs off-loaded on Tinian Island a few days before the Indianapolis was torpedoed were dropped on Hiroshima and Nagasaki on August 6 and 9, respectively.

In the flash of an instant, sixty thousand humans were incinerated, more precisely at 8:15 A.M. on the morning of August 6, 1945. According to Japanese officials from the city of Hiroshima, the cumulative death toll from the aftermath—the necrosis-caused illnesses from burns and injuries, followed by radiation sickness, cancers, and decades of birth defects—totaled 237,062. Little Boy, the first of the two atomic weapons to have ever been used in war history, was mankind's first brave step toward self-annihilation.

Three days later, Fat Man, the curious name given to the second atomic bomb, fell upon the city of Nagasaki. Japan's two torpedo factories, the Mitsubishi Steel Works and the Mitsubishi-Urakami Ordinance Works, were instantly destroyed. Some seventy-five thousand of Nagasaki's 240,000 inhabitants were vaporized. By August 15, 1945, the Japanese had accepted an unconditional surrender and the most sordid killing spree humanity had hitherto ever engaged in history was over. The lion prides of modern nationalism were, for the time being, at peace.

The atomic-bomb blast over Hiroshima:
mankind's most horrific invention.

Compared with crocodile and shark fatalities, the scope of the death toll from WWII is unimaginable. Over eleven million Axis and fifty-one million Allied military and civilians died during the war. Russia suffered the greatest losses, with over ten million troops and twelve million civilian casualties. Germany lost one-tenth of its population: seven and a half million.

We all know that WWII was preceded by WWI, which lingered on in the trenches of Europe for years. That war took another 15.1 million soldiers and civilians. Add to those two great conflicts an unbroken list of smaller conflicts and exterminations between 1900 and 1999, and most likely the overall, man-killing-fellow-man death toll has exceeded two hundred million.

The Korean War took 2.5 million; Vietnam logged between four and five million; the death camps of Auschwitz-Birkenau and Treblinka; the killing fields of Cambodia; and the recent massacres in Rwanda and in present-day Sudan's Darfur region, all remind us that *Homo sapiens* remain the greatest single danger to ourselves.

On July 16, 1945, three weeks before the United States dropped the atomic bombs in Japan, at exactly 5:29.45 A.M., *Homo sapiens* achieved a milestone in its long journey to nowhere: the Trinity test of the first detonated nuclear device was successfully completed near Alamogordo, New Mexico. For the first time in recorded history, a species had developed a tool, as a weapon, which could effectively end the existence of the species that had invented it. As J. Robert Oppenheimer said, after watching the demonstration of the nuclear blast later that morning, "I am become Death, the destroyer of worlds"—a line drawn from the Hindu scripture, the Bhagavad-Gita.

Oppenheimer realized that the strange atomic fruit born of the Manhattan Project would soon be capable of eradicating humanity from its own planet. With the invention, a decade later, of fusion-style weapons like the hydrogen bomb—a weapon over fifteen hundred times more powerful than the atomic bomb that had destroyed Hiroshima—*Homo sapiens* found themselves capable of forever changing their future and that of all known life in the planet. Indubitably, we are a cataclysmic species.

This book is not only about alligators, sharks, and panthers, but also the end of the natural world as humanity has known it since the dawn of time. There is a term in science called biophilia, which means "love of nature." For those of you who enjoy a walk in a forest or along a beach, noticing a flock of pelicans fly overhead while watching a great white egret pluck a minnow from the nearby surf, the message is clear and pressing: we are losing the battle with ourselves. It is paramount that we change.

Globally, these are our most pressing issues: overpopulation, climate change, rampant pandemics, and World War III.

Overpopulation

Nothing is more important to the future of *Homo sapiens* and the remaining flora and fauna species on our planet than human-population control, and optimistically speaking, human-population reduction. We have a choice: humanity either drastically reduces its numbers through a well-managed and effective global-wide birth-control program, or the forces of nature will handle the job for us. Historically, nature has tended to be quicker and far messier than the promotion and use of condoms, vasectomies, and birth-control pills. The historic, nature-designed, population reductions of the past have come about through plagues, disease, starvation, wars and cataclysms. Take your pick.

As of today, according to the CIA World Fact's Web site (http://www.cia.gov/cia/publications/factbook), there are 6.5 billion people on earth. At the present increase rate, over seventy-four million people are added to the world's population every year. This is a decrease from the 1989 record of eighty-eight million. Overall, the rate of population explosion has slowed since that year. Current projections indicate that birthrates should continue to diminish over the next four decades, but they still leave us with an estimated world population of nine to ten billion people by the year 2050.

It is highly unlikely we will ever reach nine billion. We have already exceeded our planet's carrying capacity by several billion and, at this point, we are not only spending all of the interest (the sustainable yield of spaceship earth) but also devouring its capital. We are a species living on credit and the bank, our planet, is about to start calling in our notes. As a species, we are bankrupt. According to many population experts and scientists, we would presently need three earths to support the number of humans we have crowded onto one. We are two earths short and neither Mars nor Venus appears to be all that hospitable at present, nor reaching them seems an affordable option, were they remotely habitable.

As we sit here in America, where we enjoy a lifestyle unimaginable to the vast majority of people in the world, it is difficult, if not impossible, to fathom the horrid conditions most people elsewhere live in. Over two billion people, one-third of the world's population, live on less than $2 a day. That's $730 a year...less than what many people reading this spend in monthly car payments.

The poorest person living in the U.S. is seventeen times wealthier than a child born in sub-Saharan Africa. Bangladesh, one of the poorest and most densely populated countries on earth, has 144 million people jammed within its 55,598 square miles. That amounts to a density of 2,590 people per square mile, with most of that land only a few meters above sea level.

The state of Wisconsin is slightly larger than Bangladesh. It has 56,154 square miles of land with a 2004 population of 5,509,000. Its population density, therefore, translates in ninety-eight people per square mile or twenty-six times lower than Bangladesh's.

To put it into another perspective, if the lower forty-eight states had a population density equivalent to Bangladesh's we would have a nation not of

Over seventy-four million hungry people a year are added to the 6.5 billion already crowded on Planet Earth.

our current 298 million people, but an astronomical population of 7.4 billion. Unfortunately, this is the direction toward which most of the world is heading.

At present, the U.S. population density, including sparsely populated Alaska, is a little over eighty-three people per square mile. Mexico, our neighbor to the south, has a density of 140 people per square mile, whereas Canada, with the second largest landmass next to Russia, has one of the lowest population densities on earth, with only nine people per square mile. But in the end, everything—from economies to global warming to health issues to war—revolves around the problems of human overpopulation. At this critical point in human cultural evolution, no sensible nation should encourage population growth of any kind.

Some organizations such as the Catholic Church do everything to encourage population growth and to discourage birth control. One Papal encyclical—*Humanae Vitae*, dated July, 1978—postulated that it was possible for the earth to feed and sustain a human population of forty billion people. While it may be theoretically possible, when one uses every green technology known to science, to accomplish such a feat, this concept is tantamount to utter dementia. We can witness what happens to a small island-nation such as Haiti, which is predominately Catholic, when poverty and a burgeoning population come together. On that western one-third of Hispaniola—the whole island is comprised of Haiti and the Dominican Republic—where resources are finite and the carrying capacity has been stretched beyond measure, the Mesopotamia Syndrome is in high gear. Forests are being stripped away, the top soil eroding into the sea, and poverty, desperation, and political instability rule supreme.

Easter Island in the Pacific collapsed for many of the same underlying causes, as did the Mayan civilization and countless other societies that overtaxed their micro-environments. Spaceship earth is a finite system.

Industrial Japan has managed to maintain an incredibly dense population of 866 people per square mile, but to feed such a huge population has resulted in the Japanese fishing fleet's being considered one of the most devastating biological killing machines on earth. Japanese fleets have taken dolphins (the mammal, not the fish), whales, squid, tuna, sharks, and virtually every living thing they can over-harvest from the oceans through the indiscriminate use of long lines or drift nets. The choice we must make is not *how many* people we can place on the planet, but *how well* they are to live while here. A classic example of quantity vs. quality....

As the population density increases in countries already stretched to the limit of available natural resources and viable agricultural lands, the average age of their inhabitants plummets. In the U.S. and the European Union, the average life expectancy is seventy-three years; in Pakistan, forty-four; and in Mali, forty-three and dropping.

The symptoms of overpopulation are everywhere and many of them greatly exacerbate global warming. Today, roughly three billion people in the world—from India to Pakistan to Malaysia all the way to South America—cook and heat their homes with wood. Burning firewood is a form of double jeopardy. When trees are cut down for firewood, one of the few carbon sinks is lost. Forests are one of only a handful of methods we still have available to safely remove excess CO_2 from the atmosphere. When trees are burned, they release CO_2, whereby the greenhouse gases are increased. Besides the climate-changing effect, another corollary is the continued desertification of local micro-environments.

Moreover, high population densities have proven to be prime breeding grounds for disease. In sub-Saharan Africa there has been a resurgence of polio, smallpox, and tuberculosis, all three of which were once deemed eradicated from the world. Organizations such as the World Health Organization, the Bill and Melissa Gates Foundation, and the Red Cross have waged nonstop battles against the myriad symptoms of overpopulation, but to little or no avail. With seventy-seven million more hungry mouths to feed on earth every year, it is impossible for supply to meet the demand, be it food, medicine, clothing, shelter, et cetera. World food production has fallen short of its capacity to feed all 6.5 billion of us for the past four years. As noble as those agencies and organizations' intentions are, they remain little more than Band-Aids on an arterial hemorrhage.

Delivering aid to the Third World without dealing with the problem of birth control is patently absurd. Most politicians avoid voicing an opinion on this topic for fear of alienating the Protestant religious right and the Roman Catholic Church, which for various philosophical reasons are pro-growth and anti–birth control. Ironically, predominately Catholic countries such as Italy, France, and Spain have some of the lowest birthrates in the world. They have simply chosen to ignore the Catholic Church's position on human reproduction rights.

Controlling populations is neither murder nor abortion: it can be done in ways so as to solely prevent unwanted pregnancies before they occur. To let the world's children be born into chronically impoverished, environmentally ruined societies is to impose on them a death sentence. "Be fruitful and multiply", no longer applies. If the human race fails to stabilize and eventually reduce its population numbers to sustainable levels, as a species we will inexorably perish and take uncountable flora and fauna with us into extinction.

Nothing, absolutely nothing, is more pressing than, and as paramount as, this single issue.

Global Warming/Climate Change

Global warming is altogether too real. The National Oceanic and Atmospheric Administration (NOAA) recently announced that September 2005 was the warmest September ever recorded worldwide ever since reliable instruments were invented, circa 1880. The Environmental Protection Agency's (EPA) Web site validates this disturbing trend: August 2005 was the third-warmest August on record; July 2005, the second-warmest on record; May 2005, the second-warmest; April 2005, the second-warmest; March 2005, the third, et cetera. The year 2005 has now officially been declared the warmest year ever recorded.

The 1990s have been the hottest the earth has seen in one thousand years. It is not the undisputed fact that the earth's oceans and atmosphere are getting warmer which has had most scientists and climatologists concerned, but the sheer rate at which these changes are taking place. The earth has cooled down and heated up hundreds of times in the past, especially during the late Pleistocene's interglacials. These changes, however, took place over thousands and thousands of years—time enough to allow plants and animals to adapt to the graduations.

With the buildup of greenhouse gases—carbon dioxide (CO_2), methane, nitrous oxide, and chlorofluorocarbons (CFCs)—the change is occurring far more rapidly. Greenhouse gases act like an invisible insulating blanket stretched across the entire earth's atmosphere. Whereas thirty percent of the sunlight that reaches the earth as shortwave radiation is reflected back into space, seventy percent of that sunlight is absorbed and then re-radiated as longwave radiation. It is this longwave radiation that becomes trapped by those gases, acting in much the same fashion as the glass panes in a greenhouse. The invisible blanket of those rare gases, measured in parts-per-million (ppm), traps in the heat generated from sunlight and warms the earth's atmosphere accordingly.

Thus far, the heat created from those gases has resulted in an overall worldwide temperature increase of just a bit over 1° F in less than one hundred years. The oceans have followed suit, also warming approximately 1° F. The largest contributor to these rises has been carbon dioxide, a by-product of the industrial revolution from the burning of fossil fuels. The levels of carbon dioxide measured in ppm have been increasing at levels unseen in the previous 420,000 years. Whereas CO_2 averaged 280 ppm for the past ten thousand years, only during the past 150 years—following the discovery and use of fuels such as coal, oil, and to a lesser extent, natural gas—these numbers have increased to over 380 ppm.

National Geographic, in its November 2004 issue on Global Warming, stated unequivocally: "We may well run out of atmosphere before we run out of oil." This is a frightening thought.

Because of a natural delay built into the sheer enormity of the atmosphere and oceans, this warming trend is expected to continue for at least another one hundred years. The 1997 Kyoto Accords on carbon-dioxide-emissions reduction will help scientists feel that a level of over five hundred ppm of CO_2 may be reached by the year 2030 or sooner. The earth has not seen this much carbon dioxide trapped in its atmosphere in fifty million years.

The results stemming from this global human experiment in atmospheric change are yet unknown. When the concept of global warming first gained the climatologists and the media's attention in the mid-1950s, the scientific and political communities' reaction was a combination of rebuttal, denial, and procrastination. In reality, very little has been done to address the issue ever since.

The Bush Administration has elected not to join the 162 nations that have signed and ratified the Kyoto Accords for fear that any reduction in the burning of fossil fuels would hurt the U.S. economy. With its millions of cars, hundreds of coal-fired power plants, and countless internal-combustion engines (trucks, locomotives, chainsaws, lawn mowers, edge trimmers, leaf blowers, outboard motors, generators, et cetera), the U.S. accounts for twenty-five percent of all carbon-dioxide emissions worldwide. Australia, using many of the same U.S. arguments, has also refused to sign the agreement.

A Swiss mountain village circa 1880: notice the location of the glacier.

Scientists now have a good idea of how that one-degree warm-up has impacted us to date. One of the most noticeable effects has been the reduction of the Arctic ice cap and the steady receding and disappearance of glaciers throughout the world.

Across the entire planet, glaciers are melting...and melting fast. In the late nineteenth century, U.S.'s Glacier National Park boasted 150 glaciers. One hundred years later, there are thirty-five. In Kenya, the famous snows of Mount Kilimanjaro are expected to disappear within the next twenty years. In the French

Alps, the still-surviving glaciers are receding farther and farther up the mountains. In Alaska's Prince William Sound, only a decade ago cruise ships were accustomed to nosing right up to the majestic two-hundred-foot high face of the Columbia Glacier. Since 1983, that three-mile-wide, thirty-four-mile-long ice river has drawn back more than eight miles. Cruise ships can no longer get anywhere near the face because the narrow passage between it and the open water is jammed with broken sheets of ice and large icebergs. What is not known is whether or not global warming will impact the two

The same Swiss village one hundred years later, with the glacier clearly retreating.

immense warehouses of frozen water on earth: Greenland and Antarctica.

Thus far, all the melting glaciers, coupled with a slightly warmer, slightly expanded ocean have resulted in a net rise of sea level between six to eight inches. As small as this rise is, it's already causing problems.

The islands of Tuvalu, sprawled across 500,000 square miles of ocean midway between Hawaii and Australia, are being swallowed up by a rising Pacific Ocean. In 2002, the people of Tuvalu threatened to sue the U.S. and Australia for excessive carbon-dioxide emissions they claim are causing the slow disappearance of their low-lying nation. In an act of goodwill, New Zealand has offered to take in those most affected by inundations, thereby avoiding the first official global warming–related international lawsuit.

As the world's oceans continue to rise, other islands and shorelines are beginning to feel the effects. Along the north slope of Alaska, an Eskimo village has had to relocate due to the rise of water levels in the Arctic Ocean. In November 2000, off the coast of Papua New Guinea, the first one thousand of forty thousand residents of the Duke of York Islands were forced to permanently evacuate their homes from the steadily rising sea levels. These "environmental refugees" may be just the start of a wave of humanity that could swell into the hundreds of millions, should the real ice caps—Antarctica and Greenland—start to slide into the ocean.

There are a host of other problems already stemming from these rising temperatures: the permafrost in Alaska is thawing and thus releasing even more carbon dioxide into the air; disease-carrying mosquitoes that were never found above one thousand meters are now bringing Dengue fever, malaria, West Nile virus, and a host of other pathogens up to thirty-five hundred meters. This insect migration is helping to deliver unfamiliar pathogens to villages and populations that have no prior natural immunity to the aforementioned mosquito-borne diseases.

*****

Another discovery relating to global warming and wildlife extinction has very recently come to light. For years, scientists have puzzled over the disappearance of dozens of frog species across the entire globe. These amphibians, whose permeable skin makes them extremely sensitive to environmental changes, are seen by scientists as early harbingers of global-warming effects. The disease plaguing frogs throughout Central and South America is the chytrid fungus. It kills them by growing on their skin and attacking their epidermis and teeth, as it simultaneously releases a deadly toxin.

In some regions of the earth, climate change, through excessive cloud cover, has led to cooler days and warmer nights, thereby allowing the chytrid fungus to thrive in areas where it was once unheard of. Just a few degrees of sustained temperature change has resulted in the loss of over sixty species of harlequin frogs, as well as the beautiful and once plentiful golden toad. The fungus is killing the frogs, but climate change is the trigger that has allowed the pathogen to thrive. The fungus grows best at temperatures only slightly cooler than those that were common in places like the Monteverde Cloud Forest Preserve in Costa Rica.

Warming oceans have also been predicted to spawn larger and more intense hurricanes but, because this is also a Florida issue with long-term and dramatic ramifications, we will look at that problem later. Floods, droughts, and famines have already weighed in on the issue of global warming. Even though we don't have computer models sophisticated enough to know exactly what's going to happen as the weather patterns change across the planet, we do know that the number of tornados have increased, that snowfall around the world is heavier and wetter than it was fifty years ago, and that Africa's Sahel region has been caught up in a drought that appears to have no end.

Recent winter wildfires in Texas and Colorado, as well as one of the wettest winters on record in the Pacific Northwest and California, may also be linked to weather changes brought about by global warming. Anecdotally, it seems everyone alive today senses the weather has somehow changed; that it's gotten much warmer everywhere in the past fifty years…and instinctually the animal in us senses that this change somehow can't be good.

The real tests loom in a not-too-distant future. There is considerable concern that, should the Greenland ice cap, which is miles thick in certain places, continue to melt away, the influx of fresh water into the Newfoundland Current could cause the Gulf Stream to change course. The dynamics of this change are complex, but the dire results do have historical precedent.

About eleven thousand years ago, the Gulf Stream did change course and both England and Northern Europe were plunged into a mini-ice age. According to scientists who have studied the ice-core samples that yielded this information, the change was neither slow nor subtle. It took only four years. A change that develops thus quickly would be somewhat akin to the recent Hollywood movie about global warming called *The Day After Tomorrow*. London would freeze every winter and places like Oslo, Stockholm, and Helsinki would become virtually uninhabitable.

Imagine European environmental refugees numbering in the tens of millions; heading southward to Spain, Africa, and the Middle East; fleeing a climate where the average temperature has dropped 10° F in a year. The concept is far more alarming when you realize that this unusual phenomenon could begin a few years from now and be firmly in place by 2015.

The single largest potential melt-problem lies on the bottom of the globe. The ice cap we call Antarctica holds ninety percent of all the fresh water in the world. Its glaciers are so thick that much of the land beneath them has sunk below sea level by virtue of the sheer weight of the frozen water lying on top of it. If Antarctica's frozen waters start melting, the ocean could rise by more than three feet, though some scientists predict it could rise as much as fifteen feet.

If you want to talk about how such an event could impact low-lying Florida, think massive. The entire Florida Keys archipelago would be submerged, as would most of Florida's West Coast. Parts of the East Coast's littoral could probably remain above the rising water, as could the panhandle and North-Central Florida, but most of Florida State would become a virtual sea. In South-Central Florida, everything below Lake Okeechobee would vanish beneath a rising Gulf of Mexico.

In other low-lying countries like Bangladesh, a rise of three feet could create fifty to one hundred million environmental refugees. Refugees fleeing to where...? Bangladesh's neighboring countries pose unspeakable barriers: Nepal is severely overpopulated; Myanmar's population has suffered under as ignominious a political regime as North Korea's; India's population is over one billion; and China is out of the question.

What are we to do with tens of millions of destitute, homeless refugees in a world that is growing warmer every decade?

Author's note: At press time, former Vice President Al Gore had just released a book and a film about this very topic titled *"An Inconvenient Truth."* For additional information about global warming/climate change, log on to Al Gore's Web site at: http://www.climatecrisis.net.

Pandemic

It is indeed remarkable that our technological prowess has inadvertently built the most efficient disease-dispersal system imaginable: the modern airline transportation system. The scenario is self-evident. A passenger boards a 747 on a long international flight with a communicable pathogen which, during its first forty-eight hours, has no obvious symptoms. In the confined, re-circulated environment of a modern passenger jet, the disease—flu virus, plague, or any number of readily communicable infections—spreads quickly and undetected throughout the cabin. The plane lands at London's Heathrow, Chicago's O'Hare, or Tokyo International and the passenger disembarks. Three days later, that passenger is dead from the disease. Meanwhile, fifty of the flight's three hundred passengers have contracted the disease, most of whom yet remain symptom-free. Some of the infected passengers go onward with layovers that span the entire globe. Others return home to Beijing, Calcutta, New York, and a dozen other major cities. The virus they are unknowingly carrying returns home with them. The disease, which a hundred years ago would have moved as slowly as a horse and carriage, now moves at over five hundred miles per hour in a system where close contact is unavoidable.

Within one week, the virus has literally spread everywhere on the planet and remains unstoppable. People are dying by the tens of thousands, hospitals are overwhelmed, and a global pandemic has begun.

Ironically, using the paradoxical logic of survival of the luckiest, those most disconnected and unplugged from the grid of modern technology are most likely to survive such a scenario. Two specific groups come to mind, in large part because they each live in remote, isolated environments and have practically no or little contact with the modern world: the first are the Bushmen of the Kalahari Desert; the second, the Aborigines of the Australian outback. Those peoples live off the land and have minimal, if any, contact with the modern world's goods and service systems.

Those of us intimately hooked up to the hardwired grid of civilization would be the most vulnerable to contracting the disease. We buy our groceries at Wal-Mart Superstores or Publix Supermarkets; our gas at 7/11, Shell, and Exxon stations nationwide; and our toiletries at Walgreens. Once the pandemic begins in earnest, we have little choice but to re-supply our food stocks and thereupon risk catching the disease or starve to death while waiting it out. As a civilization, we have become far more inter-reliant upon the network of goods and services than we were during the devastating 1917 Spanish Flu epidemic—estimated to have killed between fifty and one hundred million worldwide.

Because of this co-dependent matrix we've created, no one can predict what will happen once a new twenty-first-century pandemic occurs. Will the engineers who run our power plants refuse to come into work for fear of catching the disease? What about air-traffic controllers, medical, and police personnel; will they fail to show up to work in an effort to save their own skin?

The prospect of a partial or complete collapse of our interdependent systems looms as the worst-case scenario in the possible outbreak of a global pandemic. Within months of its onset, the modern world, with its intricately connected supply chains of food, clothing, and medicines could collapse, leaving those not yet dying from the disease soon invariably dying from hunger, cold, and lack of medical care.

Of course, overpopulation and the crowded, deplorable conditions in which many Third World people live only exacerbate the problem. The present concern is that a new strain of bird flu similar to the 1917 Spanish Flu is looming on the horizon. To date, more than one hundred people have died of the disease; all of them have contracted it directly from contact with an infected bird.

But history has shown us that a viral disease such as H5N1, or Avian (bird) flu as it is commonly called, has followed a familiar mutation pattern. Given this fact, it is likely, if not probable, that this pathogen will behave no differently than its ghastly predecessors. First the flu develops and appears in a wild population; in this case, the likely suspects have been wild ducks and geese. It, then, first mutates and jumps from a wild to a domesticated bird such as the current situation in Southeast Asia, Africa, and Turkey with their domesticated chickens, ducks, and geese. From there, it mutates once again and jumps from birds to humans, although only through direct contact with an infected bird. The last—and for the human race, the worst possible mutation—is when the virus becomes capable of human-to-human conveyance. That is currently the World Heath Organization's (WHO) nightmare, which believes that an Avian-flu pandemic is inevitable. It is exactly what did happen during the Spanish Flu epidemic of 1917.

The squalid existing conditions in large parts of India, Southeast Asia, and Indonesia have served to increase the odds of this scenario's outplay. A few years ago, we narrowly missed having a SARS epidemic, largely transmitted by the airline industry. There are equally dozens of other potentially lethal diseases still out there, which could mutate and explode into a full-fledged pandemic within months.

Ebola, dengue fever, polio, the resurgence of smallpox, tuberculosis, antibiotic-resistant infections, West Nile virus, and a host of other potentially lethal diseases wait in the wings for an opportunity to throw the modern world into a global plague. As humanity pushes deeper into equatorial jungles in an effort to take out their remaining trees and underlying minerals, we run the risk of heretofore finding undiscovered pathogens to which humanity may have little or no immunity. Ironically, the cure for these same diseases may well be locked deep within the very plants and trees we are destroying.

Ebola, or hemorrhagic fever, is just such a disease. It is now known that Ebola was first transmitted from an infected monkey to a human being in Equatorial Africa. The first outbreak of this deadly virus, with a fatality rate approaching ninety percent, occurred in Zaire and southern Sudan in 1976. Since then, it has been largely contained to that region, but sporadic outbreaks continue in Uganda, Gabon, and other sub-Saharan nations.

Ebola, with symptoms that can turn the most hardened health workers' stomachs, could still potentially break out of Africa and spread across the planet. As an overpopulated world presses into the jungles, which are the natural reservoirs of many of the world's most deadly pathogens, we run an ever-increasing risk of contracting a new Lassa, Marburg, or Hantavirus, which could forever change the world.

HIV, which currently infects over forty million people worldwide, is another instance of monkey/human contact. Like Ebola, HIV is thought to have originated in Equatorial Africa. It first appeared in the U.S.'s and Sweden's homosexual communities, one of its largest early transmitters widely held to have been a gay flight attendant by the name of Gaetan Dugas. Later evidence has shown that Dugas's excessively promiscuous activity—it has been reported that the Canadian-born Dugas had had over twenty-five hundred liaisons while infected with HIV—may have been a factor in the spread of the disease across Canada, Europe, and the U.S. Although Dugas helped spread the disease, the first cases of HIV/AIDS had occurred in Africa as early as 1959. The fact remains that the story of Gaetan Dugas, who died of AIDS on March 30, 1984, is yet another example at how effective jet travel can be for the rapid dissemination of a lethal disease.

Today, HIV is no longer considered to be a predominately homosexual disease; presently over seventy-five percent of all infections occur during heterosexual encounters. The disease continues to spread, especially in Russia, China, India, and Southeast Asia. Sub-Saharan Africa has been decimated by HIV/AIDS, with over thirty million children orphaned by this plague. It is now estimated that AIDS has killed over twenty-five million people worldwide since its discovery in 1981; the death toll in sub-Saharan Africa alone could eventually exceed one hundred million.

West Nile virus is another case of how modern technology facilitates the spread of diseases which one hundred years ago could not have spread. It is now widely held that the deadly West Nile virus arrived via a stowaway mosquito on a flight into one of New York's airports somewhere in late 1998 early 1999.

Like the bird flu, the West Nile virus has used birds to rapidly disperse across much of the U.S territory. Today, the virus can be found in almost every state in the Union and throughout most of southern Canada.

Although most of the 400,000 human infections in the U.S. have been mild, even a-symptomatic, the virus has resulted in over ten thousand infections strong enough to result in hospitalizations and, to date, more than 750 deaths. The sad thing is that this single stowaway mosquito would never have survived a transoceanic-ship crossing eighty years ago. That crossing would have taken weeks to make, not hours. The stowaway mosquito would have died in transit. West Nile virus is now so firmly entrenched into U.S.'s bird populations that eradication of the disease is out of the question. It will continue to impair or kill Americans and Canadians for centuries to come.

Along with the problems we are seeing from human race's pushing deeper and deeper into the jungles of the world, the squalor and overcrowding of many Third World slums will continue to be another breeding ground for dangerous diseases. The compromised immune systems of a poor, malnourished class of people provide the perfect living Petri-dishes for future plagues, and for bacterial and viral epidemics.

A worldwide outbreak of bird flu that might enter into the slums of Rio de Janeiro, Bombay, or Jakarta could eventually lead to a worldwide death count in the billions. Who amongst us could argue that birth control is a far less horrific means of controlling global population? One way or the other, the world's populations will be brought back into check. We, then, must come to terms with which methodology is more humane—pills or plagues?

World War III

Like many of you reading this, I grew up under the international nuclear policy known as **MAD**—Mutually Assured Destruction. I can still recall the air-raid sirens being tested on the first Wednesday of every month at noon in my hometown of Duluth, Minnesota. As though I were still in that classroom at St. Jean the Baptist School, I can vividly recall crawling under my desk and putting my arms and hands over my head in anticipation of a forthcoming nuclear blast.

Twice a year we would conduct a full-fledged drill which would lead us down into the basement of the school. There, amidst fallout shelter signs depicting radioactive symbols and stockpiles of twenty-gallon water containers, the entire student body would sit with their backs against a cold cement wall and remain silent under the stern administration of the Catholic nuns. I also remember trying hard to keep from giggling but usually ending up in detention for having broken the silence.

This was the late 1950s. The cold war was in full swing between the USSR and its communist allies and the U.S. and its capitalist coalition. For decades, the threat of thermonuclear war lingered over the world like a radioactive pall. When you think about it, it's hard *not* to admit that the concept of **MAD** was rather a concept of **MAD**-ness.

In 1965, at the peak of the arms race, the U.S. had 31,265 nuclear bombs. Some of those were considered tactical devices, capable of destroying a small city or advancing brigade. Some were absolute monsters — hydrogen bombs with an explosive capability thousands of times more powerful than either Fat Man or Little Boy.

Although they didn't have as many bombs early on, the Russians focused on size over quantity. The

A South Pacific hydrogen-bomb test in the 1950s. The island beneath the blast was vaporized.

bombs they designed and built were enormous. One of those weapons was named the Tsar bomb. It exploded north of Novaya Zemlya Island, above the Arctic Circle, on October 30, 1961, at 11:32 A.M. It remains the single largest detonation of a nuclear device in human history.

Originally, the Tsar bomb was designed for a maximum yield of one hundred megatons. This compares with the mere 15–16 kilotons of Little Boy, the atomic bomb the U.S. dropped on Hiroshima. To put it into perspective, one megaton is the equivalent of seventy-seven kilotons. After realizing that an explosion of one hundred megatons would create massive fallout and produce a blast so powerful that the plane dropping the bomb would be itself destroyed, the Soviets under Nikita Khrushchev scaled the device back to a theoretical output of fifty megatons.

The actual blast was calculated to be fifty-seven megatons and produced an energy output equal to one percent of the output of the sun over the same thirty-nine nanoseconds. The mushroom cloud the Tsar bomb created by its blast rose to more than forty miles above the earth and produced twenty-five percent of all the nuclear fallout ever created by mankind throughout the entire nuclear-testing era. In fact, had the Russians gone ahead with the original one-hundred-megaton explosion, it would have resulted in a bomb sixty-five times more powerful than Little Boy.

The Tsar bomb itself weighed twenty-seven tons and could only be delivered by a specially modified version of the TU-95 Soviet long-range bomber, the largest plane in the Soviet Air Force. An enormous parachute retarded its fall just long enough to allow the plane that dropped it to escape its massive fireball. The parachute was so large that the production of women's nylons in the USSR was halted for months so as to accumulate enough nylon material to build it.

If a bomb as large as the Tsar were dropped on Los Angeles, it would cause third-degree burns to people one hundred kilometers (62.14 miles) away from the epicenter in every direction. The Tsar's fifty-seven-megaton blast itself was so powerful that it blew out windows in Finland, some one thousand kilometers (over 620 miles) away, and created a seismic shockwave that reverberated around the earth three times. In essence, everyone living in cities as large as New York, Paris, or Moscow would have instantly been killed by a single bomb. The fallout would continue to kill for years to come. A single bomb that size would be capable of killing fifteen to twenty million people within a year of its detonation.

Needless to say, hiding under our wooden desks or placing our head between our knees would have done little to prevent the sixth-grade class of 1961 from being vaporized under a weapon that rivaled the power of the sun. As if this information isn't frightening enough, we must understand that it is indeed possible to produce weapons far more powerful than the Tsar bomb's fifty-seven-megaton yield.

The largest bomb the U.S. ever tested was Castle Bravo, detonated on March 1, 1954, with a blast of fifteen megatons. Though it was never actually tested, the U.S. also built a number of bombs known as B-41s with a theoretical yield of twenty-five megatons. These bombs were so large and unpredictable that testing them bordered on military insanity. The Castle Bravo bomb was only supposed to produce a yield of four to eight megatons. Its unexpected fifteen-megaton explosion resulted in massive amounts of fallout that, to this day, are still considered the worst radiological disaster in U.S. history.

In 1985, at its peak, the USSR had an arsenal of 39,197 nuclear bombs. With the U.S. arsenal scaling back to 22,941, and Britain, France, and China with nearly 1,085 devices, the world's total nuclear stockpile was in excess of 63,223 bombs. It is impossible to calculate the combined explosive power and destructive capabilities of this worldwide atomic arsenal, except to point out it was considerably greater than the bite of an alligator, puma, or a great white shark.

With the collapse of the USSR and the end of **MAD** per se, we have made considerable progress toward reducing our nuclear stockpiles. In 2004, it was estimated that the U.S. still stockpiled approximately 10,455 atomic or thermonuclear devices, while Russia maintained approximately eighty-five hundred. The other authorized nuclear powers have just over one thousand bombs. China has 400; France, 350; and Britain, 200. Not counting the undisclosed bombs, the world's great powers are still twenty minutes away from unleashing 20,905 nuclear devices on any given day.

From there, we turn to those states that have very few bombs but run a much higher probability of using them. India boasts having sixty-five bombs while its neighbor, Pakistan, parades across embattled Kashmir saber-rattling some forty atomic weapons. Israel denies having any, but experts contend that it harbors between 100–300 warheads. North Korea officially states it has only eight, but many nuclear scientists presume it has dozens more. It has also been suggested that North Korea, like Russia, may be building some of these weapons as large as, or larger than, the massive Tsar bomb.

We then have the "wanna-be" nuclear club, which includes nations that may already have access to both the plutonium and the scientific knowledge to build weapons of mass destruction—Egypt, Syria, Libya, Iran, Taiwan, South Africa, Germany, and Brazil. Last, but certainly not least—for we hope these countries have indeed handed them back—there are the fifteen nations that profess to have surrendered their nuclear-device stockpiles to Russia after the collapse of the Soviet Empire.

All tallied, we have more than enough nuclear bombs at the ready. All it takes is one bomb to get things started. Just as the assassination of Franz Ferdinand, Archduke of Austria, on June 28, 1914, led to the start of WWI, an ill-placed detonation of a nuclear device could trigger the release of twenty thousand bombs within weeks, if not hours. Although we no longer face the extent of annihilation resulting from an all-out war using over sixty thousand such weapons, we nevertheless are a long way from living in a safe, nuclear-free world.

Beyond nuclear technology, we enter the nefarious world of biological, chemical, and radiological (dirty bombs) weapons. Ever since the 9/11 attack on the World Trade Center, the world has been anticipating the use of one of these agents by Islamic fundamentalists or any number of related terrorist organizations. The anthrax scare that occurred shortly after 9/11 was a prime example of this kind of bio-terrorism.

Certainly, the list of potentially new and lethal agents could well exceed the length of this book, but here are just a few of the multitude of threats from these deadly weapons. On the biological end, we might look at something as simple as using an established pathogen against each other: smallpox, which has been largely eradicated and to which most people have no immunity, is a likely candidate; anthrax, a rare disease found predominately in cattle and sheep, is another; others might include bubonic plague, syphilis, various viruses, cholera, botulism, Ricin, and assorted bacteria, not to mention genetically engineered pathogens currently being developed in military labs throughout the world.

Chemical weapons have been a part of the human arsenal for thousands of years. Smoke has been used to obscure troop movements since the dawn of warfare. Mustard gas was used extensively during WWI and Sarin gas was used in 1995 in a Tokyo subway. The people who conducted that attack were a bizarre doomsday cult. These weapons, however, pale when compared with some of the experimental gases and chemical agents being produced today.

Soman, GF, VE, VG, VM, VS, VX; blister agents such as lewsite; vomiting agents such as Diphenylchloroarsine; psychochemical agents such as 3-Quinuclidinyl benzilate benactyzine; and nerve gases capable of killing millions of people within hours are all being refined and stockpiled across the globe. Once again, the list and the secrecy surrounding most of these killing or maiming weapons make one's gathering of information on them all but impossible.

Of course, all of us are familiar with dirty bombs. These are non-nuclear devices that explode using conventional explosives such as C-4, or common dynamite, while wrapped in any number of radioactive dusts or fragments. The damage done is the contamination and radiation sickness that follow, similar to the Chernobyl incident that occurred on April 26, 1986, in

Ukraine. In that tragic accident, fifty-six people died within days, but the anticipated consequences of the various radiation sicknesses may ultimately cause the death of tens of thousands.

Finally, we have a new generation of weapons produced as a direct result of our advancing technologies: laser weapons; plasma guns; weapons using ultra-high-frequency sound, rays, and beam; and computer-driven systems too complicated to describe...all designed with two missions in mind—to kill a rival tribe or nation, or to prevent one's nation from being obliterated.

A recent *Nature* program on PBS focused on two rival lion prides located in the Ngorongoro Crater of Tanzania, Africa. The two prides had come into conflict over territory and in the ensuing war one of the prides was completely decimated. Four male lions attacked and killed both males from the rival pride, whereby the lionesses were left defenseless. Their cubs were eventually destroyed by the prevailing pride and the story ended with the complete annihilation of the smaller, defenseless group.

If you want a better understanding of human nature, look to lion prides. We evolved together and both of us found it far easier to form hunting bands and tribes than to survive as individuals in a harsh, unforgiving environment. Through this process, we've become extremely aggressive and tribal, and given the technologies we now have at our disposal, the greatest threat to ourselves is ourselves.

In the Aftermath of 9/11

Amidst the turmoil of that most terrible day, it is easy to understand why the death of Robert Steele at the hands of an eleven-foot alligator on September 11, 2001, went largely unnoticed and unheralded. Death was everywhere on that appalling day. If Steele's attack had happened the day before or a month later, it would have received far more regional and national attention than it did.

Then again, there is the possibility that, had the dark cloud of the terrorists' actions on 9/11 not engulfed the thoughts and heart of Bob Steele just as it had everyone else's in the U.S., he might still be alive. Distraction of this magnitude does exact a price, and in this case it was a man's life. There were hundreds, if not thousands, of careless accidents on the day the World Trade Center towers collapsed. Humanity woke up that morning to find itself hurled into the twenty-first century by some bizarre catapult of religious insanity. It was difficult, if not impossible, to pay attention to anything else.

There isn't a person reading this story who cannot remember the morning of 9/11. Who cannot recall the exact minute when he or she first heard the incredulous news of the freak accident in New York…? The hurried phone calls to friends and relatives, the running over to turn on the T.V., the news of the inexplicable incident racing across e-mails, radios, cell phones, and office hallways almost as quickly as the explosions themselves…. Then, the disbelief that followed when, as the entire world watched, a second plane slammed into the south tower at 9:03 A.M., eighteen minutes after the first plane had set the top of the north tower aflame…. And then the Pentagon attack at 9:37 and the news that a fourth plane had crashed into a field somewhere in Pennsylvania….

Suddenly, every American realized these couldn't possibly be disconnected events. This had been no accident but a planned attack, a cruel and malicious act by barbaric individuals who held no respect for either common decency or for obeying the unspoken rules we must obey—the social contracts of civilization. A suicide mission from hell, killing more than 2,986 people, including all the nineteen terrorists who had hijacked the four planes….

Like most of us, Bob Steele and his wife, Ellen, had spent the morning watching CNN and all the news stations following the continually breaking news of the day. Who was responsible? Were there more planes still in the air, possibly harboring additional terrorists about to hijack another planeload of men, women, and children and take them careening into their death? Where would they hit next? The Golden Gate Bridge, the White House…? Where was the President…?

By noon, the events of the day were all-consuming. Replay after replay showed the planes coming in, then strangely disappearing into the buildings followed by huge fireballs fueled by the twenty-four thousand gallons of jet fuel carried in each plane. Both towers eventually collapsing from the heat of the burning fuel.... The firefighters and emergency personnel hopelessly trapped inside.... And then, throughout the day, many of the surrounding buildings falling apart, joining the dust, smoke, and rubble that just the day before had been the very lifeblood of New York's Lower Manhattan's business and financial districts.

America was at war, though answering questions as with whom and why was far more difficult. The world was in shock; the human animal was again proving to be the world's most ruthless and deadly predator. Questions and confusion regarding the amoral nature of the terrorist attacks stirred deep in the heart of every citizen. Time was suspended....

Sometime around 3:30 P.M. that afternoon, Steele told his wife he was going to take their dog out for a walk. He needed a stretch after hours of watching the horrors unfold on television, again and again, in a macabre slow motion. His terrier was equally anxious to go. Ellen Steele went into the master bathroom to take a shower while Bob faithfully got out the leash, hooked it to the dog's collar, and headed out the back door toward a short path that took them west 150 feet to a nearby bike path.

The weather was hot, cloudy, and humid. By mid-September, the summer rains had left the adjacent Sanibel River filled to near overflowing and humidity hung in the air like an invisible, damp smoke. Steele and his dog were used to it, having lived on Sanibel since 1989. Still, it seemed hotter and wetter than usual because a tropical storm was brewing to the west, which would eventually move in and inundate the lower West Coast of Florida over the next few days.

No one saw what happened. Ellen was in the shower and unable to hear her husband's cries for help until it was too late for him to be helped. The police and the Fish and Wildlife officers can only speculate what might have occurred. To recreate any alligator attack, during which the only witness has died as a result of it, becomes mere conjecture. Still, the evidence points in the same general direction.

*****

A day before the attack occurred, a neighbor, Myra Roberts, had reported that, while jogging on the same path Steele and his terrier were heading toward, a large alligator lying entirely across the path had hissed menacingly at her as she approached from the south. Roberts had moved to Sanibel just two days before and knew nothing about alligator behavior, but wisely turned around and ran back the way she came, undoubtedly at a far brisker pace. She reported her gator encounter to the local authorities, but a hissing reptile does not necessarily make it a deadly one. The Sanibel Police said they would look into it.

Normally, during the drier months of the year there is a steep bank between the water's edge and the top of the path Steele and his pet were taking to the bike path. But in the summer of 2001, the rains had all but eliminated that bank and the Sanibel River was barely a foot below the path. The path itself ran parallel to, and less than three feet from, the river's edge.

Because it's extremely unusual for an alligator to attack a full-grown adult, it is widely believed that the gator initially made its explosive lunge not at Steele, but at his twenty-pound terrier. The dog, with far quicker reflexes than an eighty-two-year-old man, must have avoided the hungry jaws of the leviathan, because it survived the attack unscathed. There are indications that Steele, possibly in an effort to protect his dog, or himself, kicked his right leg at the advancing beast in an effort to ward it off. Perhaps the far more agile terrier had dashed behind his owner in an attempt to avoid being eaten....

Getting between any predator and its prey during a full-fledged attack is exceedingly dangerous. During an all-out attack, things can and often do go wrong. A fully engaged predator—shark, panther, or alligator—is an awesome creature. Once committed to attacking, the adrenal glands inject immense amounts of adrenaline into the animal's biological system, whereupon it gives that animal unbelievable energy. Muscles are wrought with tension and the killing instinct is jammed in high gear. The animal explodes with a brief but formidable attack. If Steele, in a moment of panic, decided to kick at this exploding reptile, it was entirely the wrong thing to do. The alligator, realizing that its attempt to seize the dog had been thwarted, turned its attention to Steele. The alligator grabbed Steele's right leg just beneath the knee. Then it did what all crocodilians do: it dragged Steele back toward the water and went into a death roll.

The necropsy performed later revealed the attacking alligator to be a 292-pound, eleven-foot bull alligator. The animal's right eye was missing, possibly adding to the animal's preference for going after easy prey...like a small, unsuspecting terrier. Once the gator bit down on Steele's foot it was all over. It pulled the old man back toward the water and tumbled into a reckless death roll, separating Steele's leg from the rest of his body at the knee. In shock, Steele fell to the ground and half-slid into the dark waters of the Sanibel River. The alligator then retreated, taking Steele's lower right leg with it.

With his right leg torn off, Steele's femoral artery was severed and the arterial bleeding became uncontrollable. Lying partially in the water, Steele had only a few minutes of life left in him; as with shark attacks, the water offered no resistance to the outpouring of his ruptured artery. In the final coroner's report, the official cause of death was exsanguination: Robert Steele, with his lower leg torn off below the knee, bled to death.

Ellen Steele, upon getting out of the shower, thought she heard someone screaming. It sounded as though the cries were coming from the backyard. Fearing something was wrong, Ellen went to the back door and found the terrier, still on his leash, alone. Robert Steele screamed one last time and Ellen rushed down the back stairs to his rescue. He was only a short distance from the house, but when she got to Steele, he was already unconscious. With his legs underwater and his grave injury obscured from view, Ellen at first thought her husband had somehow fallen into the water and was drowning.

She tried to pull him out of the water but his dying body proved too heavy for her to move. She ran back up into the house and called 911. Her call was received by the Sanibel Police at 3:53 P.M. They arrived on the scene within minutes. Ellen took the four police officers down the path to where she had left her husband. They found Steele lying along the bank of the Sanibel River, apparently lifeless.

Two officers pulled Steele from the water and immediately noticed the partially amputated right leg, recognizing it as an alligator attack, not a drowning. Officers Krivas and Crandon provided security while Officer Steele (no relation) and Sergeant Phillips began to administer CPR to the victim. It was too late.

At 4:15 P.M., Commander Tomlinson and the City of Sanibel's Natural Resources Director, Dr. Robert Loflin, arrived on the scene. A few minutes later, the alligator was observed swimming on the other side of the river with what appeared to be a human leg in its mouth. Loflin spoke with Tomlinson and requested that the police attempt to shoot the animal. Tomlinson contacted Chief Phillips and received official permission to shoot and kill the alligator.

Officer Crandon fired two rounds into the alligator's head. The animal then submerged and reappeared along the opposite bank with the victim's leg still firmly held in its mouth. The rounds did not appear to have had an effect on the animal. Time and again in these situations, small-caliber weapons, unless aimed perfectly and by an expert familiar with the alligator's anatomy, seldom have any effect on a massive, bull alligator. Its skull is too thick for most handguns to be effective.

At 4:57 P.M., officers from the Fish and Wildlife Commission arrived.

Using high-powered rifles, they were able to finally kill the alligator, causing it to release the leg. The alligator was dragged from the river to near where Steele had lain earlier, but EMS had long since removed Steele's body from the scene. The severed leg vanished beneath the dark water of the Sanibel River.

Even after having been shot repeatedly with a large-caliber rifle, the alligator still showed signs of life. It is important to understand that these animals are very difficult to kill and that under no circumstances should anyone other than a trained professional attempt to shoot and kill any wild alligator. Time and again, the so-called "dead alligator" is the one that takes another vicious bite out of someone.

Once all signs of life had totally vanished from the reptile, the police contacted the neighbor, Myra Roberts, to verify if this was the same alligator she had observed the day before, stretched across the bike path not twenty yards from where it now lay dead.

Roberts arrived and said she felt confident it was the same. They opened up its stomach, but it was empty. The following day, the Lee County Sheriff's Department Dive Team successfully retrieved the missing leg. Robert Edward Steele III was laid to rest a few days later.

*****

The particular story's irony is, Robert Steele, like many Sanibel Island residents, was an avowed environmentalist. He was then the chairman of the Sanibel Vegetation Committee and a member of the Community Housing & Resource Board. The Vegetation Committee encourages island residents to focus on planting native vegetation; the Housing Board helps bring affordable housing to island residents—individuals such as the police and EMS personnel, who tried so desperately to save Steele.

Beverly Ball, a volunteer naturalist at the nearby "Ding" Darling National Wildlife Refuge, later said to a local newspaper, "I can't believe he would walk by the river with his dog, but I guess it happens. Most of the time alligators are not aggressive and they will walk away from people, but occasionally they get somebody."

In 2001, Sanibel, with its focus on nature's conservation, had a large native population of alligators. Being one of few barrier islands in Florida with an extensive freshwater system of rivers, canals, and lakes, there were an estimated two-hundred-plus alligators on the island at the time of the attack.

Mark "Bird" Westall, Sanibel's former mayor and a dedicated environmentalist, was thus quoted by the *Sarasota Herald-Tribune*: "We see alligators in the ponds all the time. Maybe because of the higher water, maybe because of the dog, the alligator came up. To me, it is a tragedy. Bob was a staunch environmentalist on the island, so it is really a tragedy for it to happen to him."

But as tragic as the incident was, it faded quickly into the background of the much larger, more shocking tragedy of the moment—the flying of commercial jetliners into the World Trade Center's Twin Towers and the missile-like use of another passenger airplane to attack the Pentagon. The television cameras were focused on the people leaping to certain death to escape the fires, on the collapsing and burning buildings, and on an empty hole in a field in Central Pennsylvania. Steele's death at the hands of a hungry alligator vanished beneath the avalanche of a far greater horror.

Robert Steele, more than anyone, believed wholeheartedly in the natural systems and ecological principles exemplified on Sanibel Island. He was dedicated to preserving alligators and knew the potential danger they presented. Being a former military officer in the Navy Reserve and a public-relations manager for General Dynamics—a corporation intimately involved with the U.S. military—the events of the morning may have distracted him more than most.

In a strange and terrible way, Robert Steele became yet another victim of 9/11.

The World Trade Center's Twin Towers before
the attack of 9/11/2001.

She Stood for Peace and Justice

In an interview published in the *Atlanta Journal Constitution* the day after Michelle Reeves's untimely death, Georgia State University Professor Paul Voss said the following about his young student: "In the best sense, she was the kind of person who would go for a swim in the middle of the night." Professor Voss knew that Reeves was free-spirited.

Voss added that Reeves had always brought a smile, a sharp intellect, and "sometimes quirky" questions to his literature class. He concluded by saying that Reeves was the kind of student all professors wish they could have. Voss, his fellow professors, and students at Georgia State (GSU) were deeply troubled by the tragic death of the bright and inspiring young woman.

A junior at GSU, Michelle Reeves was a dedicated anti–Iraq war activist, an accomplished poet, and a beautiful twenty-year-old. The youngest member of the Atlanta Poets Group, Reeves was also a dreamer and a gifted writer.

In a September 28, 2004, posting in the online journal *GI Special* (www.notinourname.net), Desmond Gardfrey, a fellow student at GSU, wrote, "She Stood for Peace and Justice." In his heartfelt tribute, Gardfrey said that Reeves was one of many students who had felt compelled to speak out for peace and against the continuation of the war in Iraq. She deeply cared about the tragedy and suffering of the Iraqi and American families that have lost loved ones in a war she had always considered unjust and non-winnable. Gardfrey concluded his eulogy thus: "My memories of Michelle will help me continue her cause: the fight for peace and justice. She will be missed."

Earlier that summer, imbued with her strong political convictions, Reeves had traveled to New York City during the Republican Convention to protest against the war in Iraq. She had also made a second trip to Washington to demonstrate against a war she considered amoral.

Reeves also expressed herself through her avant-garde poetry. Her good friend Zac Denton was also quoted in the *Atlanta Journal Constitution*: "She was extremely intelligent, loving, and socially conscious. I could see she was developing her own poetic style and voice."

Along with her father, James Reeves, Michelle Reeves had traveled to visit her grandparents in Fort Myers, Florida, in late September 2004, just before the fall semester resumed at GSU. Her grandparents, both retired, lived in an assisted-living facility in southern Lee County called Cypress Cove at Health Park. Cypress Cove lies in close proximity to a large, regional hospital called Lee Memorial Health Park. Many apartments in the complex abut a number of the small retention ponds that lie scattered throughout the larger hospital campus. It was a well-known fact that alligators thrived in all of them.

Coming from the northern Atlanta suburb of Roswell, Georgia, Reeves perhaps couldn't really appreciate the numerous warnings her father and grandparents had given her about the dangers of swimming in Florida's ponds. It was still mercilessly hot in South Florida and the cool, clear water behind her grandparents' apartment must have appeared very inviting. Several times throughout the day, Reeves had expressed an interest in taking a quick swim in the lake, but every time she was told it was not at all advisable. Alligators had been sighted in the lake recently and swimming in the pond was extremely risky.

This tale should have ended there and then, with Reeves and her father driving back to the hills of North-Central Georgia after the weekend, her entering senior year at GSU and graduating in the spring of 2005; thereafter, her finding and perfecting the poetic voice, perhaps finding a lover, a husband, a family, and all the things a woman in her twenties might wish for. It might have ended with the war in Iraq coming to a peaceful resolution and our troops returning home…but, alas.

Sometime after 2:30 A.M. on Sunday, September 26, 2004, Michelle Reeves secretly slid out of her grandparents' apartment in Cypress Cove, took off her nightgown, and went for a midnight swim. No one was awakened by the frightening sound of a young woman's scream, nor any in the household even knew she had vanished until later on that Sunday morning.

Sometime after 9 A.M., discovering that his daughter was not asleep in the guest bedroom, James Reeves went down to the water's edge in search her. Reeves must have suspected, no, rather dreaded the thought that his daughter had not heeded their warnings. At 10 A.M., behind one of the nearby apartments along the bank of the closest pond, James Reeves found his daughter's nightgown lying on the grass. He called 911.

Shortly thereafter, James Reeves discovered her floating facedown in the water a mere ten feet from the shore. After the police arrived, her naked body was recovered. According to the autopsy done the following Monday morning, Michelle Reeves had been drowned by an alligator. The cause of death was ascribed to the severe, multiple, sharp-force injuries that had been applied to her body. Her right arm had been torn off by the attacking alligator just above the elbow. There were numerous bite marks and lacerations to her upper torso. At some point during the awful struggle, Reeves must have realized her grandparents had been right, after all.

Reeves's body was removed from the scene. Fish and Wildlife

summoned a state-certified trapper to come in and kill the offending alligator. At 5:05 P.M. that same Sunday, Trapper French and his assistant, Tracy Hansen, captured and killed the responsible gator. It was a seven-foot, eleven-inch male alligator weighing 105 pounds. Reeves herself weighed 135 pounds. Once people enter the alligator's natural environment, a Florida freshwater lake, pond, or canal, even the attack of a relatively small gator can prove fatal.

As standard procedure during a fatal accident, a complete toxicology screen was conducted by a lab serving the medical examiner's office the following week. Reeves's toxicology report was negative. She had not been intoxicated, high, or on any mind-altering medications when she went for her midnight swim. Aside from the fatal injuries sustained during the attack, Reeves was simply a healthy, zestful woman with an entire life ahead of her. The autopsy shed no light whatsoever as to why a bright and sensitive girl would have done such a foolish thing. Suicide was out of the question: Reeves had always loved life with a passion.

Michelle Reeves was also a poet and a dreamer. Maybe all she had wanted to do was lie on her back in that dark, still pond and gaze at the stars on a warm, balmy Florida night. In this regard, Reeves was not unlike the English romantic poet Percy Bysshe Shelley. While visiting Italy once, almost two hundred years before Reeves went for her midnight swim, Shelley and two other people set out to sea during a stormy afternoon, where he perished at the premature age of thirty.

Shelley had been repeatedly warned by friends and fellow sailors not to set out to sea that day in his brand-new boat, *Ariel*. The weather was too threatening. Within hours of their departure, Shelley's boat foundered and sank in the storm. Along with his friend, Edward Williams, and their sailor-boy, Charles Vivian, Shelley drowned. Their bodies were found ten days later on the shoreline of the blue Mediterranean near Lerici, on the Gulf of La Spezia. It was later learned that Shelley could not swim.

In both instances, nature paid no attention to these two dreamers. Perhaps Percy B. Shelley and Michelle Reeves felt they were immune to either the whims of storms or the power of a colossal reptile's jaws. Reeves may have believed that, if she were quiet and didn't create any commotion in the pond, the alligators she had been warned about would ignore her. After all, she loved animals and the natural world around her. She also may have naïvely thought that, because she felt this way, the oftentimes unforgiving forces of nature would charitably bypass and spare her.

It did not...as it doesn't any of us. Shelley died because he, too, felt that the approaching storm would spare him and his crew. Ten miles out to sea, a raging thunderstorm overwhelmed the *Ariel* and all hands were lost. There will always be those who underestimate the natural world's savage powers and die because of them.

As romantic as is the notion that we all long to commune with nature, the fact remains that nature, in turn, cares not at all how we choose to envision it. Nature can be both the glorious sunset and the devastating eye-wall of a hurricane—beauty and the beast. As much as the people who consider themselves environmentalists, naturalists, hunters, and fishermen want to empathize with and romanticize nature, their feelings mean nothing to it. Although we may love and appreciate its exquisite canvas of plants, animals, and landscapes, we first and foremost must respect nature, lest death become the tragic result.

As we unconscionably ravish and pollute our planet, there is yet a grim lesson we can draw from these two dreamers: the consequences of our disrespect for the power and forces of nature may, likewise, deliver us to equally gruesome catastrophes in the decades and centuries to come. The unheeded pronouncements we read daily about the dangers of overpopulation, deforestation, global warming, and environmental pollution may well be as prophetic as the urging of the sailors who told Shelley not to leave port and the warning of Reeves's grandparents against her swimming that night.

Perhaps someday the destructive war in Iraq Reeves so opposed will come to an end...; people worldwide will live in true harmony with earth's natural ecosystems...; and the lofty dreams of a beautiful young woman will be at last fulfilled. Until that day, all we have is Michelle Reeves's mournful story, her poetry, her memory, and the lessons she has taught us. May she rest in peace.

In the 1930s, the beaches of Florida were already crowded. Today, Florida's environment is overwhelmed.

HOMO SAPIENS,
THE TOP PREDATOR IN FLORIDA

Eleven thousand years ago, the peninsula Ponce de León came to call *La Florida* was completely devoid of the animal known as *Homo sapiens.* Because the world's climate was still in the grip of a major ice age, the state of Florida was twice as large as it appears today. The glaciers that sprawled across northern Asia, Europe, and North America tied up so much water that the ocean levels were estimated to be as much as 450 feet lower than they are at present. The peak of this last glaciation occurred eighteen thousand years ago and it appears that the earth is still rebounding from that event, with sea levels continuing to rise worldwide.

Recent DNA studies indicate that somewhere between 12,000–14,000 years ago, a single tribe of seventy nomads crossed the Bering land bridge that had been created by the lower ocean levels and entered North America in what is presently western Alaska. Because of the lower sea levels, the land bridge spanned the Bering Strait between mainland Alaska and northeastern Siberia.

As with all migrations of prehistoric hunter-gatherers, this southward migration took centuries. Archeological evidence indicates that the first Paleolithic Native American tribes entered into present-day Florida approximately ten thousand years ago, some two thousand years after the nomads had entered North America.

It is impossible to imagine, even to speculate how pristine and unspoiled Florida must have looked one hundred centuries ago. Along the gulf side of the state, the peninsula would have extended westward another one hundred miles. All of present-day Florida Bay would have been dry land and the Florida Keys would have been connected to the mainland. Wildlife, from seals to wolves, would have flourished beyond our wildest dreams.

The American alligator, lacking any significant predator, would have probably numbered between three to seven million. The American crocodile would have been equally prolific and the manatee population could well have numbered into the tens of thousands. Florida was much cooler ten thousand years ago. Because of this factor alone, we will never surely know the true number of these populations near the end of the Pleistocene era.

Once the early Native Americans arrived, things began to change. As mentioned before, the first to vanish after the arrival of mankind was the mega-fauna. The giant ground sloth weighing over five thousand pounds were no match against the agile, spear-wielding Clovis people. Mammoths, short-faced bears, New World camels, and dozens of other species were hunted into extinction. The human overkill in the Americas had begun.

Despite those early losses, and in large part because of the small populations of native tribes, Florida remained relatively undisturbed by their presence. At the time of Florida's second invasion by the Spanish in 1513, it presumably held between 100,000–150,000 Native Americans, roughly the present-day population of Tallahassee, Florida's state capital.

Some of those tribes such as the Calusa, who inhabited much of Southwest Florida, were still hunter-gatherers circa 1500. The Calusa did not conduct any farming or herding activity; they relied instead on the bounty of nearby Gulf of Mexico, its rivers, estuaries, and surrounding forests. The Calusa survived on shellfish, manatee, porpoises, fish, whales, deer, and the once plentiful Caribbean monk seals.

North of the Calusa were the Tocobago Indians, living in the greater Tampa Bay region. Along Florida's East Coast, in present-day Miami-Dade area, lived the Tequesta. Throughout much of the state's North-Central part, lived the Timucuan, considerably friendlier to the early Spanish explorers and their accompanying missionaries than were the fierce Calusa. The Timucuan Indians raised corn, beans, squash, and various vegetables, and hunted game such as alligators, manatee, and deer. Their influence extended well into North Georgia, with an estimated total population of 200,000. The Timucuan had begun farming in Florida around the year 1000.

Several other tribes inhabited Florida, including the Apalachee, who inhabited much of the panhandle, and the Cherokee, who lived along what is now the entire northern border of Florida. Another smaller population was the Ais Indians, who lived along the Indian River. Estimates put the total number of various tribes living in Florida at the time of Ponce de León's arrival at forty-five, with almost as many languages and dialects spread amongst them.

The Seminoles, today the most well-known of the Florida Indians, did not exist in 1513. They came into being around 1700 as an assemblage of several endangered Indian tribes, including the Creeks, the Muskogees, and numerous escaped black slaves. The Seminoles stand alone amongst the Native American tribes in that, after years of warring with the U.S. government through the 1700s–1800s, they have never formally surrendered.

Everything began to change in 1513, the year Ponce de León landed near what is present-day St. Augustine. The Spanish brought two things with them that would dramatically alter the course of the peninsula over the next two hundred years: their guns and their diseases. By 1700, due to a complete lack of immunity to diseases that were practically harmless to the Spanish—e.g., the common cold, influenza, smallpox, and chicken pox—the Calusa, Ais, Apalachee, Timucuan, and Tocobago populations were quickly brought to extinction. The natives who didn't die from those diseases were captured and enslaved by the Spanish conquistadors. Some were sold off to the English while others were simply worked to death.

Even though the Indians' well-designed spearheads and bows could easily handle manatees and whitetail deer, they were no match for Spain's swords, cannons, and muskets. The die was cast early on and the lion pride from Europe soon eradicated all of Florida's native peoples.

To the wildlife of the peninsula, the next few hundred years were a blessing. Throughout the next two centuries, the three rival European powers (should we call them prides?)—Spain, France, and Britain—fought each other for the rights to claim *La Florida*. From their constant warring, Florida's overall human population fell, but its native wildlife continued to flourish. By 1771, it is estimated that fewer than ten thousand people, the majority being of European extraction, were living in Florida. The entire state's East Coast held a population of roughly three thousand people, with most of the population centered near the thriving settlement of St. Augustine.

In 1819, after the Spanish had suffered severe hardships in Europe due to the Napoleonic Wars, John Quincy Adams negotiated with Luís de Onís to purchase the east and west portions of the peninsula from Spain. On July 17, 1821, then Governor Andrew Jackson accepted West Florida from Colonel Jose Callava. The price tag for almost all of Florida was $5,000,000, or what you might expect to pay for a nicely appointed condominium penthouse on Miami's South Beach today.

By 1830, there was already talking of statehood. Shortly thereafter, in 1845, Florida was officially admitted into the U.S. The population of Florida had dropped from over one hundred thousand Indians in 1513 to sixty thousand inhabitants at the time of statehood, most of them settlers, and to the south, rebel Seminoles.

As soon as it achieved statehood, Florida began its first marketing campaign for attracting new immigrants to the peninsula. Cotton was the predominate crop near both Pensacola and Jacksonville, but the lumber barons who had already depleted most of the white-pine forests of the Midwest quickly set their sight on the yellow-pine, cypress, and live-oak forests of Florida. Over fifty percent of Florida's forests were once largely southern yellow pine. Only scattered remnants remain today.

Once again, warring factions, this time within the U.S., kept Florida's growth in check. On January 10, 1861, Florida seceded from the Union and joined the Confederacy. Thousands of young soldiers left the state to battle with the Union over the next four years, but only handfuls returned. The Civil War took a devastating toll on Florida's 1861 population of 140,000. For the next twenty years, growth in the Sunshine State was sporadic and slow.

However, during the decades of reconstruction between 1870 and 1900, Florida's population went from 187,748 to 528,542, nearly a three-hundred-percent increase. With the building of railroad lines on both the East and West Coasts, most forests were logged, phosphate and limestone mining increased, and the notorious plume hunters were decimating the southern Everglades' heron and egret rookeries in the name of fashion.

Canals were being dredged for commerce and the natural flow of watersheds diverted into channels and man-made canals. Swamps were drained, alligators hunted without mercy, and panthers and manatee brought to the very edge of extinction. Progress and wildlife seldom coexist....

Several species of animals and birds once common in Florida were eradicated. The Carolina parakeet, the Key West quail dove, the passenger pigeon, the ivory-billed woodpecker, the flamingo, and the king vulture were either exterminated or extirpated (removed from the region, but still in existence elsewhere). The disappearing mammals were the monk seal, the buffalo, and the black-colored wolf (Florida's endemic strain of the red wolf).

Various additional species of birds, including the reddish and the great white egret, would have been lost during that time as well, had the fledgling Audubon Society and the state of Florida not stepped up enforcement against illegal poaching for hat feathers. Luckily, most of these birds have been spared, at least for the time being. The Florida alligator population, suffering from the hide and meat harvest and the gathering of alligator eggs, plummeted dramatically.

Around the turn of the twentieth century, with the infrastructure in place and the U.S. experiencing a period of extreme growth, Florida was ripe for the picking. By the early 1920s, the first great Florida land boom was in full swing. Miami and the East Coast were prospering, and by 1930 Florida's population had jumped another three hundred percent, to 1.5 million. Had it not been for the 1926 and 1928 hurricanes, followed by the 1929 market crash, this number would have been higher.

The powerful and devastating storms of the late 1920s, followed by the Great Depression and WWII, helped to keep Florida's population growth in check for the next twenty years. According to the 1950 U.S. census, Florida was home to 2,771,305 people. From 1950 forward, growth skyrocketed in the Sunshine State. It became one of the world's fastest growing regions and the fourth most populous state in the nation, notwithstanding its being the 22nd largest state in physical size.

By the 1960 census, Florida's population had nearly doubled to 4,951,560. By 1980, it had almost doubled again to 9,746,961. Twenty years later, that number had increased by 6.2 million additional Floridians, totaling the state's population to 15,982,691. Today, the estimated population of Florida is 17,789,864 people, with an additional eleven hundred people pouring across the state line everyday. This phenomenal growth has in large part been attributed to two things: the invention of air conditioning and the control and eradication of malarial and most other mosquitoes.

Florida's population growth rate (2005) is currently fourth in the nation, at 2.3 percent. This growth is topped by only three western states: Arizona (3.5 percent), Nevada (3.5 percent), and Idaho (2.4 percent). Put into perspective, this growth rate is only slightly below that of Bangladesh, which has a growth rate of 2.8 percent. It is higher than Haiti, India, or Mexico. At the current rate of growth, by 2030 Florida will replace New York as the third most populous state in the nation. New York is currently experiencing an annual negative growth rate of -0.1 percent (2005).

At the present rate, Florida will double its population again in slightly more than a thirty years' time. By 2036, Florida will be approaching thirty-five million residents. Since achieving statehood, Florida, despite several of the setbacks mentioned earlier, has still managed to grow twice as fast as the whole U.S. As a result of this sustained growth, its current population density is nearly four times that of the lower forty-eight states. While this density pales when compared with the 1,134 individuals (2000 census) per square mile living in the state of New Jersey, Florida's density of 296 people per square mile falls just behind New York's 401, and far ahead of both California at 217 and Texas at 79.6 people per square mile. I seriously doubt that Florida's fragile ecosystem could possibly sustain New Jersey's present density, although we will hit that number within this century, if current trends continue.

Most of this increase is not due to an increased birthrate, but through both international (legal and illegal) and domestic immigration. Only thirteen percent of Florida's increase came from new births; an astounding eighty-seven percent came from internal and foreign immigration. Florida has the fastest-growing foreign-born population in the U.S., representing 12.8 percent of its population, while the U.S.'s average is 7.9 percent (1990 census).

Whereas Florida's landmass accounts for only 1.5 percent of the total U.S. landmass, its 7,624,378 dwelling units account for six percent of the U.S.'s total of 119,302,132 homes, condominiums, and apartments. This higher density is in no small part due to the tremendous number of mobile-home owners and seasonal occupants who arrive in Florida every November to enjoy the subtropical climate and escape the northern winters. In fact, this 17,789,864 population number takes little into account these snowbirds, along with their automobiles, consumption, and waste. In reality, Florida is already far more crowded than the census statistics would lead us to believe.

Early in the twentieth century, when Florida was sparsely populated, growth had a beneficial aspect to it. More people meant more jobs, improved services, and a higher quality of life. This is no longer the case. Growth, due to increased birthrates, illegal immigration (Florida ranks fourth in the nation), and domestic "in-migration," is no longer a boon to a state already severely overtaxed in its infrastructure and natural resources. The American mantra, "Growth Is Good," fails to apply to Florida. Growth is destroying its quality of life and should be looked at in much the same manner as cancer (i.e., uncontrolled growth), which is altogether bad and pernicious.

The negative ramifications of this explosive growth are everywhere in the Sunshine State. Highways are congested and barely serviceable, schools overcrowded, medical and emergency services strained, and the pressure on Florida's indigenous wildlife is overwhelming. As might be expected, both the crime rate and vehicular accident rate have shot upward over the past fifty-plus years. In the year 2002, 906 people were murdered in Florida. Nearly one million crimes were committed and 789,817 arrests were made. We are rapidly running out of prisons to accommodate this steady stream of prisoners.

In 2004, there were 252,902 reported automobile crashes on the highways, resulting in 227,192 injuries and 3,257 fatalities. This equates to nine deaths per day. More people mean more roads and more roads lead to more traffic and more accidents. Florida, with almost six percent of the nation's population, has just 2.8 percent of the nation's roads. The Sunshine State's highways—without either factoring in the eighty million tourists who visit it or the millions of snowbirds—already have twice the traffic of other typical U.S. roadways. Most, if not all, of our highway and roadway systems are failing, and failing miserably.

Every single day in Florida, over 450 acres of forest and 410 acres of farmland are lost to new developments, commercial buildings, and additional infrastructure. Because most of this clearing is done to add development, which in turn increases density, Florida's infrastructure will never catch up.

The end result is a continual loss of habitat for the native flora and fauna. Circa 1900, over fifty-one percent of the state would have been considered wetlands. Today, this percentage stands at less than thirty percent and decreasing at a precipitous rate. The continuous loss of wetlands parallels the loss of the wildlife that seek refuge in those remaining open spaces. Here are just some of the Florida species, both large and small, on the endangered-species list:

● **Mammals:** the Right, the Sei, the Finback, the Sperm, and the Humpback whale; the Florida mastiff, the Grey, and the Indiana bat; the Florida panther; the Key deer; the Key Largo cotton mouse; the Anastasia Island, the Choctawhatchee, the Perdido Key, and the St. Andrews beach mice; the West Indian manatee; the Lower Keys marsh rabbit; the Silver rice rat; the Key Largo woodrat; and the Duke's saltmarsh mole.

● **Birds:** The Cape Sable seaside and the Florida grasshopper sparrow; the Ivory-billed woodpecker (believed to be extinct not only in Florida, but possibly in the world over); the Kirtland's and the Bachman's warbler; the Wood stork; the Snail kite; and the Arctic peregrine falcon.

● **Fish:** the Shortnose sturgeon; the Okaloosa darter; the Smalltooth sawfish; and the Blackmouth shiner.

● **Amphibians and reptiles:** The Atlantic green, the Atlantic hawksbill, the Atlantic ridley, the Leatherback, and the striped mud turtle; and the American crocodile.

• **Invertebrates:** The Miami blue and the Schauss swallowtail butterfly; the Pillar coral; and the Stock Island tree snail.

But the real scope of the problem becomes apparent when we add both the *threatened* and the *species of special concern* to this list. We, then, find ourselves potentially losing many of the most renowned and admired mammals, birds, fish, and reptiles in Florida. A sampling of these species includes: Everglades mink, Bald eagle, Florida sandhill crane, Reddish egret, Snowy egret, Tri-colored heron, Roseate spoonbill, Limpkin, Little blue heron, Brown pelican, Osprey, Common snook, Atlantic sturgeon, Key blenny, American alligator, Indigo snake, Gopher turtle, Alligator snapping turtle, and Florida tree snail.

Imagine a Florida devoid of most species of wading birds, including the Snowy egrets and Tri-colored herons. As the remaining wetlands are drained for new subdivisions, hospitals, schools, and all the so-called necessities of modern man, those animals cannot find sufficient remnant habitats in which to survive. Estimates by state biologists calculate that, to save the remaining birds, reptiles, and mammals, Florida must set aside an additional five million acres as future sanctuaries. Lacking that commitment, envision a state comprised of freeways, parking lots, rooftops, and amusement parks from the Georgia border to Key West.... You, then, have a fairly accurate picture of the state of Florida mid-century thence.

Looking at this 1950s postcard, there is little wonder why Florida's sea turtles are on the endangered-species list.

One of the largest problems Florida faces goes far beyond its skyrocketing population, namely, the impact every individual has in this ecosystem when compared with the impact of people living in less developed or less environmentally demanding nations.

It is a well-known and often-quoted fact that, although U.S.'s citizens account for only 4.6 percent of the world's population, we control twenty-nine percent of its wealth. The average American has roughly seventeen times the purchasing power of an individual in a low-income nation such as Morocco, Vietnam, or Pakistan.

When it comes to using raw materials (lumber, iron, aluminum, cement, et cetera) and energy consumption (oil, coal, gas, natural gas, and electricity), the numbers are staggering. An infant born in the U.S. represents twice the environmental and raw materials' consumption impact of a child born in Sweden; three times that of an Italian baby; thirteen times that of a child born in Brazil; thirty-five times that of an Indian child; one hundred and forty times the impact of a child born in Bangladesh; and an astounding 280 times that of a person born in Rwanda, Haiti, or Nepal.

Using these statistics and plugging them into the population equation, the real environmental impact of Florida's current 17,789,864 people—when we add their natural-resource consumption and their waste production (garbage, CO_2, effluent, chemical by-products such as excess nitrogen, phosphorus, et cetera)—to compare with that of an individual living in Nepal, we arrive at an effective population of 4.9 billion. Florida currently has a raw materials' consumption population of nearly five billion people. By 2030, fewer than twenty-five years from now, Florida will be approaching thirty million Americans, but it will have an environmental impact population of ten billion. Given these foreboding statistics, it's no wonder that the Florida panther and the West Indian manatee are endangered.

This population boom is also having an impact on the state's freshwater resources. The water required for residential purposes per Floridian per day has been calculated at 1,318 gallons. Aquifers are rapidly becoming depleted, which in turn result in saltwater intrusions and sink holes. The latter are created when water is pumped out of limestone cavities deep beneath the surface. Sink holes are becoming a common occurrence across the state. Florida is rapidly running out of water just as millions of acres of thirsty residential lawns continue to sprawl across a Los Angeles–styled landscape.

Aside from the population and excessive immigration problems facing our state, in the twenty-first century there are several looming issues which will ultimately affect every species currently residing in *La Florida*, including our own: *Homo sapiens*.

Hurricanes

There are two trains entering a tunnel. It is not a very long tunnel, perhaps no more than a decade long, metaphorically speaking. One train has no conductor at all, but is being propelled forward by the forces of nature, the unalterable dynamics of physics and thermal energy. The other train has a conductor who refuses to acknowledge the fact that its counterpart, which existence is scientifically undeniable, is heading full throttle in his direction. A collision is imminent. The death toll could be unimaginable, the social and economic consequences dire, and the repercussions from the impact reverberate for centuries to come.

This is the scenario of Florida's rampant growth and the currently projected twenty-year cycle of intense hurricanes by the National Oceanic and Atmospheric Administration (NOAA), under the watchful eyes of Dr. William Grey, a noted expert in hurricane forecasts, plus a host of meteorology experts. Florida is on a collision course with Mother Nature and that collision will be catastrophic.

The writing is on the wall. By every known measure, the 2005 hurricane season blew away all previous hurricane records and statistics. Assuming that global warming is taking place, the 2005 hurricane season shall be remembered as the bellwether for several decades worth of storms as violent as, or worse than, Hurricane Katrina, the most damaging storm ever recorded in human history. By and large, the powers that be—the governmental authorities controlling growth, developments, condominiums, water management, building codes, evacuation planning, and insurance premiums—are either ignoring this warning shot or spinning the current situation as a statistical anomaly.

Week after week, Florida's newspapers gloss over the rising sea temperatures, melting glaciers, and rising ocean levels, focusing only on the "twenty-year cycle" and its familiar pattern of increased Atlantic storms. Nothing could be further from the truth: There were no melting glaciers during the last increase in active storms; back in the 1930s, the earth had not just experienced nine out of ten of the warmest years on record, including the two warmest ever recorded (#1 in 2005 and #2 in 1998); the Arctic ice hadn't been reduced by forty percent and carbon-dioxide levels weren't the highest they had been in 650,000 years….

This coming cycle will be greatly exacerbated by the problems associated with global warming. Ignoring that fact will not make it go away. You can spin all the official government propaganda you want to the contrary, but Mother

Nature will remain fully oblivious to the nearsighted interests of those who misinform and spin.

The 2005 hurricane season produced twenty-seven tropical and subtropical storms and shattered the 1933 record of twenty-one named storms. Fourteen of those storms became hurricanes, topping the 1969 record of twelve. The 1950 record of eight major hurricanes (category three or above) still stands, but the 2005 season missed that mark by one, ending the year with seven major storms. The 2005 season tied the 1999 one with five category-four-or-above storms and broke the record for the most category-five hurricanes in a single year with three deadly storms, all three making direct hits on the U.S.: Katrina, Rita, and Wilma.

If that weren't enough, the 2005 season produced the second storm ever to form on December 30, tying a record set in 1954 by Hurricane Alice. The storm was named Zeta because the 2005 hurricane season had exhausted the initial list of

A satellite shot of Katrina as it swept through the central Gulf Coast.

twenty-one Roman alphabetical names and NOAA had to turn to the Greek alphabet for additional names. You can only wonder which alphabet they will turn to when we soon run out of Greek letters.

The 2005 hurricane season produced the first tropical storm ever known to hit Europe when the remnants of Hurricane Vince hit Spain on October 11. Hurricane Wilma, which eventually turned toward Florida, recorded the lowest barometric pressure ever (882 millibars) breaking a seventeen-year record held by Hurricane Hugo. Only a handful of Pacific super typhoons have ever produced barometric pressure readings below 882 millibars. Wilma was also the strongest hurricane ever recorded with sustained winds of 175 miles per hour.

Hurricane Wilma holds another very alarming record, of which every Florida inhabitant must take careful note: On October 18, 2005, Wilma formed a tiny, well-defined eye in the central Caribbean Sea. Within twenty-four hours, the central pressure inside that eye dropped from a "cat-one" status of 980 millibars to its record breaking 882 millibars. In effect, overnight, Hurricane Wilma became a cat-five storm. This rapid drop in pressure (ninety-eight millibars) broke the previous record drop of ninety-two millibars set by the super typhoon Forrest in the western Pacific in 1983. No one could have forecast such a dramatic increase of intensity in so short a time. Had Wilma been a small, cat-one hurricane located just off the Florida Peninsula which erupted into a cat five in a similar time frame as Forrest's and *then* made landfall, there would have been no hope of a successful evacuation.

This is a very similar scenario to what happened during the 1935 Labor Day storm that hit the Florida Keys. Like Katrina, the 1935 Labor Day storm produced an immense tidal surge and is considered by most meteorologists the single most powerful storm to ever hit Continental U.S. It has been estimated that its sustained winds were over 170 miles per hour and the gusts exceeded two hundred miles per hour. The storm destroyed Flagler's railroad and killed over six hundred people.

The total estimated damages done by the four storms that hit the U.S. during the 2005 hurricane season are anticipated to top one hundred billion dollars (the fourth storm was Dennis, which hit the Florida Panhandle early in the season). Hurricane Katrina will likely end up being the third most deadly hurricane to ever hit the U.S., with a projected death toll of 1,383 across seven states. Only the Galveston storm of 1900 (eight-thousand-plus killed) and the Lake Okeechobee storm of 1928 (1,836 dead) took more human lives. Katrina produced one of the highest storm surges ever recorded when it came ashore at 7 A.M. on August 29, 2005. Because it remained in the gulf for several days and hit at a perpendicular angle, Hurricane Katrina produced a thirty-foot storm surge and wiped out almost everything in its path.

Since 1851, 277 hurricanes have hit Mainland U.S. Of that number, 112 have hit the state of Florida. Statistically, Florida is hit by forty percent of all hurricanes that strike the U.S. Simply stated, two out of every five hurricanes hit Florida. This number does not include tropical storms, which by themselves can cause severe flooding, spawn tornadoes, and cause extensive property damage. Florida holds the record for being hit by the most major hurricanes: thirty-seven category-three-or-stronger hurricanes since 1851. Texas is a distant second: eighteen major storms have made landfall in the Lone Star State.

With the combination of increased activity over the next two decades and a population expected to reach thirty million in the next twenty-five years, we are heading toward an unavoidable collision with the meteorological monster we've helped to create: global warming. Whenever we sit in traffic on overcrowded, congested highways, we must recognize that ours and the hundreds of automobiles surrounding us are helping build these super hurricanes. Our carbon emissions contain thousands of tons of CO_2. We are in fact creating the monster storms that will eventually spin in to destroy us.

Hurricanes can and will control growth, but they tend to be far more devastating than other natural controls such as zoning boards, improved building codes, and sound growth management. The great 1920s Florida land boom was in large part brought to its knees by the back-to-back hurricanes of 1926 (the great Miami hurricane) and 1928 (the deadly Lake Okeechobee hurricane). If the great Miami hurricane of '26 were to hit today—and it would probably be a stronger storm due to global warming—its cost could exceed one trillion dollars.

Florida is in the process of positioning itself for the Omega storm, or the storm that will pale Hurricane Katrina by comparison. Imagine the Omega storm two hundred miles south-southeast of Miami. Like the great 1935 Labor Day storm and Hurricane Wilma, the Omega storm is a well-defined but non-threatening cat-one storm as it approaches southern Dade County.

Overnight, it drops one hundred millibars and becomes a "cat-five 'cane." No one has time to evacuate and those who attempt it are trapped in traffic jams that run for miles up Interstate 95. The storm comes ashore with sustained winds of 170 miles an hour just as did the Labor Day storm of September 2, 1935, which made landfall a mere forty miles west of downtown Miami. Greater Miami, South Beach, and suburban Dade County are decimated by the twenty-five-foot storm surge and relentless winds. The cars stuck in traffic are washed or blown away.

The Omega storm tracks north-northwest, cutting across Florida. Depending on the time of year and the amount of standing water across the peninsula, the storm could gain strength just as Hurricane Wilma did when it crossed the state in late 2005. Given the worst-case scenario of its track, it could readily take out Lake Okeechobee's levees just as Katrina took out New Orleans's levees. Thousands would be trapped beneath the floodwaters flowing south through Clewiston and Belle Glade. By then, given the current trend, thousands of new homes built in the old sugarcane fields would be added to the destruction.

The storm would then continue north-northwest and eventually exit near Tampa Bay. If the winds were strong enough and their field wide enough, every mobile home in the south-central portion of the state would be destroyed. It is conceivable that the death toll could reach 100,000. The insurance losses could exceed insurers' capacity and thus bankrupt the system. No one would receive a dime in insurance claims and the U.S. government would not be able to sustain that debt as it attempted to cover the staggering losses.

The cost of rebuilding would fuel a tremendous demand on the world's remaining natural resources, especially lumber. Ironically, every time we remove a tree, we remove one of the few organic carbon sinks on earth. The process of rebuilding helps generate further global warming and thereby create larger, stronger hurricanes, which will in turn fully destroy all that had just been rebuilt. In effect, *Homo sapiens* are building its own doomsday machine.

The Omega storm regains its strength in the Gulf of Mexico, which in 2005 recorded the warmest water temperatures since the first record tabulation in 1890. The hurricane hooks north and hits the panhandle, taking out Pensacola in the process. Florida is hit twice and three large cities are directly impacted. Insured and uninsured infrastructure losses exceed one trillion dollars. The trains have met in the tunnel and the collision is worse than ever imagined.

Although the Omega storm is a worst-case scenario, it is equally doubtful that Florida could withstand one Katrina-like hurricane hitting the state per year over the next twenty years. As one area prepared to recover from the previous year's storm, it would simultaneously prepare to be itself devastated by another. For the past few years, this has already been the situation in many counties throughout Florida. One Omega or fifteen lesser storms can amount to the same untenable situation.

Florida, like California, is built on a fault line…only Florida's fault line comes by way of tropical cyclones and is far more reliable than the San Andreas Fault that lies beneath San Francisco. Our fault line has a well-defined history and is veering toward more powerful and more frequent occurrences. What has become Florida's response to this coming crisis? State and local leaders are handing out building permits in record numbers for the sake of promoting growth and prosperity for all….

For folly this unspeakable, there is no known natural law to ensure the survival of the most foolish.

A Dying Gulf of Mexico

The repercussions of the last fifty years of Florida's growth are beginning to seriously impact the state's entire West Coast, as well as Florida Bay. Bays and estuaries are caught in an endless deluge of increasing nutrients fed by inadequate sewer systems, thousands of septic systems, lawn fertilizer, phosphate mining, and an excess of golf courses. This nitrogen-rich soup is wreaking havoc on the natural controls' capacity to absorb its rampaging onrush. As a result, Florida's delicate marine ecosystems are starting to collapse. Given the ultimate failure of most West Coast estuaries, the collapse of the Gulf of Mexico will likely follow.

It is ironic that Florida boasts the largest number of golf courses of any state in the Union. With over 1,250 golf courses and hundreds more on drawing boards statewide, this statistic at first glance appears to be one Florida is proud of. But when we look at the by-products created by these hundreds of golf courses, the reality of golf's overall impact on the state cannot be measured in convenient tee times.

Golf was invented in Scotland, where it was played on windy, open fields in the summer. One of America's favorite pastimes notwithstanding, environmentally speaking golf should have never left Scotland. Every golf course, even those attempting to adhere to sound environmental practices, produces tons of chemical residuals, most of which end up somewhere in the streams, rivers, lakes, and in Florida's case, ultimately either in the Atlantic or the Gulf of Mexico.

These pollutants include fertilizer, pesticides, herbicides, fungicides, and a host of related chemicals. Golf courses and their surrounding subdivisions invariably begin their toxic journey by clearing away the native flora and fauna and by replacing those plants with imported exotics, which demand constant care. By the same token, the residential lawns (often mandatory) in subdivisions surrounding those planned golf-course developments only help to further exacerbate the problem.

Is this the future look of Florida's fabled beaches?

Grasslands are few and far between in Florida, especially in the southern portion of the state. Here is where most of these artificial, chemically maintained environments exist.

The runoff from golf courses, lawns, and commercial developments, along with that of Florida's sugar, citrus, and agricultural industries is resulting in the death of most West Coast estuaries and many of those on the East Coast as well.

The eastern outflow of nutrient-rich water from Lake Okeechobee has destroyed the Indian River/Port St. Lucie estuary on the East Coast, just as the western outflow down the Caloosahatchee River is rapidly killing the once vibrant estuary of San Carlos Bay and Pine Island Sound in Lee County. To the south, Naples Bay recently received an "F minus" by the Conservancy of Southwest Florida. The nutrient levels in the bay are so high that virtually everything in Naples Bay is dead or dying.

Charlotte Harbor received a "C minus" and remains one of the few surviving estuaries along the West Coast. The harbor suffers from an excess of phosphate loading coming from the phosphate mining operations along the Peace River, which ultimately feeds into greater Charlotte Harbor. Sarasota Bay has been caught in a seemingly endless cycle of red tide since 2004. Farther north, in the large Tampa Bay area, pollution is coming in from the air, storm-water runoff, oil spills, incoming ocean vessels, and myriad other sources.

The waters off Florida's West Coast are relatively shallow for one hundred miles offshore. As a result, these near-shore waters are far more vulnerable to the long-term effects of sustained pollution and nutrient loading. Red-tide incidents have increased dramatically in the past twenty years and the West Coast's once pristine beaches are being repeatedly shut down by local health departments due to excess bacteria levels and related health issues.

The marine ecosystem in Florida is collapsing. The postcard shots of palm trees and sandy beaches are in reality all too often being replaced by Health Department warnings informing you that entering the water could land you in the hospital. Eventually, this situation will gain visibility across the country and severely impact Florida's multibillion-dollar tourist industry. Development has a price tag. We are just now witnessing that said price tag in our watersheds and surrounding seas.

In the larger picture, the Gulf of Mexico is having serious issues of its own. There is currently a dead zone near the mouth of the Mississippi River, which encompasses an area the size of Massachusetts or roughly ten times the size of Lake Okeechobee. This lifeless, oxygen-deprived zone is growing at an alarming rate; we can only speculate that, sooner or later, it will envelope most of the gulf. As the West Coast's estuaries collapse, they create their own micro-dead zones and the degradation continues. In 2001, a huge body of lifeless, black water covered much of Florida Bay, killing everything in its path.

The fabled Florida Keys, the only living reef in the U.S., are suffering from many of the same symptoms. In 1955, in her trailblazing *A Silent Spring*, Rachel Carson wrote the following: "In the multicolored sea gardens seen from a boat as one drifts above them, there is a tropical lushness and mystery, a throbbing sense of the pressure of life: in coral reef and mangrove swamp, there are the dimly seen foreshadowings (sic) of the future."

The future for the Florida reef is no longer certain. Less than seven percent of the reef Carson wrote about in 1955 is still alive. Given the rate of decline, most corals, sponges, and a host of other living organisms will be completely gone within the next twenty years. The reefs are bleaching out or simply collapsing beneath a deluge of polluted sea water.

With an annual immigration of 370,000 people to Florida, there will not be an easy solution to this problem. The dying estuaries are already creating problems for Florida's once fabled commercial and fishing-guide industry; the boating industry will soon follow suit. Lacking any fish to catch or harvest, it's difficult to imagine selling fishing equipment or fishing licenses to anglers along either coast. The sheer numbers and demands of our species, *Homo sapiens*, are overwhelming the environmental systems of Florida. Something has to change.

A Mission Statement

With considerable authority, astronomers and scientists state that our sun has a remaining life span between four to five billion years. As a species, we are predisposed to live in the present. Our evolutionary development through the millennia has hardwired us to pay attention to the immediate. The unexpected snap of a twig on the outskirts of our camp could well be the leopard that killed one of our tribe a week ago. Most of the world's six-billion-plus people have little time to fret about changing weather patterns or overcrowded cities, states, and nations. What concerns the vast majority of people on this planet is what they are going to eat tomorrow and the day after that.

For the Western world, up until a handful of centuries ago the world was flat. The sun rotated around this flat surface, ships plummeted off the edge, and being God's chosen people, we could not have possibly evolved from monkeys. Only in the past one hundred years have we been aware of the plight of thousands of other animal species on the earth.

With the transistor's spawning of a sweeping revolution in modern telecommunications—making affordable and accessible technological marvels such as global phones, television, radio, and the Internet—our knowledge of the world has increased dramatically. If a dozen Russian hostages are taken and killed by rebels in Groznyy, we know about it within the hour. If someone dies from the bird flu in Hong Kong, his or her demise is broadcast on the evening news.

One thousand years ago, we would never have known. Two hundred years ago, we might have learned of it years, perhaps decades afterward. One hundred years ago, by using the telegraph we might have found out about it in less than one week. Today, using the technology our inquisitive brains have created, we know about everything immediately.

It is ironic that the two most important inventions of all time came about within twenty-five years of each other. One, the atomic bomb, is capable of destroying mankind; the other, the transistor, is capable of saving it. But these two are merely tools…which, in the hands of the wrong person can be used for harm as readily as they can for the betterment of society. Within a decade's time, literally all the knowledge mankind has accumulated since the dawn of time will be available to anyone capable of operating a handheld personal digital assistant like the Blackberry. From the cave paintings of Altamira to a perpetual stream of electronically digitized information in thirty thousand years…what a marvel is mankind!

But we cannot conceive of four billion years. It is just a number—

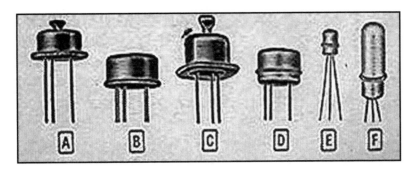

The invention of the transistor could be deemed the greatest invention of all times.

4,000,000,000—a four followed by nine zeros. As a species, we have existed about a mere 170,000 years. Geologically speaking, we are a spark, a momentary flicker of existence that means nothing to a universe which appears to be infinite in design. If we vanish, we do so by our own hand and, given the amount of sunlight left in that great candle in the sky, the forces of nature and evolutionary progression will assuredly go back to the drawing board and give intelligent life another shot at forever. We will be written off as a noble, albeit foolhardy, experiment—a dead-ended branch in the great tree of life.

There is no doubt in my heart about the ascension of our species. We are earth's most amazing and spellbinding species and our list of accomplishments will not be nullified by our failures, if indeed we end up failing. Thirty thousand years ago, we created art and, thus far, have been the only species known to do such a thing. We aspire to be God. Billions of years ago, life began with single-celled creatures capable of little more than recreating themselves. There is an undeniable logarithm to life—from bacteria to Bach.

But the time has come for us to evolve beyond the immediate. If we truly aspire to be like God, then we must change. We are overwhelming the planet with our short-term, myopic behavior and our insufferable predisposition for immediate gratification. Our actions are not only killing our fellow predators—the alligators, sharks, and panthers of this planet—but also the entire spectrum of flora and fauna. Losing a single species is like pulling teeth from the mouth of God.

At our present rate of population growth and avid raw-material consumption, it is doubtful that we will make it another thousand years. There are those amongst us who see all of this as preordained and anxiously await their private apocalypses. Fortunately, they are in the minority. Whereas such a bleak future makes for riveting headlines and impressive book sales, the more likely reality is that no one is coming back to save us from ourselves. First and foremost, we must commit to the long haul or to not at all. Doomsday-thinking will ultimately end in creating a doomsday. Western society has to bury the myths contained in Revelations and carry on…the sooner the better.

Like any well-planned organization, the human race needs a mission statement. You could say we already have a mission statement, but it's hyper-dysfunctional because the human race currently has 6.5 billion mission statements—over two billion of them go to bed hungry every night.

We are locked with ourselves in this cabin called earth; we are both the puma and the lineman. Right now, the puma—our aggressive, instinctual nature—is winning. Our pollution, our overpopulation, our neediness, and our sense of immediacy, all of which have served us so well in the past, have now come to be our worst enemy. We cannot have it all.

For every action there is a reaction. The scales have tipped because we have loaded too much weight on our side of the equation. The world we are handing to our children is not better than the world that was handed to us. Whereas fifty years ago scientists spent much of their time adding new species to their respective taxa, today they spend more time adding names to the ever-growing list of extinct species. Whether we admit it or not, we are locked into a future of diminishing returns. Only we can conquer ourselves and only we can stop this parade of human madness.

Within the next one hundred years, the world's oceans will rise by at least one meter, some say more. Most remaining icecaps and glaciers will be gone. In all likelihood, we will run out of atmosphere long before we run out of oil. Hundreds, perhaps thousands, of additional species of wild animals will vanish from their wild habitats. Many will vanish completely, victims of Leakey's prophetic sixth extinction. We are the biological asteroid slamming into our own planet.

Six decades ago, a great American, Franklin D. Roosevelt, expressed what I feel might be a good starting point for humanity's mission statement. It is known as the Four Freedoms Speech and it applies not only to the Western world, but also to all of earth's peoples and nations:

> In the future days which we seek to make secure, we look forward to a world founded upon four essential freedoms. The first is freedom of speech and expression—everywhere in the world. The second is freedom of every person to worship God in his own way—everywhere in the world. The third is freedom from want, which, translated into world terms, means economic understandings which will secure to every nation a healthy peacetime life for its inhabitants—everywhere in the world. The fourth is freedom from fear, which, translated into world terms, means a worldwide reduction of armaments to such a

point and in such a thorough fashion that no nation will be in a position to commit an act of physical aggression against any neighbor—anywhere in the world.

The first freedom will not arrive from being granted to us by any authority, but has already arrived via a world of cell phones and the Internet. In the near future, these technologies will allow anyone to communicate with everyone else in the world with ease and without regard to language barriers. Electronic translators are already being developed and, given the exponential evolution of computer technology, these are, at most, a few decades away. Our technological prowess is leading the charge to ensure that everyone on this planet has his or her freedom of speech and expression, regardless of the political machinery designed to restrict those freedoms.

The second freedom will be more difficult to achieve, given our proclivity to want others to behave and worship as we do. There is already too much 9/11 thinking in this world and this freedom will be fought for through the millennia to come. The difference between the Middle East Mullahs and the Bible Belt Pastors is negligible at best. Nonetheless, religious freedom must remain a basic freedom for all. The teaching of religious tolerance will be the key to solving this issue.

The third freedom speaks to us about sustainability, not growth. To be free from want, we must control the demands that our species places on the earth's natural systems. We cannot deforest the world and exact an endless supply of lumber. We cannot maintain the current global population numbers and expect to no longer see billions of humans living in deplorable conditions. We must not only stop human population growth; we must decrease our current numbers by over half. If we don't scale back our numbers, the immutable forces of nature will do it for us. Cataclysm is the catalyst of change. Plagues, wars, and starvation have reduced our populations very effectively in the past. They stand at the ready once again, should we fail to make this planet habitable for us and all living things.

The fourth freedom, freedom from our own warring nature, is by far the most difficult to achieve. We are who we are and our bloody history bears witness to our savage psyche. In the end, we actually have little to fear from alligators, sharks, and panthers. If you want to see the most destructive, violent animal on earth, find a mirror. Look inside of your own soul and acknowledge the fact that you are the greatest predator that has ever walked on this planet. We—with our incredible skills, intelligence, tenacity, and aggression—now stand alone at the top of the world's food chain.

At first, this book wasn't supposed to be about mankind, or man-unkind, at all. Its original title was ***Alligators, Sharks & Panthers: Deadly Encounters*** *with Florida's Top Predators.* As I gathered information and studied the brilliant biology of those creatures, I became increasingly more aware of their plight. Somewhere along the way, I realized these animals, albeit deadly and worthy of our respect, have killed fewer than thirty people in fifty-seven years. Nine people a day die on Florida's highways alone.

Halfway through this manuscript, I understood this book wasn't about them, but about us. They were here first and, left to themselves, they would be here until they, too, evolved into something new. This book, nevertheless, remains about the earth's most ferocious and lethal predator: MAN...all seventeen million of us in Florida, 6.5 billion in the world, and counting....

Four billion years hence, think about it.

This book is dedicated to the dreams and the
memory of Janie Melsek (10/26/1949 – 7/23/2004)

A Dark, Dark Shadow

George Burgess, Ph.D., Director of the International Shark Attack File (ISAF), has gone on record saying that, although overall shark attacks along the Gulf Coast of Florida are more infrequent than those along the Atlantic Coast, the sharks in the gulf tend to be larger and the sustained injuries more serious. Perhaps the only known great-white-shark attack in Florida occurred in the Gulf of Mexico on September 20, 1911. The records of that attack are sketchy but sufficient enough to allow the ISAF to include the incident in its historical records dating back to 1580.

That attack, now nearly one hundred years ago, happened south of Panama City in Santa Rosa County. It involved a ship's pilot, whose name was never officially recorded. The story goes that this particular individual fell overboard and was swallowed whole by an enormous shark some twenty feet in length. The only sharks known to reach this size are the great white and the tiger shark. Although great whites are rare in Florida, there are anecdotal and confirmed accounts of the species' being caught by anglers from the Florida Keys up to the panhandle. Typically, however, great whites show up during the winter months as they prefer cooler water temperatures.

The official Florida State fishing record for a great white shark stands at 686 pounds. An even larger great white, estimated to be over twelve-feet long and weighing over half a ton, was sighted by two anglers off Jacksonville, Florida, on March 9, 2004. Several photographs of the shark were e-mailed to Dr. Burgess, who positively identified the animal as a great white shark, or Carcharodon carcharias. Historically, it is well documented that the large, serrated teeth of great whites were used by Native Americans living along the West Coast of Florida for spear tips and arrowheads. In 1911, Florida still had a viable population of Caribbean monk seals, making the appearance of the pinniped-eating great white a far more likely event. Because tiger sharks can also grow to twenty-foot-plus lengths, and the shark was never captured, there is the possibility it was an immense tiger shark which swallowed the ship's pilot whole on that September nearly a century ago.

But it wasn't a tiger or a great white shark that cast its dark shadow on the morning of June 25, 2005, some two hundred yards off the beach east of Destin, Florida. It was a bull shark. Although the great white shark, because of its notoriety stemming from the film *Jaws*, tends to be regarded as the most dangerous fish in the ocean, the reality is, the title should belong to the smaller—but more widespread and aggressive—bull shark. From the Zambezi River, in Africa, to the mouth of the Ganges, in Asia; from Lake Nicaragua, in

Central America, to the entire Florida coastline, the bull shark has been known to attack, kill, and consume human beings.

For young Jamie Daigle, who in all likelihood had no idea how dangerous bull sharks could be, that Saturday morning in June began like so many other days along the pristine beaches of Florida's panhandle. No one had seen any sharks swimming in the region recently and there had not been warnings posted. In short, there wasn't any reason for Daigle and her girlfriend, Felicia Venable, to fear paddling out as far as they did that morning. It was just an ordinary weekend morning at a beach on a warm day in June, along Florida's Emerald Coast; nothing out of the ordinary.

Jamie Marie Daigle, of Gonzales, Louisiana, was vacationing just east of Destin with her friend when the incident occurred. Both girls were fourteen and both were swimming with boogie boards when they first spotted the shark. Boogie boards are short, chopped-off surfboards, oftentimes used to body surf. They are generally constructed out of foam and provide excellent flotation support for near-shore swimmers. Because of their length, a person swimming with a boogie board always leaves their back legs dangling or kicking in the water behind the board—a position that would prove deadly to Daigle.

Earlier that morning, a local surfer by the name of Tim Dicus had told several swimmers not to go out too far because of the potential for shark attacks in the deeper water. But he hadn't spoken with either Daigle or Venable and, seeing the water was calm and the boogie boards were easy to paddle, the two young girls decided to see what it was like out in the deeper water. The teenagers waded out in front of the Gulf Holiday Travel Park, where they were staying and proceeded to swim more than two hundred yards from shore. At this point, beyond the second sandbar, the water drops off quickly and sharks have been observed there in the past chasing schools of mullet and baitfish.

Just minutes before the attack, both girls saw the dark shadow of the shark beneath the surface. In an instant, the eight-foot-plus bull shark swam up and bit Jamie Daigle on her upper left leg. The bite was so deep, it instantly severed her femoral artery, taking so much flesh away that Daigle's femur bone lay completely exposed. Daigle's bleeding was uncontrollable. Venable screamed and started swimming frantically toward shore. It was obvious to everyone on the beach, as well as to several nearby surfers, that there had been a shark attack.

As fate would have it, Tim Dicus, the same man who had warned swimmers earlier in the day about the potential for shark attacks, was fewer than fifty yards from the two girls when Jamie Daigle was attacked. He stayed on his surfboard and paddled over to where the girl was floating facedown in a massive blood pool. The shark was swimming beneath him as Dicus loaded Daigle's body onto his board. Daigle was unconscious and had already gone into shock by the time Dicus arrived.

By this time, Felicia Venable had almost reached shore, but was completely hysterical and unable to be of any real help. Chris White, who was vacationing on the same stretch of beach, had heard Venable's screams and leapt into the water. White started swimming toward the deep water where the attack had occurred. Another beachgoer who had a raft teamed up with White and they both began towing the raft toward Dicus and his surfboard.

The rapacious bull shark was still a factor. It circled back several times and tried to bite Daigle's hand off as it dangled over the edge of the surfboard. Dicus punched the shark in the nose several times to fend it off and was never bitten by the fish.

In an interview given to a local paper later that day Dicus said, "He (the bull shark) was really aggressive. I've been here a long time and I've never seen a shark get that aggressive."

As Dicus kept a careful eye on the shark circling the water beneath him, he made slow but steady progress back toward shore with Daigle's limp body lying on his surfboard. In a few minutes, he met up with White and his friend with the raft. At that point, the three of them transferred Daigle's body into the relative safety of the raft. As it turned out, Chris White was a volunteer firefighter from Carrollton, Georgia, who had recently completed EMT training. He immediately noted the gravity of Daigle's leg wound and probably realized that her chances of surviving the bite were not good.

As the trio continued to pull the girl back to shore, the shark stayed with them. At one point Dicus yelled to White, "He's here! He's here! There's the shark!"

At that point, White looked down and saw the bull shark directly below him, behaving as if it were going to bite him as well. White said, "I looked down and he (the shark) was swimming at my feet. We all stopped swimming, just went limp vertical in the water, just dangled my legs, tried not to look like any kind of food or anything."

Dicus resumed to distract the shark, going so far as punching the fish in the nose. Luckily for all three rescuers, the enigmatic rule of sharks' rarely attacking would-be rescuers came into play. Although all three men were easy targets, the bull shark was intent only on re-biting the already bitten. No one has really put forth a viable reason for this kind of shark behavior, but it is an established fact that ninety-nine percent of all people involved in shark-victim rescue attempts never get bitten by the attacking shark. On that tragic day, the statistic held.

Once on the beach, paramedics attempted to revive the girl. Regrettably, Jamie Daigle had lost too much blood; the paramedics were unable to save her. Daigle was then taken to Sacred Heart Hospital in Destin, where she was pronounced dead. The shark that bit her swam off and was never found. The following day, the beaches along a twenty-mile stretch near Destin were closed because of the fatal attack. Since no sharks were noticed, on the next Monday those same beaches were reopened.

Three days later, some eighty miles east of where Jamie Daigle had been killed, a second near-fatal bull-shark attack occurred. In this incident, a sixteen-year-old boy was fishing in waist-deep water when a six-foot, six-inch shark severely bit the young angler in his right thigh, almost severing his leg in the process. Craig A. Hutto survived the attack in large part because there just happened to be a physician on the beach when he was dragged ashore. The doctor, noticing that the boy's femoral artery had been severed, immediately stopped the bleeding with a tourniquet, thus saving his life. Hutto's leg was amputated, but he miraculously survived much of the same type of bite that had killed Jamie Daigle. The beaches near Cape San Blas, where this attack occurred, were likewise closed for a few days after the second attack.

In 2001, a few years prior to these back-to-back attacks, little eight-year-old Jessie Arbogast was also attacked by a six-and-a-half-foot, two-hundred-pound bull shark at Langdon Beach, near Pensacola. Arbogast was left seriously brain-damaged from massive blood loss after the shark bit through his thigh and ripped off his right arm above the elbow.

Time and again in Florida, especially along the West Coast, the offending fish is the bull shark. One reason for this is, whereas great whites tend to remain farther offshore, bull sharks prefer the near-shore and intertidal waters. Able to adapt to freshwater environments, these predatory sharks swim deep into the estuaries and patrol all of Florida's Intracoastal Waterway. A full-bodied, powerful shark similar in structure to a great white, the bull shark is by far the most dangerous shark in Florida, if not in the entire world.

In a comment made to a member of the local press covering the tragedy, shark expert Robert Hueter told the interviewer that two attacks in three days were a grim reminder of the hazards of the ocean. "The ocean is a wild environment. It's not a swimming pool. And there are sometimes dangerous creatures that live there."

Those creatures include the dark, dark shadow of Florida's notorious bull shark, far and away the most dangerous animal swimming throughout our coastal waters.

The Day Janie Melsek Died

riday, July 23, 2004, 9:16 A.M.: Exactly forty-five hours after being attacked and mauled by a huge, aggressive alligator, Janie Melsek left this earth. Janie had survived the initial trauma of the alligator attack only to succumb to the bacterial infection that subsequently ravaged her immune system. The official cause of death was Systemic Inflammatory Response Syndrome. Her body, in an effort to recover from the extensive wounds inflicted and to fight off the ensuing virulent infection, was ultimately overwhelmed. Janie's vital organs, one after the other, began shutting down.

Of all the stories regarding alligator attacks in this book, this one is the hardest for me to write about. I knew Janie Melsek...thus my referring to her on a first-name basis. I live on Sanibel Island, less than a mile from whence the gator attacked her. I know the pond where the dreadful incident took place. I was even familiar with the alligator that bit her. It was known to everyone in the neighborhood and was one of the largest gators on an island teeming with large alligators at the time.

I attended the memorial ceremony held the following Friday evening, July 30, 2004, at the Sanibel Community Center and wept amidst hundreds of fellow islanders. My wife, Molly, and I held each our single flower up in Janie's memory at the end of the service, then we took our flowers to toss them into the pond where the incident had occurred. I hugged her daughter, Joy Williams. I shook hands and embraced Rusty Farst, her former boyfriend. In an outpouring of grief and tears, we all suffered Janie Melsek's loss during the bleak days following her death.

It's not to say that Janie Melsek and I were close friends, because we weren't. We were fellow islanders. We had the kind of relationship whereby we would nod to each other across the bar at the Sanibel Grill or strike up a passing conversation at the local post office on love, life, and something we both felt passionate about: native-plant landscaping. Janie Melsek was my age—born in 1949, one year before I was—and she and I shared a tremendous love and respect for the natural world. Whereas most of this book's stories have involved people who are strangers to me—their lives and deaths shown to me only through newspaper clippings, official reports, and legal documents— Janie's death from an alligator attack comes to me firsthand and far too close to home.

I know the men who jumped in the pond and tried to wrest Janie out of the viselike grip of the gator's jaws; I know them by their first names. I know the police officers who fired on the beast to kill it; and I attended the City Council meetings that followed soon after the fatal attack—well-attended meetings that forever changed Sanibel's relationship with its prehistoric predators. I also know there are people who, upon reading this story, will fully disagree with what I have to say. Likewise, I know that Janie's daughter, Joy, feels that the island's alligator population should be summarily eliminated, as do many residents and visitors to Sanibel. Nonetheless, since I'm dedicating this book to Janie Melsek and the natural world she so believed in, I won't shy away from voicing my stance.

It is important to understand that Janie Melsek was, first and foremost, a dedicated environmentalist. For years, Janie worked hand in hand with the Sanibel-Captiva Conservation Foundation's (SCCF) Native Plant Nursery. Janie had exclusively used native plants in her landscaping business, a business she had nurtured on Sanibel for more than twenty years.

Janie Melsek firmly believed in living in harmony with the natural world. In a 1997 interview with Anne Bellew of the *Islander*, a local Sanibel newspaper, Janie said:

> *My goal is real diversity, both in plant species and in the wildlife they attract. It's soon to be a new millennium and we've got to change from the pretty-blooming, exotic-flower, immaculate-yard mind-set to one that thinks future...grandchildren... community...planet...continuity...conservation. There is interdependence between plants, wildlife, and humans, which we simply cannot continue to ignore.*
>
> *You know, when I came here, I didn't know a coontie from a prickly apple, and "native plants" and "diversity of species" weren't part of my vocabulary. Through hands-on work, I've evolved from a mowing, hedging, blowing, edging—an all-noise-and-show type of landscaper—to one who can use plants that are good for and suitable in any given environment; plants that aren't so needy, thirsty, and hungry for chemicals.*
>
> *People need to think in terms of overall environment, not so much as a visual display, but rather as a deeper sense and feeling of beauty, a being a part of the whole.*

On the day Janie Melsek was attacked, I was on my way to some backwater fishing in "Ding" Darling Wildlife Refuge with a fishing buddy of mine, John Grinstead. Ironically...no, cosmically...I was telling John as we drove down Sanibel-Captiva Road that I was thinking about writing a book about alligator, shark, and panther attacks in Florida. I told John I had never come across a book that had thoroughly delved into the back-story behind those attacks. I added that I thought I could make my book both educational—by way of helping to avoid future deadly human/predator encounters—and a tool to discuss some of the larger, equally dangerous and pressing issues facing Florida's twenty-first century. The book would be titled *Alligators, Sharks & Panthers: Deadly Encounters with Florida's Top Predators.*

Later that evening when we returned from snook fishing, John and I learned about Janie. It had happened at the exact time we were driving down San-Cap Road, on our way to launch our boat. John asked me then if I had known about the attack beforehand. I told him I had no idea anything this horrific had occurred on our very island. Both of us felt the coincidence was altogether too uncanny. At the same moment, around 8 P.M. on July 21, 2004, Janie Melsek was just emerging from long hours of extensive surgery, fighting for every fiber of life left in her.

This fourteenth fatal alligator attack in Florida took place behind a seasonal rental house located off Island Inn Road, in a subdivision called Poinciana Circle. Janie Melsek, who had been retained by the owners to maintain the yard at the house, was working along the eastern edge of this single-family residence. Years before, Janie had landscaped that property for its previous owners. No one witnessed the actual attack.

In the official reconstitution of the event, it was postulated that, at the time of the attack, Janie had been trimming some native plants approximately ten feet up a low embankment. The embankment abutted a half-acre pond located due east of the house. Janie knew there was a large bull alligator living in the pond. Everyone who lived or worked in that neighborhood knew about that particular gator.

Sizewise, the alligator was a true monster. The necropsy indicated it was twelve-feet, three-inches long and weighed an astounding 457 pounds. Janie Melsek was five-foot-six and weighed 142 pounds—no match against a beast this enormous. Its size and girth would place the alligator's age at between 30–35 years, perhaps older. On more than one occasion, neighbors had seen it attack, kill, and swallow smaller alligators whole. This was an animal one surely needed to keep an eye on.

It was later learned that, since Janie knew about this particular animal, she had usually brought a "gator spotter" along whenever she worked that property's yard. That day, for whatever reason, she didn't have anyone spotting for her.

*****

At 12:35 P.M. on a clear, hot Wednesday in midsummer, Janie Melsek was bending over, trimming some plants with hedge clippers in her hands when this immense alligator exploded out of the water, ran up the low embankment, and bit down on her right arm and lower right side. Upon impact, Janie immediately let go of the hedge clippers and was then dragged, screaming and kicking, back into the murky waters of the nearby pond. This was an unusual and particularly very aggressive attack for any Florida gator to make. The fact that the alligator came so far out of the water to grab Janie quite possibly makes this the most egregious and violent fatal alligator attack on record. There wasn't a dog nearby and Janie wasn't particularly close to the water's edge.

Somehow, before Janie could be pulled under and drowned, as she was thrashing about wildly and fighting for her life, her left arm became entangled in overhanging vines and tree branches. Perhaps she grabbed for them as she was being carried back toward the water, but that entanglement kept Janie from being pulled out into the pond, submerged, and drowned by the big gator. Janie otherwise would have died within minutes. Roger Debord, who was doing some pool maintenance work on the rental house at the same time, heard Janie's scream and immediately came to her rescue. He grabbed her and tried to hold on to her, but the gator was pulling both of them into the pond. Roger had seen a neighbor, Jack David, driving by a few moments before, and knowing he was home, he left Janie and ran to Jack's house for help. It was an awful decision for Roger to make, knowing that it placed Janie in grave peril.

Roger pounded on Jack's door and told him what was happening. Jack called 911 and both men ran back to the pond. In the meantime, Jim Anholt, another neighbor who lived across the street from the pond, had also heard the commotion and ran over to the pond. Roger had already left by the time Jim arrived. At first, Jim walked right past Janie before he realized she was in there.

Jim Anholt then waded into the pond and grabbed Janie by the shirt and neck, desperately trying to keep her head above water. He was alone with her for what must have seemed an eternity.

Janie's left hand was still hanging on to some buttonwood branches just as the alligator was hanging on to her right arm and the right side of her body. Fearing for her life, she pleaded with Jim to cut her right arm off so she could get free from the gator's merciless grip. Jim told her, "No, we're not going to do that. We're going to get you out of here."

Moments later, Roger Debord and Jack David returned. Jack had grabbed a rake to pound on the submerged animal while Jim and Roger attempted to pull Janie away. Another neighbor, Steve Yetsko, arrived on the scene and grabbed Jim Anholt by his other arm, helping to keep him and Janie from being dragged deeper into the pond.

Roughly at the same time, the Sanibel police arrived. The men, working together, formed a human chain. Sergeant George Krivas slipped in front of Jim and held onto Janie, while Jim grabbed hold of Krivas's belt and Steve held on to Jim. The three men were in a life-and-death tug-of-war with a huge alligator. Janie yelled, "It has me by the butt. It has me by the arm."

In the moments that followed, more officers, workers, and neighbors joined in the human chain. The alligator had stopped pulling, but was not about to release its prey. Janie was in agonizing pain. She had been submerged in the swampy water for almost ten minutes with her head just barely above the surface.

The situation was surreal in that there was no indication that an alligator was grabbing Janie, as there was no visible sign of the attacking animal. The alligator was completely submerged beneath the murky waters of the pond and the only indication it existed was the pleas and screams coming from Janie Melsek.

After minutes of a virtual standoff, the alligator released Janie for an instant to get a better grip on her. With a half-dozen full-grown men attempting to pull her out of the pond, the moment the gator eased up, Janie was pulled free. Sergeant Krivas carried Janie back to the bank, whereupon the EMS personnel immediately began working on her. Her wounds were grave.

Upon losing its prey, the alligator finally surfaced. Fully engaged in an attack mode, filled with a tremendous burst of energy, and determined to regain its hold on the victim for a second time, the alligator opened its mouth and started rushing toward the shoreline. It was obvious to everyone that this bull alligator was going to make an all-out attempt to take its prey back from her would-be rescuers.

In a moment of self-preservation, several members of the Sanibel Police Department opened fire. Detective Crandon and Sergeant Dalton hit the alligator in the head several times with their side arms. The alligator rolled and swam away. Janie was rushed off in an ambulance, then helicoptered to the Lee Memorial Trauma Center in Fort Myers. She was still alive but in terrible condition. Most of her lower right arm had been badly mangled and she had extensive bite wounds to her pelvis and lower abdominal region. Worst of all, Janie had spent far too long a time in the bacteria-laden waters of a South Florida pond. From the moment the attending doctors began the eight-hour-surgery, Janie's prognosis was grim.

Recognizing the danger involved, the Sanibel Police draped the perimeter of the pond with crime-scene tape and secured the area. There was now an aggressive, wounded, four-hundred-plus-pound alligator in the pond. Everyone was acutely aware of the lethal danger such a beast could pose.

A few minutes later, roughly one hundred feet away toward the north side of the pond, the gator resurfaced. The bullet wounds to its head were clearly visible, but the animal was only wounded.

Lieutenant Phillips and Detective Crandon immediately opened fire on the creature, shooting it several more times in the head with their side arms. This time, one of the bullets reached the brain, killing the gator within minutes. The beast was retrieved and pulled up onto the bank through heavy ropes. It took six men to load the alligator into the pickup truck that took it away.

It was one of the largest alligators ever involved in a fatal alligator attack. Originally, it was believed the alligator had never been fed by people. Further investigation revealed that some of the past renters at the house had been seen feeding it...the same sad story, which needs to be told time and again. That alligator had learned to equate humans with food. If humans showed up along the water's edge and didn't have any food to give them, then the humans would become the food. That is how a reptile with a walnut-sized brain thinks. No matter how many times the story is told and retold, its aftermath will inexorably be the same: Given that alligator's feeding history, Janie became a mere sitting duck.

Throughout the next day, Thursday, Janie rallied. Doctors had worked on her for hours. They amputated her right hand just above the wrist and did their best to sew up the extensive wounds inflicted to her pelvic and lower abdominal region. Numerous blood transfusions and a constant intravenous drip of antibiotics staved off the infection for the moment. But late Thursday night and into Friday morning, Janie's condition started to decline. She died on the operating table on Friday morning. The doctors later conceded that, because of the extent of her wounds and her long submersion in the dirty water, her prognosis had never been good. Janie was lucky to have lived the extra two days she did.

*****

On Sanibel Island, the mood of the residents ran from a deep sense of grief to a natural desire to avenge Janie's untimely death. In the July 29,

2004, issue of the *Island Reporter*, the letters to the editor were split between trying to put this rare event into perspective—the minority opinion by far—and killing every alligator left on the island. Rusty Farst, Janie's former boyfriend and a longtime islander, still grieving his loss, said the following to a local reporter: "The Jurassic Park experiment here on Sanibel has failed...with grave consequences. Lord knows, we tried to make it work."

A posse mentality swept over Sanibel. Fellow islander Bob Steele had been killed by another large gator three years earlier on 9/11/2001. In April 2004, a seasonal resident, Jane Keefer, narrowly escaped the grip of a nine-foot alligator that had pulled her into a shallow pond behind her seawall in the Gulf Shores subdivision. After a desperate struggle, the alligator let go of Keefer and was later trapped and killed. Now, this vicious, unprovoked attack by a massive bull gator that ended the life of a well-known and well-respected native landscaper tipped the scales, to the point where islanders demanded that tangible action be taken. A public meeting was called by Mayor Marty Harrity for the morning of August 3, 2004, to discuss adopting possible changes to Sanibel's alligator policies.

Knowing there would be a large turnout, the City Council meeting was held not in the usual chambers, McKenzie Hall, which could only accommodate eighty people, but in nearby Schein Hall, which could hold up to four hundred. The extra space was indeed needed; hundreds of Sanibel residents showed up to voice their opinion.

The issue was obviously alligators: There were too many on Sanibel, and far too many large ones. The community took sides. There were those who felt that virtually all alligators over four feet in length should be killed or removed and relocated off-island; there were those who felt that the three recent incidents had been anomalies and that, overall, alligator attacks on Sanibel were extremely rare. The latter contingent warned council members that the public was still in shock over Janie's death and, given the charged atmosphere surrounding her attack, it was prone to overreaction.

Everyone had his or her opinion and everyone had his or her three-minute time slot at the microphone. In the end, coming only weeks after Janie's tragic accident, the anti-alligator faction won out: the City of Sanibel would change its policy to comply with that of Florida State. The Sanctuary Island would no longer be a sanctuary for one of Florida's top predators. Every alligator on the island was now considered guilty-until-proven-innocent.

Ever since Janie's death in July 2004, more than 125 alligators have been trapped, killed, and/or removed from Sanibel Island. An open permit allowed John French, a designated state trapper, to take over eighty large alligators within weeks of the policy change. There are so few alligators remaining outside of "Ding" Darling National Wildlife Refuge that it is now almost impossible to find one. Every alligator over four feet is in imminent danger of being reported as a nuisance and removed. Given the current policy and the fact that alligators cannot reproduce until they reach a minimum length of five to six feet, alligators on Sanibel will eventually become extirpated. Studies are underway, funded by the SCCF, "Ding" Darling, and the state of Florida to see if there is even a sustainable population of alligators left on the island.

Under the current policy, if a large alligator over four feet is seen, even without showing any signs of aggressive or nuisance behavior, a resident or visitor can call an island official in and issue that animal a death sentence...guilty of a crime by merely existing.... One Sanibel resident requested that an alligator be removed from her lake because she was planning a wedding party and didn't want her guests to have to see this dangerous predator lurking near her backyard.

In my opinion, Janie would be appalled. Janie believed in working in harmony with the natural world and alligators are an intrinsic part of that world. With the island's major predator gone, the raccoon and bobcat populations have skyrocketed. These two mammalian predators, now left unchecked, are wreaking havoc on the island's bird rookeries built near waterways that once were protected by patrolling bull gators. Within a few more years, the entire natural balance of prey and predator will be completely disrupted as a result of the newly adopted program. Just remember the wolves of Yellowstone and the subsequent ruined trout fishery that their removal engendered. Imagine "Ding" Darling National Wildlife Refuge devoid of egrets, herons, and spoonbills in the not-too-distant future, as a result of this flawed policy.

Many politicians and islanders felt that the island couldn't sustain a fourth or a fifth alligator attack. They felt that any further bad publicity resulting from another attack could permanently damage the island's vital tourist industry. There was talk that even a lawsuit could eventually be filed against the City of Sanibel for negligence if there ever were another alligator attack.

The decision was final: there were too many large alligators and they were too aggressive. Excuses for killing the island's gators were as rampant as were the hastily issued permits to kill them. While there might have been a valid argument that Sanibel's alligator population had exceeded its food supply, the taking of over one hundred large animals is another dismal study in Pleistocene overkill. Culling a few of the largest gators would have sufficed. But the posse mentality ensnared even the staunchest island naturalists and the decision was made to remove any alligator more than four feet in length if its mere sighting bothered any resident or visitor.

Ultimately, this policy, still in effect, is not only a recipe for ecological disaster on Sanibel; it's also the wrong message for a self-proclaimed "sanctuary island." In our true commitment to "living with nature," all of us must learn that said commitment also includes the possibility of our "dying with nature." Until we are willing to grant sanctuary to all of God's creatures, Sanibel will not be a sanctuary at all. Alligators had been here long before *Homo sapiens* arrived and, given our present course, they may well be here long after we cause our own extinction.

Why, then, are we killing those ancient, innocent reptiles? If someone living on Sanibel, or anywhere in Florida, is uncomfortable residing on an island that harbors large alligators, he or she should leave. If someone who rents a home or condominium on Sanibel is troubled by staying on an island inhabited by indigenous reptiles capable of injuring, even killing, a person, he or she should find somewhere else to stay. That person should seek the safety of a brave new world covered in pavement and shopping malls. The natural environment is what makes Sanibel...Sanibel, and in a larger sense, Florida...Florida, and Planet Earth...Earth.

The day Janie Melsek died was a sad day in the history of this sanctuary island, an island that takes pride in its understanding and tolerance of nature. Janie would want me to set the record straight as to why it's still a sad day here and will remain so until this killing rampage stops.... Until Florida's top predator—man—learns to live in harmony with all, and not just a part, of nature.

Following is only a partial list of the alligators that have been slaughtered since Janie's death:

Alligators Killed on Sanibel from 7/28/04 through 12/28/05

DATE	LOCATION	LENGTH
7/28/04	Sanibel Police Station Pond	9'0"
7/28/04	Dunes on Nest	10'0"
7/30/04	Bailey's Store	6'7"
7/30/04	Sanctuary Golf Course	5'8"
7/30/04	1825 Middle Gulf Drive	6'4"
7/31/04	Sunrise Circle	7'7"
7/31/04	The Rocks	6'1"
8/01/04	Eagle Run Circle	12'0"
8/04/04	Beachview Golf Club	6'0"

8/04/04	Beachview Golf Club	8'7"
8/05/04	Beachview Golf Club	8'7"
8/10/04	Sanibel Police Pickup	6'6"
8/10/04	Beachview Golf Club	6'3"
8/10/04	Beachview Golf Club	8'8"
8/10/04	Beachview Golf Club	8'8"
8/10/04	Beachview Golf Club	8'10"
8/10/04	Beachview Golf Club	7'9"
8/10/04	Beachview Golf Club	10'2"
8/27/04	Dunes Country Club	10'10"
8/27/04	Dunes Country Club	9'2"
8/27/04	Dunes Country Club	6'6"
8/27/04	Dunes Country Club	8'2"
8/27/04	Dunes Country Club	8'6"
8/28/04	Dunes Country Club	9'5"
8/28/04	Dunes Country Club	6'10"
8/28/04	Dunes Country Club	7'6"
8/28/04	Dunes Country Club	9'6"
8/28/04	Dunes Country Club	8'6"
8/28/04	Dunes Country Club	8'2"
8/28/04	Dunes Country Club	10'10"
8/31/04	Beachview Golf Club	10'2"
8/31/04	Beachview Golf Club	7'4"
8/31/04	Beachview Golf Club	10'11"
9/04/04	Beachview Golf Club	8'1"
9/04/04	Beachview Golf Club	7'9"
9/09/04	Gumbo Limbo	5'6"
9/09/04	Gumbo Limbo	6'10"
9/09/04	Gumbo Limbo	9'0"
9/09/04	Whisperwood Road	7'10"
9/09/04	Dunes Country Club	7'0"
9/09/04	Dunes Country Club	8'9"
9/09/04	Dunes Country Club	6'1"
9/12/04	Lake Murex	7'8"
9/12/04	Rabbit Road (Steele)	7'6"
9/12/04	Rabbit Road (Steele)	6'1"
9/23/04	Beachview Golf Club	7'10"
9/23/04	Beachview Golf Club	5'9"
9/23/04	Dunes Country Club	11'10"
9/25/04	Sanctuary Golf Club	7'6"

9/25/04	Sanctuary Golf Club	6'4"
9/25/04	Sanctuary Golf Club	5'0"
9/25/04	Purdy Street Pond	8'6"
9/29/04	Sanibel Police Pickup	5'8"
9/29/04	Bowman's Beach	9'6"
9/29/04	Bowman's Beach	6'6"
9/29/04	Bowman's Beach	8'10"
9/29/04	Bowman's Beach	7'3"
9/29/04	Bowman's Beach	5'8"
9/29/04	Bowman's Beach	6'5"
10/06/04	Egret Pickup at PD Station	6'2"
10/09/04	Purdy Road Pond	7'4"
10/09/04	Dunes Country Club	6'0"
10/09/04	Dunes Country Club	5'8"
10/14/04	Roseate Lane	8'5"
10/17/04	Roseate Lane	11'3"
10/17/04	Blind Pass Court (O'Connell's pool)	4'5"
10/24/04	Lake Murex Drive Front Porch	10'11"
10/25/04	Beachview Golf Club	5'9"
11/09/04	Beachview Golf Club	7'11"
11/15/04	Sanibel Police Pickup	5'11"
11/17/04	Sanibel Police Pickup	8'0"
11/19/04	Sanctuary Golf Club	11'9"
12/03/04	Rue Belle Mer	7'0"
12/03/04	Rue Belle Mer	7'0"
12/03/04	Rue Belle Mer	8'1"
12/03/04	Sanctuary Golf Club	10'0"
02/15/05	Gulf Pines Blue Heron	7'5"
02/15/05	Dimmick Road	6'7"
02/15/05	Dimmick Road	10'4"
02/15/05	Dimmick Road	5'7"
02/25/05	Birdie View—Beachview	6'8"
02/25/05	Sanctuary Golf Club	6'9"
03/15/05	Twin Ponds	6'4"
03/15/05	Gulf Pines Blue Heron	9'2"
03/15/05	Gulf Pines Blue Heron	6'5"
03/15/05	Gulf Pines Blue Heron	7'0"
03/15/05	Birdie View—Beachview	5'7"
05/04/05	Sanibel Police Pickup	7'6"
05/13/05	Twin Ponds	8'4"

05/13/05	West Rocks	6'6"
05/20/05	Sanibel Police Pickup	6'5"
05/26/05	Sanibel Police Pickup	5'2"
05/26/05	Gulf Pines White Ibis	5'4"
05/26/05	Gulf Pines Blue Heron	5'9"
05/26/05	Gulf Pines Left at Y	6'4"
05/28/05	Sanibel Police Pickup	7'10"
07/03/05	Twin Ponds—Lake Murex	10'
07/03/05	Dunes Country Club	4'
07/08/05	Beachview Golf Course	5'5"
07/08/05	Bright Water	6'
09/17/05	Bailey's General Store	9'3"
12/01/05	Open Permit Area	6'4"
12/01/05	Open Permit Area	7'3"
12/08/05	Open Permit Area	10'
12/14/05	Open Permit Area	4'8"
12/14/05	Open Permit Area	5'8"
12/14/05	Open Permit Area	6'3"
12/28/05	Open Permit Area	7'3"

Most alligators over nine feet in length were probably males, while the smaller ones were a mixture of male and female alligators. A four-foot alligator is not life-threatening. At the time of publication, the killing continued.

What You and I Can Do

From lowering our individual carbon footprint to supporting our local government in using a portion of our tax dollars to purchase conservation land for wildlife habitat, each of us can help reduce our environmental impact and change the direction Florida is heading. Following are a few helpful suggestions. For additional ideas and interesting discussion topics for book clubs and civic and political organizations, please refer to the Discussion and Debate Topics located after the bibliography.

• LOWER YOUR CARBON FOOTPRINT:

• Purchase the most energy-efficient appliances and air-conditioning units you can afford. With the rising cost of energy, higher up-front costs are often recaptured in the first few years of use.

• Wash your clothes in warm, not hot, water. Turn the thermostat down in your hot-water heater or wrap it in a thermal blanket. Better yet, install a solar hot-water heater in your home.

• Turn your thermostat higher during the summer months to reduce your cooling costs. Lower it in the winter months so as to reduce your heating costs. Install the optimum amount of insulation possible in your home or condominium.

• Buy energy-efficient, compact fluorescent bulbs to replace your incandescent light bulbs. They use only twenty-five percent of the energy for the same amount of light and can last ten times as long.

• Whenever possible, walk, bike, car-pool, or use mass transit. Lobby your local municipality to create user-friendly bike paths and better mass-transit systems to help reduce individual automobile use. Not only do our roads become less congested, the reduction in carbon emissions is substantial.

• Forgo buying another SUV and choose a smaller, fuel-efficient car that gets forty miles per gallon. Buy a hybrid or a smaller, compact car for your commuting and park (better yet, get rid of) your expensive, gas-guzzling minivan or truck.

• Plant shade trees around your home. Transpiration from shade trees helps to naturally cool your home, while their growth helps to reduce CO_2 in the atmosphere.

• RECYCLE, REUSE, AND REDUCE:

• Build a smaller home or purchase a used home. The average size of homes in Florida has increased seventy-nine percent from fifty years ago. Smaller homes are easier to maintain, less expensive to heat and cool, and cost far less to build. Used homes are recycled homes and put almost no additional demands on the world's remaining tropical forests, mines, and natural resources.

• Recycle everything. From plastics to paper and from aluminum to steel, almost everything can be recycled using today's technology. If your local garbage collection doesn't have a recycling program, lobby your representatives to start one. The savings in energy—especially the avoidance of further aluminum extraction from its raw mineral, bauxite—is astronomical.

• Reuse everything. Americans throw away tons of screws, nuts, electrical cords, and usable pieces of lumber every day. Buy a small plastic storage container and save many of these items for future reuse. Stop promoting and participating in our throw-away, planned-obsolescence culture.

• Reduce your overall consumption. Before you buy anything, ask yourself, "Do I *really* have to have it?"

• PROMOTE THE PURCHASE OF CONSERVATION LAND AND PREVENT UNCHECKED DEVELOPMENT:

• The unbridled growth Florida has experienced in the past sixty years is taking its toll both on wildlife and on our quality of life. Having a portion of your tax dollars going toward the purchase of wetlands or wildlife habitat ensures not only the beauty of green spaces for your grandchildren to enjoy, but also less traffic on the roads, less urban sprawl, and a cleaner environment.

• Insist that all new developments must be approved by voters who will be intimately impacted by them. Once sold out, developers move on and leave local residents to deal with overcrowded schools, inadequate sewer systems, and dwindling water supplies. Stop growth before it happens.

• Lobby your state, regional, and local politicians to acquire large tracts of land at market value and to turn them into regional parks and wildlife preserves in perpetuity. Do it for your children.

• JOIN ORGANIZATIONS THAT CAN AND ACTUALLY DO SOMETHING FOR OUR ENVIRONMENT:

• Get involved. There are dozens of regional and national organizations that promote sound environmental practices. The Audubon Society, The Nature Conservancy, The World Wildlife Fund, The Sierra Club, The National Wildlife Foundation, The National Geographic Society, Friends of the Earth, and the Defenders of Wildlife, to mention only a few. Log on to www.interenvironment.org and you will find a list of more than 350 reputable organizations.

• Write letters, send e-mails, and become proactive. If you don't like the term "environmentalist," proclaim yourself to be an unabashed "antidegradationist." All environmental issues are nonpolitical. Red-tide toxins affect Republicans just as readily as they do Democrats or Independents. If drilling is allowed in the Gulf of Mexico's eastern rim, the ensuing and inevitable oil spill will ruin everyone's beaches. We all breathe the same air and drink the same water; none of us want to see our world polluted.

• Vote. Use the ballot box to support politicians who promote and support sustainable environmental practices. Don't hesitate to cross party lines when you cast your vote. Remember: **the environment is nonpartisan**. Vote for candidates whose platforms include clean air, sound water management, and well-planned growth.

• Give. A portion of the proceeds from the sale of this book are going to The Nature Conservancy. Founded in 1951, this organization has been involved—nationally and worldwide—in the preservation of large tracts of habitat, whereby we can preserve and sustain Planet Earth's rich biodiversity. For information on The Nature Conservancy, log on to www.natureconservancy.org.

• In addition, an equal portion of the proceeds from the sale of *Alligators, Sharks & Panthers* will go to DKT International. This organization is dedicated not only to reducing birthrates in the Third World and emerging nations, but also to assisting in worldwide prevention of HIV/AIDS. For additional information, log on to DTK International's Web site at www.dktinternational.org.

• ADVOCATE SMALLER FAMILIES AND POPULATION REDUCTION:

• There are presently 6.5 billion people on earth and this number climbs by more than seventy million every year. It is estimated that, by the year 2050, there will be ten billion people on earth. Every Floridian born has the environmental impact of 280 Haitians or Nepalese.

• Become a staunch advocate of family planning and the widespread use of birth control, condoms, and anti-conceptive pills. Make abortion legal but rare. Zero-population growth is achieved when every couple has fewer than two children. If the world's population growth remains unchecked, the rate of animal extinctions will continue to rise. Learn to share our planet with the native flora and fauna. Remember: it's all about *quality* of life; not the *quantity* of humanity that can fit on this small planet.

• CHANGE THE RULES REGARDING THE FEEDING OF ALLIGATORS:

• Under current Florida law, feeding any wild alligator, regardless of its size, is a second-degree misdemeanor punishable by up to a $500.00 fine and/

or six months in jail. Under this current policy, very few people are reported and even fewer are prosecuted.

• There are two schools of thought regarding the changing of this law: one favors increasing the penalty to a felony with up to one year in jail and a $1,000 fine for anyone caught intentionally feeding an alligator; the other advocates decreasing the first-time penalty to a non-criminal offense punishable by a mandatory attendance at a state-operated two-hour alligator educational program. The program could be set up much like the Signal-30 highway-patrol movies shown in many high schools, which graphically illustrate what happens to people when they are in a fatal automobile accident (who can forget those images?). If people could see what an alligator-attack victim looks like (both fatal and nonfatal), they would never feed an alligator again.

Since a neighbor is the most likely person to turn in anyone seen feeding a gator, chances are that he or she will not do so if the penalty is a misdemeanor or, even more unlikely, a felony. If the first offense is a mandatory alligator educational program, chances are more people would be willing to report their neighbor's bad behavior.

• Florida should enact a state law making it impossible to file a lawsuit against a city, a county, or the state itself for injuries or death sustained by any person as a result of an attack by a wild animal in a natural environment. Florida State does not allow people to file suit against anyone when they are bitten by a shark or struck by lightning; this protection should be extended to alligator attacks. If a person wades into a lake, pond, or canal and gets bitten by a wild alligator, no one is to blame for this incident other than the very person who entered into these indigenous animals' realm.

A law to this effect would prevent further mass slaughters like the recent eradication program on Sanibel Island after the death of Janie Melsek, to whom this book is dedicated.

Selected Bibliography

This book would not have been possible without the extensive information provided by the Florida Fish and Wildlife Commission (FWC). To cite all the information included in the FWC files is beyond the scope of this bibliography. I must also recognize many of the newspapers from which specific articles—and their authors—furnished me with invaluable information and immeasurably helped me in my research. These include, but are not limited to, the following: the *Islander* and the *Island Reporter* (Sanibel Island); the *Ft. Myers News-Press;* the *Palm Beach Post;* the *Tampa Tribune;* the *Florida Times-Union* (Jacksonville); *Orlando Sentinel; Tallahassee Democrat; St. Petersburg Times; Naples Daily News* and the *Miami Herald.*

This bibliography is by no means a complete record of all sources the author consulted. The book would not have been possible without extensive use of the World Wide Web, especially Wikipedia— (www.wikipedia.org). For additional information on the various topics in this book, the titles preceded by an asterisk are the author's choices for recommended reading:

–*Alderton, David. *Crocodiles & Alligators of the World.* London: Blandford, 1992.

–Allen, Thomas B. *The Shark Almanac.* Connecticut: Lyons Press, 1999, 2003.

_____. *Shark Attacks: Their Causes and Avoidance.* New York: Lyons Press, 2001.

–Alvarez, Ken. *Twilight of the Panther: Biology, Bureaucracy and Failure in an Endangered Species Program.* Sarasota: Myakka River Publishing, 1993.

–Anderson, Robert. *Guide to Florida Alligator and Crocodile.* Altamonte Springs: Winner Enterprises, 1983.

_____, *Guide to Florida Sharks and Shark Fishing.* Ibid.

–Audrey, Robert. *The Territorial Imperative.* New York: Atheneum, 1966.

–Baldridge, David H. *Shark Attack.* Anderson, S.C.: Drake House/Hallux, 1974.

–Barnes, Jay. *Florida's Hurricane History.* Chapel Hill: Univ. of North Carolina Press, 1998.

–Benchley, Peter. *Jaws.* New York: Doubleday, 1974.

_____. Sponsored Lecture (Conservancy of Southwest Florida), Ft. Myers: 20 January 2005.

–Bothwell, Dick. *The Great Outdoors Book of Alligators and Other Crocodilia.* St. Petersburg: Great Outdoors Publishing, 1962.

–*Brown, Lester R. and Earth Policy Institute. *Plan B 2.0: Rescuing a Planet* *under Stress and a Civilization in Trouble.* New York: W.W. Norton & Co., 2006.

–Burenhult, Goran, ed. *The First Humans: Human Origins and History to 10,000 BC*, vol. 1. New York: HarperCollins, 1993.

–Burgess, George H. (Various statistics), 23 August 2005, <http://www.flmnh.ufl.edu/fish/sharks/statistics/2004attacksummary.htm>.

–*Campbell, George R. *The Nature of Things on Sanibel.* Sarasota: Pineapple Press, 1988.

_____, and Ann L. Winterbotham. *Jaws, Too! The Natural History of Crocodilians with Emphasis on Sanibel Island's Alligators.* Ft. Myers: George R. Campbell/Ann L. Winterbotham, 1985.

–*Caputo, Philip. *Ghosts of Tsavo: Stalking the Mystery Lions of East Africa.* Washington, D.C.: National Geographic Society, 2002.

–Clutton-Brock, Juliet. *Eyewitness Books: Cat.* New York: Alfred A. Knopf, 1991.

–Cochran, Gary. *Florida's Fabulous Fishes,* Rev. 4th ed. Hawaiian Gardens: World Publications, 2004.

–*Crocodiles: Here Be Dragons,* written and produced by Alan Root, 60 min., National Geographic Society videocassette, 1990.

–Danz, Harold P. *Cougar!* Athens: Swallow Press/Ohio Univ. Press, 1999.

–Davies, Ben. *Black Market: Inside the Endangered Species Trade in Asia.* San Rafael: Earth Aware Editions, 2005.

–Day, David. *The Doomsday Book of Animals: A Natural History of Vanished Species.* New York: Viking Press, 1981.

–Deurbrouck, Jo, and Dean Miller. *Cat Attacks: True Stories and Hard Lessons from Cougar Country.* Seattle: Sasquatch Books, 2001.

–Dorling Kindersley. *World Atlas.* 2nd ed., New York: Dorling Kindersley Publishing, 1997.

–*Ehrlich, Paul R., and Anne H. *One with Nineveh: Politics, Consumption, and the Human Future.* Washington, DC: Island Press/Shearwater Books, 2004.

_____. *The Population Explosion: From Global Warming to Rain Forest Destruction, Famine, and Air and Water Pollution—Why Overpopulation Is Our #1 Environmental Problem.* New York: Simon & Schuster, 1990.

–Etling, Kathy. *Cougar Attacks: Encounters of the Worst Kind.* Guilford, Ct.: Lyons Press, 2001.

–Fergus, Charles. *Swamp Screamer: At Large with the Florida Panther.* Gainesville: Univ. Press of Florida, 1998.

–Fernald, Edward A. *Atlas of Florida.* Tallahassee: Institute of Science and Public Affairs, 1981.

–Fernicola, Richard G. *Twelve Days of Terror: A Definitive Investigation of the 1916 New Jersey Shark Attacks.* Guilford, Ct.: Lyons Press, 2001.

Florida Power and Light, Miami: Pamphlet: "The Florida Panther," 1995.

–*Gelbspan, Ross. *Boiling Point: How Politicians, Big Oil and Coal, Journalists, and Activists Have Fueled the Climate Crisis—and What We Can Do to Avert Disaster.* New York: Basic Books, 2004.

–Gesner, Konrad. *Curious Woodcuts of Fanciful and Real Beasts: A Selection of 190 Sixteenth-Century Woodcuts from Gesner's and Topsell's Natural Histories.* New York: Dover Publications, 1971.

–Gilbert, Carter R., ed. *Fishes: Rare and Endangered Biota of Florida*, vol. 2. Gainesville: Univ. Press of Florida, 1992.

–Glick, Daniel. "The Big Thaw," *National Geographic*, (Sept. 2004), 13–33.

–Graham, Alistair. *Eyelids of Morning: The Mingled Destinies of Crocodiles and Men.* Greenwich, Ct.: New York Graphic Society, 1973.

–Halliday, Tim, and Kraig Adler, eds. *The Encyclopedia of Reptiles and Amphibians.* Oxford: Equinox, 1986.

–Heritage, Andrew, ed. *Dorling Kindersley World Atlas.* 2nd ed. London: Dorling Kindersley Publishing, 2000.

–*Horton, Dave, and Lee Horton. *Sanibel Island's Very Own Cartoon Book!* Sanibel: Sanibel Print & Graphics, 2000.

_____. *Sanibel Island's 2nd Cartoon Book!* Ibid., 2004.

–Humphrey, Stephen R., ed. *Mammals: Rare and Endangered Biota of Florida*, vol. 1. Gainesville: Univ. Press of Florida, 1992.

–Humphreys, Jay, in assoc. with the Florida Sea Grant College Program. *Seasons of the Sea.* Sarasota: Pineapple Press, 2001.

–Jensen, Derrick, and George Draffan. *Strangely Like War: The Global Assault on Forests.* White River Junction, Vt.: Chelsea Green, 2003.

–Klimley, A. Peter. *The Secret Life of Sharks: A Leading Marine Biologist Reveals the Mysteries of Shark Behavior.* New York: Simon & Schuster, 2003.

–*Leakey, Richard, and Roger Lewin. *The Sixth Extinction: Patterns of Life and the Future of Humankind.* New York: Doubleday, 1995.

–Levy, Charles. *Endangered Species: Crocodiles & Alligators.* New Jersey: Chartwell Books, 1991.

–Lewis, P., ed. *Special Report: Deep Trouble: The Gulf in Peril.* (Reprint of a 15-part series).

–Naples, Fl.: *Naples Daily News*, September 28–October 12, 2003.

–*Lockwood, C.C. *The Alligator Book.* Baton Rouge: Louisiana State Univ. Press, 2002.

–Lorant, Stefan, ed. *The New World: The First Pictures of America.* New York: Duell, Sloan & Pearce, 1946.

–MacCormick, Alex. *Shark Attacks: Terrifying True Accounts of Shark Attacks Worldwide.* New York: St. Martin's Press, 1998.

–Macdonald, David. *The Encyclopedia of Mammals.* New York: Facts on File Publications, 1984.

–*Maehr, David S. *The Florida Panther: Life and Death of a Vanishing Carnivore.* Washington, D.C.: Island Press, 1997.

–Maniguet, Xavier. *The Jaws of Death: Shark as Predator, Man as Prey.* Guilford, Ct.: Lyons Press, 2001.

–Matthiessen, Peter. *Blue Meridian.* New York: Random House, 1971.

*_____. *The Snow Leopard.* New York: Penguin Books, 1996.

–McCarthy, Kevin M. *Alligator Tales.* Sarasota: Pineapple Press, 1998.

–McGovern, Bernie, ed. *Florida Almanac: 2004–2005.* Gretna, La.: Pelican Publishing, 2004.

–McIlhenny, E.A. *The Alligator's Life History.* Berkeley: Ten Speed Press, 1987.

–Middleton, Susan, and David Liittschwager. *Witness: Endangered Species of North America.* San Francisco: Chronicle Books, 1994.

–Morris, Desmond. *Cat World: A Feline Encyclopedia.* New York: Penguin Reference Books, 1996.

*_____. *The Naked Ape: A Zoologist's Study of the Human Animal.* Surrey, England: Delta Publishing, 1999.

–Morwood, Mike, Thomas Sutikna and Richard Roberts, "The People Time Forgot: Flores Find," *National Geographic,* (April 2005), 6–12.

–Owen, John, and Kevin Weldon. *The First Humans.* New York: HarperCollins, 1993.

–Parker, S. and J. *The Encyclopedia of Sharks.* New York: Firefly Books, 2002.

–Revkin, Andrew. American Museum of Natural History, Environmental Defense Fund. *Global Warming: Understanding the Forecast.* New York: Abbeville Press, 1992.

–Rodgers, James A. Jr., Herbert W. Kale II, and Henry T. Smith, eds. *Birds: Rare and Endangered Biota of Florida,* vol. 5. Gainesville: Univ. Press of Florida, 1996.

–Ross, Charles A., ed. *Crocodiles and Alligators.* New York: Facts on File, n.d.

–Savage, Candace. *Wild Cats.* San Francisco: Sierra Club Books, 1993.

–Scott, Chris. *Endangered and Threatened Animals of Florida and Their Habitats.* Austin: Univ. of Texas Press, 2004.

–Shelton, James G. *Bear Attacks: The Deadly Truth.* Hagensborg, B.C., Canada: James Gary Shelton, 1998.

–Seidensticker, John, and Susan Lumkin. *Great Cats. Majestic Creatures of the Wild.* Emmaus, Pa.: Rodale Press, 1991.

–*Sleeper, Barbara. *Beneath the Blackwater: Alligators.* Minocqua, Wis.: NorthWord Press, 1996.

–Sloan, Christopher. *Supercroc and the Origin of Crocodiles.* Washington, D.C.: National Geographic Society, 2002.

–Spencer, Donald. *The Florida Alligator in Old Picture Postcards.* Ormond Beach: Camelot Publishing, 2001.

–Strawn, Martha A. *Alligators: Prehistoric Presence in the American Landscape.* Baltimore: Johns Hopkins Univ. Press, 1997.

–Taylor, Ron, and Valerie Taylor, eds. with Peter Goadby. *Great Shark Stories.* New York: Harper & Row, 1978.

_____. "Sharks: Silent Hunters of the Deep." Introduction in *Reader's Digest.* London: Reader's Digest Services, 1986.

–Tattersall, Ian, and Jeffrey H. Schwartz. *Extinct Humans.* Boulder: Westview Press, 2000.

–Thomas, Elizabeth M. *The Tribe of Tiger: Cats and Their Culture.* New York: Simon & Schuster, 1994.

–Underwood, Lamar, ed. *Man Eaters: True Tales of Animals' Stalking, Mauling, Killing, and Eating Human Prey.* Guilford, Ct.: The Lyons Press, 2002.

–Waller, Geoffrey, ed. *Sea Life: A Complete Guide to the Marine Environment.* Washington, D.C.: Smithsonian Institution Press, 1996.

–Warner, David T. *Vanishing Florida: A Personal Guide to Sights Rarely Seen.* Montgomery, Al.: River City, 2001.

–Zimmer, Carl. *Evolution: The Triumph of an Idea.* New York: HarperCollins, 2001.

Cartoon courtesy Dave & Lee Horton

313

INDEX

Comoro Islands, 88
Conservancy of Southwest Florida, 102, 282
Corbett, Jim, 155
Cory, Charles B., 196
Cousteau, Jacques-Uves, 76
Cousteau, Jean-Michel, 133, 134
Covert, William, 105–108
coyotes, 175, 200
Crespo, Robert, 112–117
Crocodiles and Alligators of the World, 21
Crocodiles-Here Be Dragons, 29
crocodilians: in Africa, 20, 248; American crocodiles, 16, 47, 50–51, 64, 120, 268; in Asia Pacific region, 19–20; in captivity, 232–233; characteristics, 16, 18–19, 23–30, 52, 98, 189; early habitats, 18; endangered species, 232; family tree chart, 22; human predation, 19–20, 23, 233; Madras Crocodile Bank, 232–233; name origins, 18; species of, 21–22. *See also* alligators; Indopacific crocodiles; Nile crocodiles
Cummings, George, 71–75
Cuyamaca Rancho State Park, 185–186

Daigle, Jamie Marie, 290–292
Dandridge, William, 76–78, 106
David, Jack, 296
Davis, Bo, 211
The Day After Tomorrow, 246
dead zones, 208, 282–283
Dean, Alf, 88
Debord, Roger, 296
deer, 15, 169, 170–171, 202, 203–204, 206–207
Deerfield Beach, 133–134
de León, Ponce, 267, 269
DEMA (Diving Equipment and Marketing Association), 133, 134, 137

Dennis, Bucky, 124
Dennis, L. Tappen, 36
Denton, Zac, 263
de Onís, Luís, 269–270
desertification, 227
de Soto, Hernando, 203
DeVane's Early Florida History, 205
Dicus, Tim, 290–292
Ding Darling National Wildlife Refuge, 46–47, 121, 261, 299
Dingwall, Fred, 184–185
dinosaurs, 24–25, 228–229
dogfish sharks, 98, 99, 233
dogs, 62–63, 164, 199, 203
dolphins, 79, 104, 240
Doña Paz, 85
Dovenbarger, Joel, 107
Dugas, Gaetan, 250
Dunn, Joseph, 91, 92
Dysard, James, 57–58

Earl, L., 20
Earp, Dave, 136–137
Eberhart, Francis (Frank), 191–194
Eberhart, Grace, 191–194
Ebola, 249–250
ecology, 148, 200, 204. *See also* global warming; wetlands
Edward Ball Wakulla Springs State Park, 71–75
Ehrlich, Anne, 227
Ehrlich, Paul, 227
elasmobranchs, 82–83, 93, 100, 101
elk, 148, 168–170, 175, 225
endangered species: cats, great, 17, 144, 151, 153–158, 197; and CITES, 157, 232, 233; crocodilians, 232; in Florida, 31, 273–274; governmental protection of, 102; manatees, 208; sharks, 102, 233. *See also* extinctions
Endangered Species Act, 196
Ennis, Tami, 138
environmentalism, 306–307

316

Author Charles Sobczak lives and writes on Sanibel Island. He has two sons, Logan and Blake, and is happily married to Molly Heuer. Sobczak is a lifetime member of the *Sanibel and Captiva Conservation Foundation* (SCCF), the President of *Lee Reefs* (Lee County Artificial Reef Association), Vice-President of *START* (Solutions to Avoid Red Tide) and an avid offshore fisherman.

Six Mornings on Sanibel was originally published in 1999 by Indigo Press. Since then it has gone on to become one of the best-selling books on Sanibel and throughout Florida. An endearing tale of two anglers who meet on the Sanibel Fishing pier, the story is most often compared with *Tuesdays with Morrie.* This heart moving story is a timeless lesson about what really matters in life. To read an excerpt go to or see the "look inside" feature at <u>Amazon.com</u>.

Way Under Contract, a Florida Story is the second novel by Charles Sobczak. The book won *The Patrick Smith Award for Florida Literature, 2001.* The novel is a black comedy about real estate agents and developers that build a condominium project in a swamp only to have it destroyed by a category 5 hurricane named Emily shortly after completion. A hilarious tale of hubris and humility before the overwhelming forces of nature. A classic "Hurricane" novel.

A Choice of Angels was conceived and written shortly before the tragedy of 9/11/2001. Set in Istanbul and Atlanta, it tells the tale of the forbidden romance between the son of a Southern Baptist Minister and the daughter of an Islamic family from Turkey. The book received a starred review from *Booklist* and went on to win *Book of the Year, 2003, Bronze,* from the review publication *Foreword Magazine.*

Excerpts and ordering information are available at <u>www.indigopress.net</u> or by calling Indigo Press, toll-free, at 877-472-8900.

ATTENTION BOOK CLUBS:
There are book discussion topics for *Alligators, Sharks & Panthers* posted on our website at www.indigopress.net.